Uncommon Friendships

Uncommon Friendships

An Amicable History of Modern Religious Thought

WILLIAM W. YOUNG III

CASCADE Books • Eugene, Oregon

UNCOMMON FRIENDSHIPS
An Amicable History of Modern Religious Thought

Copyright © 2009 William W. Young III. All rights reserved. Except for brief quotations in critical publications or reviews, no part of this book may be reproduced in any manner without prior written permission from the publisher. Write: Permissions, Wipf and Stock Publishers, 199 W. 8th Ave., Suite 3, Eugene, OR 97401.

Cascade Books
A Division of Wipf and Stock Publishers
199 W. 8th Ave., Suite 3
Eugene, OR 97401

www.wipfandstock.com

ISBN 13: 978-1-55635-836-4

Cataloguing-in-Publication data:

Young, William W.

    Uncommon friendships : an amicable history of modern religious thought / William W. Young III.

    xii + 318 p. ; 23 cm. Includes bibliographical references and index.

    ISBN 13: 978-1-55635-836-4

    1. Rosenstock-Huessy, Eugen, 1888–1973. 2. Rosenzweig, Franz, 1886–1929. 3. Lévinas, Emmanuel, 1906–1995. 4. Blanchot, Maurice, 1907–2003. 5. Kristeva, Julia, 1941–. 6. Clément, Catherine, 1939–. 7. Friendship. I. Title.

BJ1533 .F8 Y75 2009

Manufactured in the U.S.A.

To Mom and Dad

for their guidance, support, music, and love

Contents

Acknowledgments / ix

Introduction: *Interreligious Friendships and Western Religious Thought* / 1

PART ONE Eugen Rosenstock-Huessy *and* Franz Rosenzweig
- ONE The Star and the Rays: Speech and Scripture / 19
- TWO Living History: Law, Holidays, and the Unnatural Time of Humanity / 54
- THREE The Art of Education: Cultivating Humanity / 84

PART TWO Emmanuel Levinas *and* Maurice Blanchot
- FOUR Distant Companions: Art, Ethics, and Politics in Blanchot and Levinas / 121
- FIVE Insinuations: Enigmas of Responsibility / 150
- SIX These and These are the Words of the Other: Commentary and the Infinite Conversation / 173

PART THREE Julia Kristeva *and* Catherine Clément
- SEVEN Analyzing the Soul of Religion / 211
- EIGHT Keeping Time: Music, Philosophy, and the Feminine / 236
- NINE The Stranger Within: Toward a Post-Analytic Politics / 254

Conclusion: *Questioning Friendship* / 283

Bibliography / 297

Index / 311

Acknowledgments

Any book is the fruit of extensive collaboration, born of the networks of friendship, debate, and support constitutive of academic and intellectual reflection. Given the focus of this book on the place of such collaboration and friendship in modern religious thought, an acknowledgement of my gratitude to others for their contributions is especially in order.

Several colleagues with whom I have studied and taught have been central to the shape this book has taken. Peter Ochs and Gene Rogers have both provided encouragement for this project, from a distance. At Loyola College in Maryland, it was in conversation with John and Laura Betz that I first conceived the structure of this work, with the focus on these three friendships. Joel Shuman and Fr. Tom Looney, of King's College, provided support and encouragement for pursuing this project. Joe Kraus was also a wonderful conversation partner during our time at King's. At Endicott, I am extremely grateful for extensive conversations and collaborations with Rocky Gangle, as well as his friendship. These have been central to my work on Levinas, as well as rethinking the aesthetic dimensions of religious thought. Charlotte Gordon has been a wonderful conversation partner regarding the writing and shaping of the book's argument, and as with many of the friends mentioned here, our teaching and work together confirms for me the significance of interreligious friendships. I would also thank both Charlotte and Gabrielle Watling for their very helpful comments on the introduction.

Other colleagues have also contributed to this work on a number of levels. Randy Friedman has been a thoughtful, engaging, and humorous conversation partner regarding Levinas and Rosenzweig, as well as a good friend and faithful Pawtucket Red Sox fan. Mark Ryan has likewise been a constant and engaging friend, as well as a frequent volleying partner on both the tennis court and on topics of friendship, religious diversity, and ethics. Michael Zank generously provided me with an unpublished manuscript, as well as guidance regarding the early years of Rosenzweig's and Rosenstock's friendship.

A special thanks is due to my colleagues in the Society for Scriptural Reasoning. This group was my primary intellectual community for a number of years; the friendships and shared commitments of the members of the group have never been far from my mind in the work that follows. The work of this group is, in my view, one of the most hopeful signs in the development of practices of interreligious friendship, especially in terms of how this can open new paths for reflection. Among these colleagues, a few stand out. Randi Rashkover and Martin Kavka have both been wonderful colleagues, and I appreciate their many insights on the shapes of friendships, the academy, and especially on Rosenzweig and Levinas. Mike Higton, Rachel Muers, Susannah Ticciati, and Chad Pecknold have taught me a great deal; their attentiveness and openness to hearing the voices of outsiders have been inspirational. Umeyye Isra Yasicioglu has been an inspirational colleague, with both her creative reflection and attentive, patient study.

Research for this project depended on institutional support. Thanks are due to Loyola College in Maryland, from whom I received an Adjunct Faculty Research Grant in 2001 and 2002. Endicott College has provided support as well, including a Faculty Research Grant in 2006 and a course reduction in 2007. My thanks to the Robert D. Farber University Archives at Brandeis University, for access to the Nahum Norbert Glatzer Papers.

An early, condensed version of chapter 8 was published in *Cross Currents*, under the title "Healing Religion: Aesthetics and Analysis in Kristeva and Clément," in 2005. My thanks to *Cross Currents* for allowing me to retain the permissions rights for this article.

Finally, I would like to thank the editorial staff at Cascade for taking a chance on this work, which is somewhat idiosyncratic in its approach. Special thanks are due to Chris Spinks, my editor, for his encouragement and guidance through the process. Nathan Rhoads's editing has been enormously helpful. Errors, of course, remain my own.

Beyond the academy, my interest in this project developed in large part from the network of friendships that I have been fortunate to develop. It is really from these friends that I have learned to think about friendship in new ways, as well as how to practice friendship most fully. I am especially grateful, then, on many levels, for the friendships of Noora Niskanen, Avinash Rao, Logan Martin, Ethan Borg, Keith Wilde, Chad Fogleman, Dave Falk, and Nicole Merola.

My deepest gratitude is due to my parents, and to my sister Joanna, who have always provided the support for my endeavors, wherever these have taken me. Friendship, music, religion, art, teaching: the importance of all of the themes that follow was, in many ways, impressed upon me from as early as I can remember. And none of this would be possible without the love and encouragement of Melissa, my wife—my partner, lover, and friend. Our daughter, Madeleine, reminds me of the importance of listening—that I "need to put my ears on." I hope that she will have the chance to listen, herself, in a symphony of friendships as she grows older, and that others may join her in learning from the friendships that follow.

Introduction
Interreligious Friendships and Western Religious Thought

IN WESTERN RELIGIOUS THOUGHT, friendship has been one of the most central tropes of theological and ethical reflection. From Moses speaking to God "as a man to his friend,"[1] to the story of Jonathan and David and the Gospel of John, Jewish and Christian scriptures set forth friendship as the highest level of love for both one's neighbors and for God. In addition, in drawing on Platonic, Aristotelian, and Stoic traditions of friendship, Christian theology has often taken friendship as a locus for the appropriation of philosophical discourse for religious reflection. In its integration of wisdom, virtue, intimacy, and love, friendship has often served to define the ideal of human excellence, both individually and socially—in many ways, becoming an immanent form of transcendence. In a world where hostility and violence would seem to reign, friendship offers a glimpse of another world—much as in S. Y. Agnon's story where a blind friend messianically overcomes the narrator's alienation and anger, when "His two beautiful eyes shone, and I saw myself standing beside my home."[2]

Even in its transcendence, however, friendship has been subject to certain restrictions and exclusions within the theological and philosophical traditions. As Jacques Derrida argues in *Politics of Friendship*, friendship has been defined canonically as a *fraternal* relation. This suggests, first, that it is defined in a masculinist way, neutralizing or effacing sexual difference.[3] It also privileges a certain form of sameness as requisite to friendship—for instance, in Aristotle, a sameness of character, education, and upbringing, are at least as important as a likeness of gender. While such sameness is crucial for certain features of friendship to emerge, the privilege of this aspect of friendship prevents other forms of friendship from being thought in their own right.

---

1. Exod 33:11.
2. Agnon, "Friendship," 78.
3. Derrida, *Politics of Friendship*, 149, 164.

When one turns to religious conceptions of friendship, its fraternal shape changes but hardly disappears. There is little in its patristic and medieval forms that would contest the masculinist heritage of Hellenistic friendship. Moreover, an emphasis on likeness remains, though the focus shifts from upbringing to faith. One sees this, for instance, in Augustine's narrative of going to visit his sick friend, who keeps his distance because Augustine has not yet been baptized.[4] In the absence of the Holy Spirit's unity of wills, true friendship cannot occur.

Two classical texts on friendship further illustrate this point, even as they reshape the Aristotelian and Ciceronian discourses on friendship. First, in the *Summa Theologiae*, while St. Thomas Aquinas thinks that charity should be extended to all, as it is a love for God's creatures, he denies that this can take the form of friendship with non-Christians. Because non-Christians are, to varied degrees, in states of unbelief, one's love is directed to *God* as friendship, and to sinners as loved by God. Charity, as a love for God, does not allow for any reciprocity between the Christian and the unbeliever, thereby denying the possibility of friendship with them.[5]

While Thomas's approach allows for both charity and justice toward non-Christians, Aelred of Rievaulx marks the limit of friendship still more sharply. For Aelred, "spiritual friendship" is the bond that unites Christians with one another, and with Christ. In Aelred's focus on intimate friendship, he rejects the possibility that the highest levels of such friendship could be shared with "pagans and sinners."[6] Across the tradition, then, friendship is often invoked as a way to intensify and emphasize the bonds that constitute the church. Consistently, if to varying degrees, this ecclesial definition of friendship either denies or ignores the possibility of friendship with those beyond one's own religious community.

In recent years, these conceptions of friendship have been both retrieved and transformed. Particularly for those thinkers who see the church as under pressure from the secularization of modernity, these traditional accounts of friendship offer a way of thinking of Christianity as a counterculture, embodying an alternative form of community that is not defined by modern concepts or disciplines. For thinkers such as John Milbank, Paul Waddell, and Stanley Hauerwas, Thomistic, Augustinian, and Cistercian conceptions of friendship enable constructive, innovative practices of

---

4. Augustine, *Confessions*, 58–59.
5. Thomas Aquinas, *Summa Theologiae*, I.23.1.
6. Aelred of Rievaulx, *Spiritual Friendship*, 78.

community that respond to the deficits of modernity. Moreover, Eugene Rogers has recently offered a pneumatological account of friendship, drawing on more Orthodox sources.[7] While working within the tradition, these authors nonetheless turn friendship in new directions,[8] and without their work friendship would not have taken the central place in modern theological and ethical discussions that it has.

At the same time, other voices in the contemporary conversation have reshaped friendship by challenging its more traditional conceptions. Most often, this has taken place with regard to the first fraternal aspect of friendship, as its masculinist elitism has been roundly criticized. Marilyn Friedman has led the way in showing how new forms of friendship could emerge within modernity, as urban life offers alternative possibilities of solidarity and community.[9] Others, such as Leroy Rouner, David Burrell, and Gilbert Meilaender, have further rethought the limits of friendship, in part through comparative approaches to religious ethics.[10]

Even within these approaches, however, it seems that the specific possibility of interreligious friendship is often overlooked. While implicit in the work and daily life of many of the thinkers mentioned above, interreligious friendship remains untheorized, and largely ignored within religious discourse. As this remains unthought, friendship remains, on one level, within the realm of sameness. Thus, if one wishes to rethink friendship along the lines proposed by Derrida, it may be necessary to consider the shape of interreligious friendships, and the roles they play in religious ethics and theological reflection.

In our multicultural world, interreligious friendships are frequent, everyday occurrences. While such friendships may be perceived as weakening the bonds of specific religious communities, or perhaps even creating a risk of conversion, this is often not the case. Even when leading to questions about one's religious identity, faith, or practice, such friendships may ultimately intensify or deepen one's religious commitment.[11] Here, on a

7. Rogers, *After the Spirit*, 189–91.
8. See Hauerwas, "Gay Friendship," esp. 299–301.
9. Friedman, *What Are Friends For?* 231–56.
10. See Rouner, *Changing Face of Friendship*; Burrell, *Friendship and Ways to Truth*; and Meilaender, *Friendship*.
11. An excellent example, along these lines, is the friendship between John Howard Yoder and Steven Schwarzchild; see Peter Ochs's and Michael Cartwright's discussion in the introduction to *The Jewish-Christian Schism Revisited*, 12–19.

popular level, one might think of the film *Keeping the Faith*, starring Ben Stiller and Edward Norton. For their characters, their friendship, and their commitments to their respective faiths are inseparable, and work to reinforce one another.[12] For those of us for whom such friendships are a central part of our history and who we are, the demand to choose between religion and friendship would divide us from ourselves. It therefore becomes necessary to consider the significance of such friendships, and how the relation to those outside one's own tradition may, in fact be a form of fidelity to the God who created the world in which we live and move. As Eugene Rogers writes, "What does the story practiced in the Eucharist mean for those the Church has encountered as other than itself, as strange to itself: Gentiles, Jews, philosophers, nature itself—those whom human beings now name, not in order to bless, but in order to curse?"[13]

The history of modern religious thought shows that a religious exclusivity of friendship is neither necessary nor beneficial. In many ways, twentieth-century religious thought is a history of interreligious friendship, as many of the most influential and creative thinkers of the past century have fostered such relationships.[14] To tell a different story, in which religious thought and such friendships no longer oppose one another, this book explores three interreligious friendships: Franz Rosenzweig (1886–1929) and Eugen Rosenstock-Huessy (1888–1973), Emmanuel Levinas (1906–95) and Maurice Blanchot (1907–2003), and Julia Kristeva (1941–) and Catherine Clément (1939–). In each case, the friendship contributed to the development of these thinkers' understanding of their own traditions—and led to some of the most innovative reflection on religion in the twentieth and twenty-first centuries. This work often heightened these friends' sense of their religious differences, but in so doing also led to reformulations and developments within their religious thought.

While one could choose many different friendships to study, these three friendships are significant for numerous reasons. First, each friendship centers on a particular mode of study—philosophy of history and sociology (Rosenzweig/Rosenstock), phenomenology and hermeneutics (Blanchot/

12. Wright, *Religion and Film*, 129–41.

13. Rogers, "Stranger as Blessing," 277.

14. To mention just a few other instances where such friendships have shaped the scholars' work: Yoder and Schwarzchild; Jacques Derrida and Jean-Luc Nancy; Levinas and Paul Ricoeur, or (further afield) Thomas Merton and D. T. Suzuki. More recently, one could consider the work of the Society for Scriptural Reasoning, Hauerwas and Romand Coles, or Archbishop Rowan Williams and Tariq Ramadan.

Levinas), and psychoanalysis (Kristeva/Clément). The three friendships, together, thus help to illustrate how interreligious friendships have played into the study of religion across a range of disciplines and periods. Second, in each friendship both the relation itself and often the work of one of the friends has been largely ignored by ensuing scholarship.[15] This work thus functions, in some ways, as a historical midrash—recovering the voices and views of scholars on the margins of academic debate and study, who were nonetheless central to the work of their paradigmatic partners.[16] The relationships can thus further our interpretations of these works and highlight the significance of these thinkers. Third, the three friendships follow very different biographical trajectories, and thus they provide different models for how one thinks about interreligious friendship. Moreover, Kristeva and Clément provide an example of friendship between women, which has been unduly ignored through most of the philosophical tradition. Finally, as will be discussed below, all three friendships focus on aesthetic issues, and the relationship between aesthetic and religious differences is a central aspect of this study.

How is it that such friendships, in moving beyond the relational boundaries of their communities, enable their participants to develop new patterns of thought and practice? Do these friendships also change the way that we conceive of friendship itself—displacing classical models of friendship? What follows sketches an outline of these possibilities, which will then be developed in detail through examination of these three friendships. These friendships were paradigm-shifting events—opening friendship to difference, while reshaping the communal networks and symbolic systems within which these authors moved and wrote.

REVOLUTIONARY FRIENDSHIPS: SHIFTING PARADIGMS

In *The Structure of Scientific Revolutions*, Thomas Kuhn set forth an influential and controversial theory regarding the development of scientific knowledge. On Kuhn's view, scientific knowledge works as a particular form of a

---

15. This is very much the case with Clément, and to a large degree for Rosenstock as well; despite some renewed interest in his speech-thinking—and much interest in his wife Gritli—much of his later work remains unexplored. Blanchot's work has received far more extensive study, though less so within religious studies.

16. A caveat: these "marginal" scholars were and are quite central in their own countries. It is with regard to their reception in the U.S. that their work has been accorded a more secondary status, and it is that deficiency which this essay addresses.

language game, in the Wittgensteinian sense; in other words, the meaning of scientific language, and thus its truth, depends on how the language is used within particular disciplinary communities in science. Most scientific discovery ("normal science") occurs as a form of clarification, in which the fundamental presuppositions and practices of a community of inquirers serve as the basis for scientific investigation, working out the theoretical implications that follow from a groundbreaking discovery.

The most intriguing part of Kuhn's theory, however, is his analysis of how a scientific revolution (such as the discovery of DNA or the theory of relativity) leads to a paradigm shift in which the established mode of doing science no longer fits. Such a paradigm shift occurs when the results of experimentation can only appear anomalous or inexplicable within the dominant paradigm of inquiry, and lead to a point of crisis that can only be resolved by a new theory and a new approach. This new worldview, by accounting for and interpreting evidence in a way that the previous paradigm could not, becomes the language game within which scientific inquiry henceforth proceeds. As Kuhn puts it, the scientist lives in a different world after the paradigm shift, even though the world is the same.

Kuhn's theory has come under extensive criticism that goes beyond our interests here. What is intriguing in his theory is his analysis of how scientists arrive at the new theoretical discoveries that enable revolutions. He observes that those who bring about such paradigm shifts are frequently less embedded in the established discipline of scientific practice, being in some sense an outsider or newcomer to the discipline. As he writes:

> The new paradigm, or a sufficient hint to permit later articulation, emerges all at once, sometimes in the middle of the night, in the mind of a man deeply immersed in crisis. What the nature of the final stage is—how an individual invents (or finds he has invented) a new way of giving order to data now all assembled—must here remain inscrutable and may be permanently so. Let us here note only one thing about it. Almost always the men who achieve these fundamental inventions of a new paradigm have been either very young or very new to the field whose paradigm they change. And perhaps that point need not have been made explicit, for obviously these are the men who, being little committed by prior practice to the traditional rules of normal science, are particularly likely to see that those rules no longer define a playable game and to conceive another set that can replace them.[17]

17. Kuhn, *Structure of Scientific Revolutions*, 89–90.

While Kuhn glosses this outsider status as being primarily a function of how long one has been ensconced within a theoretical approach, this answer is not entirely adequate. Paradigm shifts, paradoxically, require one to both participate in a discipline *and* to remain outside of it. As he describes it, the professionalization and force of habit that constitute normal science make one resistant to change, and less likely to see anomalies as constituting a crisis (they may appear simply to be unresolved problems). At the same time, one must work intensively within a discipline, so as to grasp the anomalies in their full force.[18] Thus, in bringing about this "inscrutable shift" there may be other factors that enable such paradigm-shifting work.

While Kuhn sees the process of innovation as somewhat inscrutable, recent investigations into the relationship between friendship and creativity demonstrate the importance of friendship in the processes of creation and discovery. In *Collaborative Circles*, Michael Farrell explores the central role of several friendships in the artistic, psychoanalytic, and political activities of central figures of modernity—Joseph Conrad and Henry James, Sigmund Freud and Wilhelm Fliess, and Elizabeth Cady Stanton and Lucretia Mott, among others. In each case, the circle of friends is seen as providing support and inspiration that enable creativity, particularly by giving the friends a shared perspective over against the prevailing cultural, political, or artistic worldview, thereby encouraging the pursuit of creative innovation.[19] One could see these circles of friends as providing the marginal community that enables "paradigm-shifting" reflection. However, these friendships are still largely based upon sameness; the creative process is said to work best when the friends are of the same age, background, and common viewpoints. How might a *difference* among friends be generative and creative?

As in Kuhn's view of natural science, religious thought likewise develops through a set of interpretive practices that constitute a discursive community. It is my contention here that friendship with someone outside one's religious community often gives a thinker an outsider's perspective on his or her own tradition—thereby enabling new forms of reflection and interpretation that respond to unresolved issues within one's communal traditions of thought. Friendship, in short, gives each author an alternative fidelity in light of which to consider her discipline—shedding new light on it, and perhaps enabling a paradigm shift. The resulting shift in worldview

18. Ibid., 64.
19. See Farrell, *Collaborative Circles*.

need not mean that these scholars abandon their religious commitments, any more than Copernicus dropped his astronomical work when he rejected the Ptolemaic system. In fact, the shift in worldview through friendship may *renew* one's commitment to religion, even if the form of that commitment is irrevocably changed. Nowhere is this clearer than in the friendship of Rosenzweig and Rosenstock, as their early engagements appeared to be leading Rosenzweig toward conversion to Christianity, but actually led to his intense "conversion" to Judaism and his subsequent reformulation of Jewish thought and life.

These friends serve as outsiders to one another on several levels. First, the friends come from different religious traditions: Rosenzweig was Jewish, while Rosenstock converted to Christianity; Levinas was Jewish, while Blanchot was atheist (though from a Catholic upbringing); Kristeva and Clement, likewise, are respectively from Christian and Jewish upbringings,[20] with Kristeva more willingly adopting elements of her own religious and theological tradition, while Clement advocates a syncretism of multiple religious traditions and practices. Thus, the friendships opened the participants to alternative perspectives that they then carried into their engagements with their respective traditions of thought. They also can help us to examine how the engagement with atheism can be fruitful, even essential, in modern religious thought.

However, these authors are not simply outsiders to one another in the sense of being from different religious backgrounds. They also provide new insight for one another through their diverse scholarly approaches. As they work from varied perspectives, their friendships take on an interdisciplinary character that enables each author's innovations within her particular field of thought. Rosenstocks theory of speech enabled Rosenzweig's theological reflection, most obviously in his grammatical analysis of the Song of Songs, and Rosenstock learned from Rosenzweig's historical and pedagogical approaches. While Levinas and Blanchot both worked in continental philosophy and phenomenology, Blanchot's literary work and essays on art likewise opened a language that enabled Levinas to reconceive ethics, while Levinas's conception of exteriority led Blanchot to a break with ontology—not to mention an extenuation of his communism. Clément's attention to the body, her study of non-Western religions, and her critiques of psychoanalysis contribute to Kristeva's critical appropriation of mystical trends

---

20. Technically, Clément's family was half Jewish and half Catholic, but she identifies more strongly with her Jewish upbringing in her writings.

within Christianity, while Kristeva's focus on semiotics as the meeting of language and embodiment questions and reshapes Clément's reflections on the sacred. In each case, the interdisciplinary nature of the friendship, along with the religious backgrounds of the authors, contributes to the innovative character of their work.

These friendships clearly enabled some of the seminal shifts of modern religious thought—so are they "revolutionary," to adopt Kuhn's terminology? As the ensuing chapters will show, they are revolutionary in their impact on modern religious thought. They are also revolutionary in a deeper sense, as they establish relations across disciplinary and communal boundaries, and transform these institutions from within. As Michel Foucault has written, friendship cultivates a disciplined sociality in which the relation between two people (or more, in some cases) sets the parameters for their activity. Such a discipline runs counter to the disciplines of modernity, which work by isolating people—in the famous phrase from *Discipline and Punish*, making the soul the prison of the body. Such individuation promotes and ensures the efficient productivity of modern institutions—thus, the need for the disciplinary segmentation and ordering of the body not only in prisons, but in hospitals, armies, and educational institutions. Such institutional production of individualism lives in tension with friendship; as he writes,

> The army, the bureaucracy, administration, universities, schools, and so on—in the modern senses of these words—cannot function with such intense friendships. I think there can be seen a very strong attempt in all these institutions to diminish or minimize the affectional relations . . . I think now, after studying the history of sex, we should try to understand the history of friendship, or of friendships. That history is very, very important.[21]

While Foucault's focus is the effect of corporeal discipline on modes of thought, one could extend his approach to reflect upon the disciplinary apparatus of "religious thought" and academic disciplines. For, in most cases, scholarship proceeds in isolation from other disciplines, and religious thought occurs within a somewhat isolated group of scholars. What is lost, in such study, is the possibility of relations that cross disciplinary and communal boundaries and establish bonds between people whom religion and academic disciplines would isolate from one another. The relations of power that separate communities and confine thought within those boundaries

---

21. Foucault, "Sex, Power, and the Politics of Identity," 170–71.

remain largely unthought. By enabling modes of thought and ways of life that transgress the boundaries of modern institutions, thereby inspiring creativity and innovation within those institutional spaces as well, each of these friendships becomes revolutionary, showing how such interreligious and interdisciplinary work can establish new and alternative forms of subjectivity and community.

While these friendships are revolutionary within the modern setting, it should be noted that they also reshape the idea of friendship, opening modes of friendship that have been only rarely articulated within the philosophical and religious traditions of the West. To appreciate this fully, the distinctive form of each of these friendships should be examined, as well as how the friendships develop traditional conceptions of friendship in new ways. The particular shape of each friendship will be discussed further in the conclusion, but I would like to begin by suggesting how these three friendships modify more traditional philosophical accounts of friendship.

RESHAPING FRIENDSHIP

The friendships discussed in this study build on classic conceptions of friendship in three central ways: their pursuit of wisdom, security over against a social conformism, and the possibility of self-correction. In this, they hold to the classical view of friendship set forth by Aristotle, where friendship enables knowledge. For Aristotle, the need for friendship—a need based on neither utility nor pleasure—arises precisely because in a friend one can contemplate one's own activity and thereby come to know oneself more fully.[22] Friendship, in the Aristotelian sense, is a necessary component in the pursuit of human self-understanding (without which the specifically human desire for understanding would remain unfulfilled). However, such knowledge depends upon the likeness or identity between the characters of the friends; it is because the friends share the same identity, with a necessary equality between them, that seeing what one friend does lets the other friend know his *own* action.[23] This implies a shared conception of virtue, which involves both a shared conception of the good and shared activity. Further, as mentioned earlier, such friendships only develop over a long period of time; these relations are found only between those of similar background and education.

---

22. Aristotle, *Nicomachean Ethics*, 149 (1169b30–1170a4).
23. See Young, *Politics of Praise*, ch. 2.

In the pursuit of virtue, friendships often place one at odds with broader society. Their intimacy and security provide support for those who would challenge the norms of society and resist its deformation of virtue. This is most apparent in the Stoic tradition of friendship, where the sharing of secrets with a friend, and the trust that a friend will share in one's projects faithfully, provide security that enables one to hold to reason in the face of shifting fortune. As Seneca writes in "On Tranquility of Mind," "How good it is to have willing hearts as safe repositories for your every secret, whose privity you fear less than your own, whose conversation allays your anxiety, whose counsel promotes your plans, whose cheerfulness dissipates your gloom, whose very appearance gives you joy!"[24] By cultivating friendships as alternative communities, rooted in the pursuit of virtue, Stoics could maintain a critical stance over against conventional accounts of virtue and the common good. However, Stoic friendship requires the negation of affect in order to maintain the common bond of reason. Even if it was natural and unavoidable, any sense of emotional or affective commitment, which rendered one vulnerable to fortune and loss, must be minimized or excluded.

Lastly, in Hellenistic thought friendship provided a form of self-correction. *Parrhesia*, or frankness, was central to this practice. For the sake of one's friend, one would disagree with their actions or thoughts—often correcting them in secret, so as to protect or develop their virtue and/or reputation.[25] Frankness, then, is a way to maintain the friendship, and such criticism is seen as a form of love rather than hostility when practiced with appropriate care.

The friendships studied here all share these classical qualities. They are built around the pursuit of wisdom or understanding, and the friends for the most part supported each other in difficult circumstances and undertakings.[26] Their modes of thought often provided support and resources in challenging disciplinary paradigms and religious orthodoxy. Moreover, many of the exchanges between them often engaged in some form of criticism, in attempts to repair deficient conceptual or interpretive approaches. All the same, it is clear that the "necessary identity" of friends, the shared

24. Seneca, "On Tranquility of Mind," 88.

25. Konstan, *Friendship in the Classical World*, 103–5, 108–11.

26. While there are elements of such security in all three relationships, this was less central to Rosenstock and Rosenzweig, particularly to the extent that Rosenstock pressured Rosenzweig to convert to Christianity, and thereby reinforced the social pressure of assimilation that Rosenzweig sought to resist.

upbringing and social standing, and emphasis on reason are *not* central to these relationships. Levinas and Kristeva both adopted France as their country of residence, even while remaining somewhat critical of it; Clément and Blanchot both were more fully immersed within French culture, yet reject its hegemony in pursuit of alternative forms of community.[27] Rosenzweig and Rosenstock, while raised and educated in very similar ways, nonetheless took quite different approaches to German culture, Judaism, and history. Finally, in all three friendships, aspects of embodiment and affectivity are far more central than classical accounts would admit—as is clearest in the work of Kristeva and Clément, where a Stoic reason that closed off bodily affect would be rejected as unduly repressive. Thus, these friendships both maintain and transform traditional concepts of friendship, and are deserving of attention on both levels.

The friendships discussed in this work provide a contrast with traditional friendship in that they embody relations of difference. Even though there are "common foci of activity," as sociologists recently described the necessary components of friendship,[28] a separation marks each friendship. Rosenstock and Rosenzweig may both share an interest in grammar, but how they work with it remains very different; Levinas and Blanchot, while both thinking outside being, nonetheless reflect on art and ethics in incommensurate ways; Clément and Kristeva may both see analysis as necessary, but their relations to its practices of interpretation remain far apart. The collaboration of these friends is perhaps best understood in the words of Walter Benjamin, speaking of his friendship with Gershom Scholem: "Only the indolent are really 'influenced,' while he who really learns sooner or later comes to the point of appropriating that part of the work of another which is of use to him, in order to assimilate it into his work as technique."[29] What Benjamin describes as appropriation is, I think, the crucial element; the grasp of the other's work and thought—its internalization—reshapes the work of both parties, as one may carry it in unforeseen directions. By studying the work of these friends, this essay

---

27. Clément once again lives in France, but teaches at the Université populaire du quai Branly at the Musée du quai Branly, which is appropriately dedicated to the study and presentation of foreign cultures and art.

28. Feld and Carter, "Foci of Activity," 140–43.

29. Benjamin, *Gesammelte Schriften*, 4:502, quoted in Handelman, *Fragments of Redemption*, 20.

inquires as to the possibility of friendships of difference, and their potential for creativity, innovation, and inspiration in our times.

THE ART OF FRIENDSHIP

While the central theme of this book is the shape and significance of interreligious friendship in modern religious thought, in the course of this work the issue of aesthetics has emerged as a related, if secondary, concern. From sociological, hermeneutical, and psychoanalytic points of view, the role of aesthetics in religious life and belief becomes central to the debates between these friends. In particular, the privilege of a particular form of aesthetic expression—for instance, Kristeva's focus on verbal and visual representation—leads to a divergence between the friends, as Clément sees music as the more central and significant dimension of artistic expression, which is often confined and suppressed by signification. This aesthetic disagreement plays into their different approaches to religion; Kristeva accords a privilege to the European, and especially Christian, forms of thought and expression as modes of psychoanalytically (and politically) significant expression, while Clement's syncretistic approach is more markedly pluralistic. Similar aesthetic concerns run throughout the work of these authors, and this aspect of their work is worthy of further consideration.

This is particularly significant, I think, if one looks at the shape that interreligious or interfaith dialogue often takes. Frequently, interfaith dialogue emphasizes doctrines, conflict resolution, or perhaps seeking common ground on ethical issues. It is relatively rare, it seems, for such discussions to focus on aesthetic aspects of religious expression. Based upon this research, I would argue that any religious community is shaped, on some level, by aesthetic dimensions and commitments, and that examining those commitments may help to illuminate some of the deeper differences between disparate traditions—differences which may inform doctrinal or ethical disagreements more strongly than we often realize. For instance, in what follows, the rejection or revision of visual or static representation by Rosenzweig, Levinas, and Clément could be regarded as simply a rejection of aesthetics, seeing the valorization of art as a form of idolatry. Yet such a reading too readily equates aesthetics with its visual or poetic form. For all three authors, musicality and song, as non-representational aesthetic modalities, are highly influential, such that their work is better understood as reshaping aesthetics, rather than rejecting it altogether.

It is helpful, in this regard, to consider the recent work of Jacques Rancière, the French political theorist. In *The Politics of Aesthetics*, Rancière argues that aesthetics is, at its root, a "distribution of the sensible"—determining the relation between aural, visual, and tactile media (not to mention taste and smell, especially in the realm of food). As he puts it, aesthetics "is a delimitation of spaces and times, of the visible and the invisible, of speech and noise, that simultaneously determines the place and the stakes of politics as a form of experience."[30] As such, it involves a shaping of the material world, and the relations between individuals and their respective capacities. Aesthetics is political, in that it shapes one's relation to the world and to others—often, on Rancière's view, generating forms of inequality and hierarchy, even where equality is the stated goal.

This work examines what could be termed the "religious distribution of the sensible"—the interconnection between the theological (or atheistic) commitments and the conceptions of art for these central, influential thinkers. The connection is not accidental; in many ways, their aesthetic insights enable these thinkers to make revolutionary reevaluations of religious discourse and practice. Furthermore, the aesthetic differences between the authors are often closely linked to their religious disagreements. Thus, Blanchot's reflections on poetry implicitly bear implications for his religious reflection, and his critique of Levinas. The work of these authors can help us to consider how various forms of religious and philosophical aesthetics distribute sensibility—and the implications of such distribution for politics and community.

Finally, a note on these friendships themselves. The focus of this study is how these friendships informed—and, in many cases, transformed—the religious thought of their members. Thus, this work is far from exhaustive in its discussion of these thinkers simply on the terms of their published works. In what follows, I explore how these interreligious friendships shaped their thought, and how they can help us to understand their work more fully. My hope is that we may thereby understand such friendships more fully as well.

Moreover, in the course of this research it has become very clear that life does not fit so neatly into a conceptual framework. The events of the individuals' lives—from Levinas's imprisonment during World War II to Clément's appointment in the French ministry of culture and her travels to India—reshape and exceed their thought in ways that go beyond the limits

---

30. Rancière, *Politics of Aesthetics*, 13.

of this study. Needless to say, this has been most dramatically demonstrated in the recent scholarship and evidence set forth of Rosenzweig's affair with Margrit Rosenstock-Huessy—Eugen Rosenstock-Huessy's wife—and his extensive, passionate correspondence with her in the ensuing years. Much of this scholarship has been published during the time of this investigation, and I have made use of it in terms of the affair's impact on their thought. However, since my focus here is primarily the trajectory of these authors' work, there are aspects of the Gritli relationship, and of all of these figures' lives, that remain beyond the purview of this study.

This study proceeds through a close examination of each of the three friendships. Chapters 1–3 address the work of Rosenzweig and Rosenstock-Huessy. Chapter 1 examines their theories of speech, and how these led into their respective work on translation. Chapter 2 then examines their approaches to the philosophy of history, and their conceptions of law and life in Judaism and Christianity. Building on these theoretical materials, chapter 3 studies how they sought to put into practice their philosophy of "speech-thinking" through their respective efforts in educational reform.

With Levinas and Blanchot, chapter 4 begins by reevaluating the place of art and ethics in each author's work. In so doing, it lays the groundwork for the religious and ethical debates of their later works. Chapter 5 focuses on the notion of the enigma, which becomes central to both Levinas's reformulation of revelation and transcendence, and Blanchot's refusal of such transcendence. Chapter 6 then looks at how their exchanges played into their later views on commentary and criticism, especially focusing on how a pluralized form of interpretation becomes central to Levinas's Talmudic readings and Blanchot's later conception of literature.

Finally, chapters 7–9 explore Kristeva's and Clément's work on religion in light of their psychoanalytic and cultural training. Chapter 7 explores how both sought to revise psychoanalytic discourse, and how this ties in with their shifting conceptions of the sacred, mysticism, and shamanism. Chapter 8 focuses more directly on their conceptions of music and literature, and how these aesthetic dimensions link their conceptions of embodiment with their respective emphasis on Christian or Indian forms of religious discourse. Chapter 9 brings together the theoretical work of the earlier chapters, looking at how Clément's and Kristeva's views on religion inform their conceptions of cultural politics, multiculturalism, and the significance of religion in cultivating an ethics of hospitality.

The conclusion then explores the specific shape of each friendship, and how each can help us to rethink friendship in new ways. It also will develop the discussion of how such interreligious friendships contribute to a theological understanding of the world, as constructive forms of engagement that root one's religious commitment more deeply in the complex fabric of the world. These interreligious friendships have revolutionized the field of modern and postmodern religious thought; recognizing their transformative impact can likewise transform our vision of friendship's role in faith, hope, and love.

Part One

Eugen Rosenstock-Huessy
and Franz Rosenzweig

ONE

The Star and the Rays
Speech and Scripture

COLLEAGUES, FRIENDS, CONFIDANTS—AND YET, an infinite distance separated Franz Rosenzweig and Eugen Rosenstock-Huessy in their friendship, marked by what both saw as the universal separation of Jew and Christian. Across this distance, they engaged in one of the most productive, seminal dialogues of any two thinkers. Despite their opposition, rivalry, and occasional hostility, they remained faithful friends. Rosenstock[1] would later describe Rosenzweig as "my partner in the dialogue of life."[2] As Salomon Malka writes, "They were linked by an indissoluble friendship and an absolute hostility"[3]—even, one might add, beyond the grave.

In their friendship marked by the twists and turns of fortune, Rosenzweig and Rosenstock present a fascinating case study in how factors beyond one's control shape one's intellectual trajectory, even as one's friendships may help one to remain true to oneself within these changing circumstances. If one looked at Rosenzweig's and Rosenstock's lives in five-year intervals, beginning in 1910 at the start of their friendship,[4] one could hardly have predicted where they would be in the next stage of their lives. From his status as a rising lecturer in law and history to his work studying grammar, from his involvement in adult education to his reflections on the history of revolutions, at each stage Rosenstock's work shifted dramatically

---

1. Rosenstock-Huessy added his wife's surname to his own, as was the custom in Switzerland, Margrit Huessy's native country. For the sake of simplicity, and in keeping with much of scholarly convention, I will refer to him simply as Rosenstock.

2. Rosenstock, *Ja und Nein*, 45.

3. Malka, *Franz Rosenzweig*, 110.

4. Many writings, including some of Rosenstock's later recollections of their friendship, date its inception from 1913, the encounter in Leipzig that ultimately led Rosenzweig to intensify his commitment to Judaism. However, Rosenzweig and Rosenstock actually met and first worked together in 1910 at a meeting in Baden-Baden, amongst scholars who sensed the inadequacy of historicist methodology. See Zank, "Christlich-Jüdisches Gespräch im 1," 5–6. This is discussed further in chapter 2. My thanks to Michael Zank for the clarification and sharing his work on this topic.

from its previous emphasis. Rosenzweig's briefer career is no less remarkable, moving from his studies in the philosophy of history, "into life" in writing the *Star of Redemption* during the First World War, to running the *Lehrhaus* and translating poetry, before finally focusing on biblical translation while fighting the disease now known as Lou Gehrig's (amyotrophic lateral sclerosis, or ALS), to which he succumbed in 1929. What is astonishing, though, is that even through these transformations, each author remained committed to the issues and methodology that occupied both of them from the beginnings of their correspondence.

The distance between Rosenzweig and Rosenstock has only widened posthumously, as the reception of their work has differed greatly. While Rosenstock was better known in academic circles in Germany during the 1920s, and taught at Dartmouth until 1957 in the United States, today he is mostly remembered for his correspondence and friendship with Rosenzweig, and is otherwise largely relegated to obscurity. By contrast, Rosenzweig's work has become central to a renaissance of post-critical Jewish philosophy—though only after being largely ignored during his life. Even in recent scholarship clarifying the depth of Rosenzweig's engagement with and interest in his German cultural context, the centrality of the relationship to both of their works has largely remained unexplored.

The full story of their friendship, however, is even more complex. Since an essay by Harold Stahmer in 1986, scholars have started to wrestle with the previously concealed correspondence between Rosenzweig and "Gritli," Margrit Rosenstock-Huessy (1893–1959), Eugen's wife. This correspondence consists of over 1,500 letters, mostly between 1917 and 1922 (the letters from Gritli to Franz were, not surprisingly, destroyed by Rosenzweig's wife Edith).[5] The letters both clarify and complicate how we understand Rosenzweig's work and life in this period, as they testify to both his love for Gritli and a brief affair between them in 1918.[6] Indeed, the letters are perhaps most significant in showing Gritli's impact on one of the most profound and acclaimed dimensions of the *Star*, Rosenzweig's interpretation of revelation through a commentary on the Song of Songs. This section was, in Rosenzweig's words to Gritli, "not to you—but *yours*."[7] The letters unequivocally demonstrate how central Gritli was to Rosenzweig's work and life in this period, as he often stayed with Margrit's

---

5. Harold Stahmer, "Franz Rosenzweig's Letters," 385–409.
6. See Zank, "Rosenzweig-Rosenstock Triangle," 81, 85.
7. Stahmer, "Franz Rosenzweig's Letters," 404.

family and even wrote some crucial passages of the *Star* in her family's home in Sackenheim. She remained central to his life even after his marriage to Edith, albeit from more of a distance. While Edith's decision to exclude the remaining letters from the published version of Rosenzweig's letters was understandable, their son Rafael's generous endorsement of the letters' publication in a supplemental volume has undoubtedly benefited Rosenzweig scholars, even in complicating many received assumptions about Rosenzweig's work.[8]

Needless to say, given the focus of this work, the letters further complicate the already enigmatic friendship between Rosenzweig and Rosenstock. Rosenstock's 1960 description of their friendship, published with their exchange from 1916 in *Judaism Despite Christianity*, minimizes Gritli's role in their relationship and their work, even though he was fully aware of the letters (and the affair) at that time. Thus, a focus on their friendship risks downplaying her importance once more. However, the letters themselves testify to how much Rosenzweig identified Gritli with Rosenstock; on many occasions, he references writing to Eugen *through* Margrit. Rosenzweig frequently mentions the importance of Eugen's writings to his thought, as well as how he feels that Rosenstock has misunderstood him.[9] Recently, Zachary Braiterman has challenged the prevailing focus on Gritli, arguing that the homoerotic, masculinist conception of religion that Rosenzweig develops in his correspondence with Rosenstock—and, even in the discussion of revelation in the *Star*—objectifies and excludes Gritli, rather than making her central.[10] Finally, there is the question of how their friendship persisted despite the jealousy and emotional conflict that Rosenzweig's passion for Gritli created—as Rosenstock and Rosenzweig remained close up through Rosenzweig's death.

Thus, while recognizing that this work's focus on their friendship risks marginalizing Gritli once more, the Gritli letters actually warrant renewed examination of the Rosenzweig-Rosenstock friendship. In what follows, then, I will draw upon the letters where appropriate, to help explore and interpret the dynamic interchange in the work of Rosenzweig

---

8. See Salomon Malka's discussion of the reactions to Stahmer's essay when it was first presented; Malka, *Franz Rosenzweig*, 102–4.

9. The difference between Gritli's understanding and Eugen's miscomprehension of Rosenzweig is emphasized by Ephraim Meir in *Letters of Love*, 82–83.

10. Zachary Braiterman, *Shape of Revelation*, 229–36. While I take issue with Braiterman's reading below, there are moments in their correspondence that clearly support his view, such as Franz's references to Eugen as Gritli's "Maker."

and Rosenstock. Moreover, in the focus on how friendship affects religious thought and practice, it is clear that, beyond the *Star* itself, Rosenzweig and Rosenstock shared intellectual interests and approaches that have contributed greatly to Rosenzweig's prominence in modern Jewish thought. It is by paying attention to these other dimensions of their work that I will unpack often-overlooked dimensions of their friendship.

In the next three chapters, this work will explore how Rosenzweig and Rosenstock engaged in the study of speech, history, and education in ways that helped them to challenge established modes of thought in each discipline. The Gritli letters, I hope, will help us to recognize the provisional nature of this study, since the focus on their friendship inevitably abstracts from their lived experience, even as it shines an interpretive light on their work. What both the recent emphasis on Gritli and Braiterman's forceful response miss is the way that Rosenzweig and Rosenstock appropriate and transform each other's conceptual approaches, in ways that lead them to innovative forms of reflection and practice. While I am somewhat skeptical of Braiterman's claim that Gritli is excluded or silenced in the course of their exchange, his work is important in that it highlights the interconnections between thought, desire, religion, and embodiment for Rosenzweig and Rosenstock.

This chapter explores the centrality of speech to the philosophical and theological work of Rosenzweig and Rosenstock. Both are frequently described as "philosophers of dialogue," but this only begins to suggest their detailed engagement with particular forms of speech as the embodiment of psychological, social, and scientific relations among humanity and with God and the world. The central place of speech in their work first appeared in the course of an exchange of letters between them in late 1916, while both were serving in the German army during World War I. Rosenstock first developed his grammatical approach in his work *The Practical Knowledge of the Soul (Angewandte Seelenkunde)*, which he sent in draft form to Rosenzweig during this wartime correspondence,[11] and which he later wanted to dedicate to Rosenzweig when it was published in 1924. In a letter on his form of "New Thinking," Rosenzweig acknowledged this work as central in formulating his major systematic work, *The Star of Redemption*: "Whatever *The Star of Redemption* can do to renew our ways of thinking is concentrated in this [speech] method . . . The main influence was Eugen Rosenstock; a full year and a half before I began to write I had seen the

---

11. Rosenstock, "Biblionomics," 18.

rough draft of his now published *Angewandte Seelenkunde*."[12] Despite this acknowledgement, the relationship between these works has only recently been studied in detail, and the context for Rosenzweig's appropriation of this text remains largely unaddressed. Moreover, the "speech-method" of philosophy continued to develop in the course of their ongoing discussions and correspondence, unfolding into their concerns with translation, law, history, and education, as shall be explored further in the ensuing chapters. A brief retracing of their shared history will contextualize the development of their speech-theory.

In many ways, these authors' views on speech grow from their respective experiences of conversion, and the living speech entailed in these experiences. Both were born into nominally Jewish families living in an overwhelmingly Christian German culture. Rosenstock had converted to Christianity at the age of seventeen, finding in it a language, vitality, and universality he saw as missing from both German culture and his Jewish upbringing. In part because of their 1910 encounter at Baden-Baden, Rosenzweig decided to study with Rosenstock in Leipzig in 1913, where Rosenstock was teaching medieval history and Rosenzweig had recently come to study law. At this point, Rosenzweig had completed the dissertation that would turn into his momentous work in the philosophy of history, *Hegel and the State*, and he was wrestling with the relativism toward which historicism seemed to lead. In their 1913 encounter, Rosenstock's vitality and living faith so impressed Rosenzweig that he nearly converted to Christianity. As he would write to Rudolf Ehrenberg, "The fact that a man like Rosenstock was a conscious Christian . . . at once bowled over my entire conception of Christianity and of religion generally, including my own . . . in this world there seemed to me to be no room for Judaism."[13] Only his attendance at a synagogue during Yom Kippur services in 1913, where he heard the Jewish liturgy *spoken*, persuaded him that he could, and must, find the vitality and spirit within Judaism that Rosenstock found in Christianity. In his famous letter to Rudolf Ehrenberg, Rosenzweig chose to "remain a Jew."[14] It is, in Rosenstock's words, as if Rosenzweig "converted to Judaism,"[15] much as Rosenstock converted to Christianity, in

---

12. Rosenzweig, "The New Thinking," in *Franz Rosenzweig*, 200.
13. Rosenzweig, Letter to Rudolf Ehrenberg, in *Franz Rosenzweig*, 24.
14. Rosenzweig, *Franz Rosenzweig*, 28.
15. Rosenstock, "Prologue/Epilogue to the Letters—Fifty Years Later," in *Judaism Despite Christianity*, 74.

and through living speech. Rosenstock, however, remained unaware of the impact of their discussions on Rosenzweig until 1916. They renewed their correspondence in earnest in 1916, with Rosenstock's encouragement to Rosenzweig to publish his work on a treatise of Schelling. It was from this initial inquiry that their discussion moved toward Rosenzweig's Judaism.[16]

While the letters compiled in *Judaism without Christianity* are fascinating for the range of issues that they cover, the schematics of Rosenstock's understanding of the relationship of Christianity to paganism dominate their exchange. Rosenstock's specific concern is that, after the Enlightenment, Christianity is devolving into the paganism from which it emerged, as a disparate multiplicity of nations and peoples, with nothing to say to one another and no common life. While Rosenstock does not reduce Judaism to paganism, he distinguishes it as a particular people, while describing Christianity as being of universal significance. The crucial difference, as he describes it, is that the Jewish separation from all nations precludes its universal significance; this separation, for him, means that Judaism does not speak to all peoples. He accentuates this contrast in describing how Christ "redeems the boundless naïve pride of the Jew."[17] At this stage of the dialogue, Jewish particularity is separated from the truly universal speech of the soul. Only Christianity, in the universality of its speech, provides a force that counters such tribalism. He writes to Rosenzweig:

> "The Word became Flesh"—on that proposition everything indeed depends. While the word of man must always become a concept and thereby stagnant and degenerate, God speaks to us with the "word become flesh," through the Son. And so the Christian revelation is the healing of the Babylonian confusion of tongues, the bursting open of the prison, but also the sign on the new tongues, speech that is now informed with soul.[18]

---

16. As Paul Mendes-Flohr has pointed out, this exchange was not only significant religiously, but also gave Rosenzweig a way to address the problem of historicism that was central to much of his early work. See Mendes-Flohr, "Franz Rosenzweig and the Crisis of Historicism"; Myers, *Resisting History*, 78–85.

17. Rosenstock, *Judaism Despite Christianity*, 123. As Michael Zank has noted, Rosenstock's vehement criticism of Judaism (and Rosenzweig) at this point belies itself, most likely manifesting a form of self-hatred found amongst some assimilated Jews of the period. See Zank, "Christlich-Jüdisches Gespräch im 1," 34.

18. Rosenstock, *Judaism Despite Christianity*, 122.

In such speech—the "language of the soul"—Rosenstock perceives a healing and life for humanity that risks being lost through a misunderstanding of the importance of grammar.

Clearly, here, Rosenstock is implicitly arguing that conversion to Christianity is necessary, as it is the only the form of speech and life that provides healing and wholeness for humanity. Rosenstock maintains this privilege of Christian speech in *The Practical Knowledge of the Soul*—the work that, ironically, gives Rosenzweig the resources for rebutting Rosenstock's misconception of Judaism. In Rosenzweig's hands, the soul's speech passes through *both* the star of Judaism and the rays of Christianity. This shift has implications not only for the theory of speech, but for their understandings of God, history, and community. With this exchange in mind, an exploration of the *Practical Knowledge* and *The Star of Redemption* will show how these works continue and reshape the exchange between the authors begun in their correspondence.

MODES OF SPEECH: THE PRACTICAL KNOWLEDGE OF THE SOUL

When making reference to "philosophers of dialogue," the list of names invariably includes not only Rosenzweig and Rosenstock, but also Martin Buber, as well as figures from the movement known as the "Patmos school." As Buber's work has been the best-known, his I-Thou model of dialogue is often assumed to represent the views of the whole group. However, both Rosenstock and Rosenzweig diverge from Buber's approach in two important ways: first, the chronological priority of the "thou" over the "I" in the emergence of speech; and second, the importance of considering the mode of speech as a constitutive element of dialogue. Rosenstock first developed these themes in a draft of *The Practical Knowledge of the Soul* (*Seele*), which he sent to Rosenzweig in 1916. These aspects of speech-thinking would inform both authors' work for years to come, not only setting the stage for Rosenzweig's later debates with Buber regarding the law, but also for their work in adult education.

In the version of *Seele* published in 1924, Rosenstock constructs his arguments in response to two opponents for his theory of speech, both of whom have misunderstood the distinctive nature of the human soul. The first opponent is philosophy, and with it the human sciences, which treat the soul as identical to the mind. Identifying it with reason and with God, they abstract it from any active, social, or historical relation to the world.

The other opponent, occult science, reduces the soul to material forces, as seen in astrology's consultation of the stars for determining the fates of individuals. In this identification with mind or world, both approaches "forfeit their share of divine reason."[19] By turning to speech, Rosenstock moves beyond this dualistic opposition of first-person, egoistic idealism and third-person, impersonal materialism, toward the second grammatical person—the "you."

Before we become speakers of language, we are called *to* language. As Rosenstock writes, "The first thing that happens to the child—to every person—is that it is spoken to . . . It is first a 'you' to a powerful being outside itself—above all to its parents."[20] The child is first a "you" for another before being an "I" for itself. One is named and known before one knows, acted upon before one acts. Only in hearing others address and act toward us do we learn to respond. As Harold Stahmer describes Rosenstock's view, "It is through outside address that we gradually become a person, conscious of our identity."[21] Against Descartes, Rosenstock founds the "I" in intersubjectivity: "Our study of the soul should lead us to introduce a grammatical sentence, 'God has called me, therefore I am' to replace Descartes' '*Cogito, ergo sum*' (I think, therefore I am), which is merely pure logic."[22] The second-person "you" of grammar precedes and inspires the first-person "I." Moreover, the world about which we speak, without direct address, becomes the third-person mode of grammar—"it, he, she." For Rosenstock, the soul lives by transforming itself in speech, shifting between the different grammatical persons depending upon the situation. "Every turning point in the life of the soul becomes apparent as an inflection of its grammatical person, just as a change in its grammatical number does."[23] The full range of speech constitutes our human potential. Thus, when philosophy or the occult privileges either the "I" or third-person grammar, it loses sight of the multiple potencies of the soul. Both opponents occlude the ability to be addressed in the second person—which is, significantly, where the capacity for revelation or prophecy resides.

Rosenstock's rejection of idealism and materialism concretizes the concern about paganism expressed in his letters to Rosenzweig, as these

19. Rosenstock, *Practical Knowledge of the Soul*, 14.
20. Ibid., 16.
21. Stahmer, *"Speak that I May See Thee!"* 138.
22. Rosenstock, *Practical Knowledge of the Soul*, 27.
23. Ibid., 18.

forces infect and shape the very teaching of grammar. The Alexandrian (i.e., Greek) grammatical table exemplifies this flattening of the soul's grammatical potency. In this table, indicative conjugations take priority, and the persons are all treated as the same. "I love," "You love," and "He loves" are all taught as if they have the same meaning, even though the third person is descriptive, while the first two are modes of address that embody lived relations. As Rosenstock would later write in his 1945 essay, "Grammar as a Social Science," "In the Alexandrian list, all persons are put through the same drill. They all seem to speak in the same manner. It is here that the fatal error has crept in."[24] In short, a particular form of speech presents itself as the universal, suppressing or marginalizing other forms of speech. As shall be discussed further in chapter 3, this leveling of grammar will lead Rosenstock toward his work in revising how language is taught.

The other central feature of *The Practical Knowledge of the Soul* is its emphasis on the temporality, aesthetic, and form of community entailed by each mode of speech. Philosophers, especially idealists, emphasize freedom, which is embodied in subjunctive speech, where future possibility abounds without becoming actual. The occult, focused on what is, emphasizes the indicative, which signifies the past. Speech, however, can also occur in the imperative, and this is the proper mode of interpersonal discourse, where one person commands another to do something, especially in the imploring and commanding of love. Rosenstock associates this imperative, in its immediacy, with presence. The asymmetry of being addressed as "you" emerges when one is commanded by another; one discovers one's own agency in response. "So the 'you' is virtually discovered for the first time in the imperative which arises from the transformation love creates."[25] To recognize the "you" is to move beyond either "occult" descriptivism or idealistic voluntarism. For Rosenstock, this step was accomplished by no less than Hermann Cohen, the great neo-Kantian scholar and one of Rosenzweig's mentors: "Hermann Cohen, the last of the great German Idealistic philosophers, owes the greatness of his last work [*Religion of Reason Out of the Sources of Judaism*] to this: it speaks from the 'you' of faith. It stops being philosophy!"[26]

These different modes and temporalities of speech take a range of artistic forms, as expressions of diverse psychic modalities. For verbal arts, the

24. Rosenstock, "Grammar as a Social Science," in *Speech and Reality*, 100.
25. Rosenstock, *Practical Knowledge of the Soul*, 21.
26. Ibid.

epic (indicative), lyrical (subjunctive), and dramatic (imperative) modes of poetry correspond to each of the personal and modal aspects of grammar. Implicit in this delineation is a critique of Greek tragedy. In Greek tragedy, according to Rosenstock, the tragic hero remains in isolation, cut off from community and world. He speaks, but in monological isolation: "Answering the message of the gods from his stage between God and world, between poetry and epic, Prometheus defies the orders of the Olympians and begins to speak the pure, present-tense language of the human soul."[27] However, such defiant speech will "die away in the drama of the cross," where God and humanity enter into dialogue, revealing Prometheus's speech as "an attempt by self-awareness to be god-like instead of being a 'you.'"[28] Tragedy, then, is subsumed in the Christian dramatic dialogue, where God and humanity really speak to one another, breaking out of their isolation.

With these aesthetic and temporal features of his theory of grammar, Rosenstock articulates the break with idealism that both authors sought. However, since Rosenstock identifies full, living, present speech with Christianity, his work clearly poses a problem for Rosenzweig.[29] Why remain a Jew, when Christianity offers the overcoming of paganism and the prospect of universal fellowship in living speech? This was, clearly, a question that both authors had faced at different times,[30] but the Christian shape of *Seele* crystallizes it for Rosenzweig with particular acuity: Rosenstock's work signals a path away from idealism—but would seem to require giving up Judaism in its particularity.

While Rosenzweig acknowledges the importance of Rosenstock's work for his thought in the *Star of Redemption*, the specific nature of Rosenstock's influence is rarely discussed. However, the above features of *Seele* provide some insight into the shape of this relationship, since they closely parallel some of the more enigmatic aspects of the *Star*. In the *Star*, Rosenzweig appropriates Rosenstock's grammatical method so as to *un*-ask the "Jewish

27. Ibid., 24.

28. Ibid.

29. To clarify: on one level, the "primal speech" of all peoples embodies the multiple potentials of the soul. However, he also argues that Christianity embodies the fullness of speech, whereas other forms of thought and life tend to reduce the soul to one of its potentials. My reading here relies both on the published version of *Practical Knowledge of the Soul* and Rosenstock's distinctions between Judaism and Christianity in their letters preceding its initial drafting in 1916. See *Judaism Despite Christianity*, 149–56, 161–64.

30. Its ubiquity in German culture led to it being termed the *Judenfrage* (Jewish question), in the sense of why assimilation and/or conversion was not preferable.

question," demonstrating Judaism to be a way of speech, life, and thought with as universal a significance as Christianity—a possibility Rosenstock clearly did not envisage. The parallels that emerge from these two works show both Rosenzweig's debt to Rosenstock and his originality—their proximity and distance illustrating the uniquely creative potency of this friendship of difference.

A RELIGION OF SPEECH OUT OF THE SOURCES OF JUDAISM

The Star of Redemption is, to say the least, a difficult book, which makes a brief discussion of its structure and plan necessary. The book is divided into three sections. The first part explores the three "elements" of God, humanity, and the world. Here, Rosenzweig argues that each element has its own inner logic and identity, such that one cannot simply identify them with each other. By making each element irreducible to the others, Rosenzweig rejects an idealism that would identify them all as aspects of a totality. The distinctive identity of each element resides in its being a particular "meta"-type. First, God is "metaphysical" in the sense that God acts out of God's nature, both having an essential power and being actively free to go beyond that power. The world is "meta-logical" in that the reason that comprehends and unifies the world also surpasses it; the identity of reason with being falls apart, as logic transcends the world it grasps. Finally, humanity is "meta-ethical" in that humanity, in order to affirm and obey the moral law that constitutes ethics, must also be above the law so as to apprehend it in freedom. Each element, then, differs from the others and refuses totality, such that the three elements together elude the grasp of thought.

While resisting totality, in the first section of the *Star* the elements remain isolated. This is clearest with regard to meta-ethical humanity, which in its isolation is free, yet cannot really act. The human self is in what Rosenzweig calls its "mountainously taciturn solitude" without speech.[31] Like Rosenstock, Rosenzweig identifies this pre-dialogical self with Greek tragedy, where the character can "only debate":

> Rationally it analyzes the content of the tragic situation in endless twists and turns. Thereby it withdraws the self, defiant beyond all situations, the essence of tragedy, from view until such time as it is once more restored to the center of attention by the chorus . . .[32]

31. Rosenzweig, *Star of Redemption*, 73.
32. Ibid., 77.

Such withdrawal is volitional, an expression of willfulness over against the world and gods. Only in modern drama does dialogue emerge, particularly in the persuasion scene, where one character has authority over another.[33] Greek tragic heroes, then, do not "pose Job-like questions," but remain trapped in an isolated silence; Rosenzweig and Rosenstock here agree on the need for drama to surpass its ancient form.

How, then, does one leave this solitary "world of possibility"—"Who should summon it [the soul]—when it is deaf? What is it to do out there when it is—speechless?"[34] Only God's metaphysical, ecstatic being can break the silence, and this procession of divine speech comprises the second part of the *Star*, moving from creation through revelation to redemption. As Robert Gibbs has discussed, the three phases of interaction here correspond to the persons and types of speech in Rosenstock's grammatical method.[35] One could add, however, as their common repudiation of Greek drama suggests, that the theory of art in the *Star* also grows from the dialogue with Rosenstock. Moreover, Rosenzweig goes to great lengths not only to construct a parallel aesthetic theory, but also to link this aesthetics with biblical hermeneutics, so as to emphasize the fullness of speech within Judaism.

The heart of Rosenzweig's answer to the above question—how the soul leaves its speechless solitude—is his dialogical understanding of revelation. However, he argues this can only be reached via the indirect speech of creation. As Stephane Mosès points out, dialogue only becomes possible through the mediating negation of creation, which recognizes creatures' finite dependence on God while affirming their existent independence.[36] Creation, then, is proto-dialogue. Commenting on Genesis 1, Rosenzweig writes,

> It gives to creativity in advance the clear, active form of the *past tense* and thereby to creation its reality as time. And at a stroke it endows the Created as a whole with its appropriate form, the definite form. Each individual thing gains definition only after a detour via its membership in a category as expressed by the indefinite article.[37]

---

33. Feminist readers of Rosenzweig might be troubled by the invocation of Shakespeare's *The Taming of the Shrew* as an example of such persuasion, given the abuse Kate suffers at the hands of Petruchio.

34. Rosenzweig, *Star of Redemption*, 82.

35. Gibbs, *Correlations in Rosenzweig and Levinas*, 62–70.

36. Mosès, *System and Revelation*, 104.

37. Rosenzweig, *Star of Redemption*, 152; emphasis added.

In Genesis, creation is an act of *indicative* speech. God speaks retrospectively of creation, in the third person. The process of creative affirmation of impersonal things finds its fulfillment in the creation of humanity, where, within the third-person class of human being, Adam acquires a proper name, which lets him be called so that he may respond. The language of creation bears the features of third-person, indicative, past-tense speech, much as Rosenstock links these in his grammatical method.

The central, crucial point for Rosenzweig's system—and for his conversation with Rosenstock—emerges in his discussion of revelation. In his commentary on the Song of Songs, Rosenzweig finds the model for the dialogue between God and humanity. Beginning with God's command to humanity, calling the soul to love God, the soul is addressed as "you" first, with God being the first "I." Again, it is God's metaphysical being that frees humanity from its solitude. Like the child Rosenstock describes, the soul then finds its voice—its "I"— only in response to God's call. Here, we encounter the asymmetrical relation of the imperative, in which the soul is first a "you" in relation to authority.[38] So named, so called, the subject emerges from its third-person isolation, to a second-person grammar, and finally to the first person:

> The imperative belongs to revelation as the indicative to creation; only it does not abandon the ambit of I and Thou. That which sounded in advance out of that all-embracing, lonely, monologic 'let us' of God's at the creation of man reaches its fulfillment in the I and Thou of the imperative of revelation. The he-she-it of the third person has fallen silent. It was but the foundation, the soil from which the I and Thou sprang.[39]

One of the central arguments of Rosenzweig's view of revelation is that it transforms one's perception of creation. In the light of dialogue, the indicative, impersonal speech of creation is revealed to be revelation as well, even if it could not be understood as such: "The past only becomes visible to revelation when and as revelation shines into it with the light of the present."[40]

While this idea has been explored and clarified by many commentators, it is especially pertinent to this study for how it shapes Rosenzweig's theory of art, in relation to the sequence of creation–revelation–redemption. In

---

38. See *Star of Redemption*, 176.
39. Ibid., 186.
40. Ibid.

the "Theory of Art" section on creation, Rosenzweig discusses visual art, in which nature is given a fixed, silent, impersonal representation. Its existence is affirmed, yet speech remains impossible. Visual art, then, represents the silent world of creation prior to revelatory speech, always risking idolatry, though retaining some revelatory potential.[41]

In the section on revelation, Rosenzweig interprets music as its representative art form; like revelation, it focuses on the momentary, particularly in the harmony that "appears to make it wholly independent of the rhythmic whole." Music, like the love of the Song of Songs, is a "momentary self-transformation,"[42] denying all other moments for this one. The speech of lovers is like musical notes, utterly absorbing the hearer before passing on to the next moment. In this exclusion of duration, where one only hears what is immediately sung or played, music is like a nonverbal imperative that absorbs and thereby shapes the hearer.

For Rosenzweig, however, revelation is not simply musical; rather, it manifests a new form of poetic speech that reflects its musical intonations. The Song, he argues, is primarily lyrical poetry, the "lyrical duo-solitude of the lover and beloved." This lyrical discourse is dominated by the "I," the first-person, even as it occurs between two.[43] The mistake of nineteenth-century criticism of the Song, on Rosenzweig's view, was in treating it as epic poetry: "The goal [of historical criticism] was always to transform the lyric I and Thou of the poem into an epic-graphic He and She. The language of the revelation of the soul seemed something uncanny for the spirit of the century which recreated everything in its image, as objective and worldly."[44] The light of lyrical revelation discloses epic poetry as the objective, indicative, third-person art form that corresponds to the impersonal, monological world of creation. Lyrical melody escapes this verbal fixity, bringing speakers into a momentary, subjective union before which the world fades away.

---

41. Batnitzky, *Idolatry and Representation*, 84–90.

42. Rosenzweig, *Star of Redemption*, 163.

43. As noted in the introduction to this chapter, there is ongoing debate as to who the lovers are in this section. Building on Stahmer's work, and the Gritli letters, it would seem that Rosenzweig identifies the Shulamite with Gritli. However, Braiterman's reading of Rosenzweig's work as incorporating masks, such that this is a mask through which he constructs a masculinist relation to God, deserves consideration as well. See Stahmer, "Franz Rosenzweig's Letters," 387; and Braiterman, *Shape of Revelation*, 210–11, 230–31.

44. Rosenzweig, *Star of Redemption*, 200.

Revelation, however, is not the last word. Much as the lovers in the Song of Songs cry out, sharing the desire to share their intimacy, God and the soul cannot remain silent before the world. This is, first, because creation is already a dimension of revelation, such that the soul is called to hear God's speech in the world. More directly, God's loving imperative to the soul within revelation also calls her to love her neighbor.[45] Growing out of individual prayer, which is subjunctive, one's own voice can merge with the voice of one's neighbor, into the "we," which opens onto the future as the world of possibility. The "we," then, is the grammatical voice of community, but it is so as the integration of you, I, and she/he—all three grammatical persons are taken up into this voice. This future is the future of redemption, and the union of the "we" always remains somewhat deferred, open both to further possibility and to judgment should the community forget that its "we" is not yet final, as not all are yet included.[46]

Artistically, this redemptive unity is manifest in the dramatic, as a form of poetry that unites elements of epic and lyrical form. In dramatic poetry, one is concerned with tone and diction, but these must also be joined with the idea, so that the poem speaks to the whole human being. This significance of tone will become central in Rosenzweig's work on translation. Dramatic poetry—almost like opera—thus becomes the artistic representation of the full potency of the soul. Rosenzweig argues that the fulfillment of dramatic poetry is found in the poetic "we" of Psalms 111 to 118.[47] The life of the community, as sung in the psalm, thus comes to embody dramatic, fully dialogical speech. Thus, the cycle of art, paralleling the passage from creation to revelation to redemption, is from epic to lyrical to dramatic poetry—precisely the same progression as in Rosenstock's work.[48]

The central section of the *Star* thus not only draws upon Rosenstock's grammar, but also from his correlation of various grammatical modes, tenses, and persons to particular forms of verbal, visual, and musical aesthetics.

---

45. Rosenzweig, *Star of Redemption*, 205–8.

46. For an intriguing and helpful commentary on the relation of the "we" to judgment, see Gibbs, *Why Ethics?* 184–87.

47. Rosenzweig, *Star of Redemption*, 250–53.

48. Leora Batnitzky has argued persuasively that visual art is not idolatrous for Rosenzweig. While I agree with Batitzky on this point, she minimizes the significance of music for Rosenzweig's aesthetics. I would put the relationship as follows: visual art can be redemptive, when revelation's lyrical and musical dimensions inform and energize its stasis. See Batnitzky, *Idolatry and Representation*, 99–104.

Moreover, Rosenzweig correlates each poetic form to a particular Jewish scripture: Genesis takes an epic form, the Song of Songs is lyrical, and the Psalms are the dramatic unity of these voices. All three modes of poetry, together, give rise to the life of the community, both in their content and in their forms. Thus, the parallels between the *Star* and the *Seele* run even deeper than is often acknowledged. This raises, in my view, the question of why Rosenzweig would incorporate Rosenstock's Christian discourse so extensively into the *Star*. Stephane Mosès has asked a similar question along these lines in considering Rosenzweig's focus on the soul's dialogue with God—a personal relation that occupies a far more central place in Protestant Christianity than in Judaism.[49] Why would Rosenzweig adopt such alien terminology and conceptuality, so as to articulate the central dynamics of Judaism?

In my view, the importance of Rosenstock's work to the central section of the *Star* suggests that it is fruitful to read the *Star* as a response to Rosenstock's earlier correspondence—and, more precisely, a response to the exclusive universality accorded to Christianity. While the *Star*, obviously, is more than *simply* a response, this helps to account for the grammatical and artistic theories at its core. Moreover, Rosenzweig did, on occasion, refer to the *Star* as a "counterpart to the drawing of a cross of reality."[50] Earlier in the correspondence, Rosenzweig had expressed his frustration in trying to convey to Rosenstock the living, vital character of Judaism:

> You make it difficult for us both, because you ask me to lay bare a skeleton that can only prove through its organic life that flesh and blood grow and flow round it…you are directly hindering me from treating my Judaism in the first person, in that you call yourself a Jew too.[51]

Rosenzweig warned Rosenstock against equating Judaism with paganism, especially when Rosenstock stereotypes Judaism as the "law of the Father" over against Jesus's love in the New Testament. As Rosenzweig writes, "That is the mistake in your construction, namely that you fight against Judaism as Paganism."[52] The *Star* affirms what Leora Batnitzky terms carnal, living

---

49. Mosès, *System and Revelation*, 106.

50. Letter of August 22, 1918. See *Die "Gritli"-Briefe*, 124. Quoted in Zank, "Rosenzweig-Rosenstock Triangle," 85.

51. Rosenzweig, *Judaism Despite Christianity*, 98.

52. Ibid., 130.

Israel[53] *through* the language of Rosenstock's grammatical and aesthetic theory. This effectively constitutes an apologetic against Rosenstock's criticisms of Judaism, allowing Rosenzweig to show what he could not say in their letters. Indeed, this exchange seems particularly pertinent in understanding the principle of selection in Rosenzweig's biblical commentary: through Genesis, the Song of Songs, and Psalms, he can show Rosenstock that a full aesthetic, temporal, and verbal life is contained within Judaism, exhibiting the universality that Rosenstock could not see "from the outside."

The effect of this response is clearest in the concluding section of the *Star*, where Rosenzweig argues for the dual universal missions of Judaism and Christianity, effectively repudiating Rosenstock's universal/particular opposition of Christianity and Judaism. In effect, Rosenzweig's argument is that Jewish particularity is of universal significance, first and foremost because it prevents Christianity from lapsing into a false, hegemonic universalism. While the Christian mission spreads revelation to the world, and thereby moves the world toward redemption, Judaism's faithfulness to God prevents Christian totalization that would neglect temporality and particularity. Jews and Christians travel separate paths until the end of history; the "we" is never complete.

Rosenzweig's theory of dual universalism is intriguing, particularly because he argues that it provides a pluralistic understanding of truth. On this view, both Judaism and Christianity are ways to the truth, ways of relating to God, yet each is only partial. Neither one alone brings the relations of God, humanity, and world to completion; the truth thus remains distant. "The truth, the whole truth, thus belongs neither to them nor to us . . . the whole truth would demand not only seeing its light but also what was illuminated by it . . . And thus we both have but a part of the whole truth."[54] This partial truth, parceled out to each community, sets each on its way and demands their complementarity. This affirms, once again, the elemental separation of God and humanity, as our access to the truth can never be complete, save in the community of all of humanity. Thus, he sets forth a strong disagreement with Rosenstock, concretizing the temporal disagreement of Jew and Christian—but an eschatological bond remains.[55]

53. Batnitzky, *Idolatry and Representation*, 74–77.

54. Rosenzweig, *Star of Redemption*, 416.

55. Thus, I would disagree somewhat with Leora Batnitzky's emphasis on disagreement as constitutive of dialogue. This is central (and perhaps frequently overlooked), but it is not

Less frequently noted, however, is the connection of this theory of partial truth with Rosenzweig's understanding of God. It is only for God to have the whole truth, but this is precisely what Judaism and Christianity, *together*, represent for Rosenzweig. As metaphysical, God has an eternal, unchanging nature or power, free within God's own self-determination. Simultaneously, God goes out of God's self, extending into the world in creation, speaking in revelation. Through their two universal missions, the eternal, unchanging Star of the Jewish community and the rays of Christianity thus together model the two sides of God's being, bringing the world and humanity into the presence of God's metaphysical oneness. The star and the rays, together, are in the image of God.

In 1916, after the correspondence on Judaism and Christianity but before the *Star* was written, Rosenstock composed a litany that, he later learned, Rosenzweig agreed with as an assessment of their dialogical disagreement, while still signifying a deeper affinity between them. A few lines from the litany serve both to represent the theory of partial truth and perhaps show how they made space for one another in their lives, faithful even in and through their hostility and competition:

> Through all times his friend,
> In all places his foe,
> In the wills' whirligig equally spinning,
> In the mind's symbols relentless at war . . .
> Each other we can neither love nor hate,
> Neither tighter nor looser our dominion make.
> To him who saw all, the split overlaps.
> Life seems one's own, yet is a metaphor,
> Is in servant's shape, and Great Inquisitorial.
> God is the cross and is David's star.[56]

TRANSLATING SPEECH AND SCRIPTURE

The *Sprachdenken* (speech-thinking) of the *Star* represented Rosenzweig's break from idealism, and his turn toward a new type of philosophizing. This new, grammatical thinking led Rosenzweig away from systematic projects, and his attentiveness to the workings of language led to a lifelong interest in translation as a particularly significant project for modern Judaism. As

---

sufficient, and the many ways that both authors appropriate from one another complicate their explicit, intentional opposition. Batnitzky, "Dialogue as Judgment," 532–34.

56. Rosenstock, *Judaism Despite Christianity*, 176.

Barbara Galli has pointed out, Rosenzweig's interest in translation grew from his encounter and correspondence with Rosenstock. To communicate effectively with Rosenstock—across their different discourses, spatiotemporal locations, and religious orientations—required Rosenzweig to attend to issues of translation.[57] Translation would remain central to both Rosenzweig's thought and practice for the remainder of his life; it constituted the bulk of his later scholarship, in both the translations of Jehuda Halevi's poems, and his translation of the Bible with Martin Buber. As Galli rightly argues,[58] one can read these translation projects as nonsystematic applications of the speech-thinking central to both of these friends.

The transition from the *Star* to his works of translation can best be understood via passage through one of Rosenzweig's posthumously published works. Written as a popularization of the *Star*, *Understanding the Sick and the Healthy: A View of World, Man and God* crystallizes one of the guiding principles of the *Star*: the transition from words to names as the fundamental part of speech. In this brief work, "abstract" thinking, representing the culmination of philosophy in idealism, thinks of words as the primary part of speech, signifying the enduring, atemporal essences of things. "The 'butter in itself' is the 'idea' of butter; it is what the butter is 'essentially.'"[59] For philosophy, this essence is precisely what maintains the identity of butter over time; the idea of butter holds together the butter wished for by the customer, sold by the supermarket clerk, and the butter in the box. For such philosophy, the word thus becomes extraneous, supplementary—it is "arbitrary," as any word could be used—butter, *beurre*, etc. And yet, Rosenzweig argues, living in time, we never see, taste, or grasp, this *idea* of butter—rather, it is, in fact, the *name* of something that ensures its endurance over time: "The name is not the essence. Yet, although the name and the essence are not identical, the name is as permanent as the essence is supposed to be."[60] Speech, as an act of naming, enables continuity through the changes of time.

Names, then, carry things into the stream of time—past, present, and future. Names only indicate what things are, in terms of continuity; they do not give things freedom to change. This is why people have both a surname, which binds them to tradition and the past, and a proper name,

57. Galli, *Franz Rosenzweig and Jeuda Halevi*, 322–23.
58. Ibid., 399–416.
59. Rosenzweig, *Understanding the Sick and the Healthy*, 48.
60. Ibid., 49.

which opens to the future. The proper name indicates that a person is not entirely bound by the past, even if the surname indicates responsibility to the past. Both this responsibility and this freedom come from the other, as one is called before one can speak (one is a "you," before being an "I," as discussed above with Rosenstock).

Both common nouns and proper names point toward the Name—the name of God, in which speech finds its fulfillment. The Name, for Rosenzweig, is utterly vocative; it frees God from being a thing, or from needing to be called by another. As he writes,

> To utter God's name is entirely different from uttering the name of a man or a thing. True, they have something in common; the name of God, His proper name, and a term of designation are not identical with the bearers of these names. But except for this they differ widely. Man has a name so that he may be called by it. To be called by his name is for him an ultimate distinction. God does not have a name so that he may be called by it. To Him it is irrelevant whether His name is called or not; he heeds him who calls Him by His name as well as those who call Him by other names or those who speak to him in name-less silence. He bears a name for our sake, so that we may call Him. It is for our sake that He permits Himself to be named and called by that name, since it is only by jointly calling upon Him that we become a "We."[61]

God's name has no meaning or essence. Rather, it introduces the vocative into speech, where one can call upon God. In one person's call upon God, another can join in, or respond—the call becomes the basis for community. As what one might call a "pure vocative," however, Rosenzweig does not think the Name is confined to a particular term; rather, wherever one calls upon God, one calls upon the Name, whether in word or in silence. This means, as he explains, that the Name moves into and through other words and names, binding things together even while also binding people into a "we."

The *Buchlein*, then, attributes to names the central linguistic principles of the *Star*: moving through time, binding us to past and future in the present, developing community, and moving toward the redemption of the world. Moreover, in its vocative dimension, the Name courses through all of language—potentially making *any* word a signifier of the Name. It thereby encapsulates the central features of Rosenzweig's understanding

---

61. Ibid., 91.

of the challenges of translation, especially biblical translation, where the vocative call of revelation must resonate through the text, so as to be heard by the reader in a living way.

Rosenzweig's first major published work of translation was a collection of poems by Jehuda Halevi, which included a set of explanatory notes on his translations. While his notes to the poems demonstrate the understanding of language set forth in the *Star* and the *Buchlein*, the afterword has long been noted by scholars as Rosenzweig's clearest statement of his theory of translation. As he writes, his goal in translating the poems is not to Germanize them, but rather to reflect the "foreign" tone of Halevi's poems within the German language: "not to Germanize what is foreign, but rather to make foreign what is German?"[62] The achievement of introducing the foreign tongue into German "can lie nowhere else than where the creative achievement of speaking itself lies." This means, as shall become clearer below, that Rosenzweig fundamentally identifies speech as translation. To translate "makes foreign" the German by introducing a distant past into the present language; translation is a speech-relation that traverses (and thus establishes) both space and time. "The translator makes himself the mouthpiece of the foreign voice, which he makes audible over the gulf of space and time. With translation, moreover, one does not simply introduce one text into a new language, but rather, one "brings along with it the heritage of the general language-spirit of his [original] language to the new language."[63]

In carrying language into time, translation moves toward redemption, symbolized by the one universal language of human speech. This is not, for Rosenzweig, simply a language of objective description that sublimates difference, but rather a language that grows from the spirited discourses of the nations, including rather than suppressing their diversity. A national language (in this case, German) has the potential to include foreign tongues precisely because they are included, "at least in germ." A redemptive unity of tongues, in which people(s) speak to people(s), is possible:

> One can translate because in every language is contained the possibility of every other language; one may translate if one can realize this possibility through cultivation of such linguistic fallow land; and one should translate so that the day of that harmony of

---

62. Rosenzweig, "Jehuda Halevi: Ninety-Two Hymns and Poems," 170.
63. Ibid., 171.

languages, which can grow only in each individual language, not in the empty space between them, may come.[64]

This goal of redemption is significant, for while Rosenzweig emphasizes the foreignness of translation, his goal is not ultimately one of exile.[65] Rather, it is through the sojourn of foreignness, and the creation of real relations of difference, that a deeper, non-hegemonic unity among peoples is possible.

For Rosenzweig, both leading the way and blocking the path is Martin Luther, whose German translation of the Hebrew Bible stands as one of his greatest cultural achievements. As Rosenzweig describes, the power of Luther's translation is precisely his willingness to stretch the German language to accommodate the foreign spirit of the text. This was, precisely, not an assimilation of the text to the target language: "it [the Hebrew text] was not washed away without further resistance . . . instead it actively engaged in this development, and by this itself remained preserved in its originality."[66] While Luther's willingness to translate with a sense of the foreignness of the text garners Rosenzweig's praise, a tension remains insofar as Luther's reading of the Bible is a Christian one, figurally shaped by the New Testament. This becomes a more pressing issue in Rosenzweig's biblical translation with Buber, but it shapes his work on Halevi as well.

For the Halevi poems in particular, Rosenzweig describes two central difficulties for the translator. First, he stresses the importance of translating the meter of the poetry, as well as its words and rhyme scheme. Whereas rhyme can be copied, meter carries with it a "marked foreignness," such that translating the meter will stretch the language more radically than simply attending to a literal, word-for-word translation. Only when the meter is adequately translated will the poems be fully translated into the German language—something which prior translators of Halevi had failed to do. The second task of the translator is to convey the "heritage" of Halevi's language—namely, the biblical text, as Halevi quotes from the Hebrew Bible throughout his poetry. The translator cannot, in Rosenzweig's words, "suppress the innuendos of language." This task is rendered easier, initially, by Luther's having translated the Bible into German; citation of Luther's translation will let readers recognize the citation as such. Of course, in

---

64. Ibid., 170. See also Gibbs, *Why Ethics?* 293–97.

65. This qualifies the exilic aspect of translation which Peter Gordon emphasizes in his discussion of Rosenzweig's translation theory. See Gordon, *Rosenzweig and Heidegger*, 218–20.

66. Rosenzweig, "Jehuda Halevi," 172.

citing Luther, one may lose the meter, or in retaining the meter, one may lose Luther—it seems impossible to translate both levels of meaning simultaneously. Moreover, to have the text bear the innuendos of a Jewish reading, as opposed to the christocentric innuendos of Luther's language, adds another level of complexity for which the translator remains responsible.

Faced with these contradictory demands, translation must seek to accomplish both, for the translation of this text is far from a mere act of scholarship. As Rosenzweig says at the end of the afterword, Halevi's poems were initially composed to be spoken, or even *sung*—they are liturgical poetry, sung by the cantor and congregation. They are meant to be the language of revelation and redemption: the poems translate biblical revelation into the life of the community, making it spoken to the congregation. When one reads the poems, and recognizes their close relation to the Song of Songs and the Prophets, the importance of meter becomes clearer: to lose the meter would be to lose the lyrical and dramatic feel of the poems—their *musicality*—which is precisely the spoken element of revelation. Clearly, Rosenzweig does not expect that his translations will be used in worship, but he does want his translation to bear this capacity for revelation to future readers, whether they hear it or not. The goal of the translation, then, is ultimately to translate poetry such that the poem may translate God's speech from the past to humanity for future generations. To translate in a way that failed to recognize this level of address would run counter to a hope for redemption.

In his translation of the poem "Life," Rosenzweig conveys these multiple levels of significance in his emphasis on the material dimensions of the poem. The poem begins with what is a strangely distant speech—a speech that, in recognizing the vanity and transience of the world, is subject to death and emptiness. It is, as he terms it in the notes, a "soliloquy of the human with his soul." However, Rosenzweig notes the break before the last six lines, where God's presence as redeemer leads into a renewed emphasis on life:

> Before God, powerfully swift, calls me to rest and of life's
>   Bond I am bound in dark shrines.
> Because my Redeemer lives, He will still bless
>   His memory and so incorporate me
> "Into life!" to the living, rejoicing souls,
>   Still living in life's ground—Yours.[67]

---

67. Rosenzweig, "Life," in *Franz Rosenzweig and Jehuda Halevi*, 94.

Strikingly, in the note Rosenzweig describes these lines as "a floating away of immediate—I might say musical—power . . . with its unceasing repetition of the same motif, following one after the other more and more closely . . . it is reminiscent of the vanishing finales of some of Beethoven's slow movements."[68] The lyrical, musical dimension surges forth, breaking the human soul out of its isolation and death—into life, much like revelation in the *Star*.

Beyond the musical dimension, the poem also testifies to Rosenzweig's intertextual concern. The language of the last few verses evokes scripture— "Because my Redeemer lives" recalls Job 19, and the surrounding verses evoke both Psalm 115 and 1 Samuel 25. Rosenzweig also manages to maintain both the acrostic form, in which the opening letters of the poem spell Jehuda Halevi, *and* the rhyme within the verses—even while translating to German. The poems harken both back to the *Star* and forward to his translation with Buber, while testifying to the continued importance of speech-thinking.[69]

Rosenzweig's work in translation culminated in his biblical translation with Martin Buber, a project that was central to Rosenzweig's scholarship and correspondence until near the end of his life. As throughout his work, the focus on the tonal, musical elements of speech predominates, especially in two essays on translation, "Scripture and Word" and "Scripture and Luther."[70] In "Scripture and Word," Rosenzweig accentuates the segmentation of scriptural phrases by breathing marks, as the rhythm of the text. The poetic dimensions of the biblical text must be recognized, and translated, in their distinctive rhythms. However, Rosenzweig also recognizes that the lyrical moment of speech is not the only one; rather, it inspires and informs prosaic speech. As he writes,

> Even today the language of every child is originally lyrical and magical, the enraptured outburst feeling and the powerful instrument of desire . . . But the child only becomes an adult when through this *Ursprache* there breaks the unlyrical and unmagical fullness of the word, equally alien to song and proverbial saying alike—a breakthrough that like every genuine revelation is perceived only

---

68. Rosenzweig, "Jehuda Halevi," 232.

69. See Galli, *Franz Rosenzweig and Jehuda Halevi*, 329–33, 341, for the connection with Rosenstock.

70. Everett Fox argues that there is a shift in Rosenzweig's translations, which come to differ more strongly from Luther's reading over time. See "Rosenzweig as Translator," 377.

in retrospect, and avoids being assigned to a particular moment of the past.[71]

As in the *Star*, speech begins in lyricism but moves to drama, where law and community emerge. The Bible's prose builds from this lyricism, even if it is not determinative for biblical speech as a whole. As with the Halevi poems, a translation that lost this dimension would lose the capacity for revelation.

"Scripture and Luther" is perhaps Rosenzweig's best-known essay on translation. In it Rosenzweig emphasizes both the transformative impact of Luther's translation of the Bible for Christianity, and its subsequent stasis within the community. Moreover, he finds in Luther's work a tension between the two approaches to translation discussed above. At times, perhaps in passages that seem clearer, Luther's concern is to render the language as naturally in German as possible, not least because of his strong commitment to revelation being *for us*. Only on occasions where he sees the form as particularly noteworthy does he introduce Hebraisms and "foreign" rhythms into the translation. In other words, his focus on the formal elements of the text was always already shaped by his doctrinal commitments. Because Rosenzweig recognizes translation as both for the present community and for future readers as well, he argues that the act of translation must be more radically open to the importance of form:

> And if we believe that not only a passage called to our attention by a particular circumscribed doctrine but any human utterance may conceal the possibility that one day, in his time or in my time, God's word may be revealed in it, then in that case the translator must, so far as his language permits, follow the peculiar turns of that potentially revelation-bearing utterance, whether by direct reconstruction or by implication.[72]

The possibility of speech between God and humanity, as the fundamental dimension of biblical prose and poetry, requires attention to the form of Scripture in greater detail than Luther allowed; it must be phrased so that it can be *spoken*. Attention to the diversity of genres, wordplay, and intertextuality must occupy the translator if this dimension of the text is to be "audibly legible." Again, Rosenzweig adopts a musical metaphor to describe the goal: "It is only when it [the Scripture] is freed from the

---

71. Rosenzweig, "Scripture and Word," in *Scripture and Translation*, 45.
72. Rosenzweig, "Scripture and Luther," in *Scripture and Translation*, 64.

monotonous gray of the usual piano reduction that this whole wealth of voices and tonal colors becomes, precisely through this notation of it in full score, audible, legible—audibly, legible."[73] The Bible, for Rosenzweig, is symphonic. Thus, it is clear that the grammatical forms of speech remained central throughout Rosenzweig's work on translation, but his tonal focus modifies his approach. [74]

What is not yet clear in his writings on translation is exactly why Rosenzweig thinks that all speech can participate in the redemptive work of translation. This becomes clearer in his essay on "The Eternal"—Moses Mendelssohn's translation of God's name, in Exodus 3:14. Mendelssohn was perhaps the single most influential Jewish intellectual of the eighteenth century, and strenuously defended the rationality and universality of Judaism, thereby laying the groundwork for Jewish liberalism in Germany. Mendelssohn translates the Name as "The Eternal" to signify God's eternal being and providence; for him, this name designates these attributes better than "the Lord" as a translation of *Adonai*. However, even in rejecting "the Lord" (the translation preferred by Calvin, so as to express God's sovereignty), Rosenzweig argues that this perspective still influenced Mendelssohn, as he sides with God's eternal immutability rather than with God's proximity to the believer. In this emphasis on eternal sovereignty, both Calvin and Mendelssohn lose the *vocative* dimension of the name. As Rosenzweig writes, "The Hebrew *Adonai* . . . possessed (and still possesses in Jewish mouths) precisely this inward resonance, charged with a fundamental tone of vocativeness, of direct address and petition, and accordingly was used in post-biblical prayer literature predominantly in the vocative."[75] He argues that this vocative dimension is central to both the "digrammaton," the primeval form of the name that only occurs in exclamations, and the Tetragrammaton, distinguishing divine names from all other names. The Tetragrammaton, for Rosenzweig, is both vocative and epithet; it is a call to the wholly other, but also a call to the one who "bends down to be essentially present."[76]

For Rosenzweig, the true significance of God's name (as in *Understanding the Sick and the Healthy*), is that it lets us call upon God. Moreover,

73. Ibid., 66.

74. Fox, "Franz Rosenzweig as Translator," 382–83; and Braiterman, *Shape of Revelation*, 115–18.

75. Rosenzweig, "The Eternal," in *Scripture and Translation*, 106. See Batnitzky, "Translation as Transcendence," 109.

76. Rosenzweig, "The Eternal," in *Scripture and Translation*, 112.

Rosenzweig hypothesizes that the Tetragrammaton is the earliest of the divine names, most central precisely because it is both vocative and epithet. As both, the Tetragrammaton introduces the vocative dimension into descriptive, nominal language. It is, one could say, the introduction of the foreignness of calling upon God into the mute speech of creation. The revelation of the Name is a translation into human speech, and perhaps the inspiration for translation within human speech as well.

In his work on translation, the full impact of Rosenzweig's speech-thinking becomes apparent. Speech-thinking includes both speech and writing as modes of encounter. Moreover, the task of the translator, in seeking to transmit the possibility of revelation, even for an unknown audience in the future, demands attention to the forms of textual specificity and distinctiveness, such that nothing is lost. Speech-thinking, then, while a being-present in encounter, is an extensive being-present, listening in a way that bears responsibility for both past and future. As Rosenzweig makes clear in "Scripture and Luther," his work is critical of *Wissenschaft*, the scientific study of religion epitomized by historical criticism, not because it is critical, but because it is not scientific *enough*. Its focus on objectivity flattens out the range of discursive forms that enable relation and fails to convey the full, living sense of revelation to which the Scriptures' poetic and aesthetic dimensions testify. By studying and translating the text of Scripture in its diversity—epic, narrative, lyrical, dramatic, imperative—Rosenzweig seeks to recapture the vitality of its speech both for his own community and for the future. As Leora Batnitzky argues, translation should "defamiliarize" the reader, creating gaps that require the recognition of divine otherness.[77]

While Rosenzweig's work on translation bears strong resonances of his engagement with Rosenstock and his work, the dialogue between them only continued to develop, with Rosenstock's later works on Scripture and translation bearing the spirit of Rosenzweig's work. Turning to Rosenstock once more, in his later work, will illuminate the parallel trajectories of their views on speech-thinking in relation to Scripture.

CHRISTIAN SPEECH: THE CROSS OF REALITY

In his later work Rosenstock elaborates the grammatical theory of speech described *in nuce* in *Angewandte Seelenkunde*. As with Rosenzweig, Rosenstock sees Scripture as the embodiment of the full life of speech, though

77. Batnitzky, "Translation as Transcendence," 115.

he focuses primarily on the speech of the Gospels. Rosenstock interprets the central dogmas of Christianity, and its canonical Scriptures, in ways that respond to the historical criticism prevalent in late nineteenth- and early twentieth-century theology. Again, it is by attending to the particular imagery of his thought that the parallels with Rosenzweig emerge most clearly. Moreover, like Rosenzweig, his theory of speech centers on the issue of translation, which was a central concern through much of his life—not least because of his split between German and American academia. As Rosenstock writes in "Biblionomics," his first foray into scholarship as a child was a work of translation, and he retained this interest into his later years.[78]

As was discussed earlier in the context of *The Practical Knowledge of the Soul*, Rosenstock argues that the dramatic form is the fulfillment of speech, taking up the diverse modes and persons of lyricism, imperative, and narrative, and thereby carrying past and present into the future. The importance of drama is its movement through time. The implicitly Christian character of this drama, referred to as the "Drama of the Cross," is not spelled out, but Rosenstock's later work shows that his dramatic emphasis highlights his belief in creation's participation in the Triune life of God. Living speech is in the image of God, precisely by reflecting the Trinitarian movement of speech through space and time.[79]

Classically, the relations of the Trinity are described as follows: the Father begets the Son, the Son obeys, and the Spirit proceeds from their love, spiraling outward while binding them together (either from both Father and Son (*filioque*), as in Western Christianity, or from the Father through the Son (*per filium*), in more Orthodox approaches). In some ways presaging the narrative approaches to Trinitarian thought of recent years—for example, those of Karl Barth, Hans Urs von Balthasar, and Robert Jenson—Rosenstock highlights several features of these relations. He especially highlights the work of the Spirit, as the union between the Father and the Son. The Spirit, uniting them, is the bond between these generations, representing their inner life and outward movement into the world. As he writes, "The very meaning of the term Holy Spirit is lost if we forget that the Holy Spirit opens the spirits of the different times to each other."[80] In the Trinity, then, one finds analogates to space and time: the relations of

---

78. Rosenstock, "Biblionomics," 14.
79. Wilfrid Rohrbach, *Das Sprachdenken Eugen Rosenstocks*, 177–78.
80. Rosenstock, *The Fruit of the Lips*, 31.

Father and Son figure past and future, bound together in the present of the Spirit, which extends both inwardly and outwardly into space.

The goal of human speech is to embody these relations—or, more theologically, to participate in this divine life. The guiding image of Rosenstock's speech-thinking is the "Cross of Reality," yet the cross is best understood as analogous to the Triune life. The Cross of Reality clarifies the relations of the different types of speech suggested in his early work. The horizontal axis of the cross is time, from past toward the future. This intersects the vertical axis of the present, which is both inward life and life extended outward into community.

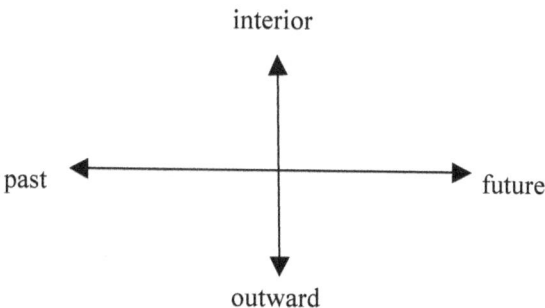

It is important to note that both the future and outward axes of the cross require difference for their constitution. The future must be open to something different than what has come before, and the "outward" element of speech must move beyond the established bounds of a unified community—seeking agreement in dialogue where only disagreement is present. Living speech, at its fullest point, will unify these vertical and horizontal axes, moving in four directions at once, fulfilling the various modes of expression of the soul. For Rosenstock, living speech is found only in Christ, whose speech takes up the modes of speech that would only proceed in a single direction. He writes, "He overcame man's dividedness by living once for all the specific law of the human kind, namely, that man can progress from fragmentariness to completeness only by surviving the death of his old Adam, his old allegiances, and beginning new ones."[81] For Rosenstock, Christ is the Word in that he embodies the fullness of speech.

To participate in the living speech of the spirit—and thus to embody the Cross of Reality—requires living in both past and future, both

81. Rosenstock, *Christian Future*, 66.

locally and beyond one's present community. In several essays, Rosenstock describes the Holy Spirit's work of binding generations as translation. Speech's responsibility to multiple audiences means that, at its core, speech is an act of translation. As he writes of the Gospel of Luke,

> *To be inspired means to translate.* By fixing his attention on this seam between the times, Luke became the first human being who was able to see the spirits of the periods together [i.e., Jesus and the disciples, in parallel missions] and to envisage them as subservient to one spirit, the Spirit of all Spirits.[82]

In "The Generations of the Faith," an essay I will return to below, he makes the connection even more strongly: "Could it be that any future doctrine of the Holy Spirit may have to start with the mystery that we all are required to translate, from the days of Adam to the last judgment?"[83] These later writings of Rosenstock bear testimony to his commitment to the connection between translation and speech, as well as the divine origin of both, which similarly informed Rosenzweig's translation and scriptural interpretation.

Much as Buber and Rosenzweig were met with puzzlement when their speech-oriented translation of the Bible was published, Rosenstock's interpretation of the Gospels stands as a work that scholars trained in historical criticism could only regard with bemusement. It is, one could say, the Word made *very* strange. At times, Rosenstock rejects the conclusions of historical criticism outright, but more broadly his rejection is of its method of treating the Gospels as objective, historical documents—rather than together comprising the source of Christian speech that enables participation in the Cross of Reality. This idiosyncratic interpretation is, I think, best understood as an interpretation of the Gospels as translations of Jesus's speech, in ways analogous to Rosenzweig's principles of scriptural interpretation discussed above.

Rosenstock argues for the unity of the four Gospels based upon the different modes of speech, time, and community that each embodies. Together, they take up and unify the diverse modes of speech and life of humanity, showing how they can be brought together in a nonsynthetic unity. Specifically, Luke's Gospel is a narrative, telling the third-person story first of Christ, and then of Paul, in their respective missions of the Spirit. His Gospel thus extends into the past. Matthew's Gospel is primarily

---

82. Rosenstock, *Fruit of the Lips*, 30.
83. Rosenstock, "Generations of Our Faith," 6.

imperative, as the reader is called to follow Jesus as his savior; this Gospel opens toward the future. Mark, writing from within the early Christian community, in intimate fellowship with Peter, writes the lyrical, subjunctive Gospel, opening the inward space of subjectivity. John, lastly, writes in the abstract indicative, beyond the cycle of history, speaking of Christ as the one who is eternal, yet who comes into the world—thereby moving out into the world. Each Gospel thereby constitutes one axis of the Cross of Reality.[84]

As each Gospel takes up a particular mode of speech and life, it opens new possibilities for that form of life that would otherwise have remained impossible. Luke's Gospel, on Rosenstock's view, takes up Judaism's messianic desire for salvation, which denies the finality or accomplishment of redemption. By writing narratively, Luke shows that this redemption has been accomplished in Christ, and in Paul's mission. John's Gospel adopts the language of Greek poetry, thereby redeeming this language that Platonism saw as dangerous. Mark's Gospel shattered the cosmology of his time, revealing Jesus to be the true Son of God. His work thus broke with the political systems of antiquity, where emperors would be identified as gods. Such natural power is broken by the power of "fellowship," where people are brought together in a new community. Lastly, Matthew's Gospel transgresses the bounds of tribal ritual, where victims are sacrificed, by allowing the victim to speak.[85]

By so unifying these communities, temporalities, and modes of speech, the Gospels take up and transform—perhaps, one should say, resurrect—the artistic, religious, scientific, and customary modes of human speech. The Gospels thus integrate the full range of human speech. Whereas Rosenstock diagnoses various pagan cultures to be "sick" because of the predominance of one mode of speech over others, the Gospels heal speech by introducing the "foreign" spirits of the other modes of discourse into each of them, moving these various discourses and peoples toward unity. The Gospels, in a sense, are mutually translating, allowing each language to speak with the others in a redemptive manner. As Rosenstock summarizes,

> The Evangelists reversed the cross of grammar into a grammar of the cross. One man [i.e., Jesus] had lived from fiat to *factum est*, from "Go out into my world" to "It has been done, my father," from listening to the call through poetry to story to summing up,

---

84. Rosenstock, *Fruit of the Lips*, 85.

85. Ibid., 57–72.

completing his whole life as one grammatical cycle. The Gospels depicted this cycle."[86]

The noteworthy aspects of Rosenstock's grammatical interpretation of the Gospels are the following: First, his theory provides a way to understand, and affirm, the unity of the biblical canon. He strongly rejects the attempt to link three "Synoptic Gospels" when this is done to the exclusion of John (Rosenstock sees John as an apostolic author). However, within this unity, there is still space for attention and listening to what is distinctive in each Gospel—its particularity of form, audience, and history. The best way to understand this approach is, I think, to see each Gospel as a translation of Jesus's life into speech, and together they translate the life of speech for the church. Moreover, to see this unity in the canonicity of the Gospels is to enter into relation to it; each "primitive" discourse (art, religion, manners, science) is a dimension of our humanity today. Reading the four Gospels as a unity provides us with a way into living speech, moving between the diverse modes of human speech as the early church did. This requires listening to the Gospels as revelation, orienting one's own generation to earlier and future generations and congregations, in the life of the Spirit.

One might question, however whether this schematic approach, along with Rosenstock's guiding emphasis on holistic unity, ultimately distorts his interpretation. The rigidity of such a schema, it seems, is less attentive to the rhythms and dimensions of other forms of speech than, say, Barth's interpretation of "secular parables," or Frei's or Lindbeck's more *ad hoc* approach to listening to other communities. This may be most apparent in his exclusive view of Christianity as a universal faith. Thirty years later, Rosenzweig's theory of partial truth still seems to have fallen on deaf ears. In *The Fruit of the Lips*, Judaism remains a particular form of speech, rooted in the past and devoid of universality on its own terms. Moreover, both in conversation with Rosenzweig and in his scriptural hermeneutics, Rosenstock is far less attuned to the intertextual resonances and rhythms of the text, preferring a systematizing order to the dissonant interplay of Rosenzweig's translation.

While *The Fruit of Lips* indicates the biblical impetus for Rosenstock's focus on translation, he does not restrict the importance of translation to the Scriptures. Rather, translation is also the activity that constitutes tradition. A highly illuminating example of the role of translation is "The

---

86. Ibid., 84.

Generations of Our Faith," a lecture given on the occasion of the publication of a new translation of Calvin's *Institutes of the Christian Religion*. For Rosenstock, the *Institutes* are best understood as a translation of the Protestant spirit into scholarly, indicative discourse. The danger for this mode of speaking is to lose the sense of freedom—the future—that comes from hearing the imperative of God's freely given command. "He [Calvin] wanted the poor minds of the mere indicative to learn of the true God who blesses and curses, who denies and demands."[87] Calvin's work, then, attempts to infuse the scholarly indicative, in which relation is absent, with the relational dimension of divine speech.

Interpreting the *Institutes* as a translation, Rosenstock argues, renders comprehensible its most notorious feature—Calvin's doctrine of predestination. While largely of the same spirit as Luther's *sola gratia*—that God's free election justifies people through faith—this doctrine takes on a far more sinister appearance when Calvin draws out the (apparently) logical consequence that God also elects some to reprobation. His logical explication inverts scholastic rationalism, leading it to the unfathomable mystery of God's secret decree. The doctrine of predestination, then, is a "heroic effort of translating man's temporality and so-to-speak non-existence and God's eternal existence into the purely spatial concepts of reason."[88] Linking Lutheran piety with scholastic thought, Calvin informed each's speech with the spirit of the other.

While Calvin's work serves as a translation that opens the theology of his time to the future, ongoing translation is a central feature of a living tradition; this, for Rosenstock, is the importance of Battles' new translation. In a number of cases, Battles' translation may not be philologically correct, yet Rosenstock argues that his interpretations are appropriate—for example, in substituting "plan" for "economy" in speaking of God, given the ways that "economy" is understood in modernity. In a more general sense, translation is ongoing even within thought; while Calvin's doctrine of predestination may have been necessary at his time, it may likewise appear overly rationalistic, lacking in vitality and freedom. One sees the importance of ongoing translation in the work of Karl Barth, whose doctrine of election (in II/2 of the *Church Dogmatics*) breaks with Calvin—in Rosenstock's words, acting as a "translation of predestination into life."[89]

---

87. Rosenstock, "Generations of Our Faith," 9.
88. Ibid.
89. Ibid., 14.

Clearly, translation embodies living speech for Rosenstock as for Rosenzweig. In one's obedient listening to the other, and finding freedom in responding, it builds community across generations. "The Generations of Our Faith" is particularly noteworthy because, as with Rosenzweig's work with both Jehuda Halevi and Moses Mendelssohn, translation provides a way of understanding the vitality of previous theological work, without thereby accepting it as the last word. Still, even with this implicit parallel, it is surprising when Rosenstock invokes Rosenzweig as a way to understand what moved Calvin to "translate" the *Institutes*. Describing Rosenzweig as a "great man of Calvin's stature and suffering" who "has described these secrets of the soul's trembling, as Calvin has trembled innumerable times," Rosenstock then quotes Rosenzweig's note on Jehuda Halevi's poem "The Compulsion" (*Der Zwang*):

> Man seeks his honour in action. But there is in every such action a moment when man loses courage, precisely because he has staked all of it. If at this point a compulsion did not come, which did not help the action to be born, it would never see the light of the world. But this compulsion comes. The human has a right to it, which is recognized by God.
>
> All praying is, in the last resort a prayer for this compulsion, all thanking a thankfulness for it. But the bashfulness, which surrounds the prayer, has its basis here.[90]

With this citation, Rosenstock affirms in 1961 the mutual commitment both thinkers made nearly fifty years earlier: to philosophize only on the basis of speech. Yet, we see here that their commitment to speech-thinking goes deeper than merely aural speech or dialogue in any simplistic sense. Speech is, at its root, already translation—projecting oneself into past and future, into broader community, and into mutual relation. Both authors, in their shared commitment to this intellectual discipline, find the resources for renewing and transforming their traditions, so as to address both the present and the future.

However, the depth of their agreement on speech-thinking only serves to highlight the divergences of their thought. While both thinkers develop a form of speech-thinking, they disagree regarding its implications for their community. We have already seen this in terms of Rosenzweig's application of grammatical thinking and aesthetic theory to the Jewish Scriptures

---

90. Rosenzweig, "Jehuda Halevi: Ninety-Two Hymns and Poems," 268. Quoted by Rosenstock, "Generations of Our Faith," 6–7. It is should be noted that this essay was published after Rosenstock had discovered Rosenzweig's letters to Gritli in 1959.

and liturgy in the *Star*. To be sure, Rosenzweig's aesthetics incorporates other components, from uncanniness to an emphasis on form,[91] but these components are organized and shaped on many levels by his exchanges with Rosenstock. Each learns from the other while adapting the other's thought to address the issues that are most pressing for him. The complex dynamic of mutual commitment and sustained disagreement, however, does not stop with speech-thinking. It extends into their work on history, law, and education, where their respective work shows both the depth of their engagement and the transformative freedom they find there. As the ensuing chapters shall show, while their correspondence and grammatical thinking form the basis of their friendship, their work in these related fields maintains their proximity even in their separation.

---

91. As Leora Batnitzky and Zachary Braiterman have emphasized. See Batnitzky, "Rosenzweig's Aesthetic Theory," and Braiterman, *Shape of Revelation*, 50–61.

TWO

Living History
Law, Holidays, and the Unnatural Time of Humanity

> You evidently have no idea how different all things Jewish are. Renascences, doctrine, study, Law—everything has a different positional value, even though the number is the same. This goes also for economy, although here the relationship between the Jews and the nations is quite direct, and doubtless revolutionary. The Sabbath *is* a world revolution.[1]

FOR BOTH ROSENSTOCK AND Rosenzweig, the "new thinking" of speech illuminates the temporal character of human reason and society—the passage from generation to generation, and the need for translation so that generations and peoples may speak to one another. As speech-thinking moves from "you" and "I" to "we" and "they," it unfolds into politics and social theory. Together, both authors proposed an alternative approach to social theory grounded in social interaction and language, rather than the isolated, atemporal data of natural science. The spirit of this approach is perhaps best captured in Rosenstock's claim that humanity does not live in the natural time of physics, but rather in an "unnatural" time of creation constituted by the world of speech.[2]

As we shall see, this approach to social science opens new avenues of thought across the spectrum of social sciences. Its clearest impact, however, is in the field of history. Rosenzweig began his career as a philosopher of history. Rosenstock and Rosenzweig first met in 1910 as part of a discussion group in Baden-Baden that addressed the problems of the philosophy of history and the general malaise of their culture. Their encounter confirmed and deepened Rosenzweig's doubts regarding the historicism of his mentor, Friedrich Meinecke, and led him to study with Rosenstock in Leipzig in

---

1. Rosenzweig, letter to Rosenstock, August 25, 1924, in Glatzer, *Franz Rosenzweig*, 135.
2. Cristaudo, "Revolution and the Redeeming of the World," 10.

1913.³ His later work continues this interest in the historical dimensions of his "new thinking."

Rosenstock likewise began his academic career as a historian of law, but left academics because he saw the historical approach as too confining for his thought. Much as both authors sought to restore the vitality of language through their dialogical approaches, they also articulated views of history as *living* history, shaping the present and opening possible futures for humanity. Speech-thinking becomes a social science through the study of the modes of speech that constitute various forms of community: biblical narrative, law, calendars, and liturgy.

In exploring the parallels between their views on social science, the question of how they view the relations between different communities becomes central. In particular, given their early, contentious debates over the relationship between Judaism and Christianity, the history between these communities remains important. It highlights the significant and highly contested messianic and redemptive dimensions of their thought. While Rosenzweig seeks to articulate a conception of Jewish life and thought that would reshape the relation between Judaism and the nations, his messianism carries a high cost in terms of embodiment. As shall be discussed below, while there are changes in Rosenstock's view that indicate that he took Rosenzweig's formulation of Judaism and its place in the world seriously, traces of his early supersessionism and his synthetic, totalizing approach to history nonetheless mark his later views. These issues, along with their shared methodology, give us further insight into the shape of their friendship, as well as the fruits and weaknesses of their theological conceptions of history.

THE TIME OF REVOLUTION: ROSENSTOCK'S PHILOSOPHY OF HISTORY

Looking back fifty years later, Rosenstock recalled Rosenzweig's importance for his investigation of history:

> It is clear to me today, fifty years later, that in 1913 I planted the germ of the "Star" in Franz; and conversely the metamorphosis of my own esoteric works, from a kind of St. George-and-the-dragon approach into the worldly form of revolutions, was promoted

---

3. See Stahmer, "Christianity in the Early Writings," 32–34; Myers, *Resisting History*, 78–83; Hollander, *Exemplarity and Chosenness*, 167–70.

thanks to Franz's grounding in the methods of scientific historical investigation.[4]

It was in their letters of 1916 that the calendar emerged as central to a living, speech-oriented conception of history. For Rosenstock, the calendar embodies the living, speaking life of a community that is often overlooked by historians. As Wayne Cristaudo has written of Rosenstock's view, "The calendar gives us a clue to those events that have been significant enough to be marked in our collective memory as creating the rhythms of our common era."[5] While still at the front in Verdun during the First World War, he first envisaged one of his historical projects, *Out of Revolution: The Autobiography of Western Man*, a study of the history of European revolutions. When, after emigrating to the United States in 1933, Rosenstock finally wrote this work in 1938, he argued that the changes in the calendars of European nations during their revolutions disclosed the potential constellations of political and economic relations that constitute the history of human society.[6]

In *Out of Revolution* Rosenstock argues that calendars embody the living time of society, which differs markedly from the natural, linear time of the natural sciences. One of the fundamental mistakes of the social sciences, on his view, is to understand social time on the objective model of physics or biology. This is a mistake because the calendar develops through speech as people determine which days should be commemorated as holidays, which are thus accorded profound significance by the community. Calendars thus shape the world of time in which people live and by which they express themselves. He writes, "Mankind has always, with the ultimate tenacity, cultivated its calendar ... A day introduced into the calendar, or a day stricken out of the calendar, means a real change in the education and tradition of a nation."[7] Calendars form a record of living history, navigating between the materialist, finely detailed histories of specialists that lose sight

---

4. Rosenstock, *Ja und Nein*, 115, quoted in Harold Stahmer, "Franz Rosenzweig's," 396.

5. Cristaudo, "Revolution," 2.

6. At least in part because of his training, Rosenstock concentrates on European history. There is no question, however, that he views his work as being of universal significance, and there is no methodological reason or internal principle that would preclude the study of other cultures in a similar light, though it would clearly complicate the synthetic aspect of his project.

7. Rosenstock, *Out of Revolution*, 8.

of the life of communities, and the sweeping generalizations of popular history that lose sight of the influence and agency of individuals.

The holidays recorded in the calendar are political instruments, and the changes in holidays that follow political revolution thus mark and signify the development of a new political culture. As Rosenstock writes,

> The calendar and its holidays, the monuments and fashions of a country, the words and names of its speech, are equally important sources in this book. By emphasizing their bearing on the moulding of a nation's or a class's memory and—by that—its character, the teacher of history can steer between the two extremes of our present history-writing—the confusion of endless detail and the charlatanism of cheap and irresponsible constructions.[8]

Revolution is what Rosenstock terms a "disease of speech," one of the four ways that the cross of grammar can collapse upon itself. Speech becomes diseased when it no longer establishes relations between the inner life of thought and the outer world of the community, nor between the past of tradition and the future of the individual. Revolutions occur when social speech becomes decayed, as a response to tyranny in the sense that one aspect of human life, once embodied in the social time of the calendar, suppresses other modes of speech and life.[9] A revolution overturns this order, rejecting the past and establishing a new order of social relations that lets the repressed elements speak (though potentially suppressing other aspects of life). Because new holidays embody this new political order, the respective calendars of different societies and periods manifest these revolutionary changes.

Through his historical study of revolution, Rosenstock makes several controversial if compelling arguments that illustrate the social and historical dimensions of speech-thinking. First, he argues that European revolutions constitute a "cycle of speech"; each revolution is in dialogue with the previous ones, and builds upon their developments. While a national event for Germany, England, France, or Russia, each revolution thus bears significance for Europe as a whole. Second, he argues that this cycle of secular revolutions responds to and grows from the cycle of papal revolutions from 1000 to 1500 CE, moving from the age of the church to a secular age and opening the way to what he envisages as an age of "economic" coordination. Third, Rosenstock analyzes the cycle of revolutions as the passage

---

8. Ibid., 706.
9. Rosenstock, *I Am an Impure Thinker*, 10–19.

through the various forms of government and political expression (tyranny, monarchy, democracy, aristocracy) available to human society, such that together they embody the whole of political life available to a European thinker.[10] Exploring some excerpts of his analysis will illustrate these arguments and the centrality of calendrical time within his methodology.

For Rosenstock, the transition from papal, religious revolutions to the cycle of secular revolutions occurred in the Protestant Reformation in Germany. Both in the person of Luther and the reshaping of church/state relations, this revolution opened a path toward the English, French, and Russian revolutions that followed. When Luther left his monastic order and married in 1525, he became a stranger to the established order, as there was no recognized citizenship apart from one's military duty. In effect, the recognition of his marriage by the state established the category of citizen within German culture. On Rosenstock's view, the transitional category for the Reformation was the establishment of the "cultivated" individual, whose scholarship and learning enabled the interpretation of Scripture. This educated person found a voice and political standing in the university under the protection of Frederick the Wise. By establishing the university as an autonomous forum within which deliberations about church doctrine could take place, the German princes challenged and limited the authority of the church. This marked the beginning of a shift from the universal authority of the church—accompanied by the local, limited authority of secular rulers—toward a universalization of secular authority and localization of church rule. This reversal would continue in the subsequent revolutions. The sovereignty of the interpreters and the princes both stood over against the influence of the Catholic Church; in each case, however, checks were placed upon such interpretation by other members of the congregation or neighboring princes. The German revolution, then, was "a democratic party in the Church and a monarchical party in matters of government,"[11] democratizing the church into a "priesthood of all believers" while reinforcing subservience to royalty.

On Rosenstock's view, Luther's teaching and ministry parallels the work of the prophets of Israel, overturning the established order of princely servitude to the church in the name of equal servitude of all before God. Of course, with his doctrine of "two kingdoms," Luther did not directly overturn the social hierarchy, but rather shifted the relations within that

10. Cristaudo, "Revolution," 8.
11. Rosenstock, *Out of Revolution*, 438.

hierarchy. As prophetic, his mission was also Pauline, seeking a reform of the church in its universality. Rejecting the visible form of the church, Luther sought to establish a universal church as invisible, and to create a common law to which all people (both lay and ecclesial) would be subservient.[12]

In this Pauline mission, and in his continued care for scholarship, Rosenstock argues that Luther was in fact continuing and extending central features of earlier papal revolutions. These revolutions, running from 1000 to 1500, had radically reshaped political life in Europe. The first of these was the emperor's reform of the church, in which he invoked the figure of Paul as a universal reformer over against the church's identification with Peter as bishop of Rome.[13] This movement toward universality filtered into the liturgy and calendar with the insertion of All Souls' Day into the church calendar—a day on which all of humanity is equal before God in the face of death. As in Dante's *Divine Comedy*, All Souls' Day "reveals how men can be equal in the eyes of the Creator."[14]

In the next revolution, a struggle over investiture first led by Gregory VII, the papacy appropriated the figure of Paul to signify the universal ministry of Rome and its freedom from imperial power, effectively reversing the hierarchy between emperor and pope. Henceforth, popes acted as representatives of Rome and for the universal church; as both Peter *and* Paul, the pope subverted the emperor's claim to apostolicity. This "undermined the kingdoms of the earth," revealing their finitude and transience. It also introduced the possibility of freedom. Humanity was placed between two allegiances; as Rosenstock writes,

> The papal revolution introduced the principle of dualism into the political world . . . Theoretically, all philosophers praise liberty. Practically, it can exist only when every human soul has two loyalties. Every monism leads to slavery. The modern democracies are leading to slavery, because they have no guarantee against the monocratic tendencies of popular government.[15]

This imperative that Rosenstock locates in living between two loyalties will occupy us later in this chapter.

---

12. Ibid., 392.
13. Ibid., 505–7.
14. Ibid., 508.
15. Ibid., 543.

In light of this history, Luther's claim of the Pauline heritage through the notion of justification by faith challenged the universality of the visible church, even while remaining faithful to one of the central ideas of the earlier revolutions: where Gregory revolted against the emperor and earthly kingdoms for the sake of ecclesial freedom, Luther's revolution was for the freedom of each Christian to stand before God, as on All Souls' Day. In Protestant churches, this principle has since been affirmed by the practice of celebrating Luther's posting of the Ninety-Five Theses on what has been *re*named Reformation Sunday.[16]

If Luther's stand against the Roman Catholic Church marked the beginning of secular revolution, the connection between the calendar and revolutions becomes clearest in the culmination of the secular cycle, the Russian revolution. Here, the tendency toward universal secular government and the localization of the church reaches its apotheosis, dissolving local institutions in the interest of national economy. Rosenstock sees the Russian revolution as a protest against the fundamental horror of modern industrial life: the alienation of the worker. However, Rosenstock also notes that Marxism does not address the deepest aspects of this alienation, its atomization of time. In the form of the factory shift, capitalism divides time into hours, breaking up the unity of daily life. Beyond Marx, Rosenstock locates the real outrage against the laborer of capitalism: "He is degraded because his boss does not care for his past or his future, and because he is deprived of the power to weave past and future into his own day of work."[17] By defining the worker in terms of her labor, and abstracting this labor from her lived situation, neither capitalism nor communism allows humanity to reproduce itself in speech and community. This inner alienation remained unreconciled within Marxism, and Rosenstock saw this social deficit as requiring the development of new forms of labor and adult education, as shall be discussed further in the next chapter.

Dissolving all of the aspects of local community by which a worker could conceive her past and future, the Russian Revolution universalizes the realm of labor as the public realm. For Rosenstock, this revolution gave power to the world of labor, which had been suppressed by the inefficient local economy that preceded the revolution, as well as the Orthodox Church's lack of concern for worldly transformation. Labor's dominance over life is evident in the calendar forms proposed in the early years of

16. Ibid., 449.
17. Ibid., 84.

the Soviet Union. Early proposals suggested there be *no* days of rest or holidays, with a complete focus on labor, before settling on six-day weeks, with the sixth day being a day of rest. However, since the day of rest was determined by the factory schedule, one's day of rest was entirely private, and labor thereby constituted the public life of the community. While this was eventually changed to make for a common day of rest, this calendar's effect was to break family and religious ties. Holidays—May Day and Lenin's Day—celebrated the victory of labor, and the holidays of local communities or the church were abolished. The reversal of the papal revolution was now complete: in making a day of rest (the Sabbath) an individual event, with labor and the economy constituting public and universal life, the calendar effectively inverted the universal church and local economy.[18] Rosenstock recognizes that this constellation of politics, leisure, and economy in fact continues the capitalist trend, as "holidays" become private days of leisure, without any common or shared life. The shift to a new politics and new calendar, then, is not therapeutic in and of itself. We will return to this point below, in addressing Rosenstock's diagnosis of the ills of modernity and the required treatments.

The Protestant Reformation and the Russian Revolution illustrate how the maintenance and/or changing of a calendar embodies the politics of a community. Calendars embody the speech of a community, extending into its past and opening its future. The danger within any community is that the calendar will exclude or suppress particular ways of life (and particular groups of people as well), and it is when social life becomes deaf to the voices it excludes that revolution may result.

A recent example from American culture may help to illustrate Rosenstock's argument. Within the past thirty years, the United States has adopted Martin Luther King Jr.'s birthday as a holiday, to commemorate and valorize his work (and the work of many others) in the civil rights movement. Perhaps more than any other holiday in contemporary America, this holiday is taken as an opportunity for teaching contemporary history to its youth. There are frequently calls to make it a day of public service as a living commemoration of King's work to transform American public life and to hold the American nation to the promises embedded in its founding ideals. Here, more strongly than with any religious holiday, the public, unifying, historical dimension of the calendar is most evident in American life.

18. Ibid., 121–24.

Of course, the holiday to honor and remember King was not a given; it represented a real change in the United States' self-understanding. To honor King also requires recognizing the nation's terrible history of racism, which is far from finished. There were many difficulties in establishing the holiday. When Virginia (where I grew up) recognized Martin Luther King Jr.'s birthday as a holiday, it also maintained the holiday recognizing Robert E. Lee and Stonewall Jackson, so that for many years (until 2000) the holiday was called "Lee-Jackson-King" day—an oxymoronic name in just about every sense. This illustrates a community's resistance to changing the calendar, but more deeply it shows the extent to which holidays do constitute the world in which we live, and how calendars mark different, conflicting ideologies and political systems.

The ideological and political elements of calendars demonstrate the motivated character of any narration of history. If a calendar is how a community narrates its history, this is invariably a selective and interested representation. Rosenstock recognized that when people tell their history they will often tell it in a way that protects the interests of their group. This can involve renaming and reshaping the calendar, but it can also involve giving different names to the same events (again, in the United States, one might think of the difference between the "War between the States" and the "Civil War," or the different names given to Civil War battles). For Rosenstock, the revolutionary period in England illustrated the interested character of narration, which extended from Cromwell's overthrow of the king in 1648 through the king's return in 1660, to the overthrow of James and the recognition of William as monarch in 1688. Traditionally, these are named the "Rebellion," the "Restoration," and the "Glorious Revolution," thereby separating the initial series of events involving Cromwell from the revolutionary events that followed.

Rosenstock, however, argues that these names don't adequately capture the connections between these three events. The Rebellion led to the execution of the king because he refused to give up his claim to be the head of the church. The king thereby maintained the unity of the church in its "public spirit." This public spirit was then passed on to Parliament in the passage from the Restoration to the Glorious Revolution, when it was via Parliament's authorization that William acceded to the throne. The church remained subject to the state, as it had been in its Anglican form, but through these several steps of revolution it went from being subject to the king to being subject to the public's representatives. By calling Cromwell's action "rebellion," the later historians deprived his actions of any legitimacy. As Rosenstock describes it,

> The limelight of consciousness was concentrated on the final act because consciousness of the foregoing stages was neither wished nor accepted. English memory is *scarred* by the preceding acts, the Parliamentary War, the Cromwellian Commonwealth, and the Restoration of the Stuarts. Any such scar in a nation's life obstructs truth. Scars produce myths and legends. Every myth is the self-defence of a body politic which cannot bear to see its wounds re-opened and bleeding once more. By fixing unswervingly on 1688, the English avoided touching their scar.[19]

Names may take on the emphasis of living speech, but as myths they can also deceive; Rosenstock here highlights the political consequences that such names bear, and how they can lead to misinterpretation. Separating Cromwell from William III concealed the continuity of the English Revolution with other European revolutions. By highlighting all of these events as a single cycle of revolution, Rosenstock demonstrates that the British revolution brought about a national church within a unified nation, thereby moving toward the French Revolution in its universal humanity and further localizing the church. In a similarly mythical fashion, the German Reformation named its preceding period as "medieval," thereby obscuring its own roots in the preceding papal revolutions whose spirit still moved Luther.

The problem of naming spills over into historical documentation itself, particularly in the form of periodization. Under the humanizing, secular influence of the French Revolution, nineteenth-century historians wanted to find antecedent roots for the French Revolution outside of the German Reformation. On Rosenstock's view, this led to the invention of the Renaissance, as a period of humanistic, cultural renewal in Italy.

> Since the leading class of writers like Humboldt did not even mention the destinies of the Church any longer, the cut needed no longer to be simultaneous with Luther. It was transposed to 1450. History-writing Humanism was now purified from any respect for religion.
> . . . In pointing this out we are not trying to break up real periods in history-writing; we are merely opposing an unanalyzed, self-confident naïveté of certain experts. They honestly believe in

---

19. Ibid., 337.

the prejudices of their own time! Yet they think themselves unbiased by any faith or creed![20]

With each revolution, a new view of history emerges, diminishing prior accomplishments and effacing their significance in the interest of the prevailing movement of the present. Historians remain susceptible to the spirit of their culture, and may not see the real significance of the primary names and periods each society develops through its own calendar. As Rosenstock writes, "Periods like that of Humanism or of the Industrial Revolution are afterthoughts, not born of original, contemporary experience . . . They lack the candour and elemental greatness of the historical calendars built up immediately in the wake of revolutions."[21] To naively accept one's prejudices precludes the dynamic grasp of history that Rosenstock envisages, as one can no longer hear prior generations in their own voices.

By studying the shifting calendars and names of European history, Rosenstock hopes to deepen our understanding of the historicity of modernity. For, if each of these revolutions informed the ones that followed, then we are children of *all* of these revolutions, regardless of nationality; together, they constitute the spirit of Europe (or, more exactly, the *Christian* spirit of Europe, an important qualification in light of Rosenzweig's work). In understanding the dynamic relations between these different revolutions, Rosenstock articulates the relation between these different potentialities of humanity: "Not one of these national revolutions is local in purpose or result . . . the tree planted in such a national area bears fruit for all mankind."[22] The significance of this dynamic history should not be lost, as Rosenstock was writing in the shadow of and in opposition to the nationalism of the period (and, not least, that of National Socialism). To argue that each nation influenced others, and that the dialogue *between* nations represents the true European spirit, is a vehement rejection of the nationalism that would have repressed the connections and dynamics between different national, ethnic, and historical communities.

Rosenstock thus sees the historian's task as unifying the histories of different communities. Each community or nation tells its history in its calendar and in naming its holidays; it thereby participates in what he terms the "self-revelation" of humanity. Only when these different calendars and

20. Ibid., 702–3.
21. Ibid., 705.
22. Ibid., 712.

memories are brought into conversation—to speak to one another—does the unity of humanity emerge:

> The historian is the physician of memory . . . As a physician must act . . . so the historian must act under a moral pressure to restore a nation's memory or that of mankind . . . The historian regenerates the great moments of history and disentangles them from the mist of particularity.[23]

Where nationalism substitutes myth for history, history must explore and unite the concrete, linguistic historical records of different communities. These communal histories may themselves be repressive, forgetting some things and concealing others. However, Rosenstock envisages that by uniting the different memories of the nations a scientific history could truly emerge that would overcome the dangers of nationalism, creating a common life through which we could move into the future. We will explore Rosenstock's view of the future after a discussion of Rosenzweig's parallel treatment of the Jewish liturgical calendar, and its constitution of Jewish history.

ROSENZWEIG'S HISTORY: THE CALENDAR AND REDEMPTION

While Rosenstock established the calendar and liturgy as material for philosophy in their correspondence, Rosenzweig first worked out the social, liturgical, and linguistic constitution of community in the third section of *The Star of Redemption*. As the liturgy constitutes the Sabbath, the Sabbath founds the week, which grows into a cycle of festivals that comprises the year. This liturgical cycle builds the varied dimensions of communal worship and thereby the time of the Jewish and Christian communities. Each community, in its liturgical and calendar-based time, thus moves toward redemption along its particular path of participation in the truth. Rosenzweig's articulation of the sociological, temporal, and theological significance of the liturgy, calendar, and history is significant for understanding his particular application of new thinking—especially in his interpretation of law—and for comparing this approach to Rosenstock's sociology of the European nations. It is with these questions in mind that we turn to Rosenzweig's discussion of the Jewish year in the *Star*.

---

23. Ibid., 696.

In the third part of the *Star*—"The Configuration"—the liturgy establishes the time in which the Jewish and Christian communities live. For Rosenzweig, it is through the liturgy that these communities bring eternity into time.[24] The hour and the week draw humanity from the transitory passage of time toward participation in eternity. The hour and week are not natural, in the sense of being simply a given; rather, Rosenzweig argues that time is "wholly human": "the week with its day of rest is the proper symbol of human freedom,"[25] as it embodies the rhythm of human life, moving from labor to contemplation. The rhythm of the week is meant "to mirror . . . the eternal, in which beginning and end come together, by means of the ever repeated present."[26] As the embodiment of creation, the week thus serves as the material for revelation, which occurs through the cycle of weeks that make up the year. In each year, the cycle of revelation moves toward redemption, though it requires repetition in deferring its final completion.

For Judaism, which maintains its eternity in distinction from all other nations, the liturgy is the language of creation; the celebration of Shabbat draws together the elements of creation, and the bread and wine celebrate the creativity of humanity as the image of God's creativity. As Rosenzweig says, with the reading of Scripture in the morning one enters into revelation. The core of the Sabbath occurs in listening to the reading of Scripture and the sermon. The sermon is meant to be solely exegesis on the Scripture, in the sense that in the sermon one should still hear revelation, and not the speech of an individual or even a culture. The sermon thereby enacts the lyricism of the Song of Songs, drawing the hearers into revelation. Both the reading and the sermon should, he argues, unite the congregation in "absolute listening," where no one prepares to speak before hearing the end of what is being said.[27]

While the yearly cycle of Sabbaths is important, Rosenzweig emphasizes that the Sabbath takes on its revelatory significance while remaining only one day of the week. Only if the day of rest flows into the week of labor does its contemplation serve as revelation that moves toward redemption. As he writes, "A way must be found from the sanctuary back into the

---

24. Batnitzky, "Philosophical Import of Carnal Israel," 136.
25. Rosenzweig, *Star of Redemption*, 291.
26. Ibid.
27. From my own very limited experience of giving a sermon, replete with snoring, smoking, and talking, Rosenzweig's idea of "absolute listening" sounds like a pipe dream.

workaday world. The year, all of life, is built upon the shift from the holy to the profane, from the seventh to the first day, from perfection to outset, from old age to early youth."[28] The shift to youth—and the integration of the Sabbath with the week as a whole, as its perpetual renewal—will both become central factors in Rosenzweig's work to revamp Jewish education, as shall be discussed in the next chapter.

The cycle of Sabbaths, each a "festival of creation," creates the spiritual year, taking the community through festivals of revelation and redemption. The festivals' variation occurs through the weekly readings of different Scriptures, and the passage through different festivals. The festivals of revelation are the Passover, the Feast of Booths (Sukkot), and the Feast of Weeks (Shavuot). Together, they draw the congregation into the eternal history of the Jewish people, opening a time that is distinct from other nations. Within this cycle of feasts, there is a progression into the world, as the Feast of Booths serves as a foretaste of redemption; however, in the transience of the dwellings it also serves as a reminder that this redemption has not yet been reached. As Rosenzweig writes, "In this festival of redemption there is no present redemption. Redemption is only a hope, only something expected in the source of wanderings." [29] The reading of Ecclesiastes further accentuates the transience of the present dwelling.

The anticipatory character of redemption—its being not yet fulfilled—becomes even clearer in the feasts of redemption: the days of Awe, Rosh Hoshanah, and Yom Kippur. Here, redemption is enacted as each person stands alone before God in confession and penitence, and yet united with all others in the community: "God lifts up his countenance to this united and lonely pleading of men in their shrouds, men beyond the grace, of a community of souls . . . this God of love, he alone is God!"[30] In bearing humanity over the border of creation that death marks, revelation carries one into common life. At this point, however, the unrealized character of this hope reemerges, as the Feast of Booths carries one back into the year and the world, such that the rest of this Sabbath does not lose its rhythm.[31]

---

28. Rosenzweig, *Star of Redemption*, 313.

29. Ibid., 321. For more on this "not-yet" dimension of redemption, and its connection with meontology, see Kavka, *Jewish Messianism and the History of Philosophy*, 148–51.

30. Rosenzweig, *Star of Redemption*, 327.

31. For more on the incompleteness of redemption, see Batnitzky, "Philosophical Import of Carnal Israel," 136–37.

On Rosenzweig's view, the significance of the Jewish calendar is that it sets the community apart from all other nations. Living by it makes the Jewish people a holy people. They are also "eternal" in that their time is not that of the nations. This separation becomes the basis for an alternative politics. To live by this calendar, far from the finality of redemption and in the midst of the journey to freedom, frees one from being bound to one's land. Likewise, living between the tongue of one's nation and the Hebrew language, one is never fully immersed in the language of everyday life. The liturgical language and the cycle of holidays carry one out of the national life of community. The political aspect of this is most apparent in Rosenzweig's argument that holy war is a concept of the past for Judaism. Since all present wars are experienced as political, and thus unjustified, "the Jew is practically the only human being who cannot take war seriously, and this makes him the only genuine pacifist."[32] Where Hegel defines war as necessary for the state—as the staking of life that commits the people to the universality of reason—Rosenzweig sees such politics as beneath the purview of Judaism. In the *Star*, it is the refusal of war that constitutes the life of the Jewish people.

Such a position was hardly uncontroversial, particularly given that Rosenzweig wrote much of the *Star* while still serving in the German army. His opposition to nationalism had led him to criticize his teacher, Hermann Cohen, for his support of German entry into the war. Rosenzweig's focus on speech and learning and his desire to define Judaism over against the nations placed him in conflict with the Zionist movement, even as he agreed with its criticisms of Jewish assimilation. A Jewish state, as a state, did not do justice to his view of what Judaism calls its people to be.

The calendar is significant because it represents the most embodied, concrete aspects of Rosenzweig's description of Judaism. It is precisely in this symbolic embodiment that the Jewish people incarnate eternity. This is particularly significant, I think, for illuminating Rosenzweig's highly controversial claim that the Jews are a "blood-community," which for some readers may evoke the Nazi racist ideology that emerged after Rosenzweig's death. While I think that Peter Gordon gives a compelling argument that blood symbolizes the force that flows and gives Jewish life its continuity and eternity, thereby distinguishing Rosenzweig's view from such racism, it

---

32. Rosenzweig, *Star of Redemption*, 331.

should also be noted that Rosenzweig articulates this "blood" as taking the form of the liturgical calendar, emphasizing its symbolic aspect.[33]

Much as the Jewish people live via their calendar, Rosenzweig views the Christian calendar as formative for Christian life and community. The essentially Christian act, here, is the unifying of brother with brother in the love of *caritas*. The cultivation of this bond of love occurs through the Christian liturgical year. As with the Sabbath, Sunday founds the Christian week, yet there are crucial differences: Sunday is the beginning of the week, where the Sabbath is its close; Sunday sets Christians on their journeys, while the Sabbath reminds the Jewish people of the goal they seek; Sunday returns to creation, making the Christian the "eternal beginner,"[34] while the Jewish Sabbaths anticipate redemption. The cycle of Christian festivals constitute the year of the "sanctification of the soul," with Christmas, Easter, and Pentecost serving as the festivals of revelation that build upon creation.

While Christian worship points toward redemption, Rosenzweig argues that there is no festival of redemption proper to Christianity; it is always on the way, working through the world. Redemption, for Christianity, is signified by baptism, where the church gives one a new birth, that starts one on the path to redemption. Baptism is individual, but it also has a communal dimension; when the church blesses the cycles of national festivals, it blesses and enters into the life of the nations, taking them up in the time of redemption as well. This journey through these festivals becomes the Christian participation in redemption, even though such participation remains a foretaste that defers its own completion. While both Judaism and Christianity are thus anticipatory, Rosenzweig's description of Christianity as "setting on the path" emphasizes that it is just starting, whereas Judaism's anticipation has, in some sense, already reached its goal. This point is worth bearing in mind, given that Rosenstock will attempt to use Rosenzweig's own work to argue that Judaism is more a religion of the past than of the future.

Out of Revolution and the final sections of *The Star of Redemption* show how both friends sought to revitalize the social sciences and the historical method through their study of calendars. Their goal, as Rosenstock stated,

---

33. See Gordon, *Rosenzweig and Heidegger*, 206–14. The calendar and liturgy are not mentioned in his discussion. Leora Batnitzky's discussion is also helpful here; see *Idolatry and Representation*, 72–75.

34. Rosenzweig, *Star of Redemption*, 359.

was to avoid excessive generalizations, and it is clear that Rosenzweig likewise saw a focus on ritual as providing an embodied dimension to Jewish history. That said, questions remain about the overall implications of this approach, especially in terms of its attention to embodiment. This has become a central point of contention in recent Rosenzweig scholarship. Most notably, Martin Kavka has criticized Rosenzweig's treatment of the neighbor as effectively instrumentalizing love of neighbor so as to build the chorus of voices toward redemption.[35] The preceding discussion of the congregation, as involved in an "absolute listening" that denies any internal difference, highlights and illuminates how Rosenzweig, despite his intentions, conceives a highly idealized form of embodiment, lacking in real alterity.

That said, it seems to me that when one locates Rosenzweig's account of Judaism within its broader context in Rosenzweig's work, there are ways to recover a certain degree of otherness at work. For, unlike Rosenstock, Rosenzweig does not see a complete synthesis between different calendars as possible or desirable. More exactly, where both see Christianity as unifying, Rosenzweig emphasizes that Judaism defers such completion. The Jewish calendar—as it would be lived by German-Jewish people (or other diasporic communities)—would introduce a difference within its members' lives, unsettling the unity and identity of the surrounding culture in which they live. This is perhaps clearest in Rosenzweig's letter to Rosenstock, where he explains how his living Judaism displaces his commitments to the German state—even when, while serving in the army, those commitments appear to be largely intact.[36] Likewise, the difference between the Christian and Jewish calendars serves as a continuous fragmentation of identity, as the "not-yet" of Judaism undermines the Christian hope for completion, which reminds the Christian how far she remains from redemption.[37] Kavka is right to highlight the highly restricted form of embodiment set forth by Rosenzweig, but it would seem that Rosenzweig essentializes (and almost nihilates) Jewish identity, so as to fragment the totality of German culture that confronts him.

---

35. Kavka, *Jewish Messianism*, 154–56.

36. Rosenzweig, *Judaism Despite Christianity*, 136–38.

37. Eric Santner highlights the "stuckness" of Rosenzweig's conception of Judaism, and the political import of its dislocation of totality; see *On the Psychotheology of Everyday Life*, 127–28.

For Rosenstock, the speech-thinking approach to history likewise carries both positive and negative aspects. Positively, it creates a way to see history as alive—with significance for our lives today. It also emphasizes the interactions between different nations and historical periods, countering an ideological or nationalist bias that might emerge. These were especially important aspects of the method for Rosenstock, both when he conceived the work at Verdun, and when he wrote it in the shadow of the Nazi rise to power. Both authors, then, conceive of a dialogical approach to history as a way to avoid the mythical thinking that would erase historical difference.

All the same, as with Rosenzweig, the degree of Rosenstock's abstraction is often far too high to be persuasive. Moreover, the systematic dimension of Rosenstock's use of the calendars further problematizes his approach. The neat harmony into which he fits the religious and secular revolutions—which then likewise fit into the shape of a cross—is highly reductive in its reading of the particular events themselves. For instance, Luther's revolution may grant sovereignty to the princes and create the life of the university—but does the historical significance of those achievements remember, let alone redeem, the suffering of the peasants whose rebellion was brutally crushed? Furthermore, it is striking how Judaism, while inspiring messianism, is seen as largely disposable by Rosenstock—especially after the "messianic" French Revolution universalized citizenship.[38] The problem, it seems, is that a historian who is a "physician of memory" would need to neglect or forget a great deal of suffering to so starkly schematize and unify history. Rosenzweig's emphasis on irreducible difference, over against Rosenstock's schematic unity, would seem to hold out the possibility of greater attention to particularity, even if Rosenzweig himself fails to perform this consistently.

To see that both thinkers encountered similar pitfalls in their attempts to revise historical study is striking. Both were attempting to develop approaches to history that would help to create a vitality for their religious communities. Bearing these questions in mind, exploring how they sought to vivify law and faith in the contemporary setting will clarify the transformative dimension of their accounts of history, and further illuminate the problems just raised.

---

38. Cristaudo, "Revolution," 3.

LAW, HISTORY, AND THE POLITICS OF REDEMPTION

Rosenzweig's emphasis on the "ahistorical" character of Judaism is often misconstrued. Where it is seen as either setting Judaism outside history or defining Jewish identity in purely racial or ethnic terms, it is then criticized for its political naïveté. While these views have been somewhat put to rest by Peter Gordon's work, his reading of Rosenzweig raises an equally problematic alternative. As Gordon argues, Rosenzweig's view of Jewish identity (and community) can be construed as decisionist—a founding of a community that rests upon nothing other than a free, sovereign decision, not unlike the decisionism of Carl Schmitt's political theology.[39] There are levels on which I would agree with Gordon's reading, as shall be explained below; however, if one attends to the ways that Rosenzweig sees Jewish community as constituted through the liturgical calendar and through law, important qualifications must be placed upon this parallel. By examining Rosenzweig's debate with Buber over the significance of law, the specifically messianic dimension of Jewish identity can be highlighted—a dimension which places Rosenzweig closer to Walter Benjamin's conception of redemption than to Schmitt's theory of sovereignty.

Rosenzweig's letter to Buber titled "The Builders" began an intensive correspondence between the two men from 1922 through 1925 on the subject of law and commandment. In the letter, Rosenzweig responds to Buber's lectures on Judaism and questions Buber's placing of the Law outside of what is essential for the modern Jew. While commending Buber for an approach in which, in terms of seeking knowledge or wisdom, "nothing Jewish may be excluded as alien,"[40] Rosenzweig then questions whether Buber remains consistent on the question of Jewish practice. By telling his audience to "take cognizance of the Law with reverence,"[41] Buber has effectively reduced the importance of *doing* and *studying* the Law. Buber's focus on the "inner power" of Judaism becomes, in the end, divorced from the practices that distinguish Judaism from other peoples and constitute the temporality of Jewish life—in many ways, the very practices that makeup the calendar discussed in the preceding section.

Rosenzweig disputes Buber's approach by arguing for a positive understanding of Law: not as a set of precepts, but rather as a way of life

---

39. Gordon, *Rosenzweig and Heidegger*, 215–16.
40. Rosenzweig, "The Builders," in *On Jewish Learning*, 75.
41. Ibid., 77.

in which external and internal observance are united. He critiques the division of life into the spheres of "forbidden" and "permissible" actions, arguing that even those things that are permissible "must be given a Jewish form." Taking two examples of observance, he writes,

> For those who eat Jewish dishes all the traditional customs of the menu as handed down from mother to daughter must be as irreplaceable as the separation of meat and milk; and he who refrains from opening a business letter on the Sabbath must not read it even if somebody else has opened it for him. Everywhere the custom and the original intention of the law must have the same rank of inviolability as the law itself.[42]

The positive aspect of Law, for Rosenzweig, is its uniting thought, will, and practice, creating an integrity and unity both within the believer and between the believer and tradition. To be sure, there is a retrospective dimension, as tradition and the "original intention" become the ground for renewal. Yet Rosenzweig argues that through this positive sense one "experiences the Joy of being able to be Jewish even in the every-day and generally human aspects of one's material existence."[43] There is a freedom, here, in that one becomes free to act, as well as to create an "internal union" between one's belief and practice.

As with other aspects of his thought, Rosenzweig presents his approach as navigating between the liberal and orthodox forms of Judaism. Where liberalism would dispose of the particular precepts and practices of Judaism in the name of a core ethical sensibility, and Orthodoxy emphasizes the prohibitive, negative aspects of the Law, Rosenzweig rejects both options. For him, liberalism separates Jewish knowledge and wisdom from practice, and thereby reproduces internally the very alienation that its emphasis on assimilation strives to overcome. Orthodoxy, by contrast, seeks to emphasize the external precepts and prohibitions that set the Jewish community apart—yet, ironically, it thereby allows the "permissible" sphere of life to remain untouched. Moreover, Rosenzweig rejects the claim that one keeps the Law because God "imposed it upon Israel at Sinai"; rather, for Rosenzweig, one keeps the Law because this is how one may live freely in response to God's command. For Rosenzweig, the Law (*Gesetz*) must

---

42. Ibid., 83.
43. Ibid., 84.

become *command* (*Gebot*), "which seeks to be transformed into deed at the very moment it is heard."[44]

Rosenzweig's description of the significance of doing the Law is enigmatic; he cautions against a simple return to tradition as a "lie in deed." He thus agrees with Buber that the "inner power" of Judaism must be captured, but sees this as embodied in the Law's transformation into commandment, rather than its negation: the Law must become the new, *living* law of commandment. The Law gives what he calls "our independence from history or, to put it positively, our eternity," which sets the Jewish people apart from other nations. Yet this eternity is not outside of time—rather, it "*gives simultaneity to all moments of our history.*"[45] As the Law becomes command, it places the hearer at the base of Sinai—with others, throughout history, but also thereby recapitulating the whole history of Judaism.[46]

Buber's replies to Rosenzweig succinctly rejected the very premises of Rosenzweig's argument. As he wrote in explaining why he would not want to publish a reply to "The Builders,"

> I do not believe that revelation is ever a formulation of law. It is only through man in his self-contradiction that revelation becomes legislation. This is the fact of man. I cannot admit the law transformed by man into the realm of my will, if I am to hold myself ready as well for the unmediated word of God directed to a specific hour of life.[47]

For Buber, God is "not a Law-giver," but rather law emerges as something humanity formulates in the absence or the breakdown of immediacy. Law would seem to be connected far more to the I-It realm, which Buber describes as threatening the presencing of the "unmediated" word of God that could break in in an I-Thou moment. Indeed, Buber's responses make clear that for him law is a human construction, which blocks hearing and communication rather than enabling it. While he also admits the possibility of command as immediate speech, he sees the Law as something that each

---

44. Ibid., 85.

45. Ibid., 90; emphasis added.

46. The passages quoted here give Rosenzweig's account a decidedly traditionalist flavor. Recently, Martin Kavka and Randi Rashkover have argued that Rosenzweig's noncognitive understanding of revelation leaves open the possibility that alternative interpretations of a divine command would be possible for Rosenzweig. Their view is, I think, consistent with Rosenzweig's logic, though not the view he himself sets forth. See Kavka and Rashkover, "Toward a Modified Jewish Divine Command Theory," 401–3.

47. Martin Buber, letter to Rosenzweig of June 24, 1924, in *On Jewish Learning*, 111.

person must scrutinize to determine if it applies to him or her in a particular moment—rather than taking it as a whole, as Rosenzweig argues.

On a theoretical level, Rosenzweig agrees with Buber that revelation and commandment are not reducible to law. As is clear from the preceding discussion, Rosenzweig wants to make law something new, creating a unity and presence for the believer beyond prohibition.[48] While Rosenzweig agrees with Buber on the conceptual level,[49] Buber's consistent replies raise the question of whether or not his approach, with its emphasis on the totality of the Law as giving a form of identity, is more legalistic than Rosenzweig would want to admit. Based upon the rhetoric of "The Builders," Buber has a strong case. However, Rosenzweig's last (published) reply in *On Jewish Learning* points to a different possibility. Here he admits that revelation cannot become legislation, because "then the original self-interpretation of revelation would have to give way to human interpretation."[50] He then rephrases his view, saying, "I believe in the right of the Law to prove its character as an exception against all other types of law."[51] If the Law, as commanded, suspends the human sovereignty constitutive of other laws and draws together people across space and time, then it holds a redemptive, messianic possibility, as shall be discussed further in this chapter's conclusion. It is perhaps only through Buber's insistent refusal that we glimpse this dimension of Rosenzweig's approach.

CHRIST, HISTORY, AND THE CHRISTIAN FUTURE

In light of Rosenzweig's discussion of the significance of Judaism for a redemption of law, Rosenstock's discussion of the future of Christianity provides an illuminating contrast. Like Rosenzweig, Rosenstock sought to bring Christian life into the modern world and to create a unified sense of existence grounded in a relation to Christ. Much as Rosenzweig's account of law seeks to integrate different dimensions of Jewish life, Rosenstock sought to create a living unity in modern life that would simultaneously give meaning and purpose to history.

In his 1947 work, *The Christian Future, or the Modern Mind Outrun*, Rosenstock sets forth a christological conception of history. As in *Out of Revolution*, Rosenstock envisages history as creating a sense of unity among

---

48. Braiterman, *Shape of Revelation*, 83–85.
49. Rosenzweig, letter of July 16, 1924, in *On Jewish Learning*, 116.
50. Rosenzweig, letter of June 5, 1925, in *On Jewish Learning*, 118.
51. Ibid.

the diverse temporal, national, and vocational potentialities of humanity. History, as the Cross of Reality, reflects the living truth of Christianity. He argues that to the extent that our lives involve breaking out of the past—and, in a sense, dying to one life and rising to another—we live in a new creation that reflects and shares in the life of Christ. In short, the narrative of Jesus's crucifixion and resurrection gives a shape to history that lets us make sense of events in our world and our lives.[52]

Rosenstock identifies the distinctive contribution of Christianity to historical thinking as eschatology. It is the *second* coming of Jesus, and the belief in that future event, that creates the community of the church. This event breaks people out of a simple loyalty to the past, or being trapped in their present; as a call to community beyond that which has been and is, it opens the future and the possibility of progress, in part by establishing a connection between different epochs and nations. On this basis, Rosenstock argues that the modern conception of progress, which eclipses eschatology and treats progress as a purely immanent process, does not really allow for any future because it remains rooted in existent divisions and energies. The loss of eschatology is, for Rosenstock, a loss of the living significance of faith.[53] As embodied in the Apostles' Creed, Rosenstock sees Christian faith as speaking to how we may die and be born again within our everyday life, such that reality reflects the gospel story through which we may find ourselves made into new creations.[54]

While Rosenstock thus argues for a Christian unity to history and the world, his approach is less dogmatic than it initially sounds. For, with the ways that Christianity has transformed the world, the Christian task has changed as well. If, in early generations, the task was either to draw Christians out of the world, or to make the world a Christian realm (which is how Rosenstock interprets the first two millennia of Christianity), the task now is to renounce the world of Christianity itself. This requires what he calls a "nameless" Christianity, which recognizes that the Spirit blows where it will—not least outside the realm of the visible church.

A "nameless" Christianity would be one in which the pattern of division, death, and resurrection would be discovered within our own lives. In this, and in the connections that such resurrection draws between generations, Rosenstock sees the Spirit uniting the movements of history. Like the

52. Rosenstock, *Christian Future*, 102–3.
53. Ibid., 67–78.
54. Ibid., 98–112.

bond between the Father and the Son, the bonds between generations and nations give new life where death had seemed to reign. Yet Rosenstock is emphatic that such unity must be found in the midst of our lives—uniting our work and our private leisure, and informing our public and inward selves.[55] Such life may only be found, he argues, in moving outside the established dogmas and ecclesial forms. He describes this new age thus:

> A third form, the listening Church, will have to unburden the older modes of worship by assembling the faithful to live out their hopes through working and suffering together in unlabelled, undenominational groups, thereby to wait and listen for the inbreak of a new consolation which shall redeem modern life from its curse of disintegration and mechanization.[56]

For all his idiosyncrasies,[57] this conception of an active, nameless faith is not far from Bonhoeffer's influential (if still controversial) suggestion of a "religionless Christianity."[58] Like Bonhoeffer, Rosenstock recognizes that the established forms of Christianity have, in many ways, failed to address the modern age, thereby contributing further to the disharmony and alienation of Christians as well as others.[59] It is in adopting a new form that he hopes Christianity's teaching—which he sees reflected in the daily rhythms of life—can gain new traction for engaging and redeeming the world.[60]

As part of this "nameless" Christianity, Rosenstock argues that the pattern of the Cross of Reality extends beyond the bounds of Europe. In particular, he interprets Lao-Tze and Buddha as manifesting the inward and external dimensions of the Cross, which are complemented by Abraham's affirmation of history and Jesus's opening of the future. In these four

---

55. Bryant, "The Grammar of the Spirit: Time, Speech and Society," in Bryant and Huessy, *Eugen Rosenstock-Huessy*, 253.

56. Rosenstock, *Christian Future*, 127.

57. For instance, Rosenstock argues that the commute between work and home offers a way for the modern worker to unify the different aspects of his life (*Christian Future*, 23). As somewhat of an expert on lengthy commutes, the ridiculousness of that claim leaves me speechless.

58. Bonhoeffer, *Letters and Papers from Prison*, 281–82, 285. Harold Stahmer notes the parallel in his introduction to *Christian Future*.

59. Cristaudo, "Revolution," 11.

60. Beyond the possible parallel with Bonhoeffer, Rosenstock cites the early work of Hans Urs von Balthasar with great approval, esp. *Apokalypse der Deutschen Seele* (*The Apocalypse of the German Soul*). See Rosenstock, *Christian Future*, 128. Bryant (n. 55) criticizes the comparison with Bonhoeffer—wrongly, in my view.

founders Rosenstock locates a figure for the potential of all humanity—no longer a strictly European vision.

While Rosenstock's attempt to interpret non-Christian religions from a Christian perspective is noteworthy, his systematic account leaves much to be desired. In introducing his account, he writes, "The Cross is not an exclusive symbol of the egoism of one group; it is the inclusive symbol of the reunification of man, and every spark of life is welcome unless it refuses to die in time. Even the primitive cultures must be included eventually."[61] Needless to say, even though he does not mean to reduce Taoism or Buddhism to a "primitive culture," they nonetheless occupy what appear to be preparatory stages in the drama of humanity. While he readily admits that these are just sketches, such sketches always run the risk of degenerating into caricatures, particularly when shaped by his schematic of cruciform reality. In this light, his discussion of Abraham is particularly interesting, not least because he draws extensively upon his early correspondence with Rosenzweig. As Rosenstock describes, he had equated Abraham's sacrifice with Agamemnon's sacrifice of Iphigenia, and Rosenzweig "came down on me with terrific energy."[62]

Drawing on Rosenzweig—and declaring his own earlier view to be wrong—Rosenstock now argues that Abraham's offering amounts to the *end* of pagan sacrifice. When Isaac's death is refused, it shows God's refusal of violence, opening a peaceful form of faith that breaks with both sacrifice and warfare. This creates, on his view, a "supreme loyalty"—a belief in a past that goes beyond nation or creed, to a fundamental unity of humanity. "And, my friend continued, for this reason, Israel always has considered the act of not slaughtering Isaac as the great spiritual revolution. God's final purpose of man stood revealed as peace, not war."[63]

This passage is noteworthy, for it is one of the clearest places where Rosenzweig's thought clearly impacted Rosenstock's own work. Yet, oddly, Rosenzweig is not mentioned by name, and one may end up wondering just how well Rosenstock heard his friend's argument. For, while Rosenzweig does clearly see Judaism as living its sacred history anew, this is not simply a past—it also opens a future. Even in its interiority and history, Rosenzweig clearly argues for Judaism as a form of public expression that opens a future—not only for itself, but also for others. Again, Rosenstock's

---

61. Rosenstock, *Christian Future*, 172.
62. Ibid., 182.
63. Ibid. See also Rosenstock, *Judaism Despite Christianity*, 133–35.

penchant for classification and the fixity of images limits the more engaging and provocative dimensions of his thought. Such classifications create a sense of rationality, and almost a necessity to the unfolding of history. However much he may protest against Hegel, Rosenstock seems to privilege the synthetic unity of historical development over the contingent and particular events that would constitute its manifold.

One might argue that reading history from a Christian perspective must give some such narrative form, thereby reducing the place of contingency within history. However, it would seem that Barth's typology, and even more strongly Frei's narrative approach to history, both allow for a stronger sense of contingency within the movement of time than Rosenstock's cruciform system.[64] Must a unified conception of history be purchased at the cost of the multiple, complex identities of those engaged in its movements and struggles? Or can history be told in ways that give contingency its due, without subsuming it under a dialectic that predetermines its movements?

MESSIANISM, ESCHATOLOGY, AND HISTORY

Since Scholem's influential essay on the messianic idea in Judaism, Rosenzweig's view has frequently been criticized for its apparently passive, apolitical stance. For instance, Emil Fackenheim rejected Rosenzweig's approach as one that renders Jewish people—individuals, and not just the people as a whole—vulnerable to death and destruction. For Fackenheim, historical engagement is required in the aftermath of the Shoah in ways that Rosenzweig neither articulated nor could have foreseen.

Recently, Gregory Kaplan has raised important questions regarding the adequacy of Rosenzweig's conception of redemption with regard to the question of eschatology. As Kaplan points out, Rosenzweig's dual-covenant approach emphasizes the antagonism between Judaism and Christianity until the end time—at which point this difference is overcome in a somewhat ambiguous form. The goal of such antagonism is twofold: it reminds Christians that redemption has not yet been accomplished, thereby serving as a critique of idolatry, and it creates a space into which "pagans" (that is,

---

64. One could also include Stanley Hauerwas's recent writings, which emphasize contingency as well. See Hauerwas, *Performing the Faith*, 111–34. On Frei, see Mike Higton, *Christ, Providence, and History*, 155–76; and William Young III, "Identity of the Literal Sense," 616–19.

everyone who is neither Christian nor Jewish)[65] may find their way into redemption. As Kaplan describes, this creates an irregular geometry, as the star and the rays remain oddly incomplete. The whole of history is greater than the sum of its parts.

Yet, more importantly, Kaplan highlights the limits such a conception of history places on Jewish identity and life. The constant differentiation from the nations and peoples of the world amounts to a "non-linear, a-temporal determinism," in which Israel's eternal life disrupts the existence of the nations.[66] Such a role, whose purpose is to "implode history," nonetheless essentializes and constricts Jewish identity. As Kaplan puts it, whereas "the Christian 'way' follows a centrifugal course by extending its reach . . . the Jewish 'life' follows a centripetal force by closing in on itself."[67] As Kaplan notes, this would seem to separate Jewish life from any sort of individual embodiment, making inhabitation of the world "unreal."

By contrast with Kaplan, Dana Hollander has recently defended Rosenzweig's conception of the messianic against Scholem's criticism. As she argues, Rosenzweig's conception of Jewish identity is as a form of "messianic interruption" of the course of human history. Jewish history, as "eternal," is construed primarily as a contrast to both Christian and secular history, countering their tendencies toward totalization. Rosenzweig thus refuses a progressive view of history, not as an escape from history but rather so as to reconceive it.[68] By standing in an immediate relation to redemption, Jewish messianism undercuts and critiques any universalism that would seek to subsume particularity under its conception, enabling what Hollander terms a "messianic epistemology."[69]

Hollander's work suggests an alternative way of conceiving the Jewish place in history that might respond to the concerns raised above. First, it is clear that in the exchange with Buber Rosenzweig emphasizes the ways that eternal life must be embodied in the form of the Law, as the Law becomes command. Thus, whereas Kaplan demonstrates the dualism at work in Rosenzweig's early (1913) conception of Jewish identity, by the 1920s there is an attempt to ground eternity in *doing*, sacralizing not just Jewish history

---

65. This reduction is perhaps clearest in Rosenzweig's treatment of Islam. See *Star of Redemption*, 171–73, where he reduces al-Ghazali's theology to a form of stoic thought.

66. Kaplan, "In the End Shall Christians Become Jews," 516.

67. Ibid., 517.

68. Hollander, "On the Significance of the Messianic Idea," 559–62.

69. Hollander, *Exemplarity and Chosenness*, 176, 182–83.

but the practice of everyday life. Moreover, in this letter Rosenzweig seems to build upon the ways that "eternal" life is only lived through the Jewish calendar, which once again incorporates a historical dimension rather than subsuming it.

Buber's reply to Rosenzweig indirectly highlights the innovative aspects of Rosenzweig's approach. Rosenzweig does not see the Law (as command) as something that divides, but rather as what makes redemption possible. This is seen, first, in his sense of doing as surpassing the forbidden/permissible opposition. Moreover, doing the law makes one both a "child" and a "builder," following in one's ancestors footstep while re-marking their footprints for those who are yet to come. And, most intriguingly, Rosenzweig does not see this path as a permanent division from other peoples. Rather, as the Law becomes a Jewish form of life, permeating one's whole existence, it thereby enables the sharing of existence with other peoples—albeit in a different mode.

This suggests, then, that Rosenzweig's view of history is more of a combination of the "static" and "catastrophic" forms of redemption than Scholem recognized. However, I do not think it would be enough to say that Rosenzweig conceives Judaism as a "continuous interruption" of the forces of history. While that, like Hollander's argument, would counter Scholem's concern, the question of essentialism raised by Kaplan remains in force. Rosenzweig's engagement with Buber shows, in my view, that he conceives of identity less as something settled than as a *form of becoming*; Jewish identity, insofar as it is responding to a command, is always in process, and never fully settled. If this were not the case, there would be no grounds for Rosenzweig's theoretical agreement with Buber. Moreover, "The Builders" suggests that this process, by which daily life becomes the embodiment of sacred history, is a form of continuous exodus, reshaping the life shared with other nations and peoples.

It does seem that Rosenzweig's view in "The Builders" remains essentialist on some levels, particularly in its embrace of tradition as the source of innovation. This is perhaps most the case in Rosenzweig's brief but highly stereotyped references to the domestic role of Jewish women.[70] Yet Rosenzweig's own process of development, as well as his sustained conversations with Rosenstock and others, suggest that his view of Jewish history and community may be more engaged with the world than it first appears.

---

70. Rosenzweig, "The Builders," in *On Jewish Learning*, 84–85.

It is, in my view, his struggle with this issue—more than the specifics of his answer to it—that remains salutary for us today.

At this point, one can return to Gordon's claims regarding the character of redemption for Rosenzweig—in particular, the decisionist nature of Jewish identity.[71] While it is true that Rosenzweig turns away from the state as a vehicle of redemption, and that the social realm takes priority, the parallel with Schmitt's political theory is only partially correct. As Rosenzweig writes in a letter to Buber, "God is not a Law-Giver," such that obedience to a command does not operate within the terms of political sovereignty. I would argue, instead, that Rosenzweig's conception of law-following, as a set of practices and forms of speech that place oneself outside of a nation, are a form of placing oneself—and one's community—in what Giorgio Agamben terms a *remnant*, as an act of witness to the forgotten underside of history.[72] This form of identity, which undoes the divisions of law, would challenge the supremacy of sovereignty, creating a conception of history that avoids both a fascist theory of sovereignty and a liberal, "progressive" view that fails to really meet fascism's challenge.

In raising this possibility, I would thus suggest that Rosenzweig's messianic conception of history constitutes a form of thought similar to Benjamin's "Theses on the Philosophy of History." For, if the historical task is to retain an image of history that threatens to be erased, and thereby to "turn away from the world and its affairs," then both Benjamin and Rosenzweig saw an alternative conception of history as necessary.[73] As such, Rosenzweig's religious conception of witness—so central to the *Star*'s discussion of revelation—might also be at the heart of an alternative, messianic conception of politics.[74] On this point, both are not far from Rosenstock's idea of breaking nationalist images of history as a redemptive, materialist practice.

However, this point also raises one of the central differences between Rosenzweig and Rosenstock. While their thought on history and law is remarkably similar, Rosenstock's view of the historical task, as a recapitulation

71. See Gordon, *Rosenzweig and Heidegger*, esp. 110–13 and 214–18.

72. Agamben, *Time that Remains*, 56. This is the subject of my essay entitled "The Worklessness of Love: Agamben's Messianic Redemption," which argues that Rosenzweig's conception of redemption is much closer to Agamben's interpretation of Benjamin than is often realized.

73. Benjamin, "Theses on the Philosophy of History," 258.

74. In this, I am largely in agreement with Eric Santner's reading; see *On the Psychotheology of Everyday Life*, 55–60, 114–17.

of history as a totality, risks becoming a progressive, totalizing view. Not surprisingly, despite his efforts to see historical change as restoring a balance or integrity to human life, this leads to an inability to truly locate the suffering and destruction that such historical "development" has wrought. While one can agree with Kaplan and Scholem that Rosenzweig's views share many of the risks of Rosenstock's work, Rosenzweig's emphasis on moving outside history introduces an irresolvable tension *within* history—not to mention within his own life and work. For Rosenzweig, Jewish life is exilic and unified, dividing itself in its very integration.[75] Perhaps one could even say that Rosenzweig's emphasis on a dual place within history—within and beyond the nations—serves to better imagine the freedom that Rosenstock evokes in the "divided loyalty" of humanity discussed in *Out of Revolution*.

Like Benjamin, both Rosenzweig and Rosenstock sought to counter the violent, coercive aspects of modern life—from assimilation and cultural hegemony, to the industrial exploitation of labor. For Benjamin, the exemplary way to counter the force of "mythical" violence that both led to and supported the rise of fascism was through the "divine" violence of education.[76] Similarly, in seeking to put into practice the redemptive potential of speech-thinking, both friends turned to work in the field of education. It is to see speech-thinking in practice—and how they extended their religious thought into the world—that the next chapter will turn to Rosenzweig's and Rosenstock's efforts in adult education.

75. Rosenzweig, *Judaism Despite Christianity*, 136–37.
76. Benjamin, "Critique of Violence," 298.

THREE

The Art of Education
Cultivating Humanity

IN TIMES OF CRISIS, the pursuit of wisdom can appear to be a luxury, irrelevant to if not a distraction from the pressing problems of the day. When social transformation beckons, study and reflection may appear to be a selfish, bourgeois refusal of Marx's call to change the world, rather than merely understand it. Thus, the question of how philosophy can think responsibly in times of crisis becomes a pressing issue. This was the question that both Rosenzweig and Rosenstock faced after November 1918, in the chaos and turmoil of postwar Germany and the early years of the Weimar Republic. How could philosophy contribute to the renewal of German—or German-Jewish—culture and political life, so as to respond appropriately to the crises of modernity that had fractured society?

For both thinkers, the answer to this question was shaped by their sense that the sociopolitical crisis was also a symptom of an intellectual crisis—such that without a new understanding of the world, it could not be adequately repaired. The logic of speech discussed in chapter 2 provided the requisite "new thinking," in Rosenzweig's terms, but speech-thinking would only be effective if it shaped others' *learning*. Educational reform therefore became the central focus of Rosenzweig and Rosenstock in response to the political and intellectual issues of their time. In many ways, it became the embodied form of their intellectual solidarity, and a testament to how deeply both were shaped by their early encounter and exchanges with one another. It was through education that these friends sought to move, in the closing words of *The Star of Redemption*, "into Life."

While both became involved in educational reform, and built their endeavors on the shared philosophy of speech-thinking, the issues that engaged them differed significantly. Broadly speaking, both sought to address issues of assimilation in education, but the types of assimilation were different. Rosenstock was concerned with the homogenization of learning through an objective, static model that reduced speech to its cognitive and scientific potential, to the detriment of other aspects of human life. Paralleling this, he saw an abstraction of scholarship from life and work, such that intellectual life and labor could not be integrated. These concerns led Rosenstock into varied forms of involvement with adult education in both Germany and the United States. He also developed innovative forms of language instruction later in his career. On his view, teaching had to learn to speak anew—responsibly addressing its audience, shaping its listeners' futures, and carrying their history, so that people could become "new creations," bearing the multiple voices and dynamic history of humanity. To reduce education to "just the facts" as the conveyance of information was what he termed a "sin against the Holy spirit," the unforgivable loss of social life, culture, and humanity that assimilated all aspects of existence to a scientific model.[1]

For Rosenzweig, the issue of assimilation centered more directly on the relations of the Jewish community to its surrounding German culture. As Paul Mendes-Flohr has discussed, identification with and support of German culture and learning (*Bildung*) became one of the primary avenues of assimilation for German Jews in the early twentieth century.[2] While assimilation had become central to Jewish cultural life, it had not led to the anticipated widespread acceptance and integration. As World War I ended, despite widespread assimilation and the support and participation of many German Jews in the war effort, ostracism and outright anti-Semitism remained prevalent factors of social life. In Rosenzweig's view, one effect of this was the loss of a specifically Jewish culture, or else a sense that Jewish culture was derivative from and secondary to German culture. This assimilative emphasis shaped Jewish education: the teaching and scholarship of Judaism followed the historical-critical approach dominant in liberal Protestantism. This did little to advance a sense of Judaism as a living, communal faith, or to cultivate a distinctive cultural and religious voice in the cultural conversation of Germany. Further, while Rosenzweig thought Orthodox Judaism and Zionism correctly recognized the need for a distinctive Jewish identity, they were misguided in seeking separateness—either from other Jews, or from other ethnic and political communities.

By contrast, Rosenzweig sought a form of scholarship that would build Jewish culture and community, integrating its internal identity, so that Jewish people could speak constructively within their surrounding

1. Rosenstock, *I Am an Impure Thinker*, 189.
2. Mendes-Flohr, *German Jews*, 28–34.

culture. These issues led Rosenzweig first to critiques of established practices of Jewish education, and then to founding and directing the *Freies Judisches Lehrhaus* (House of Jewish Learning) in Frankfurt am Main in the early 1920s. Thus, the programmatic vision of speech-thinking led both thinkers to pedagogical innovations on the personal and classroom level, as well as to developing institutions that tried to address the sociopolitical aspects of education. It is in their respective applications of this shared philosophical vision that the fruits of their friendship emerged most fully, continuing even into Rosenstock's work in the United States in the 1930s and 1940s.

Indeed, one could argue that Rosenstock's and Rosenzweig's educational theory and attempts at implementation may most clearly present the contemporary relevance of their work for today. The political and social impact of their educational transformation is perhaps clearest in the opposition it engendered; the Nazis closed down both the *Lehrhaus* and the *Akademie der Arbeit* (Academy of Labor, Rosenstock's adult education program founded as part of the University of Frankfurt am Main) in the 1930s. In the *Lehrhaus*, Rosenzweig sought to integrate learning and religious life, culture and community. He thereby envisioned a public space through which the Jewish community could engage and enrich the broader German culture. In many ways, one can see Rosenzweig as wrestling with issues similar to the recent discussions of public space, plural voices, and particularity among Jeffrey Stout, Stanley Hauerwas, Alasdair MacIntyre, and their interlocutors. How one creates a multi-vocal, democratic, civically responsible culture that thrives through giving space to its dissident groups is a challenge that many cultures still face today, and education is central to this process. Rosenstock likewise explored issues regarding the social divisions of labor and education that still beset our attempts to construct vibrant, flourishing communities.

Alternatively, one could describe the issues Rosenzweig faced as centering on the problem of ethnicity and nationality. As Andrew Wachtel has described, "multiculturalism" may be a misnomer for the challenge our culture faces. Rather, the difficulty is constructing a national identity that integrates the multiple ethnic or religious communities that play an integral role in its development, without bringing about their dissolution.[3] Like translation, education provides a way to welcome foreignness into a community—not in the name of assimilation, but rather in practicing an openness to alterity. One could read Rosenzweig's work as wanting to

---

3. Wachtel, *Making a Nation*, passim.

construct a form of Jewish identity that would, in its own right, be treated as a central component of German culture and life. In the aspirations, limits, successes, and failures of their projects, Rosenstock and Rosenzweig give us material for reflecting on these issues. Moreover, as many American universities and colleges turn to adult education as an additional source of revenue, how one teaches in the adult educational setting is an issue of great import for higher education today, and both thinkers' work provides food for thought on this front.

This chapter will explore the educational initiatives that Rosenzweig and Rosenstock undertook, building on their speech-thinking as well as their religious and historical reflections. It will first examine their proposals for curricular changes, which reflect their philosophical rejection of a Cartesian, egocentric approach to education. It will then examine their work in developing institutions of adult education that sought to integrate life and learning, from the *Freies Judisches Lehrhaus* and the *Akademie der Arbeit* through Rosenstock's work with Camp William James in Vermont. Exploring the parallels will shed light on each author's somewhat idiosyncratic educational proposals, and show how they sought to implement social transformation through educational renewal.

ZEIT IST: A SCHOLARLY RENEWAL OF JUDAISM

1917 was a central year in Rosenzweig's development. The *Star* was beginning to take shape, there was a marked shift in his relationship with Gritli and Eugen, and Germany's fortunes took a dramatic downturn in the war. It was at this time that Rosenzweig wrote his first proposal on Jewish education, *Zeit Ist*,[4] as an open letter to Hermann Cohen. This letter was widely circulated and received significant attention in the Jewish community. While its ambitious proposal would not come to fruition as Rosenzweig had envisioned, both his program and the enthusiastic response of many leading figures signal the issues the Jewish community was wrestling with at this time.

Rosenzweig opens the letter by expressing to Cohen his sense that the "Jewish world" is being lost for the German-Jewish community, implying this is due to the trend toward assimilation. Cohen himself, of course, had argued that the Jewish people were simply one of many ethnic populations within Germany—and, therefore, could be just as much good Germans as

---

4. "It Is Time," in Rosenzweig, *On Jewish Learning*, 27–54.

Prussians or Bavarians. However, what has been lost for Rosenzweig is the unity of lived religious experience; the "Jewish sphere" "exists only in the synagogue," cut off from working, family, and intellectual life.[5] Relegated to the margin of social life, largely through the dynamics of assimilation, Jewish life had grown weak, and Rosenzweig sought to redevelop its independence from the surrounding German culture. The sense of disappointment and loss expressed in this letter may have been exacerbated by Rosenzweig's sense that the German leadership, in handing power to the military, made the "world-historical" significance which Rosenzweig had ascribed to the war a vain hope, further necessitating a break with German culture.[6]

In response to these dashed hopes, Rosenzweig argues for a revitalization of the Jewish community through religious education. In a sense, one could say that he advocates a return much like his own, following his near-conversion to Christianity several years before. However, this would miss some of the subtler dynamics of this essay, where, while rejecting assimilation, an *integration* of German and Jewish culture within the Jewish community remains central. To understand this, it may be helpful to place *Zeit Ist* in its intellectual context.

Since the "Parnassus" affair in 1912, many German Jews had advocated a return to Judaism. For some, this grew from a sense of the desiccation of liberal or secularized Jewish life—often reversing previous generations' antipathy toward traditional Judaism. This return was often expressed through a romanticization of East European Jewry, and Hasidism in particular. The widely popular reception of Buber's work on the Baal Shem Tov, as an "oriental" Judaism that could avoid the decadence and crises of Western industrial culture, was one form of such romanticism.[7] A similar shift can be discerned in paintings within the Jewish community, particularly of the ghetto. Whereas, in the early 1800s, perhaps inspired by a combination of realism and a focus on emancipation, the Jewish ghetto in Frankfurt was often depicted as small, crowded, and dingy, paintings in the late 1800s and early 1900s romanticized its history. At a time where many of Frankfurt's Jews no longer lived in the ghetto area, it was now painted as spacious, bright, and clean—in short, as a place of enlightenment on

---

5. Rosenzweig, *On Jewish Learning*, 28–29.
6. See Mendes-Flohr, "Franz Rosenzweig and the Crisis of Historicism."
7. Mendes-Flohr, *Divided Passions*, 77–109.

its own terms.[8] While this vision of the Jewish community may have been Rosenzweig's goal, *Zeit Ist* recognizes that the required steps to that goal are more complex than a simple nostalgic romanticism.

Rosenzweig begins his proposal by noting how Jewish education must differ from Christian educational programs that had been its models in modernity. While Christian education may try, in his words, to develop "religious feeling through influencing the intellect," the very seat of religious feeling has disintegrated in Judaism. "Consequently, the task of Jewish religious instruction is to re-create that emotional tie between the institutions of public worship and the individual, that is, the very tie which he has lost."[9] The curriculum of the school, then, seeks to direct study toward liturgical life—as in the *Star*, leading through speech into the community that prefigures redemption.

To effect this change, Rosenzweig envisioned a radical, innovative, and ambitious curriculum. It was most radical in its emphasis on Hebrew instruction. At this point—years before translating Jehuda Halevi or the Bible—he argued that to read the Bible as a Jew required reading it in Hebrew; to read it in German was, effectively, to read it *as* a German. Moreover, since the prayer book gives one the "inner life" of Judaism, Hebrew is essential for this aspect of learning as well. As he writes, "And even though in the case of the Bible both possibilities [reading in German and Hebrew] must be admitted, because both Jew and German share in its possession, the language of Jewish prayer is different; of the language of Hebrew prayer we may state quite categorically: it cannot be translated."[10] The loss of identity that translation risks becomes clearer later in the letter: "Language and meaning are co-related, and we underestimate the intimate relation existing, even before Luther, between Christianity and the German language, if we think that Jewish contents can be clothed in German language without admitting connotations foreign to them." [11] Developing

---

8. The chronological display of paintings at the Judengasse Museum in Frankfurt am Main excellently illustrates this trajectory. In particular, one might examine Anton Burger's 1872 painting *Judengasse in Frankfurt* as an early work of romanticization.

9. Rosenzweig, *On Jewish Learning*, 28.

10. Ibid., 30.

11. For a critical reading on this point, see Derrida, *Monolingualism of the Other*, 82–84. Derrida criticizes Rosenzweig for presuming that being "at home" in both German and Hebrew is a living possibility. While Rosenzweig privileges the idea of a "natural" language, that he does so in the context of education suggests that he sees this as something that must be learnt—such that, in response to Derrida's questions, the educational program Rosenzweig articulates is precisely for those who *lack* the language.

Hebrew instruction is necessary for building a "Jewish world" that is not just a "preliminary step" toward the broader German culture.

Given the youth of the students—Rosenzweig envisions their beginning at age nine—pedagogy becomes a central concern. Here, the innovative aspects of his curriculum emerge. He proposes to teach Hebrew through its application—the student learns "by its actual use, the Holy Tongue as a living language."[12] This avoids the ways that traditional grammatical instruction abstracts from use and reifies grammatical structure. One teaches through a series of short texts from worship, including the Shema, benedictions, and oft-cited scriptural passages. As Rosenzweig points out—somewhat presaging Wittgenstein's later thought—such use-oriented learning is how one learns one's mother tongue, progressing "from its application to the rule." Grammatical instruction follows in the later years of the curriculum, but one begins from the everyday usage, which shows how the language lives in liturgical speech.

Of course, in using brief passages, the principle of selection becomes important. Rosenzweig argues that texts should be selected based upon the Jewish liturgical calendar: "the student can be taught the most important customs and institutions related to them."[13] The calendar serves as an initial, if partial, introduction to biblical history, through festivals and the order of services, but more significantly introduces students to the practice of Jewish culture. Through the calendar, a student's individual study becomes linked to the life of the community, and to the "eternal" life of the Jewish people, as discussed in chapter 2.

In the ensuing years of study, Rosenzweig argues that more Jewish history should be incorporated into the lessons. This builds upon the calendrical and linguistic syllabus of the first year. The reason is to "engage" the stories, not in the "pale imitation" of translation and distant history, but in their "originality and presence." As Rosenzweig writes, "Instead of the lame words, 'Where art thou?' from the Paradise story, and 'Here I am' from the sacrifice of Isaac, he [the student] will remember the concise and concentrated Hebrew terms."[14] His method seeks to revitalize history, countering the tendency of historicism to teach it as simply past, relative, and irrelevant. In the later years of the curriculum, this comes to include

---

12. Rosenzweig, *On Jewish Learning*, 34.
13. Ibid., 31.
14. Ibid., 34.

midrash, medieval thinkers like Jehuda Halevi, and Jewish philosophy. The goal, in later years, is that a student "shall recognize Judaism not only as his own world, but also as a spiritual power to be guarded as such in his own life."[15] Rosenzweig's curriculum integrates a diverse array of theological positions and modes of expression from the Jewish tradition, rather than privileging one movement or sect.

Clearly, in spanning such a range of texts, as well as organizing them to cultivate a connection with Jewish worship and community, this is an ambitious educational program. The financial and pedagogical challenges it posed shall be discussed shortly. However, what is most striking is how Rosenzweig's proposal applies the philosophy of language and sociology that he and Rosenstock had developed over the previous several years. Teaching language through use, as opposed to the Alexandrian form of rule-based conjugation, was central to this view. Moreover, as seen in the last chapter, the calendar was central to both Rosenzweig's work in the *Star* and Rosenstock's work on revolutions. Thus, the curricular reforms that Rosenzweig proposed were, to a significant degree, outgrowths of their turn toward speech-thinking and emphasis on the living dimension of history as it is remembered in the community. He argued for an educational approach that would enable the calendrical sociology and messianic understanding of history described in chapter 2. Ironically, for all of his emphasis on separation from the German culture, Rosenzweig developed this possibility through the methods he had developed in dialogue with Rosenstock.

How students would accomplish such an ambitious project by meeting two hours a week is a legitimate question. In the letter's conclusion, Rosenzweig chose to concentrate on an equally pressing problem: who would teach this unorthodox curriculum to the students? Given the depth of learning required in philosophy and history, Rosenzweig argued that a higher level of training was necessary than high school teachers received. However, university training posed a different set of problems, and it is in preparing teachers that the difficulties of assimilation become most evident. The problems are twofold: first, there is the question of who receives religious education, and second is the nature of theological scholarship. In both respects, Rosenzweig sees dangers in following the model of the German Protestant community, as the modern Jewish community had been doing. As only rabbis were receiving high-level theological training (much like Protestant ministers), the broader Jewish community had been

15. Ibid., 41.

cut off from intellectual religious debate. There is, for Rosenzweig, no intellectual Jewish community in the theological sense. Thus, steps must be taken to constitute a public sphere of religious discourse—a concern that will later be carried into his work with the *Lehrhaus*.

The second problem—the character of scholarship—was more difficult to resolve, and Rosenzweig only obliquely gestures toward its solution. While recognizing the scholarly value of "Protestant treatment" of the "Old Testament" [i.e., historical criticism], he says that the extension of this model to scholarly study of Judaism would be dangerous for the community. He gives the following example:

> Scholars with great sagacity and erudition, but little understanding and sympathy for the peculiarities of Jewish religious thinking, will then apply their methods to Halakhah and Aggadah, to philosophy and Kabbalah, surprising us with the results of their inner criticism, as they have surprised us in the past with the separation in Psalm 72 of the supposedly inconsistent elements of "Jewish chauvinism" and "prophetic universalism," or with the elimination of the Suffering Servant from the great Messianic prophecy concerning the history of the Jewish people and all mankind (Isaiah 40ff).[16]

The problem he diagnoses is source-criticism's tendency to divorce different strands of thought within a text. This loses the sense of how the text, as a whole, lets these different voices coexist and dialectically play off of one another, teaching the community through the redactor's voice. His concern, then, is that this model of scholarship would fragment Jewish tradition and prevent students from finding the integrity and vitality that he seeks to convey. Training scholars on the extant university model would therefore be counterproductive.

So as to invigorate scholarship in the Jewish community, Rosenzweig proposed to Cohen the founding of an Academy for the Science of Judaism. Funded by the community with the mission of training teachers in Jewish education, this academy would enable study of a wide range of aspects of Jewish life. Significantly, Rosenzweig saw this as a way to integrate Orthodox and Reformed Judaism, by establishing faculty trained in complementary disciplines and methodologies (a similar idea would later guide the *Lehrhaus*). Through these professorships Jewish scholarship could be established on equal footing while remaining independent of the liberal Protestant influence that dominated university life. This would both enrich

---

16. Ibid., 45–46.

the broader academic debate and help to develop the level of theological discussion within the community.

Calling on the community to fund several new professorships at the end of a costly and devastating war seems ambitious enough. Yet the most ambitious part of Rosenzweig's plan was the creation of a group of teacher-scholars. As students of the Academy, they would go on to serve a hybrid role: teaching the Jewish youth in the educational program described above, yet receiving enough support that they could devote a significant amount of time to scholarship. This, on Rosenzweig's view, was essential for several reasons: 1) it linked scholarship to the community, making it responsive to the students and the synagogues; 2) it helped to create a common discussion and understanding among the different segments of the Jewish community; and 3) perhaps most importantly, it reconstituted the community's public intellectual life, as the teachers would be "equal" in status and learning to the rabbi, while serving different roles in the community.

When *Zeit Ist* was published, it was very well received, and supporters backed the founding of the Academy. However, several events sidetracked the plan, most notably Hermann Cohen's sudden death in 1918. Funding for teacher-scholars—and capable individuals—became difficult to find. As the Academy devolved toward more traditional academic scholarship and teaching, by 1920 it had become dissociated from the life of the community.[17] Rosenzweig's interest waned. It was around this time that he began to turn to the idea of a *Lehrhaus*, with a focus on adult education instead. While the Academy was short-lived in its realization, and perhaps never really lived up to Rosenzweig's expectations, *Zeit Ist* shows how Rosenzweig saw speech-thinking as enabling an integrative reform of education that could harmonize religious, intellectual, and social life, strengthening a sense of identity and countering the trend toward assimilation. As we will see, a similar impetus drove Rosenstock's attempts at education reform—if, again, with very limited success.

MAGNA CARTA LATINA: RE-FORMING SPEECH

Chapters 1 and 2 demonstrated the ways that a reconsideration of spoken language, in its temporality and relationality, runs counter to the mechanistic thrust of modernity. Language is neither learned nor spoken in isolation, and both Rosenzweig and Rosenstock saw the abstraction of its

---

17. See Zank, "Franz Rosenzweig, the 1920s," 241.

objective aspects from its relational dimensions as a fatal error. As we have seen, their work to counter this approach led to the *Star*, their thoughts on history and revolution, and Rosenzweig's interest in pedagogical reform.

The issue of teaching was likewise central to Rosenstock's work. The role of language in curricular development is best illustrated by his *Magna Carta Latina: On The Privilege of Singing and Keeping a Language Alive*. Rosenstock wrote this initially as an alternative Latin textbook for his own son, who struggled with more traditional methods of learning Latin.[18] It would later be used at Dartmouth, in the 1930s and 40s (where Rosenstock taught), as well as at other schools such as the Hartford Seminary. For the sake of brevity, I will highlight the aspects of this work that are most pertinent to this discussion.

The most eye-catching change in *Magna Carta Latina* is its approach to conjugating verbs. Whereas many students may still have the "amo, amas, amat, amamus, amatus, amabant" pattern roll off the tongue many years later, Rosenstock reverses the order. The pattern is third person (*amat*), second (*amas*), and finally first person (*amo*). Of course, this reversal is entirely in keeping with the approach of speech-thinking, in which one cannot say "I" until called "you" by another, as was discussed in chapter 1. Personal speech emerges from the epic, impersonal third person of the past. By treating the persons as basically the same, and overlooking the relational dimension, Rosenstock argues that the Alexandrian grammar that structures the teaching of language gives it a false rigidity, impersonality, and mechanistic quality.[19] *Magna Carta Latina* reorders grammar in light of how language is spoken.

There are other significant innovations as well. Rosenstock selects texts vastly different from standard, "classical" Latin texts. As in *Zeit Ist*, the principle is to see language in its use, and to begin with short, manageable passages; Rosenstock thus frequently opts for medieval texts. The traditional preference for "golden," "pagan" Latin, had the consequence that Latin "is treated as a language separated from all our speech by two thousand years."[20] This reaffirms the view of Latin as a dead language, separating it from our present and the future. In selecting medieval texts, Rosenstock argues that "it is practical to go to the roots of our own life by means of

18. Rosenstock, *Magna Carta Latina*, ii.

19. See ibid., 24. For more on the problems with the Alexandrian grammar, see Rosenstock, "Grammar as Social Science," in *Speech and Reality*, 98–114.

20. Rosenstock, *Magna Carta Latina*, iii.

the central Latin texts that any educated member of our modern society should be able to read—texts so close to the center of our civilization that all national literatures impress us as radii extending from this center."[21] Drawing from Benedictine worship, as well as law and literature, *Magna Carta Latina* unifies the disparate sources of modern life, showing their common historical roots within the Christian and European traditions. The text also begins with a selection of Latin choral texts, helping to make the liturgy more comprehensible while retaining its traditional form. Like Rosenzweig's pedagogy in *Zeit Ist*, Rosenstock seeks to move through the religious practice of language, and an understanding of its social significance, toward a more abstract and rational grasp of its principles.

Far from being a dead language, Rosenstock sees in Latin the ways that language adapts and finds life in new social and political contexts. With the rise of the Christian church, Latin became ecclesiastical, oriented toward church life; it then was adapted as a language of politics and royalty, before becoming a scholastic language in the medieval period. Its "death"—the rumors of which were greatly exaggerated—arose with the collapse of medieval church-state structures, as it became an academic language. In other words, "pure" Ciceronian Latin arose in the sixteenth century, as a historical construct and result of varied shifts in language and culture.[22] By showing how Latin was used through history, Rosenstock brings it into greater proximity and relevance for students, developing their motivation for learning.

Like many of Rosenstock's endeavors, *Magna Carta Latina* found a small but enthusiastic audience. Without a clear articulation of why it approaches language as it does, the value of its pedagogical approach is not readily apparent. However, its design is clearly structured around both the idea of speech-thinking and Rosenstock's "revolutionary" view of history. The methodological resemblance to Rosenzweig's *Zeit Ist* is even more significant, as both thinkers sought to revitalize the teaching of language and tradition in similar ways. These works, then, provide a glimpse into how their shared philosophical outlook shaped their approach to education and social reform. However, to fully understand this outlook, it is necessary to explore their work with alternative adult educational models: the *Akademie der Arbeit*, work camps in Germany and the U.S., and the *Freies Judisches Lehrhaus*.

21. Ibid., iv.
22. Ibid., 194–97.

WORK AND EDUCATION: ROSENSTOCK'S INTER-WAR TEACHING

Despite being one of the most promising young scholars in Germany as World War I neared its end, Rosenstock's career did not follow the expected academic trajectory. As he described many years later in an essay titled "Metanoia: To Think Anew," the crises of German society called him to find a new way of teaching. At war's end, he had opportunities to work as a professor, within the church, or as part of the government. In his view, as attractive as these options were, none was satisfactory:

> ... It became clear to me that by accepting any one of these offers I would become a parasite of German defeat. The country was heading towards disrepute, defeat, poverty, and I would get on top of this corpse. I would shine either as undersecretary or a religious editor or as a university teacher. And I would have to wave a flag which had proved to be uninspired, unprophetic, and would make other people believe that I believed in its message when I did not.[23]

To accept these offers would be to "sin against the Holy Spirit"—the one unforgivable sin. What this meant for Rosenstock was that it would be refusing to listen, to know what mode of speech and practice the new situation required. To undergo *metanoia*, transformation, is to be cast into a new life, breaking with patterns and with one's own will.[24] With this in mind, he sought an alternative path.

The new life that Rosenstock found centered initially on industry, but this led toward an interest in adult education. Carrying him outside established academic channels, this was a path that would extract many personal costs, as well as frustrations with projects that remained unfinished or met resistance. However, it provided him with a series of ventures through which he could extend speech-thinking into practice. From his work at the Daimler factory to the *Akademie der Arbeit* and Camp William James, adult education provided a field for the integration of diverse activities of the human spirit, uniting disparate potentials and communities, and it was this unitive function that drove much of Rosenstock's work.[25]

---

23. Rosenstock, *I Am an Impure Thinker*, 187.

24. Ibid., 189.

25. Beyond the projects discussed here, Rosenstock also served as the vice chairman of the World Association for Adult Education from 1929 to 1933.

Rosenstock often described these endeavors as creating, in the words of William James, an "army at war with nature"—an unfortunate phrase in the postindustrial era. However, an understanding of what he meant by "nature" clarifies this vision. As he wrote in "Arbeitsgemeinschaft," an early piece for *Daimler Werkzeitung*, the journal he published for the Daimler factory workers, the law of nature is to create differences that are oppositional, and which cannot coexist. The task of human labor, then, is to unite those elements of life that are opposed, or separate, "according to nature." Work, acting "contrary to nature" (Rom 1:20), is "spiritual work," because, like the Holy Spirit, it creates a unity out of differences—in which difference remains, but they are held in relation to each other.[26] This was especially significant, at this early stage, as a response to the crisis in Germany at the end of the war, with soldiers returning defeated from war and in need of ways to be reunited with the rest of society. Highlighting this spiritual and theological aspect of work at the start illuminates Rosenstock's vision of adult education, and helps to explain his responses to the conflicts and opposition that he encountered over the next several decades.

After working at Daimler for a couple of years, Rosenstock's work in the 1920s focused on two central projects: work camps, and a brief period of leading the *Akademie der Arbeit* in Frankfurt. The work camps were always closest to his heart; he had coauthored a piece arguing for their creation, as an "industrial army," in 1912 before the turmoil of the war.[27] After the war, Rosenstock saw the camps as a way to do work that would repair the problems of society—addressing issues of poverty and relating the educational system to the activity of labor. One of the central ideas of the camps, as he conceived them, was to make people from different segments of society into coworkers, giving them a sense of the different social classes and helping to overcome class division.[28] Furthermore, by linking work with education, and also with service to the community, he sought to overcome the egoistic pointlessness of modern labor: "Not unemployment but the condition of being nothing but an employee was the evil from which escape was sought."[29] The camps made service possible for intellectuals and elites, and brought intellectual life and culture to the working class

---

26. Rosenstock, "Arbeitsgemeinschaft," 89–90.

27. The 1912 essay is entitled *Im Kampf um der Erwachsenbildung*; see "Army Enlisted against Nature," 272.

28. Simmons, "Bridge-Builder in Quest for Community," 134–35.

29. Rosenstock, "Army Enlisted against Nature," 272.

as well. Rosenstock would continue working with such camps in Germany from 1928 to 1930.

Of course, this is hardly the vision of German labor camps that first comes to mind for most readers. As Rosenstock admitted in 1934, this initial vision became horribly distorted and destroyed by government involvement, especially with the rise of National Socialism. Workers were segregated by age and class, and the fellowship and intellectual life collapsed. Camps were also militarized, losing the open and nonhierarchical character that he saw as essential, and far worse was to follow. We will have to consider later in this section whether the seeds of this perversion tainted Rosenstock's own vision or became a problem at a later date. However, the vision of work camps as an integrating force in society would remain central to Rosenstock's understanding of how to repair the ills of industrial society and labor.

The second major component of Rosenstock's work with adult education during the 1920s was his brief period of directing the *Akademie der Arbeit*. Following a discussion in September 1920 of his ideas on education, he was appointed as leader of the Academy for its first year, which began in May 1921. The curriculum was wide-ranging, with courses ranging from principles of work and psychology to sociology, political economics, law, and history. One hundred ninety-eight students enrolled, and, in addition to the regular coursework, Rosenstock established "work groups" for student discussion in which all students participated.[30] He taught courses in economics, law, and history.

Almost from the date of his hiring, Rosenstock encountered difficulties and problems. The *Akademie* faced numerous challenges, among the most significant being the diverse backgrounds and levels of preparation of its students, as well as the lack of a common pedagogical model. Rosenstock's attitude toward this puzzled his colleagues. Somewhat Socratically, he thought that the students brought with them "unformed concepts" from their work experience, and that the teacher's task was to draw these out of the students by involving them in the educational process. In his view, the lack of an established program was a strength, as it created a space for a new sort of interaction.[31] Breaking with the standard model of education, he conceived the Academy as an institute that would bring together academic scholarship and work life, allowing these different human faculties to speak

30. Antrick, *Akademie der Arbeit*, 138–40.
31. Ibid., 31.

with and learn from one another. Effectively, he sought to create an educational model in which workers would be equal with teachers, rather than a hierarchical one. As he wrote, "The worker should become a co-worker (*mitarbeiter*) in spirit, not a student."[32]

The work groups were essential for this plan. In them workers would master, discuss, and *teach* a particular topic. They would no longer be students—listeners (*horern*)—but would be involved in the process. Rosenstock emphasized this aspect of the *Akademie* as a "counterweight" to balance lectures and create a dynamic dialogue amongst the participants.[33] The model fits, on many levels, with his speech-philosophy: once addressed in lectures, the "hearers" could find their voices and become speakers; through the conversation, different aspects of human life are united, rather than being divided in their traditional roles. Finally, the model creates an integration of work with the intellect, creating new possibilities of service, *verifying* intellectual life through the relationship.

Of course, as might be expected, many faculty of the *Akademie* were not enthusiastic about having students "verify" their ideas. The work group model was an implicit, if unstated, challenge to the adequacy and hierarchy of lecture-based university pedagogy. However, the methodology of Rosenstock's approach was not clearly laid out, and many faculty who were used to the university model sought to revise the curriculum. Dr. Hugo Sinzheimer, also a law professor, led the criticism of Rosenstock's leadership. Sinzheimer spoke out about the problems many faculty saw in trying to teach in this new environment, complaining about a "systematic lack in the pedagogical plan." He sought to emphasize lectures as a primary form of instruction.[34] Rosenstock clearly took it personally. In an unpublished essay, he described how the conflict between him and Sinzheimer threatened to ruin the work of the first year. The deeper problem that he saw, however, was that the proposals of Sinzheimer and others for a more university-based model were not appropriate for the audience of the Academy—in Rosenstock's view, this restored hierarchy by "making coworkers into students."[35] A university-modeled pedagogy was, in Rosenstock's view, an irreparable error, aligning the Academy too closely

32. Rosenstock, "Akademie der Arbeit," 148.
33. Ibid., 151.
34. Antrick, *Akademie der Arbeit*, 31.
35. Rosenstock, "An die Mitarbeiter der Akademie der Arbeit."

with the university and depriving it of its distinctive calling. Defeated, Rosenstock left after the first year.

Today, from a variety of perspectives, both epistemological and pedagogical, one can conceive justifications for Rosenstock's approach, particularly in terms of the need for diverse learning styles for nontraditional students, as well as incorporating their experience and practical knowledge into the classroom. However, it seems that his rationale was never adequately conveyed in practical terms, and the work groups were subsequently dropped from the curriculum. In later years, he would attribute the conflict to problems with labor unions and Marxists,[36] but the pedagogical conflict seems to have been central.

The *Akademie der Arbeit* would continue its work through 1933, when it was closed by the Nazis. It reopened after the war, and still serves as an adult education program in the University of Frankfurt today. Like much of adult education, the Academy's focus is primarily on educational and professional advancement. The curricular, social, and personal synthesis that Rosenstock envisioned as a way of reintegrating the fragmentary life of modernity has faded from view.

STRANGER IN A STRANGE LAND: CAMP WILLIAM JAMES

In part because of his involvement with the Academy of Labor and the work camps, when the National Socialists gained control of the German government in 1933 Rosenstock was forced to emigrate to the United States. At this time he was still very involved with issues of adult education, publishing several articles on the topic. After teaching briefly at Harvard, he moved to Dartmouth College, where he would teach for the rest of his career. In the United States, Rosenstock returned to the academic setting, beginning with his work *Out of Revolution* in the 1930s. However, as World War II approached, and with the persistence of the Great Depression, he saw his students at Dartmouth struggle with finding their place in the modern world, and began to consider how alternative educational models might address the social ills of America.

At Dartmouth, Rosenstock was working primarily with the elite youth of America. This meant, effectively, that they had been divorced from the work of industry and agriculture, gliding through an ethereal world of academia and management in the midst of great turmoil and suffering.

---

36 Rosenstock, "Biblionomics," 24.

Privilege effectively led to alienation. Teaching no longer would "lead to something out of the classroom": the focus on objective and scientific learning left students ill-prepared to address the social and political problems of their day. Ignoring how history repeats itself, historians repeated one another, losing a sense of what history might teach students for the crises they and their communities faced. To really educate, as he said in a 1939 lecture at Dartmouth, required "a jump outside ourselves . . . Otherwise we fall flat, by the self-centeredness of our professional routine."[37] But how does one jump outside oneself, into the future that calls for new action?

An initial step for Rosenstock came through advisory work for the Civilian Conservation Corps (CCC), part of the "alphabet soup" of Franklin Roosevelt's New Deal. Through organizing a conference on the CCC at Dartmouth, Rosenstock was able to become involved in thinking about the transformative potential of the CCC. He saw it as providing a potential remedy to American education, which "made our schools factories for the mass. The school withdraws the children from private homes to which they never return."[38] If education did not cultivate or regenerate social and communal connections, then it would effectively industrialize citizens. The CCC, with its potential service to communities, could counter this trend. Some of his connections from this meeting, as well as his time at Harvard, provided him with the support to help develop Camp William James, an alternative work project that ran from 1940 through to Pearl Harbor in December 1941.

The work of the camp began with Harvard graduate Frank Davidson, who met with Rosenstock in 1939. In the words of Jack Preiss, he was concerned about the "widening segregation" of American society,[39] its isolation in what Jeffrey Stout has recently termed "enclaves" of isolated, monological voices.[40] Learning from Rosenstock about the work camps in Germany, Davidson decided to try to join the CCC in an effort to integrate the separate strata of American youth. This was a radical endeavor: the CCC was structured to include only the most impoverished youth, and this often meant those with no college education whatsoever. On one level, there was good reason for this policy—many individuals

---

37. Rosenstock, "Teaching Too Late, Learning Too Early," in *I Am an Impure Thinker*, 102.

38. Rosenstock, "What They Should Make Us Think."

39. Preiss, *Camp William James*, 7.

40. Stout, *Democracy and Tradition*, 114–15.

and families were in dire need of the program's meager financial support. However, the unintended consequence was that the CCC reinforced the social isolation of its participants, placing them in self-contained work projects with few ties to communities or opportunities for personal and social enrichment. This conserved resources economically, but did not conserve or regenerate social and intellectual bonds. The contrast with Rosenstock's view of work camps as enabling social integration could not have been starker. Frank Davidson, in fact, was the first college-educated member of the CCC, and was looked upon with some trepidation and puzzlement by its administration. Davidson wrote a letter to Rosenstock describing his early experience:

> I have had to forget a vocabulary and learn a new one . . . Beyond that, I have had to invent and stick to a "hard luck" story. I am probably the only person in camp (excepting the educational director) with a college education . . . There is an utter lack of integrated intellectual or recreational activities. The fellows think and talk only of sex. A few men have mentioned the situation as a sad one, and I hope to get them to cooperate, eventually, to initiate some voluntary activities in the camp, and perhaps later in one of the nearby communities.

Despite these difficulties, he saw potential in the camp itself:

> I have never felt so sure of my own personality as I do now. Manual labor is a great and important thing, and I am glad to have been forced to get along in what would have ordinarily been an uncongenial group . . . The CCC comes closer than I thought it would to William James' idea of an army against nature. The spirit of the place is really pretty good, despite a total lack of leadership.[41]

While Davidson worked through the CCC, several recent graduates of Dartmouth were also involved in community service in rural Vermont, working for room and board on farms in Tunbridge and the surrounding area. In this area they saw rising rural poverty, as well as an exodus of the youth to cities and more prosperous areas. Through experience and conversations with the community, they realized the deep need for labor, and for an infusion of youth to sustain the community.

With Rosenstock's guidance, the graduates sought to develop an alternative work camp that could remedy the abstraction of college life, the

---

41. Preiss, *Camp William James*, 12–13.

pointless, isolated labor of the CCC, and the deep economic and social needs of Vermont's rural communities. In 1940 they managed to reopen an abandoned CCC work camp in Sharon, but designed it to address the problems they diagnosed. Rosenstock wrote,

> The jobs we do are in response to obvious community needs . . . in working on farms in and around Tunbridge, we are helping to overcome a shortage of seasonal agricultural labor: we are helping to limit the absurdity of young men without respected employment on the one hand and farmers without sufficient support to keep their families and communities going, on the other. Secondly, we have accomplished a few jobs designed to conserve land and water resources for future generations: this work is outside the ordinary economic system, but it is the kind of work that will enable this section of the United States to look forward with confidence to a future in which there shall be an economic system. For poor land means poor men.[42]

To accomplish these goals, several steps were taken. First, they set up an advisory committee from the local community, to make sure that the projects met actual community needs, and to build community support for the project. Second, the graduates joined the CCC, and the camp included both "regular" and college-educated CCC members. The goal, then, was to integrate them in their work, and also thereby create a richer social life and bond for all the members. On December 14, 1940, Camp William James opened, with two of James's children in attendance.

Rosenstock played several roles in the setup of the camp. His connections with several of Roosevelt's political supporters played an integral role in getting the president's support for the camp. On a more regular basis, he would occasionally give lectures for or to the workers, and held extensive discussions with many of them, along with devoting much time and expense to establishing the camp. He also worked extensively to try to develop a sense of fellowship within the camp. His role remained informal, for both bureaucratic and political reasons. Because he had not received U.S. citizenship he could not be employed by the CCC, and, despite having left Germany under the threat of Nazi persecution, his German background made both townspeople and some government officials suspicious of his actions. Even when he was personally defended on a number of

---

42. Rosenstock, "Purpose of William James," 2.

occasions against charges of being a German spy, political expediency often kept Rosenstock's official role to a minimum.[43]

Rosenstock's primary interest was the sociality of the camp. This had three dimensions to it: first, to unite intellectual life with labor; second, to bring together different and often segregated classes of American society; and third, to develop working relationships between different communities and age groups. He organized dinners, speakers, and square dances to try to create these relationships, and was very critical of the standard practice of the CCC in failing to recognize the importance of these dimensions. As Rosenstock wrote to Dan Goldsmith, one of the campers, in 1945,

> The true experience of the work service must be in how to rebuild a community. And a community is not represented by a soldiers' barracks or a logging camp, but by a long-range society of all age groups, both sexes, and all classes. We implied . . . that the unemployed individual, in the work camp, must find comrades from all walks of life because he cannot survive his segregation outside of it. We now add the second rule—that the camps cannot be set out anywhere in the country as in a vacuum. Unfortunately, this is the very link by which our educational system has been broken out of the chain of each community. In the work service, the harm done by the isolation of our high school and college system is to be repaired. For under our present educational system, youth dreams its dreams of the future *outside of and against the home community*.[44]

Work camps might serve to employ people, and to conserve economic resources. However, for Rosenstock, without attending to the bonds of community, and the ways that our economy can often see these as either convertible to capital or impediments to economic development, such work loses its spiritual sense and leads to the division and collapse of the community, rather than being an activity through which a community may become whole. As he put it in "The Purpose of Camp William James," "Pigeonhole a man and he loses his stature."[45]

In practice, the camp was only a marginal success. Integrating the different groups of workers proved difficult, and in spite of successful dinners

---

43. For a discussion of the political conflicts that the Camp encountered, and the ways its opponents tried to use Rosenstock's emigration against him and the project, see Preiss, *Camp William James*, 138–56.

44. Letter to Dan Goldsmith, March 14, 1945, in Preiss, *Camp William James*, 224. Rosenstock's emphasis.

45. Rosenstock, "Purpose of Camp William James," 6.

and dances there was still extensive isolation from the broader community. "Integration," at this point, was still limited to whites, with no attention to racial discrimination as part of its work. Moreover, the local efforts were often undermined by bureaucratic oversight in Washington, as CCC officers sought to retain control over the direction of the camp, which directly challenged the model on which many of the CCC camps were conceived. There were also differences within the group as to direction, and the importance of local commitment. Some members wanted to rejuvenate and work farms that had become dormant, having been closed when they were no longer economically viable. Others wanted to work more directly for the benefit of established farmers in the area. Despite President Roosevelt's support (which was limited due to other political concerns, such as the impending war), Camp William James lost its status as a CCC project early in 1941. The camp was closed later in the year after one last attempt at farming, shutting down completely with the U.S. entry into World War II after Pearl Harbor. Once again, a project with such promise suggested an alternative approach to education—yet was unable to make a lasting impression.

In evaluating Rosenstock's work with Camp William James and with alternative modes of education more broadly, several notable trends stand out. First, there are a number of levels on which his approach to education resonates with recent educational, philosophical, and cultural movements in the United States. The focus on the connection between division of labor and social segregation is especially interesting, as it suggests a comparison with the cultural criticism and communitarian environmentalism of Wendell Berry. Like Berry, Rosenstock sought to repair the isolation, economic and social drain, and environmental destruction of rural and small-town America. Rosenstock's description of the loss of youth, and of workers in agriculture more generally, could be taken almost verbatim from Berry's work thirty to forty-five years later, when the problems have only intensified due to technological industrialization of agriculture.[46] By highlighting how the separation of labor isolates different segments of society, and the effect this has on community, Rosenstock helps to trace the roots of this problem.

Moreover, in thinking about how an economy creates or destroys social conditions, one could draw connections between Rosenstock's emphasis on work that addresses the local needs of a community and the idea of "local economy" that has informed much of Berry's recent work. A local

---

46. See Berry, *Unsettling of America*.

economy, in which people work with, and buy from, their neighbors, from local farmers to other businesses, seeks to be as communally self-sufficient as possible, but also seeks to develop solutions to its particular problems, rather than relying on general policies that cannot repair particular issues.[47] In a sense, one could say that Berry's vision of local economy, along with Rosenstock's practice, represents a reversal or renewal of an earlier historical moment: where in *Out of Revolution* Rosenstock saw economies becoming more global, with politics being localized, in his later practice he breaks with this systematic vision to work locally with the troubled communities of Vermont.

However, one of the most intriguing connections here has to do with the connection between segregation of work and social segregation. Again, there is a profound confluence with Berry, whose singular contribution to discussions of race and class is to ask how racism relates to our culture's denigrating attitude toward manual labor in the United States. The desire of Americans to be free from manual labor, and the tendency to look down on those who do it, is closely connected with racism.[48] Albeit with regard to class, Rosenstock also saw the segregation of work as one of the most significant dividing lines of American culture, and the camp provided one model for unifying those groups that have been separated, and allowing them to engage with and renew one another.

On another level, one can look at the work of both Rosenzweig and Rosenstock and ask about their contribution to educational theory. First, it is clear that for both education is a central component, if not *the* central component, of building community. Second, however, both emphasize a decidedly non-hierarchical view of education—seeking to counter specialized, isolated knowledge, in favor of how it relates to other disciplines and even other economic professions and social strata. It is striking to see how, whether in the *Lehrhaus* (which will be discussed below), the *Akademie der Arbeit*, or Camp William James, the teacher's knowledge is not privileged; rather, it gives voice to others, so that they too may speak. Along with the focus on understanding, critical thinking, incorporation of diverse perspectives, and personal involvement, their emphasis on non-hierarchical instruction suggests that they see education as central in the building of self-reflective, polyphonic communities.

---

47. See Berry, "Damage" and "The Idea of a Local Economy."
48. See Berry, *Hidden*.

If there is a weakness to Rosenstock's approach to education, it may be in the difficulties raised by his tendency toward historical generalization. As we have seen, this affected his relationship with Rosenzweig, to the point that Franz often felt Eugen did not really recognize him as an individual. It likely played a role in his failure to adequately conceive a pedagogical structure that addressed the specific concerns of both students and faculty at the *Akademie der Arbeit*. In the later work at Camp William James, Rosenstock does seem to have become more attuned to particularity—emphasizing the importance of work with the community, and relating on a very personal basis to the students involved, including extensive counseling and support.

The question, however, should be put to Rosenstock's theory, not his behavior. For, in many ways, to think in terms of "potentialities of the spirit," and what they can contribute to the broader social dynamic, tends to define people by their roles—and by how those roles can fit into the broader group. He tends to think largely in collective terms.[49] My sense is that, as with many aspects of his theory, the reasoning here is theological, and particularly draws upon Pauline pneumatology. As in 1 Corinthians, the body of the community is made up of many members, and each has a role—and, as Paul warns, those who prophesy should not speak in tongues, and there is no need to privilege one role over the others.[50] The Holy Spirit works through the body as a whole, integrating each person's particular function.

While Corinthians may illustrate and explicate his view, it also highlights the problem more concretely. For, if people are located according to social function, then the particularities of their activity, and other aspects of their lives, may be ignored. Rosenstock privileges social interplay between different tasks over their place in an individual's life, even while saying it is important to "pass through" each stage of the spirit. Pigeonholing may lead to a loss in stature—yet, at times, it seems that Rosenstock himself was vulnerable to this criticism. Someone who can play multiple roles, and perhaps even feels that living between roles *is* her role, may be without place or misunderstood. The engaged struggle and debate between different aspects of community, as an element of political life, may still be undervalued on this approach.[51] One may even wonder if Rosenstock's

---

49. This is most apparent in his lecture, "The Social Function of Adult Education," where he explicitly privileges the cohesion of the group over individual development.

50. 1 Cor 12:12–31.

51. Here I am thinking of the work of Sheldon Wolin and radical democracy. Wolin's

theory does not really account for how someone engages in as many debates, communities, and disciplines as he did—or, alternatively, the plural engagements and approaches taken by Rosenzweig. At the least, the social and communal dynamic tends to override such individual dynamism in Rosenstock's theory.

For example, shortly before the dissolution of Camp William James, there was a debate as to how the camp members should carry on their work in the community if the CCC closed the camp (which it did). While this debate was going on, several non-college members of the camp went out and arranged housing and work in the community for the college members. This initiative and civic engagement were pretty much unanticipated by the college members (as well as by Rosenstock)—almost as if it were not a task the non-college members would or could do. Fremont Smith, who led the initiative, expressed both his sense of confinement and frustration, which would shortly lead to his staying in the CCC and leaving the camp: "Jes wanted you to know we could get things done, too . . . Well, you got your house, by Jesus. Now go live in it."[52] If the Spirit blows where it will, then there may be a need to balance the social interaction of different voices, practices, and communities with the dialogical interplay of such voices in the multifaceted lives of individuals. Such balance, it seems, remains underdeveloped in Rosenstock's work.

THE *FREIES JUDISCHES LEHRHAUS*

> Teaching and study have both deteriorated. And they have done so because we lack that which gives animation to both science and education—life itself.[53]

In 1920, as the Academy for the Science of Judaism tended toward more traditional academic scholarship, Rosenzweig distanced himself from this project. He remained interested in educational issues, though his focus shifted toward adult education. His initial foray into this field was a letter to Edward Strauss, translated as "Toward a Renaissance of Jewish Learning." The German title, *Bildung und Kein Ende*, suggests that the relation of Judaism to its surrounding culture (*bildung*) and the cultivation

---

critique of Platonism, with its limitation of participatory struggle, could perhaps apply to Rosenstock in an analogous manner; see Wolin, *Politics and Vision*.

52. Preiss, *Camp William James*, 156.

53. Rosenzweig, "Toward a Renaissance of Jewish Learning" in *On Jewish Learning*, 60. For a more recent translation, see Zank, "Franz Rosenzweig, the 1920s," 227–39.

of Jewish culture remain central issues for Rosenzweig—though to say they are "without end" raises the question of their goal.[54] However, assimilation is a less central focus in this letter. Rather, here Rozenzweig describes a renewal of adult education as a way to integrate and unite diverse aspects of Jewish individual and communal life, which, after emancipation and in modernity, have become alienated from one another.

The path to overcoming these forms of alienation lies in what Rosenzweig terms "Life." Life unites the whole range of disciplines, politics, and practices of human life, letting them blend as aspects of a whole individual. The crucial move this lets Rosenzweig make is that he conceives being Jewish not as a part of one's identity, nor an aspect of one's humanity that one has, like a nationality; rather, being Jewish is the particular mode of humanity that one *is*.

> The Jewish human being finds his limitation not in the Frenchman or German but only in another human being as unlimited as himself: the Christian or heathen. . . . His Judaism must, to the Jew, be no less comprehensive, no less all-pervasive, no less universal than Christianity is to the Christian human, or heathenism to the heathen humanist.[55]

The problem that Rosenzweig diagnoses is that when Judaism (or Christianity, for that matter) is treated as an aspect of one's life, a religious "sphere" of existence separate from family, politics, or culture, then the unity between these different aspects of life is lost. Without "Life," the law, the Jewish home, and synagogue are "parts" of life, but no longer "the single platform of a real and contemporaneously lived life."[56] As segments of life, these coalesce into segments of the community, causing division between those devoted to different aspects of life. Assimilated and Orthodox, Zionist and anti-Zionist, work and home life, all become separate, isolated, and opposed spheres of Jewish existence, with nothing to bridge the gaps. Religion and education are divorced, "in keeping with the spirit of the culture-obsessed, pigeonholing 19th century." [57] While the struggle for equal rights, after emancipation, has given the Jewish community a common concern, it does not help to cultivate a distinctively Jewish life,

---

54. Zank notes that the title plays on Ecclesiastes 12:12 in "Franz Rosenzweig, the 1920s," 241.

55. Rosenzweig, *On Jewish Learning*, 57.

56. Ibid., 61.

57. Ibid., 63.

or unite the fragmentation individuals and communities faced. Jewish "individuals" remained divided within themselves, and from one another. Likewise, it is, I think, because Zionism also failed to address such internal alienation that Rosenzweig remained a non-Zionist in his politics.[58] All of these programs have value in his eyes, but they do not lead to the unifying, creative force of Life.[59]

In his letter, Rosenzweig envisions the *Lehrhaus* as creating a space in which these particulars could be harmonized and integrated—much like Rosenstock's focus on integrating different aspects of the German (or later, American) community. However, in order to do this, Rosenzweig sees the *Lehrhaus* as needing an innovative pedagogical approach. Over against a set, fixed curriculum, he proposes a discussion-oriented format: "This movement would begin with its own bare beginnings, which would be simply a space to speak in and time in which to speak."[60] He argues for a public discussion space, in which the desires of different participants can be spoken, and the *Lehrhaus* can then design programs that respond to these desires. There are two significant aspects to this. First, with the discussion room, a public, inclusive learning space is developed. This avoids the hierarchy of a lecture, and the abstract speech of those whom Rosenzweig labels "stuffed shirts," who fail to create speaking relations. Moreover, it creates an equality, or interchangeability, between teachers and students: "The teacher able to satisfy such spontaneous desires cannot be a teacher according to a plan; he must be much more and much less, a master and at the same time a pupil . . . He must be capable of something quite different—he himself must be able to 'desire.'"[61]

By beginning from desire, and from Life, the public, open discussion creates a bond among the discussants and brings together different aspects of life and community. "The discussion should become a conversation"[62]— joining those who have been separate or isolated. This "bookless start" can then incorporate other forms of learning (history, text study, philosophy),

---

58. For more on his relation to Zionism, see Rashkover, *Revelation and Theopolitics*, 175–80.

59. It is important to note how this may involve a shift from the conception of life and redemption in the *Star*. See Kavka, "Ethics of Verification," 21–23.

60. Rosenzweig, *On Jewish Learning*, 68.

61. Ibid., 69. See also Brenner, *Renaissance of Jewish Culture*, 79–80. For a strong interpretation of how this connects with exegesis, see Rashkover, *Revelation and Theopolitics*, 106–7.

62. Rosenzweig, *On Jewish Learning*, 69.

but these all derive and grow from its sociality. In breaking with hierarchy and creating a conversational speech, the movement would begin to respond to the problems of alienation.

On the basis of this letter, along with his other philosophical work, Rosenzweig was invited by Rabbi Nehemiah Nobel and others to found an adult education program in Frankfurt-am-Main. The *Lehrhaus* was formed through the revision of an existing *Volkschule*, which had been run by Eugen Meyer.[63] Rosenzweig described this as a "modern beth ha-Midrasch," a school at once traditional and modern. He named it the *Freies Judisches Lehrhaus* to signify that all were welcome. Moreover, the curriculum took the vague proposal of *Bildung und Kein Ende* and gave it definition that spoke to Rosenzweig's belief that "nothing Jewish is alien to me."[64]

In his address on the opening of the *Lehrhaus* on October 17, 1920, Rosenzweig describes the rationale for the course prospectus. The prospectus sets up a series of contrasts: classical, historical, and modern Judaism, with each containing two "opposed" subjects: the Law and the Prophets, Haggadah and Halakhah, and the Jewish world and the Jewish person. Whereas historical approaches separate these elements of Judaism, here these contrasts function dialectically: "The contrasts are put in solely for the purpose of being bridged."[65] The goal, for Rosenzweig, is to discover the inner relation that unites these different aspects of Jewish life, and makes them parts of the whole, both for individuals and the community.

In seeking this inner unity, Rosenzweig also constructed an intentionally diverse faculty. In this address, he mentions that many teachers are not specialists in the study of Judaism—rather, they include chemists, physicians, and other professions. The reason is that a new sort of learning is required because of the alienation that marks modern Jewish life. Rosenzweig does not reject this alienation, but says that for those who experience it (including himself), they must "lead everything back to Judaism."[66] Therefore, teachers who are engaged with the modern world can lead students in integrating this into a Jewish life. This path—between assimilation and traditionalism—sought to humanistically retain engagement with the surrounding world without sacrificing any particularities of Jewish life.

63. Glatzer, "Frankfort Lehrhaus," 6–7.
64. Rosenzweig, *On Jewish Learning*, 69.
65. Rosenzweig, "On the Opening of the Jewish Lehrhaus," in *On Jewish Learning*, 100.
66. Rosenzweig, *On Jewish Learning*, 98.

Beyond their diverse professions, Rosenzweig saw the faculty as creating a public discourse that could create conversations between different sects within the Jewish community. He designed the curriculum so that students would hear lectures by teachers from the different sects of the community. Thus, Rabbi Nobel, the Orthodox rabbi, taught Halakhah, while Rabbi Seligmann, the liberal rabbi, taught Haggadah, giving students a sense of their different approaches to the Talmud while setting forth both as voices within a common tradition. Zionist and anti-Zionist views were also incorporated.[67] By doing this, different perspectives within Judaism—and their relation to the tradition—could be elaborated upon and discussed within a common framework of learning. It modeled, in a sense, a "generous orthodoxy," to borrow a phrase from the work of Karl Barth. As Nahum Glatzer points out, one of Rosenzweig's goals was to overcome provincialism within the community, and the faculty was constructed with this in mind.[68]

Rosenzweig's other focus with the *Lehrhaus* was the development of work groups. These ranged from high-level studies, such as a group exploring Cohen's posthumous *Religion within Reason Out of the Sources of Judaism* to introductory Hebrew study. These also provided an alternative learning format, as they sought to be "teacherless teaching" (*lehrerlose lernen*), to use Rosenzweig's phrase.[69] The goal was to create a forum in which students who merely listened in the lectures could become more involved.[70] Over the coming years, he would see these groups as the heart of the *Lehrhaus*, more so than the lectures. Indeed, these groups became central to the intellectual life of the community, bringing together Martin Buber, S. Y. Agnon, Gershon Scholem, Nahum Glatzer, and many others. Rosenzweig would continue to meet with work groups at his house on 10 Schumannstraße even when he could no longer lecture or attend the *Lehrhaus* itself.

From 1920 until the summer of 1922, Rosenzweig taught in the *Lehrhaus* before his ALS became too debilitating. At the end of 1922, Rudi Hallo took over the operations and direction of the school, though Rosenzweig remained involved. During this period, he lectured on a range of topics, most notably the "Science of God, Man, and World," an

---

67. See Rosenzweig, *"Gritli"-Briefe*, August 22, 1920.
68. Glatzer, "Frankfort Lehrhaus," 15–16.
69. Feidel-Mertz, "Lernende Lehrer," 113.
70. Kern-Ulmer, "Franz Rosenzweig's *Jüdisches Lehrhaus*," 209–10.

attempt to explicate the central ideas of the *Star*. What is most notable about these lecture notes is their dialogical format, involving questions and responses, in an attempt to draw students into the topic.[71] To help with this, Rosenzweig also relied upon Rudi Hallo, Rudolf Stahl, and Martin Goldner to "lead the chorus of questions," so as to draw the audience into discussion.[72] He also frequently used concrete examples to explicate his concepts, clearly attempting to engage his audience and draw them into the study. As Feidel-Mertz writes, "'Jewish learning' was based at all times on dialogue and discourse, that one learn from another."[73]

In the early years of the *Lehrhaus*, Rosenzweig was very enthusiastic about the project. Despite expressing some concerns to Gritli over projected enrollments and financing,[74] his commitment was quite strong. Late in 1920, he invited Eugen to participate in a panel on speech as testimony, and emphasized in his letter that the *Lehrhaus* was open to the public, both Jewish and non-Jewish, as the Talmud directed (it is not clear if Eugen accepted). A letter a few months later, in February 1921, gives some sense of their divergent perspectives at this point. The background to Franz's letter is a proposal that Eugen had made regarding the study of nineteenth-century Jewish history; this may have been for a lecture, but more likely he was encouraging this as a course of study for Rosenzweig. Rosenzweig emphatically rejects this, as running counter to the tenor of his current work and of no interest to him whatsoever. He makes it clear that academic study must be done in Frankfurt—with his *Lehrhaus* students. As he writes, "Habilitation comes only in one form: *Here*, for Philosophy, in the student-dependence of the *Lehrhaus*."[75] The sort of historical study Rosenstock proposed was, in Rosenzweig's view, tantamount to death.

The differences between their approaches to education are also starkly apparent in a letter to Gritli from September 1921, shortly after Eugen had started directing the *Akademie der Arbeit*. Rosenzweig attended an event with Rosenstock, with several lectures given. As will be recalled from the previous section, Rosenstock emphasized that the workers should also become teachers, and speak, rather than just receive lectures. Rosenzweig

71. See Rosenzweig, *God, Man, and the World*, 53–61, for a good example of his question-based presentation.
72. Feidel-Mertz, "Lernend Lehrer," 113.
73. Ibid., 113.
74. Rosenzweig, *"Gritli"-Briefe*, October 15, 1920.
75. Ibid., February 3, 1921.

describes the worker's speech as "horrible," and criticizes the sort of spontaneous, undirected speech that Rosenstock advocated. He writes to Gritli that things work better at the *Lehrhaus*, because there are conversations between teachers, which create a structure into which students can enter, rather than an unformed, haphazard discussion.[76] While both emphasized work groups, Rosenzweig maintains some sense of hierarchy to give order to the learning. There is clearly disagreement bordering on antagonism between Rosenzweig and Rosenstock at this point; one year later, when Rosenstock had been ousted from the *Akademie*, and was in the process of leaving Frankfurt, Rosenzweig's tone shifted markedly to a more sympathetic and supportive view.[77]

The *Lehrhaus* reached its zenith in 1923, as enrollment expanded to 1100 students. It would become the model for other cities, as Cologne, Wiesbaden, Mannheim, and Breslau also founded *Lehrhauses*.[78] After this point, due in part to the economic crisis and spike in inflation, the number of enrollees diminished. By 1926, Rosenzsweig wrote to Eduard Strauss that the *Lehrhaus*'s structure of lectures and work groups had become a failure; the lectures were to bring in students and provide support for the work groups, but this no longer worked.[79] The *Lehrhaus* shifted to more informal, occasional courses and lectures after 1926. It would continue to function, and took on renewed importance in 1933, with the Nazis' rise to power. Buber took over its direction, and Glatzer describes its work, until 1938, as central to helping the Jewish community deal with the changes and persecutions of those years. It was closed in 1938, though a *Lehrhaus* was reopened in Frankfurt in 1982,[80] and many have opened in other cities in Germany and worldwide since then.

As Rosenzweig noted in *Bildung und Kein Ende*, the goals of Jewish adult education were substantially different from those of the German adult education movement Rosenstock worked with.[81] As just discussed, the pedagogical structure of the *Lehrhaus* differed from the model of both the *Akademie* and the later camps that Rosenstock developed. In particular, Rosenzweig emphasized the mediating role of teachers, to help develop

76. Ibid., September 29, 1921.
77. Ibid., September 8, 1922.
78. Brenner, *Renaissance of Jewish Culture*, 90–99.
79. Letter of January 28, 1926, in *Gesammelte Schriften*, 2:1083–84.
80. See Kern-Ulmer, "Franz Rosenzweig's *Judisches Lehrhaus*," 202–14.
81. Rosenzweig, *On Jewish Learning*, 67.

and bring hearers into conversations, rather than simply direct speech by workers without some introduction to the language of the disciplines. Helping students to learn patterns of inquiry and speech, and modeling these for them, so they can become part of the disciplinary conversations, is as crucial for an educational approach based upon speech-thinking as it is for more traditional educational approaches. Perhaps this emphasis on mediation was a central reason the *Lehrhaus* model was more successful and more widely accepted than Rosenstock's approach.

However, on the level of vision, there are deeper parallels between their educational work that should be noted, as they are highly relevant for today. Both Rosenzweig and Rosenstock saw education as a potential solution for the problems of social alienation, fragmentation, and segregation, because education creates a public space in which different speakers, practices, and communities can enter into relation to one another. Through education, there can be differences of labor, but as these are related to one another, they need not become *divisions* of labor that divide society or reinforce existing segregations.

It is also quite striking how, within their respective institutions, both rejected the traditional model of university teaching as overly rigid and hierarchical. While the roles of teachers and students were not dissolved, they could be exchanged. A doctor becomes a theologian, and a philosopher a Hebrew teacher, and both become students as well. Israel Steinberg wrote of his experience at the *Lehrhaus* that he learned much from the teachers, more from his colleagues, and the most from his students.[82] Moreover, the educational institution, in constructing multiple learning environments, developed a range of social orders in which students could engage—from role-bound learning, to group work, to individual study, and exchangeable roles within the classroom.

What is significant, here, is that the educational programs that Rosenzweig and Rosenstock developed were responding to social deficits: a sense of alienation and individual isolation, or a sense of confinement to one's role without any broader purpose or engagement. The importance of this engagement becomes more notable when one recognizes that these are the social conditions that Hannah Arendt and others have diagnosed as the soil in which totalitarianism can take root. In an industrial society defined by rigid labor roles and individual isolation, these educational programs sought to give both group experience and defined roles for social practice.

82. Feidel-Mertz, "Lernende Lehrer," 116 n. 23.

They also sought to increase intellectual, and communal, participation by individuals, countering the tendency toward "depoliticization" in society.[83] This is, one could say, democratic in an unorthodox sense, as it seeks to create a balance or interplay between the different forms of social organization, and the respective social and intellectual capacities that can flourish in these settings.[84] It also gives the public more access to intellectual life, and relates scholarship to concrete, communal issues and practices. It is by enabling these diverse activities and creating spaces for interaction between them that both thinkers sought to bring about an intellectual and communal renewal. To the extent that our society faces similar social deficits today, the approaches they adopted are worth studying, for both their innovations and the pitfalls they encountered. More specifically, with the growth of adult educational programs in the last few years, primarily in terms of professional advancement and for financial growth for institutions, their emphasis on educating for the good of the community, and the integrity and wholeness of the students, raises an important question about both the goals and practices of adult education as it is practiced today.

For the purposes of this work, though, what should be stressed is that even through their disagreements, different practices, and the tensions and antagonisms they experienced, the shared intellectual vision of Rosenzweig and Rosenstock did, ultimately, shape much of their practice. Speech-thinking, if it was to be effective, had to bring *others* to speech, and this led them to practice very similar sorts of social analysis and repair in their communities. Moreover, the parallels in their pedagogical approaches are more fully understandable in light of the shared intellectual view discussed in the previous chapters. Their decisions are not simply idiosyncratic or haphazard, but grow from their shared commitment to the New Thinking's linguistic philosophy. This helps us to situate Rosenzweig's work, and to recognize his distinctive contributions—both within their friendship and growing out of it.

Rosenstock and Rosenzweig's educational work confirms the quixotic character of their friendship. Their interactions with each other—in speech and via letters—are marked by hostility, antagonism, and a certain level of competitive jealousy regarding Gritli. Their religious disagreements were pronounced, and remained so throughout their lives. Nonetheless, in their

---

83. See Bourdieu, "Against the Policy of Depoliticization," 38–52.

84. Much of my analysis here is applying the social theory, and its political consequences, as developed by Steven Ney and Mary Douglas in *Missing Persons*, esp. 104–6, 125.

forays into various scholarly fields, they acted on a shared vision and sought to transform their disciplines and communities in remarkably similar ways. It is clear, I think, that their friendship shaped their religious and scholarly engagement, and gave them the perspective, vocabulary, and impetus to do the creative and innovative work that they did.

As contemporary Jewish thinkers and communities take renewed interest in the *Lehrhaus* model, a historical irony of their work is worth noting. As discussed in previous chapters, Rosenzweig and Rosenstock both saw Judaism as an "ahistorical" religion, standing outside of history and culture while Christianity engaged with history and politics. And yet, when one looks at the trajectory of their work, Rosenzweig's *Star* and his educational work have become central to global religious and philosophical discussion, while Rosenstock's work sits mostly outside the flow of scholarly history and interest. This is in part because, his theory notwithstanding, Rosenzweig was the more historically rooted and attuned of the two thinkers. As his thought spoke to the concerns of his community, it also resonates with the lived concerns and religious and intellectual puzzles of other generations. Rosenstock, as perhaps too schematic of a thinker, never found the traction that would engage with a broader community, nor the ability to reach subsequent generations in substantial numbers. By considering their relationship, and their work in tandem, we can bear in mind both the strengths and the difficulties that their speech-thinking carries with it.

Part Two

Emmanuel Levinas *and* Maurice Blanchot

FOUR

Distant Companions
Art, Ethics, and Politics in Blanchot and Levinas

WHERE ROSENZWEIG AND ROSENSTOCK's friendship was cut short by Rosenzweig's early death, the friendship of Emmanuel Levinas and Maurice Blanchot spanned nearly seventy years. From their meeting in Strasbourg in 1926 until Levinas's death in 1995, Blanchot and Levinas remained close friends, even while living apart. They introduced one another to ways of thought that would prove central to their work and life; Blanchot introduced Levinas to French literature, while Levinas guided Blanchot in his early readings of Heidegger. As Levinas had emigrated to France from Lithuania, he found a valuable acceptance and welcome within France on Blanchot's part. As Blanchot would write, they agreed to speak intimately (*tutoie*) to one another, as a "pact" that they upheld throughout their lives.[1] As will be discussed further, both often spoke highly of one another, and their writings show great respect for one another's work, even in their extensive disagreements.

Over the course of their lives, their friendship was marked by numerous twists and turns. Controversially, in the 1930s and during World War II Blanchot worked as a journalist in a number of far-right French publications, and even served as a literary editor for one that was sponsored by the Vichy government. These writings and activities have led many to question the roots of his later affinity for Judaism. Yet, even as he worked for *Nouvelle Revue Francaise*, Blanchot also helped Levinas's wife and daughter to find refuge and avoid persecution (Levinas's sons, however, did perish at the hands of the Nazis).[2] During World War II, Levinas was by contrast in a prison camp, having been captured very early in the war. Later, their involvement in politics often led to divergences, yet throughout they remained committed to their friendship.

---

1. Blanchot, *Pour l'Amitié*, 35.

2. See Lescourret, *Levinas*, 121. One of Blanchot's early novels, *Aminadab*, bore the name of one of Levinas's lost sons.

The friendship between Levinas and Blanchot is particularly striking when one considers the contrasts in their lives and work. Blanchot was avowedly atheist, while Levinas practiced Orthodox Judaism throughout his life. Levinas's public image grew over the course of his career, through university teaching and Talmudic readings, while Blanchot maintained a discreet, reclusive existence, letting his work be his sole public image. Even while remaining anonymous, Blanchot was more extensively involved in French politics—especially active against the Algerian War, and in the uprising of May 1968. What drew them together was, in many ways, what Michel Foucault called "the thought from outside"—a way of thinking that challenged literature, philosophy, and religion to hear and respond to the call of otherness.

Because of the complex interchange of ideas that occurred over the course of their careers, Blanchot and Levinas provide an exemplary friendship for study. Their religious differences, in many ways, pushed each toward a rethinking and radicalization of his thought. Blanchot's atheism, and his literary narration of the horrors of existence, made any simple theism impossible for Levinas. Conversely, Levinas's interpretations of Judaism, along with the ethical imperative that drove his phenomenology, pushed Blanchot to rework his criticisms of religion. Furthermore, Levinas's commitment to philosophy and Blanchot's literary discipline repeatedly challenged each other's thought, as fidelity to the friendship called into question the sufficiency of their modes of reflection. Theirs was a sober fidelity, as they vigilantly strove to attend to otherness—both conceptually, and with regard to the other thinker in particular.

Levinas's and Blanchot's writings demonstrate, then, how an interreligious exchange can inform and transform thinking. To highlight this, the next three chapters will focus on three central topics. First, this chapter explores how Blanchot's conception and practice of art informs Levinas's conception of aesthetics, enabling his break from Heidegger and his thought of saying as a form of ethical responsibility. It also reverses this, to show how Levinas's conception of sociality plays into Blanchot's approach to community. Chapter 5 then develops the concept of the enigma, which becomes increasingly central in their later work and in their interpretations of one another. The enigma becomes central to their interpretations of responsibility—both reinforcing Blanchot's atheism and enabling a new conception of revelation for Levinas. Finally, chapter 6 studies how Blanchot and Levinas turn to commentary as a practice of writing that embodies the separation and "plural speech" that both envisage as central to ethics and politics.

Part of the difficulty in thinking about the relation between Blanchot and Levinas lies in the philosophical polarization of ethics and aesthetics, which are often sharply separated and opposed. As a result of this separation, readers frequently privilege one discourse over another—for instance, treating ethics (and perhaps religion) as "higher levels" of existence, an approach which tends to denigrate artistic and aesthetic pursuits, or reduce art to a means to ethical life. Alternatively, one may reject the emphasis on ethics, in quasi-Nietzschean fashion, and turn to art as a discourse and activity that frees the subject from the constraints of personalism or ontology. In either case, one modality of existence becomes subordinated to the other.

This tendency to hierarchize has shaped the study of both Levinas and Blanchot. Even while recognizing the importance of each to the other, a reader's focus on art or ethics results in the privileging of a certain mode of thought. For instance, in a recent study, Lars Iyer argues that Levinas's focus on God and ethics, from *Totality and Infinity* onward, circumscribes alterity—actually becoming a form of "impatience" in its focus on a particular, human other. Iyer argues that Blanchot's recognition of the impersonal, inhuman form of alterity carries us beyond humanism into solidarity with the material of the world, and it "brings with it the possibility of an experience that may open any determination of the relation to *autrui* (the other one) to a dying that exceeds all measure."[3] For Iyer, Blanchot conceives neutral, impersonal alterity through Levinas's work—but thereby challenges the limit of Levinas's conception of exteriority.

Conversely, Jill Robbins argues that even while Levinas and Blanchot share an emphasis on the relation to alterity through speech, there is a difference in how this conversation proceeds. For Robbins, Blanchot's emphasis on infinite conversation, in its neutrality, loses the concrete welcome of the other in her particularity. The other is "frozen," without the mobility and freedom signified by the face.[4] As Robbins writes, "In *The Infinite Conversation* Blanchot is as it were the poet who thinks poetry can do the job of the ethical in responding to the impossible . . . Blanchot's conversation may be nontotalizing, but it is still *not yet ethical* in Levinasian terms."[5]

3. Iyer, *Blanchot's Communism*, 87.
4. Robbins, "Responding to the Infinity between Us," 78.
5. Ibid., 79; emphasis added.

Here, the very materiality of literature becomes a potential roadblock to ethics, whose responsibility to the unique other surpasses Blanchot's neutral relation. Depending on one's reading, then, either Levinas determines and circumscribes Blanchot's thought of the outside, or Blanchot neutralizes the exteriority of the face.

The opposition between these readings points to the need for rethinking the relation between Levinas and Blanchot, by rethinking the relationship between what *they* term ethics and art. Both were involved in a careful rethinking of these concepts, finding in them a significance that unsettles their everyday sense. As Levinas refigures ethics, and Blanchot distances art from the realm of aesthetics, a different relation between their works emerges. As William Large puts it, "Their friendship undercuts this opposition . . . It is possible to read Blanchot philosophically, without betraying him; or better, this betrayal is a testimony of his friendship, the presence of Levinas in his work."[6] And, I would add, to read Levinas with an eye to aesthetics testifies to Blanchot's presence as well. The enigmas of responsibility and demands of conversation require *both* art and ethics as mutually conjoined yet exclusive facets of existence. By exploring how Blanchot's conception of literature relates to politics and ethics, and how Levinas finds both music and literature to be aspects of existence that open onto alterity, this chapter will show that Levinas and Blanchot both revalue those aspects of existence that they are generally thought to downplay.

ART AND EXTERIORITY IN BLANCHOT'S EARLY WORK

The connection of art with exteriority in Blanchot becomes manifest in the influential collection of essays titled *The Space of Literature*. "Literary space" is the modality of existence unique to literature, as Blanchot describes how within art there is a movement of spacing or distancing that unsettles any project or appropriation. In *The Space of Literature*, he describes how poetic language manifests this feature of the work of art:

> In poetry we are no longer referred back to the world, neither to the world as shelter nor to the world as goals. In this language the world falls silent; beings with their preoccupations, their projects, their activity are no longer ultimately what speaks. Poetry expresses the fact that beings are quiet. But how does this happen? Beings fall silent, but then it is being that tends to speak and speech that wants to be. The poetic word is no longer someone's word. In it no

---

6. Large, *Emmanuel Levinas and Maurice Blanchot*, 101 n. 4.

one speaks, and what speaks is not anyone. It seems rather that the word alone declares itself.[7]

Focusing on the work of poetry, Blanchot sees its language as expressing silence, bringing the absence and shattering of the world into view. With reference neither to shelter nor the past, nor to goals nor the future, poetic language is beyond time. In the absence of the world, the speaker and the object both recede on the hither side of being.

This going outside of being raises the question of the temporality of art. Art is associated with the future, as it opens a space for activity, yet rests beyond any limited project or intention. In its impersonality, it speaks to each reader, here and now, yet refuses capture in the present, resisting appropriation. As a work, it becomes detached from its creator; even while bringing the past into view, it frees itself from history. Poetry, as art, thus extends throughout time, while exceeding everyday temporality.

In this temporality, art refuses to be productive; here, the idea of worklessness so central to Blanchot's later writing emerges. In its separation, art cannot serve a politics or program—even though it may be appropriated by one (and does not protect itself from such appropriation). It thus remains unjustified in the struggles of the world, even when a project does adopt it. "Granted, art has as its goal something real: an object . . . Which is to say, an object of contemplation, not of use, which, moreover, will be sufficient to itself, will rest in itself, refer to nothing else, and be its own end."[8] Even while existing beyond the world, art nonetheless emerges within and through the world. This "disappearance" of art "even when it is disguised as useful presence, belongs to the essence of art."[9] Ironically, the art which refuses the world, and remains unjustified by it, also *gives* us the world—creating a public space, as it enters museums and symbolizes agendas. The very prospect of success in the art world—shows, criticism, praise—may also make the appearance of art's worklessness that much more difficult to grasp.[10] Art, then, emerges within and through the world, while existing beyond the world's productivity.[11] It dissimulates itself in the museum setting or within the confines of the "book"—the totalized,

---

7. Blanchot, *Space of Literature*, 41.
8. Blanchot, *The Space of Literature*, 212.
9. Ibid., 206.
10. Ibid., 202.
11. Collin, *Maurice Blanchot*, 40–41.

consumable text that emerges from the poetic writing. For Blanchot, art exists as a trace within the order and time of the everyday, while remaining irreducible to this form.

In this unique temporality, art and poetry present themselves to us in the activity of reading. In a sense, the artwork is more dependent upon its reader than its creator for its existence. Reading, however, is not just uncovering or disclosing the meaning(s) of a text. The reader "relieves" the book of an author, carrying the work out of its original context and temporal setting. As Blanchot writes,

> Reading makes of the book what the sea and the wind make of objects fashioned by men: a smoother stone, a fragment fallen from the sky without a past, without a future, the sight of which silences questions. Reading gives to the book the abrupt existence which the statue seems to get from the chisel alone.[12]

Reading gives "abrupt existence" by allowing the work to show itself as what it is; it "lets it be itself," beyond context or goal. Blanchot associates reading with freedom that "welcomes, consents, says yes"—reading is affirmation of existence itself. In the timelessness of the work, a murmur emerges that shows the limit of the world in which we live: death itself. Reading is like conversing with Lazarus—who has been dead for three days, "if not forever." Reading provides no relief; rather, it affirms life in the face of death's weight. Reading does not just show us the timelessness of the work—it shows the timelessness of death that each of us faces, to which each of us is singularly called. Like the light beyond the door of Kafka's law, reading is an impersonal, anonymous rupture of being—and yet, it exists uniquely for each reader.

From this, Blanchot concludes there is a lack or void at the core of any artistic work. The impersonality of art—its ability to call to anyone, anywhere, in its mute gaze—unhinges the solidity of the world, and thereby fissures the identity of the viewer or reader. The murmur of art opens the reader to the anonymity or impersonality within her. She, like the work, is carried beyond projects and out of the world. Art's distance from the world, its separation, opens a distance within and between us as well.

Art's challenge to the world's totality is central to "The Gaze of Orpheus," one of Blanchot's most influential essays. For Blanchot, the poet is like Orpheus, who desires to see Eurydice—to make present the "night" of death into which she has fallen. In his failure, Orpheus represents how

12. Blanchot, *Space of Literature*, 193.

art calls us to an impersonal, anonymous, yet singular existence.[13] In drawing Eurydice up from the underworld, he brings her death to light. However, he can only do this indirectly, by not gazing upon her. He sees her, and death, in the light of day—not for herself. Art, in creativity, keeps concealed the "other night" of death, a darkness beyond harmony or balance with the day.[14] It is only in art itself that Orpheus (the artist) relates to her (the unique one)—when he impatiently seeks to grasp or possess her, she slips away. Through art, then, we relate to what is impossible and unpresentable, even as it resists our appropriation.

In this reflection on both reading and creativity, the homeless, exilic character of art shines forth. It is a movement of impossibility, which, like death, gives rise to possibility. Without art, there would be no world; in its ceaseless murmur, things give themselves. It discloses to us the impersonality at the heart of unique subjectivity, which Blanchot describes as "I am he who is not." This anonymity is the condition for all singularity, giving the movement of time in a patience that makes space for the time of the world, and for politics as well. The theme of a mode of existence that goes beyond description or classification becomes central to Blanchot's notion of community, particularly in *The Unavowable Community*, which will be discussed later in this chapter. Art, in its impersonal patience, is the condition for both the passivity of responsibility and addressing one another in fraternal solitude. Its refusal of the world thus constitutes a condition for Blanchot's rethinking of politics.

ART IN LEVINAS'S EARLY WORK

As mentioned before, the priority of ethics as "first philosophy" in Levinas's work is often taken as a denigration of aesthetics. While differences remain between Levinas and Blanchot—particularly regarding the relationship between impersonal and personal being—art is a distinctive, central modality of existence for Levinas's work. Moreover, his reading of art unfolds in conversation with Blanchot, such that the exteriority of Blanchot's artwork is more central to Levinas's ethics than is often recognized.

The early work that illustrates art's centrality most clearly is *Existence and Existents*, published in 1947. While the work was largely overlooked by

---

13. Collin, *Maurice Blanchot*, 64.

14. Blanchot, *Space of Literature*, 171–73. See also Hill, "Affirmation without Precedent," 64–67.

the French academy, Georges Bataille reviewed it positively,[15] and Blanchot draws upon this book in writing both *The Work of Fire* and *The Space of Literature*. *Existence and Existents* develops the thought of the *il y a*, "there is," and focuses on the passage from neutral existen*ce* to personal being (existen*ts*). In so doing, Levinas is working in close proximity to Blanchot; in the course of his argument he cites two of Blanchot's early novels, *Aminadab* and *Thomas the Obscure*. What is more, Levinas develops his argument against Heidegger through an analysis of art that resonates strongly with Blanchot's conception of the poetic work discussed above, such that art becomes a mode of *separation* that discloses beings in their singularity.

Existence and Existents proceeds as a subtle inversion of Heideggerian ontology via several different modes of questioning. It reworks how we think of art, the relation between consciousness and existence, and reflects on the conditions of *Dasein*, our ecstatic mode of temporal existence. Levinas continues to develop the issue of escape, which was central to his earlier questioning of Heidegger in *De L'évasion* (1931). He works phenomenologically, developing his argument through an analysis of the temporality of everyday events.[16] While the seeds of his later work on the face, insomnia, fecundity, and eros are already present in this work, his focus on fatigue, sleep, and art gives *Existence* its particular shape. Through these analyses, he moves toward the thought of alterity and the face in *Totality and Infinity*. As he writes in the concluding lines of *Existence*, "The event which we have been inquiring after is antecedent to that placing [in Greek and philosophical ontology]. It concerns the meaning of the very fact that in Being there are beings."[17] By thinking the ontological difference, not in terms of Being as other than beings, but in terms of the emergence of beings (existen*ts*), Levinas lays the groundwork for his later focus on ethics and the singular relation to the other.

In his analysis of fatigue, Levinas lays out how artistic existence illuminates our being separated from ourselves. As a lethargy of the subject, fatigue exemplifies the temporal extenuation that constitutes our being. Generally, we would think of fatigue as derivative of activity; we labor, and

15. Bataille's review is translated by Jill Robbins and published in her *Altered Reading*, 155–80.

16. As John Drabinski argues, Levinas is combating Husserl's anti-intellectualism, through the very analysis of these embodied states and actions that undo the privilege of consciousness. This makes it an "anti-phenomenology," or "to practice phenomenology otherwise than Husserl." See Drabinski, *Sensibility and Singularity*, 61–62.

17. Levinas, *Existence and Existents*, 106.

make an effort, and feel fatigued as a result. However, Levinas suggests that fatigue may in fact be more fundamental than labor. In his view, fatigue is a "condemnation to being,"[18] in which one no longer possesses oneself. It brings out the impersonal existence of the moment, and thus sets the conditions in which labor can bring forth an existent, active subject. In other words, it is *from* fatigue, and in this self-delay, that the working subject is born.

To illustrate the temporal relationship between fatigue and effort, Levinas turns to music. As he points out, in listening to a melody, the particular, specific notes blend together into a smooth, ceaseless flow; time passes by, without consciousness of a particular moment. Music is "like a game," in that each note gives itself over completely to its annihilation, for the sake of the melody. "The different instants of a melody only exist to the extent that they immolate themselves in a duration, which in a melody is essentially a continuity."[19] In melody, where notes fall away from themselves into the melodic whole, we find an artistic analogue to the evanescence of fatigue. By contrast, effort brings particular instants to consciousness and concreteness, making them stand out, much as digging a hole or fixing a window makes that place and material shine forth in its difference. Effort, in opposition to the play and flow of music, is "the very effecting of an instant."[20]

Over against effort, fatigue is like an incessant murmur, flowing in a way that calls for the assuming of existence in labor or effort. Labor or effort folds time back on itself so as to bring its momentary singularity to light, in *separation* from the flow. The dialectic of existence begins in the rumble of fatigue, from which effort surges forth, only to fall back into fatigue so as to surge forth once more. "Fatigue does not arise in it [effort] as an accompanying phenomenon, but effort as it were lunges forward out of fatigue and falls back upon it."[21] Whatever work we do, we remain bound to the flow of time in which our work proceeds, and into which we collapse when the day's work is done.

If effort and existing as a subject come forth from fatigue, then this situates the subject in a field of impersonal anonymity. Levinas highlights

18. Ibid., 24.
19. Ibid., 21.
20. Ibid., 23.
21. Ibid., 19.

this aspect of fatigue; when I am fatigued, it dislocates me, disclosing the non-coincidence of the subject with itself.

> It [fatigue] is not the solitude of a being forsaken by the world with which it is no longer in step, but of a being that is as it were no longer in step with itself, is out of joint with itself, in a dislocation of the I from itself, a being that is not joining up with itself in the instant, in which it is nonetheless committed for good.[22]

In this move, Levinas begins to unsettle *Dasein*; fatigue discloses a subject who is not simply thrown into the world, but rather one fundamentally unsettled within itself. The non-coincidence of the subject, in its time being out of joint, leads toward the anonymous *il y a* that questions the limits of the ontological difference.

The *il y a*, for Levinas, is not simply nothingness; rather, it is the "nothingness of everything that is," the hither side of what we know and experience in the world. It is horrifying—the loss of the world, and of the existents that we know and engage everyday, including ourselves. It thus exposes us to the outside of existence, while weighing on us, and showing that in our existence there is no escape.

> *There is* is an impersonal form, like in "it rains," or "it is warm." Its anonymity is essential. The mind does not find itself faced with an apprehended exterior . . . What we call the I is itself submerged by the night, invaded, depersonalized, stifled by it . . . The disappearance of all things and of the I leaves what cannot disappear, the sheer fact of being in which one participates, whether one wants to or not, without having taken the initiative, anonymously.[23]

The *il y a* is horrific because it exposes us to the necessity of being: that it will be, even when I will not. It therefore moves us beyond Heidegger's being-towards-death, in which one is anxious about one's being, in conceiving the *impossibility* of not-being. In this anonymity, one no longer is concerned with one's "own" death, "participating" in unceasing existence: "horror turns the subjectivity of the subject, his particularity qua entity, inside out. It is a participation . . . in the *il y a* that has 'no exits.' It is, if we may say so, the impossibility of death, the universality of existence even in its annihilation."[24]

22. Ibid., 24.
23. Ibid., 53.
24. Ibid., 57.

What is striking in Levinas's argument is the role that art plays in his conception of the *il y a*. Existence's ceaselessness, beyond death, is illustrated in *Macbeth*,[25] and modern art shows the *il y a* in its dark radiance. The argument regarding art is particularly significant:

> The investigations of modern painting in their protest against realism come from this feeling of the end of the world and of the destruction of representation which it makes possible . . . In contemporary painting things no longer count as elements of a universal order which the look would give itself, as a perspective. On all sides fissures appear in the continuity of the universe. The particular stands out in the nakedness of its being.[26]

What modern art discloses is the materiality of things—their existence, their being in ways that cannot be grasped as part of the world of the subject. As de Vries writes, "Art disengages the artist and the beholder from the light of day, in which ethics, human agency, interiority, and economy are firmly situated."[27] In this matter without or beyond the form in which we grasp things in intentionality, things revert to their nothingness, and we see the *il y a* shine forth in the "nocturnal space" that darkness fills. Levinas references Blanchot's *Thomas the Obscure* as expressing the horror that the *il y a* evokes.[28]

The connection of art with the notion of *il y a* is a significant point, given the chronology of the essays in *Existence*. A portion of the introduction, and chapter 3, section 2 (the central discussion of *il y a*) were previously published as an essay in *Deucalion*. Section 1 of chapter 3 is the part of the essay devoted to painting. The connection developed here suggests a link between a critique of Heidegger's conception of art and the attempt to pass beyond the ontological difference. To see art as carrying us outside the world—and, as exposing the incessance of being rather than nothingness—directly confronts the "earthly" dimension of art in Heidegger, for whom

---

25. "In *Macbeth*, the apparition of Banquo's ghost is also a decisive experience of the 'no exit' from existence, its phantom return through the fissures through which one has driven it" (ibid., 57). As Hent de Vries writes, "modern poetry (from Baudelaire to Rimbaud to Celan) serves Levinas as a sounding board in the attempt to articulate the desire for a way out of Being, out of the *il y a*, and out of the realm governed by the ontico-ontological distinction. Modern tragedy, by contrast, supplies him with an interpretive model for the permanent failure of any such striving" (*Minimal Theologies*, 451).

26. Levinas, *Existence and Existents*, 50.

27. Vries, *Minimal Theologies*, 420.

28. Levinas, *Existence and Existents*, 58.

art shows forth the concealment that makes existence possible. This is a tenuous connection, given that Levinas wrote much of these essays while a prisoner of war, and explicitly requests pardon for not engaging publications between 1940 and 1945. However, cross-referencing Blanchot may help to clarify this connection; the works published by Blanchot in 1947–48, *The Work of Fire* and especially *The Space of Literature*, demonstrate significant familiarity with Heidegger's 1936 lectures "On the Origin of the Work of Art," suggesting its circulation in Levinas's intellectual milieu. In light of the parallels between Blanchot's conception of the exteriority of art, and Levinas's analyses here, it becomes clear that both are working toward a critique of Heidegger, by distancing their work from his conception of art.

While close to Blanchot, Levinas modifies his account of art slightly. He emphasizes modern art because of its nonrepresentational character. As it draws colors, lines, and elements out of their connection with objects, and lets them stand apart, it creates a separation from the world. In so doing, it reveals not the earth—as Heidegger finds in Van Gogh—but *sensation*, which gives the "impersonality of elements."[29] Sensation is an event, neither merely a subjective feeling nor a feature of the object. Sensation, for Levinas, is not perception; it is an event, the appearance of time, which Levinas connects most directly with *musicality*. As already discussed with regard to fatigue and effort, Levinas associates music with an impersonal stream of existence, as the notes dissolve into the melody. Here, he describes it as the basis of sensation, and as an aesthetic modality that informs *both* visual art and poetry:

> In music this way a quality can divest itself of all objectivity—and consequently of all subjectivity—seems completely natural . . . And it may enter into relations and syntheses that no longer have anything in common with the order of objects. Colors, whose bond with things is more intimate, detach themselves from them, especially in painting that takes itself to be revolutionary.[30]

29. Ibid., 47.

30. Ibid. Or again (on modern painting): "In the representation of matter by modern painting this deformation, that is, this laying bare, of the world is brought about in a particularly striking way. The breakup of continuity even on the surface of things, the preference for broken lines, the scorning of perspective and of the 'real' proportions between things, indicate a revolt against the continuity of curves. From a space without horizons, things break away and are cast toward us like chunks that have weight in themselves, blocks, cubes, planes, triangles, without transitions between them. They are naked elements simple and absolute, swellings or abcesses of being. In this falling of things down on us, objects attest their power as material objects, even reach a paroxysm of materiality" (ibid., 51).

Distant Companions 133

From this, Levinas then extends the discussion of musicality into poetry. The musicality of poetry is manifest in the ambiguity of poetic language, its proliferation and multiplicity of meaning. This ambiguity leads to a recognition of the materiality and existing quality of the words themselves. In this sensibility of language, there is a premonition of the *saying* which will precede all thematic *said*, in the rhetoric of *Otherwise than Being*. By so conceiving language, Levinas sees in modern poetry the manifestation of the *il y a*, and thus a possibility distinct from Heideggerian poetics. This inversion is significant: where Heidegger sees all art as essentially poetic, by foregrounding music Levinas highlights how art may carry us outside, beyond Heidegger's conception. In all of this, Levinas seems to be inspired by Blanchot's work. However, the focus on music sets him slightly apart, and it remains a central aspect of art and literature in Levinas's later writings as well, as shall be discussed below.

Through this conception of art, Levinas rethinks the situated, historical being of humanity in a way that contests the being-there of *Dasein*. While the conscious self always discovers itself thrown into a situation, and thus cast out of itself toward the world and into past and future, Levinas argues that the subject has a presence, or a "here," prior to such "being-there," and this is found in sleep. In sleep, we find: 1) the embodied location and temporalization of the conscious subject, which emerges from impersonal existence into hypostatic being; 2) a singular, unique mode of existing that is a condition for *Dasein*, and for the ego; and 3) the conception of time that lays the groundwork for Levinas's thought of the relation to the other.

Sleep is an embodied, local activity that is a condition for the work of consciousness. Whereas in insomnia the subject is open to the impersonal murmur of the *il y a*, sleep gives the subject the rest from its fatigue that lets it reengage in labor. It is a *base* for consciousness; "The summoning of sleep occurs in the act of lying down. To lie down is precisely to limit existence to a place, a position."[31] By thus taking a place, standing under a position, consciousness becomes hypostasized; it moves out of the general stream of existence, into personal being. This "work of being" of resting prevents the destruction of the subject.

Levinas locates this "placing" as prior to *Dasein*: "The here (of sleep) precedes every act of understanding, every horizon and all time. It is the very fact that consciousness is an origin, that it starts from itself, that it

31. Ibid., 66.

is an existent."[32] Sleep, one could say, is the spacing of the time in which *Dasein* comes to be—much as the movement of the tongue spatializes time, in Derrida's reading of Husserl in *Speech and Phenomena*. Rhetorically, Levinas also associates consciousness with creation—the unprecedented coming-into-being of form, from the chaos and darkness of *il y a*.[33]

While consciousness breaks from the *il y a* through positioning, and becomes located in an instant, this is not ultimately a form of freedom. For, the subject who takes place remains rooted there—"enchained," as Levinas says. "The enchainment to oneself is the impossibility of getting rid of oneself. It is not only an enchainment to a character or to instincts, but a silent association with oneself in which a duality is discernible."[34] Here, Levinas draws once again upon his earlier reflections in *On Escape*, seeing the subject's solitude and *Dasein* as still trapped within the confines of being.

While it does not give freedom, the solitary bond with oneself gives the *concept* of freedom. Levinas now invokes alterity and sociality as the modes of transcendence that can free the subject. "The dialectic of the social relationship will furnish us with a set of concepts of a new kind. And the nothingness necessary to time, which the subject cannot produce, comes from the social relationship."[35] Alterity frees the subject by injecting time into consciousness, through the redemptive resurrection of the *instant*. The subject can give neither time nor redemption to itself; it depends on the other for both.

To think of time as given by the other, in sociality, requires rethinking time as beyond the world of the everyday. From what we have seen thus far, time exists as either the unending, indeterminate flow of existence, or the duration and instantiation of *a* being. Neither of these forms of time, however, can address the suffering or burden of the subject—its need to escape its solitary confinement. In its duration, the subject's relation to the world is one of use, or enjoyment, such that the world is for it[36]—our relation to the world condenses or effaces time. Levinas argues that when we see things as for our use, we use them to overcome the delay of time—to work more quickly, fulfill desire and overcome lack:

32. Ibid., 68.
33. Ibid., 75. See Katz, *Levinas, Judaism, and the Feminine*, 24–25.
34. Levinas, *Existence and Existents*, 89.
35. Ibid., 96.
36. Levinas analyzes this relation extensively in ibid., 27–44.

> Tools serve this yearning for objects as wages. They have nothing to do with ontology . . . In modern civilization they do not only extend the hand, so that it can get at what it does not get at of itself; they enable it to get at it more quickly, that is, they suppress in an action the time the action has to take on. Tools suppress the intermediary times; they contract duration.[37]

The absence of a tool, or its brokenness, therefore does not simply show us the tool in its being; rather, it introduces a delay into the subject, reverting to the fatigue that characterizes existence. Such delay causes suffering, which, in the worldly view, is to be compensated later and thus forgotten.

As compensation forgets the instant of suffering, the utility of the world renders suffering useless. It remains irrecuperable, and unredeemed. In a transition that points toward the later essay "Useless Suffering," Levinas writes, "For it is not enough that tears be wiped away, or death avenged; no tear is to be lost, no death be without a resurrection . . . Pain cannot be redeemed . . . There is no justice that could make reparations for it. One should have to return to that instant, or be able to resurrect it."[38] Suffering is redeemed in the gesture of the caress, where one touches the other in *compassion*, without forgetting or suppressing the instant. Suffering remains, the instant is present, and yet compassion redeems it through the relation to the other across this distance.

Alterity, then, introduces another mode of time—the time of *pardon*. The other, as "what I am not," introduces what is not myself into my consciousness, and thus frees the subject from its confinement. It gives the subject its death, by relating it to its non-being, and yet also lets it remain itself, rather than become part of some *tertium quid*. The relation to alterity, as compassion, gives new life to the instant, letting the subject recover itself while freed from its solitude—it is freed to be something it could not be on its own. One's ownmost possibility, then, is in relation to the other.[39] The social relation to the other is not a part of a community, or a fusion, nor is it a common commitment to a third thing. Rather, it is the "fearful face-to-face situation of a relationship without intermediary," beyond the being-with of *Dasein*. One is in proximity to the neighbor, but this must be conceived in aneconomic and asymmetrical terms; to avoid this "leveling,"

---

37. Ibid., 92.
38. Ibid., 93.
39. Ibid., 94–95.

a thought of heterogeneity becomes central, through which instants and subjects can be thought in their singularity rather than their similarity.[40]

This detailed analysis of *Existence and Existents* highlights several central points. First, it demonstrates the proximity between Levinas and Blanchot in their thought in the 1940s, a period which has received less attention than the later engagement in *The Infinite Conversation*, *On Maurice Blanchot*, and *The Writing of the Disaster*. Levinas's analysis of art, and his thought of the *il y a*, are both very close to Blanchot's contemporaneous work on literary space; moreover, Levinas takes Blanchot's novels as epitomizing existence. For instance, he references *Aminadab* as depicting the leveling of fraternity that effaces alterity.[41] Conversely, Blanchot's reflections on sleep, as the form of existing in the night that makes consciousness possible and hides the darkness of night, reference and draw extensively on *Existence*.[42] Thus, despite the difference in emphasis, there is significant resonance between their works at this stage as well.

Existence and Existence is thus preparatory not only for *Totality and Infinity*, pointing toward both the analysis of the face and the phenomenology of eros (with the caveat that here, Levinas thinks eros primarily as compassion). Its emphasis on sociality also points toward Blanchot's later thought of community, particularly *The Unavowable Community*, where Blanchot conceives a community beyond the utility and fusion of ordinary community. By reading Levinas's later work in light of *Existence*, and its relation to Blanchot's early literary criticism, their proximity with regard to sociality will become clearer. Where Levinas argues for a sociality that goes beyond the solitude of the subject—and thus implicitly breaks with Blanchot's literary focus—the politics that Blanchot develops on the basis of literary experience nevertheless bear a strong resemblance to Levinasian responsibility. Finally, while Levinas seeks to go beyond ontology and art, it is only in light of and through Blanchot's conception of art as exteriority and separation that Levinas can move toward the time of the other. Across their distance from one another, their proximity remains.

---

40. Ibid., 99.
41. Ibid.
42. See "Sleep, Night," in the appendices to Blanchot, *Space of Literature*, 266.

LITERATURE, FRIENDSHIP, AND THE UNAVOWABLE COMMUNITY

While Levinas and Blanchot both address the status of art as part of their sustained resistance to Heideggerian nihilism, their reflections on art go beyond mere theory. For both authors, the question of literature becomes a question of how one speaks or writes in the shadow of the Shoah: whether literary testimony, as poetic, can remain in solidarity with those who suffered and died in the camps, or involves an essentially unethical forgetting. They recognize that this event gives them both pause in their philosophical and literary endeavors. Yet what is particularly intriguing, in the course of their reflections, is the surprising reversal that ensues from this "absolute interruption" of history. Where one would expect Levinas to turn ever more forcefully away from aesthetic and literary expression, literature and poetry become central aspects of a response to its shattering violence. By contrast, it is Blanchot—defender of the exigency of art—for whom at least a modality of expression must be silent in the Shoah's aftermath. As he would write in *After the Fact*, "I will say there can be no fiction-story about Auschwitz,"[43] and more broadly, "There is a limit at which the practice of any art becomes an affront to affliction."[44]

The renewed significance of art emerges in two of Levinas's works published in the 1970s—*Noms Propres* and *Sur Maurice Blanchot*, collected and published together in English as *Proper Names*. The essays on Blanchot span nearly twenty years, from 1956 until 1973, and reflect the continuing inspiration Blanchot provided for Levinas's thinking regarding literature. As Levinas describes, in Blanchot's work literature "recalls the human essence of nomadism."[45] In their separation from the world, and their break with the everyday, literature and poetry open the question of the beyond—resisting the domination and power of language, letting "the incessant murmur of that distancing reappear."[46] While recognizing Blanchot's atheism and his resistance to ethical language, Levinas sees his literary voice as necessary for opening the possibility of an ethical and theological vision. As he writes, the "authenticity of art must herald an order of justice, the

---

43. Blanchot, *Vicious Circles*, 68.
44. Blanchot, *Writing of the Disaster*, 83.
45. Levinas, *Proper Names*, 137.
46. Ibid., 132.

slave morality that is absent from the Heideggerian city."[47] It is, moreover, in the separation and distance of Blanchot's work, that the possibility of revelation emerges; the "God of justice" can be thought in the reworking of art that frees it from Heideggerian enrootedness and indifference.

Levinas's reflections on Blanchot's literature set Blanchot at a distance from Hegel, in part by recognizing how Blanchot's thought moves in such close proximity to Hegelian dialectic. By repeating Hegel, Blanchot's neuter points beyond the system, freeing poetics from its dialectical servitude to philosophical reason. In this freedom, Levinas sees Blanchot's neuter as opening a dimension of *saying* that exceeds consciousness—and thus, the possibility of ethics. As he writes, "Poetry, in Blanchot's view, transforms words—indices of a manifold, moments of a totality—into signs set free, that break through the walls of immanence, disrupting order."[48] Blanchot's literature manifests the vulnerability of language, its exposure to alterity, even as in its neutrality it does not pass beyond being; rather, poetry introduces alterity within the realm of the same.[49]

Levinas's reading of Blanchot recognizes that the work of literature or art takes its proper form in its distance from the world. Levinas's reading of *The Madness of the Day* highlights the obscure, other darkness in which Blanchot's literary works operate, through confounding reversals and inversions of emotions and experiences. Madness calls out from the "extreme consciousness" of recognizing its own inescapability, the suffering of the happy (much like that found in another of Blanchot's stories, "The Idyll"). Still, it is precisely in the *saying* of this work—its conveyance of a relation to the other—that Levinas thinks that escape from the inescapable remains the truth of Blanchot's work. Even where catastrophe reigns, saying transcends its cosmological form, creating the separation that enables proximity and responsibility.

The importance of Blanchot's work for Levinas's sense of poetics emerges clearly in several of the other literary essays published in *Proper Names*. Many of these essays, resonating strongly with the language of the enigma, saying, and vulnerability, epitomize the centrality of these concepts for Levinas from 1965 onward (as shall be discussed further in

---

47. Ibid., 137.

48. Ibid., 146–47.

49. In this, one can see the emergence (or further development) of the more "inclusive" relation to otherness that William Large emphasizes as drawing Levinas's thought closer to Blanchot. See Large, *Emmanuel Levinas and Maurice Blanchot*, 32–36.

the next chapter). In his reading of S. Y. Agnon, Levinas highlights the enigmatic quality of Agnon's work, as it gestures toward a near-nostalgia for a Jewish world that has disappeared. However, Levinas argues, the literary depiction of this does not let this world lay dormant. As Jill Robbins writes, this literature has a "trace-structure," which becomes "the way the other signifies."[50] Agnon's stories resuscitate biblical language, and give it life—not simply in what is said, but in the *saying* of the story (which, in Agnon, may be highlighted by obscurity and unexpected reversals):

> A reference to biblical or rabbinic writings, the repetition of the master formulation, a variant or an echo—and suddenly the word, without imitating any model, signifies both in the context of the passage in which it occurs and, in counterpoint, in the scriptural context, oriented toward an unrepresentable past. Such is the enigmatic modality of a resuscitated language, beginning again within its own trace![51]

The story thus "redoubles the enigma," introducing a break within ontology.

What stands out in his reading of Agnon is Levinas's emphasis on the musicality of language—the song within what is said introduces a "sur-reality" to language. "Poetry signifies poetically the resurrection that sustains it: not in its theme, but in its song."[52] The resonance with the earlier discussion of music, from *Existence to Existents*, is clear. This musicality becomes even more pronounced—and significant—in Agnon's later work, where the stories come to deal with the Shoah's destruction. Where Agnon's writing questions why God would create Israel, in a world where people seek its destruction, Levinas responds that the writing (or saying) highlights how the law of love transcends death. Love of neighbor—as the good for which one will even die—transcends death, and thus can even live beyond it. A life of solidarity and justice, living for the law "worthy of the supreme sacrifice," is what cannot be killed—the indestructible humanity that evil is always trying to destroy. Poetry signifies *saying*, the root orientation to love that cannot be crushed by the weight of being.[53]

The saying of poetry likewise informs Levinas's appreciation of the work of Paul Celan, as poetry which refuses rootedness and turns it toward an exilic wandering. Like Blanchot's work, Celan's poetry gestures toward

50. Robbins, *Altered Reading*, 139.
51. Levinas, *Proper Names*, 9.
52. Ibid., 12.
53. Ibid., 11–12.

a way of life that refuses to remain ontological. Its "pre-disclosive" dimension sets forth a language of proximity, as the poet's dedication to the poem "desubstantiates," or de-nucleates, the poet at the very moment of speaking or writing. This suggests, for Levinas, that there can be a break within humanity—language creates separation, and thus singularity, without effacing the general commonality of humanity. In letting "otherness's ownness speak," poetry thus gestures toward an otherwise than being—poetic language turns toward the saying, beyond the confines of the said.[54]

Finally, Levinas's essay on Roger Laporte reads as indirect praise for Blanchot, as Levinas references him in reflecting on the "precise writing" of Laporte. Laporte's book *A Still Small Voice* sets forth a form of writing that waits for the unexpected, hoping for the other to come, while letting the other be. This writing, on Levinas's view, allows the event to take place, disclosing the time that Levinas evokes as the central feature of Blanchot's work, as well as that of Laporte. The time that "no longer flows into common time,"[55] the time of ceaselessly dying, creates separation between people, as a condition for proximity. Here, though, Levinas gestures more directly toward a religious dimension: Laporte's writing manifests a "need for the absolute," which goes beyond a "traditional theology of transcendence." What Levinas is gesturing to, here, is alterity as a relation to the other that cannot be thought within the spatiotemporal frame of the world; even transcendence, as a "world-behind-a-world," remains deficient. Rather, as Levinas writes, Laporte's writing "accomplishes a movement beyond being, and beyond the thought in which being looks at and reflects itself."[56]

What is striking in Levinas's discussion of these authors is how poetry becomes the way beyond being. Far from foreclosing ethical responsibility, poetry is the form of speech in which the saying unsettles—weakly, and as a trace—the order and hegemony of the said. It is through poetics, and especially through musicality, that Levinas envisages the transcendence of saying—which, in other works, he associates with the passing of God. In this affirmation of literature, Levinas's writings resonate throughout with Blanchot's conception of literature, and of the neuter's alterity. While Levinas always turns the neuter in the direction of responsibility, taking and keeping his distance from Blanchot, there is little question that Blanchot's writing plays a central role in Levinas's rethinking of ethical

54. Ibid., 44 (quoting Celan, n. 17).
55. Ibid., 91.
56. Ibid., 93.

responsibility, in the period up to *Otherwise than Being*. Yet why, one might still ask, would Levinas see Blanchot's literature as so closely linked to the possibility of ethics?

An early hint of this affinity is found in Levinas's essay on Proust, which dates from 1947 (reprinted in *Proper Names*). In response to Sartre's dismissal of Proustian psychology, Levinas rehabilitates Proust's conception of literature as setting forth an alternative conception of communication—and with it, an alternative conception of community. Levinas takes up Sartre's charge that Proust deals with psychology on an empirical level, by arguing that the literary redoubling of these psychic states effectively acts as a transcendental reduction: there is an ambiguity to his description of a world where "realization does not sacrifice virtuality."[57] Through this, the strangeness of the I from itself, the "dialogue with the other in the self," is set forth for the reader. Such strangeness does not abandon the subject to solitude. Rather, much like in *Existence and Existents*, the separation of the subject within becomes the condition for a rethinking of sociality:

> But if communication thus bears the sign of failure or inauthenticity, it is because it is sought as fusion. One sets out from the idea that duality should be transformed into unity—that the social relation should end in communion. This is the last vestige of a conception identifying being and knowing—that is, the event by which the multiplicity of the real ends up referring to one sole being . . . One does not see that the success of knowledge would in fact destroy the nearness, the proximity, of the other. A proximity that, far from meaning something less than identification, opens up the horizons of social existence, brings out all the surplus of our experience of friendship and love, and brings to the definitiveness of our identical existence all the virtuality of the non-definitive.[58]

The resonances within this passage are striking; the challenge to knowing, and the emphasis on proximity, hearken toward the ethics of nearness found in *Otherwise than Being* and beyond. Yet the first part of the passage is perhaps more striking, as Levinas rejects a view of society, friendship, or love based upon union or fusion of the parties (it is also, as far as I know, one of the few references to friendship in Levinas's work). This description of Proust's poetics could as well describe Blanchot's work; a community that refuses fusion, a sociality that neither demands nor relies upon

---

57. Ibid., 100.
58. Ibid., 104.

sameness, becomes his focus in the quasi-autobiographical series of essays, *The Unavowable Community*. It is to Blanchot's literary community that we now turn.

LITERARY POLITICS: THE UNAVOWABLE COMMUNITY

The Unavowable Community foregrounds the political dimension implicit in Blanchot's literary and social engagements. Through a reading of texts by Bataille and Marguerite Duras, it remembers and thereby rethinks the significance of several of the most central moments of Blanchot's life—the friendship with Bataille, his involvement with the *Declaration of the 121*,[59] and his contributions to the student revolt of May 1968. As throughout much of his life, Blanchot carefully veiled his involvement behind pseudonyms and anonymity, and he only obliquely gestures toward his involvement in these events within this text. Yet the thought of worklessness (*désoeuvrement*), and its reshaping of friendship and community, gestures toward a Levinasian form of proximity—not to mention Blanchot's own proximity to Levinas himself.

In the reading of Bataille, Blanchot counters some aspects of a critique of Bataille set forth by Jean-Luc Nancy in "The Inoperative Community." The argument is nuanced, as it largely agrees with Nancy's conception of friendship while challenging the subsumption of Bataille under this concept. Blanchot argues that there is a worklessness, or inoperativity, at the heart of friendship, which emerges most clearly in the death of a friend; as a friend dies, one may stay with her, even hold her hand, and yet remain separate—as one may neither do anything for them, nor die in their place. Death refuses unity or fusion—the principle often thought to underlie community—rendering impossible a "being-in-common" that would assimilate and efface its members' singularity.[60] For Blanchot, Bataille's work and life thought this inoperativity as fully as anyone, most notably in the Acéphale group.[61] This group—which considered performing sacrifices of volunteers, but did not[62]—was one of the central targets of Nancy's critique, yet Blanchot argues that Bataille saw the group as a success, *only*

---

59. The "Declaration" was a statement signed by 121 intellectuals, arguing for a right to refuse to support the war in Algeria. It was a strong protest of de Gaulle's censorship and statism. Blanchot was widely believed to be the anonymous author.

60. Blanchot, *Communauté Inavouable*, 17–20.

61. Large, *Emmanuel Levinas and Maurice Blanchot*, 106.

62. Goldhammer, *Headless Republic*, 184–87.

in its failure. The knowledge and unity of the group—and thus of any sacrificial economy—was only illusory, indicating an absence at the heart of community.[63] For Blanchot and Bataille, the crucial move is thus to affirm this absence and separation as the condition for community. The relation to non-knowledge, which lets the other be other, is what makes friendship possible: as Blanchot puts it, "Friendship: friendship for the unknown, without any friends." Beyond the unity of the individual, friendship testifies to a "sharing" that separates the friends from themselves, opening them to the neuter and the obscure singularity of the other.

In his reading of Duras, Blanchot likewise draws out the anonymous otherness at the heart of any relation, even that of love. Love is unsettled by the "double dissymmetry" between self and other, the distance that remains even where lovers become one.[64] It was this veiled equality—a solidarity of those who remain in solitude—that led to the "communicative explosion" of May 1968. As Blanchot describes, the events of the student revolt were "without project," with each having the freedom to speak, and write—a liberty, equality, and fraternity which unsettled all established or projected communities. It was, in short, a different thought of France. This community, this "being-together," manifested a "manner of *communism* never lived, would not recuperate or revindicate any ideology."[65] The invocation of communism bears several dimensions of significance—not least Blanchot's affinity for the thought of Robert Antelme (discussed below), and the challenge the events of 1968 posed to the authority of the French Communist Party.

In his discussion of 1968, Blanchot describes the event as "The Saying expressed in the said."[66] While one should read this statement in light of Blanchot's own interrogation of Levinas, the phrase provocatively associates Levinas's ethics with a certain thought of communism, as a solidarity rooted in one's vulnerable humanity. Blanchot, moreover, relates the events to a certain form of messianism, like the call of the Jewish people to the "arid solitude" of the desert, in which the distinctions and hierarchy of the social fall away. This is, in many ways, a form of community that cannot be vanquished—a relation to the eternal, beyond any particular election,

---

63. Blanchot, *Communauté Inavouable*, 33–34.
64. Hart, *Dark Gaze*, 220.
65. Blanchot, *Communauté Inavouable*, 53. See also Iyer, "Workless Community," 64–65.
66. Blanchot, *Communauté Inavouable*, 53.

law, or society. As Sarah Kofman writes of Blanchot, in writing of her own father,

> In this unnameable 'place,' he continued to observe Jewish monotheism, if by this, with Blanchot, we understand the revelation of the word as the place in which men maintain a relation to that which excludes all relation: the infinitely Distant, the absolutely Foreign. A relation with the infinite, which no form of power, including that of the executioners of the camps, has been able to master, other than by denying it, burying it in a pit with a shovel, without ever having encountered it.[67]

Kofman's gloss on Blanchot points toward a significant aspect of his work on art and politics, one which brings out with heightened clarity the importance of Levinas for his thought. While Blanchot engages, almost continuously, with notions of the sacred, his work undoes the notion of the sacred as origin, ground, or unity. Indeed, his interrogation of unity as the last idol is a refusal to accept the sacred as the final word. Such unity, ultimately, would exclude or assimilate foreignness, conceal our vulnerability, and restore sovereign power, rendering friendship and the "community without community" impossible.

What Kofman's reading points toward, then, is that the *break* with the sacred is at the heart of Blanchot's atheological-political writings. This is, ultimately, close to what Levinas means by *holiness*, as the break with totality that opens one to alterity. To be sure, there is a paradoxical or enigmatic quality to this holiness, which for Blanchot can only emerge in the refusal of religion. Yet, holiness is as much a break from traditional theology for Levinas as it is for Blanchot. As Blanchot writes, "If Levinas pronounces or writes the name of God, he does not pass over into religion or theology, nor does he thereby conceptualize it."[68] The speech of literature opens a path to holiness through its passive resistance to the working of power, rendering all projects and powers doomed to their failure. Within that failure, like flowers among the ruins, a faint hope for redemption lies.

LEVINAS ON ANTLEME: THE OTHER WITHIN THE SAME

In light of the preceding reflections on Levinas, literature, and politics, I would like to conclude this chapter with an imagined conversation. It

---

67. Kofman, *Smothered Words*, 34–35.
68. Blanchot, "Our Clandestine Companion," 49.

concerns a particularly surprising lacuna in Levinas's work—specifically, Levinas never directly addresses Robert Antelme's *The Human Race [L'Espèce Humaine]*. *The Human Race* is the story of Antelme's confinement in the Gandersheim concentration camp and the prisoners' long, horrific march at the end of the war. Antelme, like Levinas, was one of Blanchot's closest friends, evoked with great fondness in the late text *Pour L'Amitié* and elsewhere. Indeed, Antelme's proximity to Levinas was apparent to Blanchot, who placed his discussion of *The Human Race* immediately after his commentary on Levinas in *The Infinite Conversation*. Even in Blanchot's late work, such as *At the Instant of My Death*, echoes of Antelme's story remain.[69] Given the centrality of the Shoah to so much of Levinas's thought—including his reflections on literature—and how profoundly this work affected Blanchot, Levinas's silence on this work is puzzling, to say the least. How, then, should one hear Levinas's silence—or imagine what might Levinas have said?

The Human Race is an urgent, passionate appeal for human solidarity, growing from the choked desire to speak that Antelme and his fellow prisoners felt upon leaving the camps. Written between 1945 and 1947, the story recounts the various degradations and humiliations to which the prisoners of Gandersheim were subjected—from beatings, nakedness, and forced desecration of churches to the lice, hunger, and roll calls that became their daily bread. *The Human Race* is, in many ways, a story of *dying*—not least because of the paradoxical status of the prisoners, through whose degradation the Kapos, SS, and German civilians define their superiority. It is the darkest of irony that, as the end of the war approaches, the SS find themselves needing to kill the prisoners—so as to leave no record of what has been done—and yet, in their undying cowardice, needing the prisoners to remain alive so as to have a reason to flee the final battles.

While the evil done to the prisoners is almost unspeakable—such that Antelme admitted that any testimony must remain fictive—the force of the novel lies in its articulation of the shared humanity of victim and perpetrator that the camps sought to destroy. As Christophe Bident describes, the story's language recognizes the events by letting them escape; the poetic dimension of *The Human Race* is a crucial aspect of its truth.[70] Through the prisoners' degradation, the SS sought to reduce the humanity of the

---

69. Blanchot's discussion of Antelme is taken up in chapter 6, in discussing his approach to commentary.

70. Christophe Bident, *Reconnaissances: Antelme, Blanchot, Deleuze*, 76, 80–81.

prisoners to nothing—beating them until there was no resistance, shattering any sense of virtue through the Kapos' criminal corruption, cramming prisoners into rail cars until one's limbs were hopelessly entangled with others, depersonalizing them through the roll call that makes one's name no longer one's own. As Blanchot would write later of this roll call, "The prohibition against having anything of one's own and against keeping anything having to do with oneself is pronounced by the proclaiming of the name or of that which takes its place."[71] This process of degradation represented the biopolitics of national socialism, as it was through such dehumanizing that the SS sought to produce their own sense of power and superiority. Nowhere does this shine forth as vividly as the bright, clean, and strong thighs of the SS, which the "master race" and their collaborators would show with pride, in contrast with the gaunt, all-too-human skin and bones of the prisoners.

Despite this, Antelme and his fellow prisoners found humanity, fraternity, and dignity where it would least be expected, often only in the steam of their own piss into a urinal—which meant they were still alive, and gave a moment's respite from their surveillance. As Jacques Rancière writes, "the writing evinces the specific form of resistance that Robert Antelme wants to highlight: the one that transforms the concentration camp's reduction of life to naked existence into the affirmation of fundamental membership of the human race, even in its most basic gestures."[72] The SS's aura of invincibility is constantly exposed as an illusion, providing no more protection than the prisoners' rags. When Allied bombs fall, the prisoners see the SS quiver in fear, and the natural world's solidity refuses to bend to the Führer's will:

> A railroad car that is railroad car, a horse that's horse, the clouds coming in from the west—all the things that the SS cannot contest are royal things; everything up to gravity itself, thanks to it SS men may fall to the ground . . . The wind which wafts the west into our faces doublecrosses the SS, so do the four letters *SNCF* which he didn't even notice . . . Trees haven't dried up and died just because the SS decided they were not men.[73]

The continuous production of a mythical sovereignty through the prisoners' degradation belies the SS's irreducible vulnerability. They can no more

71. Blanchot, *Step Not Beyond*, 38.
72. Rancière, *Future of the Image*, 124.
73. Antelme, *Human Race*, 45.

make themselves superhuman than deny the humanity of the prisoners. A simple (yet courageous) gesture of humanity pierces the Nazi myth of superiority: when a German gives Antelme bread, a handshake, or says "*Langsam!*" (Slowly!) as he works, Antelme writes, "Against that handshake there was nothing that could prevail."[74] In the end, human solidarity remains—as Blanchot puts it, the indestructible that is continuously being destroyed. The story closes with Antelme speaking to an unknown Russian, shaking his hand and saying "*Wir sind frei*" (We are free), turning the language that had silenced and divided them into a site for common humanity.

The most haunting aspect of Antelme's work is the parallel that he crafts between the hierarchy of the camps and the class structure of society. This gives the story a "hope which seems terrible," as Blanchot wrote to Bataille.[75] Far from a flat or rigid Marxist analysis, the narrative rather draws one into the connection—showing, to paraphrase Benjamin, that the state of exception exemplified by the camps is the rule of modern life. When Antelme is sweeping in an office, he is hastily dismissed by the office girl, and then is told "*Weg!*" (Get out of the way!) by a civilian in leaving; Antelme comments that the real meaning is, "I don't want you to exist." In the disdain of that dismissal—its refusal of recognition, the denial of Antelme's face—he sees the underlying dynamic of social division:

> I shrugged it off. Here, perhaps, it [*Weg!*] did not have overmuch importance. But there in its purest form was that disdain which is the world's affliction, such as, more or less camouflaged, it still reigns in human relations everywhere—such as it reigns yet in the society we were removed from. It was clearer here, however. We provided a disdainful humanity with the means of revealing itself completely.[76]

It is in confronting this disdain—both within the camps and beyond—that Antelme came to be a "necessary counterideal,"[77] in Sarah Kofman's words, against the Nietzschean ideal of a will to power. While never completing another novel, Antelme would become outspoken against the Algerian war and worked to transform Marxism within France as well (he was expelled

74. Ibid., 75.
75. See Bident, *Reconnaissances*, 89.
76. Antelme, *The Human Race*, 51.
77. Kofman, postscript to *Smothered Words*, in Dobbels, *On Robert Antelme's The Human Race*, 122.

from the French Communist Party for being excessively internationalist).[78] The exigency of recognition, as an extension of friendship beyond distinction, drove Antelme's work and thought through the rest of his life.

In this light, the question of Levinas's silence regarding Antelme returns to the fore. Clearly, there are strong resonances between Antelme's work and the poetics set forth in *Proper Names*, as *The Human Race* testifies to a human solidarity and ethics that unsettles the being of the world in which we live. Antelme's refusal of transcendence, set forth in a dramatic contrast of Jesus's crucifixion with the impersonal dying of the camps,[79] further fits with Levinas's prophetic account of responsibility and consciousness, in its recognition of the faces of those whom society makes faceless. Moreover, Levinas expressed an affinity on several occasions with a certain spirit of Marx,[80] which would seem to parallel Antelme's own unorthodox form of Marxist thinking. Levinas's silence regarding Antelme, then, is highly enigmatic.

If one cannot know if Levinas read *The Human Race*, then how should one read Levinas, in light of this question? What I would argue, here, is that one read Levinas as having read Antelme, and read his thought in that light. As Eleanor Kaufman's work has shown, particularly within French thought the form of address of another's work provides an oblique affirmation of their thought, and such appropriation can take forms ranging from delirious praise to silence.[81] As Blanchot and Levinas both emphasize, the address to another exceeds what one says of them; to address another's work need not be through direct, "face-to-face" engagement. It is conceivable, then, that Levinas's work bears traces of an engagement with Antelme. I would suggest, even, that the adopted rhetoric of *Otherwise than Being*—being-hostage, vulnerability, hunger, nakedness—echoes Antelme's work, taking up his language and giving it life, much as Agnon's writings revive the language of Scripture.[82] Both Levinas's conception of subjectivity in *Otherwise than Being* and the politics of justice in the book's conclusion testify to the saying that speaks throughout Antelme's work.

Moreover, to read Levinas as having read Antelme would contest—and begin to repair—certain divisions within Levinas's thought. For, if literature

78. See Antelme, "Principles Put to the Test," 23–26.
79. Antelme, *Human Race*, 187–88.
80. Kearney, "Dialogue with Emmanuel Levinas," 33.
81. Kaufman, *Delirium of Praise*.
82. See Young, "Betrayals of Vulnerability."

opens an alternative society, based on separation rather than unity—a proximity that neither assimilates nor disdains the neighbor—then it suggests a way to see Levinas's thought as more materially redemptive. There is, in Levinas, a tendency to fix or reduce alterity to certain conceptions and positions; as Randy Friedman has pointed out, these are often gendered, thereby reifying the masculinity of the responsible subject. It also might help with conceiving the concrete, economic questions that would grow from an account of Levinasian responsibility.[83] To read Levinas in light of Antelme would work to counter such reductions, demanding recognition of the other's humanity beyond such distinction. One might say, then, that in recognizing Antelme's exclusion one could read Levinas in a way that counters the exclusions by which ethical responsibility constitutes itself. The vigilance that Levinas demands of us might also be demanded of his work, by interrogating the limits and shape of the community that he seeks to define.

We have seen, to this point, how art and community have been intertwined in both authors' works—and, through that, the intertwinings between the authors themselves. There is, one could say, a hidden, subversive solidarity that emerges in their distance from one another. However, within the preceding discussion, there has also been a subtle shift. For, whereas Blanchot's and Levinas's early writings both emphasize separation, their later works shift to an emphasis on multiplicity, in which diverse voices and levels of significance overlap and work through one another. Perhaps this is nowhere clearer than Levinas's discussion of music, which shifts from being the impersonality that enables separation (and thus, only indirectly sociality) to the form of saying that constitutes responsibility. This shift in responsibility unfolds largely through Blanchot's and Levinas's conversation regarding the notion of the enigma, which transforms their thought on ethics, writing, and religion. On the basis of the preceding discussion, we may now attend to the role of the enigma in their work.

---

83. See Dussel, "'The Politics' by Levinas."

FIVE

Insinuations
Enigmas of Responsibility

THE LAST CHAPTER EXPLORED the interventions that Blanchot and Levinas made in one another's work in terms of the relationship between art and ethics. They provided one another with a voice from outside, testing and challenging the limits of their thought, even while affirming its provenance. As was discussed, Blanchot's work gave Levinas a language for thinking art beyond the Heideggerian work, while Levinas's thought of separation injected a form of alterity into Blanchot's notion of politics. While the latter sections of the chapter gestured toward the implications for their thought of religion, with Levinas's reading of Agnon and Blanchot's invocation of messianism, the broader significance of religion in their work requires further attention.

The next two chapters will explore the significance of religion more directly, though with an emphasis on its relation to their friendship. This chapter addresses the notion of the enigma, which becomes increasingly central to both authors' writings, beginning with Blanchot's 1960s essays that would later be published in *The Infinite Conversation*. These essays comprise Blanchot's response to Levinas's idea of the infinite in *Totality and Infinity*. As the ensuing discussion shows, Levinas took up this figure of the enigma in his intriguing essays "The Trace of the Other" and "Enigma and Phenomenon," and then further developed this thought in his second major work, *Otherwise than Being*. In these essays, the enigma becomes central to Levinas's conceptions of transcendence, revelation, and responsibility, enabling significant modifications in his thought of the relationship between Judaism and philosophy. These writings on the enigma then formed a crucial starting point for Blanchot's later reflections, as he returns to this figure and Levinas's own thought in *The Step Not Beyond* and *The Writing of the Disaster*.

For both authors, the enigma provides them with a new way to conceive responsibility. As, in Levinas's terms, an enigma "insinuates" a certain thought even while not presenting it, it thereby calls for a certain form of subjectivity that differs from philosophical cognition. This becomes essential to his idea of revelation, and gives him a way to articulate the relationship between the saying and the said, as well as the relation of ethics to justice. For Blanchot, the enigma likewise opens a new thought of responsibility by exposing us to the neuter, rendering responsibility anonymous and making transcendence impossible. The enigma thereby pluralizes responsibility—reworking the responsibility of poetry from his early work—and allows Blanchot to challenge the residual theological and monological elements of Levinas's thought. Ultimately, as one traces the enigma through the course of their writings, it reveals the enigmatic character of their friendship itself: a consistent attention to one another, a respectful appropriation of the other's work—and yet, ultimately, a separation that emerges in the very intimacy of their encounter.

While this chapter focuses primarily on their later work, where the enigma becomes central, it will be helpful to see how it becomes central by beginning with Blanchot's early writings on the responsibility of literature. This brief discussion of *The Work of Fire* links us back to the aesthetic concerns of the last chapter, while showing how Blanchot's conception of literature leads into an ambivalent, almost contradictory form of responsibility. This will give us a vantage point from which to see how the enigma complicates their later conceptions of responsibility, religion, and writing.

LITERARY ENIGMAS: BLANCHOT'S *WORK OF FIRE*

> Poetry is a means of putting oneself in danger without running any risk, a mode of suicide, destruction of self, that comfortably leaves space for the surest affirmation of self. It is right to recall it, because this criticism is demanded by literature itself and because in truth this has meaning and value only as passion lived by the writer, in the imposture to which he feels himself an accomplice . . . While bad faith is being accomplished, it is just as much the advance of a good faith, too good ever to accept itself, as the irresponsible game of imposture that refuses to be engaged and take real risks.[1]

Blanchot's earliest discussions of responsibility center on the responsibility of the poet. In his literary criticism, he frequently analyzes works in terms of their enigmatic character. In so doing, his writing considers what

---

1. Blanchot, *Work of Fire*, 142.

one could term the darker, abyssal side of the enigma, which becomes the condition for the responsibility and subjectivity which Levinas foregrounds. Literature, for Blanchot, is enigmatic because it 1) unhinges existence, 2) creates separation within being, and 3) creates the relation between speech and silence, breaking with both the active utility of everyday language and the utter passivity of speechlessness. While creating this separation, literature retains a worldly form, and it is this internal difference that renders both it and the writer enigmatic.

The enigma of literature comes to light in the series of studies in *The Work of Fire*, first published in 1949. In these studies, Blanchot considers the relationship between literature and existence in several central literary figures. This focus can first be approached through Blanchot's reading of the differences between René Char and Charles Baudelaire. Both poets think through the abyss between poetic figures and existence—yet the implications of the abyss differ dramatically for the poets themselves.

In his study of Char, Blanchot explores how Char's poetry is a "revelation of poetry," breaking with existence. Poetry, here, is less speech in the form of verse or meter than "all that is refusal in us"; it "escapes us because it is our absence rather than our presence."[2] The language of poetry hollows out the world in which we live; the images, descriptions, and turns of phrase of the poetic imagination bear us away from everyday reality, creating a distance and emptiness within things. Poetic language differs from everyday speech because it gives the world to us in the world's absence. Language gives both the materiality of the being and the flow from which it comes into being; the poem's images "reproduce a call" that draws the poet "into the intimacy of things and their total presence."[3] Beginning from things in the world, poetry "receives from their presence the irreality that makes this presence possible,"[4] thus moving beyond the world. As Blanchot says, the poet exists as an effect of the poem, in the movement *beyond* of poetic language. The poem "opens the future," giving time to the poet that goes beneath the everyday flow of events and things—but this movement beyond is never fully complete.

In reflecting on Baudelaire, Blanchot sees his failure as a poet as manifesting a fundamental, essential possibility of poetry. Drawing from Sartre's analysis of Baudelaire's "bad faith"—in Sartre's view, not living up

2. Ibid., 102–3.
3. Ibid., 108.
4. Ibid., 104.

to the vocation of the poet—Blanchot turns this in a different direction, by noting that Baudelaire's bad faith can be read as a function of his fidelity to the contradictory demands of poetry. Baudelaire confronts the abyss of language, in which words founder and are lost—yet also sees the demand for form, the need for finitude in order to make the dream real, as "first the infinite's principle of questioning."[5] Without form, particularity and concreteness, the questioning, restless movement of thought would halt. As Blanchot describes,

> And the infinite in the finite—undoubtedly that is something easy; but to hold these two movements together, to compose them, to realize one by the other, if that implies a great effort, the work of art finds exactly there the most precious resources, and one sees in the end that the unexpected, far from opposing the expectation of rhythm, is perceptible only in this expectation, that *vagueness agrees with the most exact language,* just as the obscurity of dream, to express itself, finds all that is necessary in language's transparency.[6]

The precise form of Baudelaire's poetry incarnates an infinite questioning. In its ceaseless oscillation between infinite and finite, Baudelaire's work signifies the endless process of dying. The nothingness of death does not even serve as consolation: "we do not have death in front of us, but existence that . . . is always in front, and, as low as I sink, is always lower, and . . . infests this unreality with an absence of reality."[7] As dying is endless, dispersing the finitude that would be a limit and a closure, Blanchot sees Baudelaire as exposing a poetic possibility that unsettles Heidegger's authenticity of *Dasein*: "Heidegger's 'being-for-death,' far from characterizing authentic possibility, would thus represent for Baudelaire only one more imposture."[8] In all this, then, both Char and Baudelaire manifest a poetic possibility very close to the conception of art (and the *il y a*) discussed in the last chapter.

While both Char and Baudelaire exhibit the possibility of literary existence, Blanchot highlights the dramatic difference in their respective lives. Baudelaire's poetry disclosed a form of existence beyond Heidegger, but his life betrayed this poetic possibility—he was "half disloyal to poetry—to

5. Ibid., 141.
6. Ibid.; emphasis added.
7. Ibid., 149.
8. Ibid.

which there is no half-loyalty."⁹ Unable to "live poetically," in the uncertain space of sheer existence, he lapsed into "social conformism": "In a word, Baudelaire retreats before what he calls the abyss and what Sartre calls existence, and he seeks guarantees on the side of a truth or of an objective, moral, social, or religious authority, what Sartre and Baudelaire both call being."¹⁰ On the other hand, the "overflow" of Char's poetry leads to his political commitment and revolutionary partisanship; as Blanchot writes, the poem

> puts us in contact with all that is sovereignty in the world, in opposition to all that is *fait accompli*, weightiness of fate, fossilization of man. That Char's poetry, the closest to the essence of poetry, has led him to the struggle of the partisan in the world, that it has continued to express itself in this action, to be this very action without losing anything of the purity of its essence, that is what "verifies" it as the ability to overflow the economy of creation, to enlarge the blood of acts.¹¹

Char becomes politically engaged; however, Blanchot also argues that there is an impersonality to his poetry, in which it "speaks for itself"—*refusing* commitment, even while leading to it.

How is it, then, that poetry leads to Baudelaire's "dandyism," Char's partisanship, and beyond both of these possibilities? This puzzle—really, this enigma—illuminates the significance of literature's separation from the world. In making the world absent, poetry introduces a modality of existence that pulls the subject out of everyday language and life, thereby creating a space *for* engagement. The freedom of literature makes commitment possible. At the same time, however, the conditions of such engagement also demand that one not be engaged. Concrete involvement and fleetingness are *both* demands of poetic existence, and the same language that calls one into responsibility and engagement can be the occasion for irresponsibility, refusal, and conformism. The bad faith of literature, its refusal to be in the world or its deceit, is a condition for its truth. In the difference between Char and Baudelaire—and in recognizing that both are fundamentally forms of poetic existence—Blanchot highlights the *enigmatic* character of

---

9. Ibid., 134.
10. Ibid.
11. Ibid., 106.

literature: carrying us beyond the everyday world and signifying nothing, it is all the same the condition for responsibility and involvement.[12]

This enigmatic engagement of literature—both impelling and resisting involvement with the world—is likewise a noteworthy feature of surrealism. In thinking of surrealism's significance, Blanchot sees it as liberating language from function: "that rational constructions are rejected, that universal significations vanish, is to say that language does not have to be used, that it does not have to serve to express something, that it is free, freedom itself."[13] This freedom is not simply a freedom of language, but in language, for those whose speech is freed from utility, such that surrealist art effects a social revindication. Like the Cartesian *cogito*, surrealist language cannot *not* think of itself, thereby transcending its material conditions. The freedom of the surrealist project places it at a distance from any concrete political agenda or movement. Blanchot sees surrealism's affinity with Marxism as a commitment to revolution in the name of poetry. The pursuit of human freedom, such that history is accomplished, would open the space beyond the world in which poetry can take place. As he writes, "Thus, the service that surrealism expects from Marxism is to prepare for it a society in which everyone could be surrealist, but especially in which the aims of surrealism would be led to good, in all their purity, without misrepresentation or falsification."[14] It is in this sense that Blanchot says the "most uncommitted literature is at the same time the most committed"—it must recognize the distance between its realization and the conditions of the society in which it takes place.

In these reflections, Blanchot accords poetry a twofold significance: first, it signifies the becoming-totality of the world, its completion and presence to itself. Second, poetry introduces a form of alterity that transcends the everyday, while enabling a responsible engagement through such separation. Poetry thus demands a dual response—being in the world, but not of it, secularizing and rendering immanent a classic form of transcendence. It thereby gives the possibility of responsibility, through its contradictory demands to the poet. Thus, even in Blanchot's early writings, responsibility has an enigmatic character. However, at this point, it is still largely unitary—one's response either is or is not attentive. As Levinas and

12. For a helpful discussion of the ambiguity of writing in "Literature and the Right to Death," see Critchley, *Very Little, Almost Nothing*, 48–56.

13. Blanchot, *Work of Fire*, 88.

14. Ibid., 96.

Blanchot think through the enigma more directly, the unitary character of responsibility will come undone, multiplying into irreducible difference.

THE ENIGMA IN LEVINAS'S TRANSITIONAL PERIOD

As discussed in the last chapter, Levinas's early work illuminates an ambivalence to being, gesturing toward an exteriority that would transcend ontology. In many ways, this was close to Blanchot's conception of art. In the period following *Totality and Infinity*, the notion of the enigma (*l'énigme*) becomes central to Levinas's language, as a way to unsettle ontology. This is, in part, an attempt to go beyond Heidegger's ontology through phenomenological practice. This shift is notable on several levels. First, these essays develop shortly after Blanchot's invocation of the enigma as an aspect of fragmentary writing in the essays later published in *The Infinite Conversation*.[15] Second, it is in terms of the enigma that Levinas articulates the trace as the mode of "nonmanifestation" of alterity and transcendence. This enables a rethinking of the dynamics of revelation and the prophetic signification of language. Third, the enigma provides Levinas with a way of situating alterity within phenomenality, or the saying within the said, and thereby within both language and the subject, moving toward the reworking of responsibility and language in *Otherwise than Being*.[16] The enigma thus becomes a central figure for thinking through the distinctive account of alterity and responsibility that emerges in *Otherwise than Being*. While *Otherwise than Being* is often read (rightly, in my view) as a response to Derrida's "Violence and Metaphysics," the importance of the enigma to this work suggests that it may also be fruitfully read as continuing the engagement between Blanchot and Levinas. These two readings are not opposed; after all, one might recall that perhaps the most central term of Derrida's thought—*différance*—itself functions as an enigma, in its verbal/nominal and spatiotemporal ambiguity.[17]

This section traces Levinas's discussion of enigmas in the post-*Totality* period. It will begin with a discussion of two central essays, "The Trace of the Other" and "Enigma and Phenomenon," initially published in

---

15. While *The Infinite Conversation* was published in 1969, many of the central essays were published in the early 1960s, prior to "La Trace de l'Autre" and "Énigme et Phenomenon." *The Infinite Conversation* is addressed further in the next chapter.

16. And, toward an "inclusive" relation to alterity; see Large, *Emmanuel Levinas and Maurice Blanchot*, 58–60.

17. Derrida, "Différance," 7–10.

1963 and 1965. Building from these essays, it moves to *Otherwise than Being*, where the language of the trace and enigma is taken up once more. However, there is an important shift in *Otherwise than Being*, as Levinas accentuates more strongly how the enigma, in its passivity and openness to its own ruin, gives itself over to phenomenality, representation, and consciousness. This enables Levinas to situate the language and rationality of philosophy as oriented toward justice, restoring an ethical significance to philosophy after deposing the sovereignty of its reason.

In "The Trace of the Other," Levinas introduces the trace as a form of existence that upsets or unsettles the order of being. It first appears in what he calls the Work (*l'Oeuvre*), evoking Blanchot's discussion of the work of art. A Work, on Levinas's view, unsettles the order of consciousness, because its finality, impersonality, and separation from the world gesture beyond the subject. It is, as he says, a "being-for-after-my death."[18] Like poetry in *The Work of Fire*, the Work undoes Heideggerian being-towards death. This opening beyond oneself has the character of *liturgy*—an offering of oneself. Insatiable desire impels this "ethical liturgy," where satisfying one's desire increases one's hunger, much like Sonia's "insatiable compassion" for Raskolnikov in *Crime and Punishment*. Desire's movement toward the other indirectly manifests alterity, in its overturning of consciousness and its egoism. Levinas terms this appearance a trace—an appearance that could not be fully present, because the other who is desired only appears in the movement toward them. The trace *of* the other appears in the response *to* the other. This is a trace that appears as the "third person"—the Illeity—of the other, distancing alterity irreversibly from the subject, and thereby calling one to a unique subjectivity.

As the non-apparent, the trace institutes a reversal of signification, presaging the enigma's modality of manifestation. While the trace does not appear as such, but only in its withdrawal, it can "play the role of a sign."[19] It becomes part of the order of language and being—losing its abstraction and transcendence in the process. However, the trace also upsets the order of signs, "making an entry" into signification that undoes the totality of phenomena; the trace remains a "surplus on the inevitable paralysis of manifestation."[20] As the trace temporalizes appearance, it introduces a delay or difference into appearance that cannot be grasped. This difference

18. Levinas, "La Trace de l'Autre," in *En Découvrant*, 190–92.
19. Ibid., 199.
20. Ibid., 194.

inverts signification; whereas traces may become signs, now all signs become traces as well.[21] Rather than being ontological, in the trace language turns toward the otherness beyond being.

"The Trace of the Other" clearly aims to extend phenomenology beyond ontology; however, while rendering the thought of the trace as theoretically possible, its phenomenological possibility remains in question. It is not clear, at this point, how a subject would be aware of a trace; like Inspector Clouseau, one may stumble on a clue, but not recognize it. This problem highlights the importance of "Enigma and Phenomenon," the 1965 essay where Levinas more directly addresses how a trace may appear to the subject. A trace is, as he writes, an "insinuation"—something that presents itself indirectly, that "manifests itself without manifesting itself."[22] As an example, Levinas discusses a knock at the door—where, when it is answered, no one is there; one cannot know who knocked, even as the knock remains present to one's mind. A trace thus appears only in its dissimulation—appearing as other than it is, an *enigmatic* mode of appearance. Whereas a phenomenon appears in clarity, and gives itself as present to consciousness (even if only fully appearing in apperception), an enigma unsettles the transcendental ego, rendering uncertain its grasp. Its withdrawal from representation pulls the subject out of itself, into proximity to the other.

An enigma becomes central to Levinas because of its "extra-ordinary duplicity," which allows a dimension of subjectivity to emerge that remained hidden within the phenomenal field. Interrupting the ordinary flow of time, the enigma "deranges" the phenomenon, and thus the ego's consciousness of the world. The self (*Moi*) emerges as responsible in response to this enigmatic call, as one may find oneself obsessed by or drawn to what one cannot master. This is not imposed on the self by the enigma, since its "exorbitant sense" disappears in its appearance. Rather, the enigma's passive withdrawal leaves it to the subject to respond—or not. The enigma may be treated as nothing, reduced to a sign—or be that which "fissures" being. Much as the trace could be refused, the enigma of language may either call one to responsibility or become the site of conscious mastery. It is this irreducible ambiguity that calls forth the subject's responsibility, beyond the limits of knowledge. As Levinas writes, "Language is the possibility of an

21. Drabinski, *Sensibility and Singularity*, 157–60.

22. Levinas, "Énigme et Phenomène," in *En Decouvrant l'Existence*, 208. Translations are drawn from *Emmanuel Levinas: Basic Philosophical Writings*.

enigmatic equivocation for better and for worse, which men abuse."[23] This enigmatic discretion makes ethics possible, as the subject may be uniquely for the other: "The response to the assignation of the Enigma is the generosity of sacrifice outside of the known and unknown, without calculation, as going to the Infinite."[24] Precisely because one does not know whether one is responding to the infinite or not, the enigma opens the subject to a responsibility that eludes self-interest—what Levinas will come to term dis-inter-estedness.[25]

As ethical responsibility becomes a "going to the Infinite," the enigma opens the possibility of a relation to transcendence. Here, transcendence is not an overwhelming or even a saturation of the phenomenal field, but rather a differential absence within phenomenality that testifies to another possibility.[26] It is like the slight, whispering voice that Elijah hears in the cave—rather than a voice from on high. As Hent de Vries writes, "For Levinas, the trace, enigma, and ambiguity all hint at a modality of transcendence which is essential in a world that has come to know good reasons for atheism and therefore can no longer believe in any single form of the presence of the absolute."[27]

As the trace of Illeity, the enigma's dissimulation reveals a beyond of phenomenality, a *saying* or relation prior to what discloses itself in thematic content (what Levinas calls the *said*). This saying, for Levinas, is the register in which revelation occurs. Levinas's discussion of revelation here is striking: the burning bush does not, in his view, overwhelm Moses, but rather hints at a trace of God:

> Such is the duplicity of oracles: extravagances are lodged in words that guarantee wisdom. A lover makes an advance, but the provocative or seductive gesture has, if one likes, not interrupted the decency of the conversation and attitudes; it withdraws as lightly as it had slipped in. A God was revealed on a mountain or in a burning bush, or was attested to in Scriptures. And what if it were a storm! And what if the Scriptures came to us from dreamers! Dismiss the

---

23. Levinas, "Énigme et Phenomène," 208.
24. Ibid., 215. See Drabinski, *Sensibility and Singularity*, 163–65.
25. See Levinas, *Ethics and Infinity*, 99–100.
26. And thus, a less forceful call, in my view, than Jean-Luc Marion finds in Levinas. This may mark a central aspect of Levinas's shift in language. See Marion, "Voice without Name."
27. Vries, *Minimal Theologies*, 513.

illusory call from our minds! The insinuation itself invites us to do so.[28]

"Duplicity" leaves it up to the subject to interpret what has happened. Theophany only occurs in the response to this "appearance"—that is, in the responsibility that follows from it. As Levinas writes, "It is up to us, or more exactly, it is up to me to retain or to repel *this God without boldness,* exiled because allied with the conquered, hunted down and hence ab-solute, thus disarticulating the very moment in which he is presented and proclaimed, unrepresentable."[29] The truth of God, for Levinas, is a "persecuted truth," which "remains with the contrite and humble."[30] Precisely because transcendence may or may not appear—its modality of the "perhaps" (*peut-etre*) is undecidable—it demands a response from the subject, either of hospitality or exclusion.

This enigmatic transcendence manifests a divine passivity—its weakness, and its submission to the force of representation. Such weakness, it seems, is a condition for revelation. It is precisely in such passivity that the trace of God is "allied with the conquered"[31]—persecuted, impoverished, calling for a response in its very silence. As the enigma of the Infinite breaks with the correlation of consciousness, a different correlation establishes itself: in responding to the passive, "persecuted" trace of God, the subject of responsibility thereby turns toward those who are passive and persecuted, in the *human* realm. As Levinas writes, "A You (*Tu*) inserts itself between the I and Illeity."[32] Here we encounter one of the fundamental points of Levinas's thought: to respond to the enigma is to become a prophetic subject, as the recognition of the trace is a response to persecution—which may be and often is ignored. By contrast, to take the enigma merely as a sign, as something for consciousness, is the reduction of the subject to egoism, ontology, and the logic of the Same. Ontology would efface the enigma, and thereby conceals the radical nature of responsibility from view.

The enigma thus becomes a central notion for thinking of the trace, and responds to several related problems regarding alterity. As an appearance in which alterity is manifest in its withdrawal, the enigma lets Levinas

---

28. Levinas, "Énigme et Phenomène," in *En Decouvrant l'Existence,* 208.
29. Ibid.; emphasis added.
30. Isa 57:15. Levinas, "Énigme et Phenomène," 209.
31. Ibid., 208.
32. Ibid., 216.

conceive alterity's emergence within the realm of the same, while remaining other.[33] Moreover, if God passes in an enigmatic trace, then God's enigmatic, passive "incarnation" evokes the subject's response to persecution, and thereby turns the subject toward ethics and prophecy. The weakness of divine manifestation is linked to human persecution; the trace of God appears only in the response to human persecution, because divinity reveals itself in weakness. Ironically, then, the connection between God and the face of the neighbor becomes clearer in the very obscurity of the enigma. However, the role of language and the character of the responsible subject remain largely undefined. It is with these questions in mind that we turn to the enigma in *Otherwise than Being*.

VULNERABLE SUBJECTIVITY: THE ENIGMA IN *OTHERWISE THAN BEING*

The notion of the enigma remains central in Levinas's second major work, *Otherwise than Being*. However, Levinas's discussion shifts in several important ways. First, the enigma's appearance calls for a rethinking of subjectivity—in terms of both its persecuted character and its materiality. Second, while "Enigma and Phenomenon" largely conceives the enigma as a surpassing or departure from phenomenality, *Otherwise than Being* recovers a positive—albeit secondary—ethical significance for language, ontology, and appearance. While Levinas adopts a new language for several of the crucial arguments of *Otherwise*, the centrality of the enigma to the programmatic and concluding chapters warrants scrutiny, to help frame the notions of substitution, persecution, and vulnerability that become the central ethical themes of his later work.

The programmatic opening chapter of *Otherwise* introduces the notion of a beyond to being, as found in a saying that exceeds and precedes the said. The said, for Levinas, is what *is*—what can be predicated or made present to consciousness. In any act of consciousness or communication, however, there is a temporal dimension that escapes, even in constituting this moment. Levinas calls this temporal extenuation *diachrony*—a "lapse of time which does not return"[34]—and it indicates a modality of subjective life beyond or prior to consciousness. It is at this level, in the *saying* beyond

---

33. Large, *Emmanuel Levinas and Maurice Blanchot*, 142–45.
34. Levinas, *Otherwise than Being*, 9.

what is said, that Levinas locates the subject's ethical responsibility. This saying, however, is a "primordial enigma":

> Essence [which can be thematized] fills the said, or the epos, of the saying, but the saying, in its power of equivocation, that is, in the enigma whose secret it keeps, escapes the epos of essence that includes it and signifies beyond in a signification that hesitates between this beyond and the return to the epos of essence.[35]

The "hesitation" of the sign is enigmatic—opening a mode of transcendence, but also thereby setting forth the thematic consciousness that may mask or forget that which precedes it. The enigma can call the subject to something that exceeds and subverts its intentionality—a responsibility "from a 'prior to every memory,' an 'ulterior to every accomplishment,' from the non-present par excellence, the non-original, the an-archical, prior to or beyond essence."[36] Thus, as we have seen before, the enigma holds together Levinas's conception of responsibility as transcendence, particularly in conceiving the relation of the saying and the said, as the beyond being "always shows itself enigmatically."[37]

The saying of ethics is a moment of *witness*—when a command sounds "in the mouth of the one who obeys."[38] As a response prior to consciousness or intention, witness is enigmatic, as the other speaks *within* the subject. It is a time where the subject is without identity, torn from itself, in a movement that "detaches itself absolutely." Witness, then, is a saying that unsettles the order of the said, giving a sign *to* the other. This sign's relationality opens a dimension of signification—both by and of the subject—that goes beyond a cognitive relation or understanding. Like the trace, an enigma may become a sign, yet it injects a moment of ambiguity into the order and clarity of language. This reorients linguistic signification in terms of what Levinas calls prophecy. Prophetic language manifests itself in the said; as Levinas writes, it may become information (a reduction to its content), or may be a form of "glory" for the Infinite. Through its enigmatic manifestation, prophetic speech guards its infinity: "Transcendence owes it to itself to interrupt its own demonstration."[39] Without taking the

---

35. Ibid., 9–10. For a helpful discussion of delay, see Purcell, "On Hesitation before the Other," 18–19.
36. Levinas, *Otherwise than Being*, 10.
37. Ibid., 19.
38. Ibid., 149.
39. Ibid., 152.

risk of reduction to a thematic statement—or even to what Levinas calls "ideology and sacred delirium"—the transcendence of responsibility could not exist. Its passivity and weakness can only emerge as a trace within the order, unsettling and reorienting it while risking complete effacement or cooptation.

To this point—not only in *Otherwise than Being*, but perhaps throughout Levinas's corpus—the passage from the saying to the said has remained problematic. Levinas consistently discusses this passage in negative terms—for instance, as a "betrayal" of transcendence by representation.[40] However, the enigma of responsibility helps Levinas to reorient this passage in more positive terms, a move which revalues philosophical discourse and rationality. Levinas notes that the *third*—in the sense of a third person—is always already present, in the relation to the other. This is, in part, because in substituting oneself for the other—even to the point of being responsible for one's persecutors—ethical responsibility must be open to the other's responsibility for *other* others. Thus, the relation of proximity—the nonthematic relation to alterity—would "signify as an enigma," because it must relate uniquely to more than one other: "The third party introduces a contradiction in the saying whose signification before the other until then went in one direction."[41] This introduction of distance demands an ordering, a "comparison of incomparables," as Levinas says.[42] Order and rationality become necessary so that others may live together—to give others an "equal footing as before a court of justice." Justice thus becomes the orienting of rationality in light of the transcendent signification of proximity. What is particularly important here is to note that this "contra-diction"—as the saying turns against itself—is ab-originally internal to responsibility: "In the proximity of the other, all the others than the other obsess me, and already this obsession cries out for justice, demands measure and knowing, is consciousness."[43] It is because revelation is always enigmatic that it enables *both* responsibility to the unique one, *and* calls for the political response of justice before multiple others. The enigma's singular multiplicity embodies the unique contortion of responsibility between singularity and generality.

The necessity of this "contra-diction" helps to explain both Levinas's rhetoric and his emphasis on skepticism as a necessary moment of rationality.

40. On this, see Young, "Betrayals of Vulnerability."
41. Levinas, *Otherwise than Being*, 157.
42. See Ciaramelli, "Comparison of Incomparables."
43. Levinas, *Otherwise than Being*, 158.

In *Otherwise*, Levinas contorts language to turn it away from an everyday or thematic signification—to show the saying at work and concealed within the said. For language to witness to alterity requires both a moment of recognition and its negation; the *movement* of thought, more than what is thought, becomes the passage of transcendence. The logical and temporal movement of skepticism represents the movement of saying within philosophy. Even when it is refuted, the passage through this thought does not simply restore truth, but rather dislocates it:

> The skeptical discourse, which states the rupture, failure, impotence or impossibility of disclosure, would be self-contradictory if the saying and the said were only correlative, if the signifyingness of proximity and the signification known and said could enter into a common order, if the saying reached a full contemporaneousness with the said, if the saying entered into essence without betraying the diachrony of proximity . . . But the skeptical saying undone by philosophy in fact recalls the breakup of synchronizable, that is, the recallable, time. Then, the trace of saying, which has never been present, obliges me; the responsibility for the other, never assumed, binds me; a command never heard is obeyed.[44]

In its revocation of the said—by stating its "rupture"—skepticism evokes a saying that lies beyond it. Yet this invocation must likewise be unsettled, to gesture toward the saying's irreducible temporal difference. Skepticism, and its refutation, amount to an "unsaying of an unsaying of the said," as D. H. Brody puts it, recognizing the link between this contortion of language and an enigmatic form of representation.[45] In a sense, it restores the enigma to itself.

While concluding Levinas's discussion, skepticism thus plays an integral part in his argument. It shows how, despite appearances, discourse "qua discourse belies the very claim to totalize"[46]—showing the impossibility of totalization, and that it can be oriented toward a possibility that remains beyond conception. As Blanchot later writes, "Language itself [for Levinas] would be skepticism; thought of in this sense, indeed, it would not allow satisfaction with absolute knowledge or allow transparent communication."[47] The logic of skepticism, as the possibility of an

---

44. Ibid., 168.
45. Brody, "Emmanuel Levinas," 184.
46. Levinas, *Otherwise than Being*, 170.
47. Blanchot, "Our Clandestine Companion," 47.

un-saying that does not revert to cognition, makes justice and prophecy conceivable by turning language against its cognitive form. While, in its thematic moment, the violence of discourse is not eradicated, its reduction and limitation as a "just violence" situates consciousness within the purview of ethics. This opens language to that which transcends its force, much like the plural speech that Blanchot gestures towards in *The Writing of Disaster* (as shall be discussed below). Justice demands the enigma of discourse so as to address each other singularly yet equally, in a responsive speech accomplished in its incompleteness.

This passage from ethics to justice highlights all the more the significance of the enigma for Levinas. It is, in a sense, the middle term, the way of thinking difference as irreducible alterity rather than dialectical opposition. Enigmatically, alterity insinuates itself into consciousness, while the conscious ego exits itself into responsibility for alterity. The enigma ultimately discloses the enigmatic character of the subject itself—for, the subject is no longer purely a center of consciousness and agency, but also vulnerable, responsible, and called beyond itself to a responsibility it did not choose. The subject, within and beyond being, becomes the enigmatic form of transcendence par excellence. Blanchot takes up this idea and thinks it through in ways that both respond to and further question Levinas's conception of responsibility.

THE ENIGMA AND THE NEUTRAL: BLANCHOT ON RESPONSIBILITY

First published in 1973, *The Step Not Beyond* (*Le Pas Au-Délà*) takes up both the conceptual and formal problematics first articulated in *The Infinite Conversation*. It thus parallels the shift within Levinas's language, in response to the challenges posed by Blanchot's queries regarding neutrality and plural speech. Returning once more to the Eternal Return, writing about writing, a prolonged meditation on the incessance of dying, *The Step Not Beyond* carries the reader through a meditation on these central terms by submitting the reader to these experiences. Indeed, these figures represent the problem of the non-identical: on one level the terms operate according to a very similar logic, exhibiting and letting us name the movement of fragmentary writing. On another level, however, the differences between return, writing, and dying—not to mention their separation by the *recit* that interrupts Blanchot's argument—prevents their synthesis into a concept of the fragmentary that would, in its unity and presence, efface their multiplicity. Their proximity to one another, and doubling of one another, gives these words an enigmatic quality that multiplies and fragments their significances.

The Eternal Return of the Same takes up the priority given to repetition in the essays on Nietzsche from *The Infinite Conversation*. In *Step*, however, the Eternal Return becomes a way of thinking the impossibility of presence, even within that which seems self-identical. One would think that that which recurs eternally could capture the stability of presence; however, recurrence dislocates this, as origin and completion remain always beyond; the Same *will have been*, but its diachrony means that it is not.[48] Blanchot's use of the future anterior hints at the significance of Derrida's work for this book, as the diachrony of being fissures its seeming totality. As past and future infect one another, the present becomes obscure; the enigma of dissymmetric recurrence inverts one's view of presence, rendering it as an effect of difference.[49]

The diachronic fissuring of presence opens onto the neuter, whose patient ebb and flow are most evident in Blanchot's conception of anonymity. The anonymous neuter, "borne by the *il* that always speaks the name forgotten in advance,"[50] is that which gives the possibility of naming, even while rendering it impossible. The name, as a figure of unity, is also the figure of a political hegemony; names exhibit the "desire to dominate the neuter."[51] Blanchot evokes the naming of the camps, where the name or number becomes the effacement of any singularity in the radical, shameful exposure to a public with no liberty or reserve.[52] Against this, the "passive insistence" of the neuter undoes the force of the name, by remaining beyond it. Ultimately, this resistance fragments the name's unifying presence, turning it into "the non-unity and non-presence of the nameless." In other words, despite its attempt to capture anonymity, the name becomes the mask through which the neuter slips beyond thought. "Signaling to us across signification," while being dissimulates and confirms its nonpresence, the anonymous "welcomes the enigma of being without being's being able to lessen its own enigma."[53]

48. Blanchot, *Step Not Beyond*, 23.
49. Ibid., 42.
50. Ibid., 35.
51. Ibid., 83.
52. Ibid., 38.
53. Ibid., 35.

The neuter, as both sign *and* withdrawal from signification, mirrors Levinas's thought of the enigma's negativity: the "enigma of the neuter, enigma that the neuter reduces even in making it shine in a name,"[54] points to a fragmentary, non-unitary operation of language. This, for Blanchot, is found in the singular power of the name of God—which, far from opening transcendence, turns language back toward its own materiality. The Name's "power of non-designation" shows the failure of language, even while seeking to recuperate its meaning. This taking of weakness for power, the drawing of strength from sickness, can only always fail—an "incurable cure" that forever calls forth further speech. What unsettles and refuses the power of the Name is the worklessness of writing, which Blanchot takes as a figure for dying. As a movement without beginning, dying is not captured or stopped in death. Rather, like the evaporation of water from the road after a summer rain, it only ends through its own movement, without ever really ceasing. As a "normal anomaly," dying/writing cannot be subsumed under a rule. The neuter excludes both immanent presence and transcendent absence, enigmatically remaining within a fragmentary totality—a step *not* beyond. There is, then, a *refusal* of transcendence that characterizes the enigma for Blanchot, putting his work at a distance from Levinas, who sees the enigma as opening a new form of transcendence within sensibility.

As Christophe Bident describes, the poetics of the neuter "is directed toward the attempt to rediscover a just relationship with the world."[55] While accepting Bident's claim, one might note that the justice of the neuter and its refusal of an unjust violence remain concealed in *The Step Not Beyond*. It is in light of this demand for justice that Blanchot returns to the enigma in *The Writing of the Disaster*—in large part, as a critical reading of Levinas's *Otherwise than Being*. It is in heeding the call of the disaster—beyond question or concept—that Blanchot conceives a way of thought and action that would "answer for that which escapes responsibility."[56] While *The Step Not Beyond* thinks the enigma in parallel with Levinas—without engaging his work directly—Blanchot's last return to this figure extends the infinite conversation with Levinas. Engaging with Levinas's conceptions of responsibility, passivity, and saying, *The Writing of the Disaster* exposes Levinasian responsibility to its outside—writing, the accidental, dying.

54. Ibid., 69.
55. Bident, "Poetics of the Neuter," 26.
56. Blanchot, *Step Not Beyond*, 123.

The disaster is, for Blanchot, the "break with the star"—that which undoes any cosmological totality or final word. Its withdrawal microfractures any idea of unity, fissuring it irreparably. The disaster, a "rip forever ripping apart . . . this is what seeks, forming an enigma, to be written, in order to separate us (not once and for all) from the unitary imperative which is necessarily always at work."[57] In its refusal of unity, the disaster denies any progressive or linear philosophy of history;[58] its discontinuity demands an alternate form of reading, as becomes clear in Blanchot's discussion of etymology and myth.

The disaster's separation is rhythmic—always double, never unified, incessantly pulsing without end. "Rhythm's enigma" is dangerous, as it introduces a gap within the subject. Always differing from itself, rhythm separates by "disengaging the multiple from its missing unity."[59] It is in thinking the multiple *as* multiple, in its dispersal, that Blanchot deflects alterity and singularity away from Levinas's view. For Blanchot, the unity of the Name, history, and monotheism all serve to efface the movement of writing/dying, thereby foreclosing ethics even in calling it forth. To think rhythm's enigma is to think the multiple that goes under the name of the unity, since an enigma *must* be multiple in order to be one.

The separation of rhythm creates a relation between thinking and dying. More exactly, as thinking always reduces dying, it is only able to call dying as an "unspoken thought." In the "unbridgeable un-relation" of thinking and dying, the murmured movement of the *il y a* is in play. This un-relation takes an enigmatic form, giving itself to the thought it refuses. There is, here, a form of "downward ascendance," carrying thought beyond any question while giving rise to the question. This enigma, where one thinks in "the absence of the question,"[60] opens speech to a relation without relation—the "separate abiding" of patience that Blanchot names *friendship*.

As the enigma recedes from thought, it undoes its power, revealing a passivity at the heart of the subject. The disaster cannot even be experienced, but rather is undergone (*subissement*) in a passivity beyond patience. Much like Job's passivity as he undergoes the disaster both in his own loss and his friends' miscomprehension, one is passive before the neutral, dispossessed

---

57. Blanchot, *Writing of the Disaster*, 75.
58. See Hart, *Dark Gaze*, 154–57.
59. Blanchot, *Writing of the Disaster*, 112.
60. Ibid., 30.

of all power—even the power to be patient.[61] Passivity, then, is a refusal beyond consciousness or will, an "abstention . . . which precedes all decisions." Such passivity falls "outside of being"[62]—and, not surprisingly, into engagement with Levinas.

The absolute demand of passivity renders responsibility unconditional. Blanchot describes the ambiguity of this responsibility in a moment that recalls Derrida's thought of the impossible. On the one hand, in the other's weakness, the "pure nakedness of supplication," the other dispossesses the subject, exposing one to a responsibility or "awkward weakness" where one "cannot do anything"—a speaking or saying as radical exposure.[63] Yet, even as the other becomes one's master—in Levinas's terms, I become responsible for my persecutor—one must return to knowledge, so as to "refuse, resist, or combat" the domination that would destroy passivity. Like the name whose "presence" maintains the anonymity of the neutral, the labor of language and consciousness maintain the passivity of dying beyond being. Responsibility must be plural in order to be itself—it must be conditioned and reciprocal in order to be absolute. Blanchot is, here, both with and against Levinas at the same time.

Blanchot's description of the "two languages" necessary to think responsibility is, in many ways, very close to Levinas. It parallels the saying/said distinction, particularly in the dispersal of the said into justice by the secret movement of saying. However, it is at this point that the neuter also turns responsibility away from Levinas's view, particularly regarding the unsubstitutability of the subject. To "sustain the enigma of what is announced in the term 'responsibility'"[64] demands a recognition that one's utter dispossession before the other renders one nameless: one's election is purely contingent, and could have been anyone. This is what Blanchot terms *happenstance singularity*: the stranger within oneself responds, exposing the subject to namelessness, exile, and the vulnerable wandering of alterity. In short, the subject undergoes the abandon at the heart of election, as one is consigned to what is unassumable.[65]

This displacement of subjectivity has great significance for Blanchot: as a moment of solidarity outside negativity, it enables a recognition and

61. For more on patience in Blanchot, see Young, "Patience of Job," 604–6.
62. Blanchot, *Writing of the Disaster*, 17.
63. Ibid., 22–23.
64. Ibid., 26.
65. Ibid., 18.

community beyond speech's violence. This political dimension was highlighted in the discussion of *The Unavowable Community* in the previous chapter. Blanchot's central point is that responsibility places the subject beyond being, outside the work of sovereignty and consciousness:

> But when the other is no longer the remote, but the neighbor whose proximity weighs upon me to the point of opening me to the radical passivity of the self, then subjectivity—subjectivity as wounded, blamed, and persecuted exposure, as vulnerability abandoned to difference—falls in its turn outside of being . . . Then subjectivity, in the same capacity as the other and as the face, is the enigma which troubles order and breaks with being: it is the exemption of the extraordinary, exclusion from the domain of that which can appear, exile from the realm of experience.[66]

The subject thus not only responds to the enigma, but *becomes* enigmatic in its very response. Blanchot highlights the undecidable aspect of responsibility: the disaster *pluralizes* responsibility, as the subject must respond as, for, and not-as itself and the other. Enigmatic and fragmentary, the subject's response remains incomplete, always put into question. The infinite, multiple demands of responsibility render the subject infinitely other than itself.

Yet, if the infinitude of responsibility renders the subject infinitely passive, then an ethics that attends to this infinity must recognize or submit to it as well. For Blanchot, this occurs in fragmentary writing—which, as discussed before, distances us from dying. Here, we see why a simple privilege of ethics over art would be wrong, as it would attempt to unify and thematize the multiple. One could even argue that the fragmentary form of *The Step Not Beyond* and *The Writing of the Disaster* exhibits Blanchot's response to the multiple—a response that must be both occasional and incomplete. Fragmentary writing introduces the neutral into the language of dialectic, insinuating the thought of the fragmentary through discontinuous juxtapositions that ruin interpretation.

The enigma of subjectivity not only makes writing an exilic, fragmentary practice,[67] but also reshapes the movement of reading. As in other works (most notably "The Gaze of Orpheus") Blanchot rereads an established myth, contesting its reception and opening alternative meanings. In *The Writing of the Disaster* he rereads the story of Narcissus. No

---

66. Ibid., 24.
67. See Davies, "A Fine Risk," 209.

longer a story of narcissism where one is obsessed with oneself, Blanchot instead highlights Narcissus's not-being himself, as he fails to recognize his own reflection. Narcissus, for Blanchot, is the story of desubjectification or misrecognition: the "adventure of the I" is displaced, becoming anonymous and exposed to the neutral. Beneath the myth of unity, the story of Narcissus testifies to our non-coincidence with ourselves.[68]

Blanchot further reworks our practices of reading through a scathing yet profound critique of etymology. To present an etymological argument—for example, Heidegger's reading of *aletheia* as "un-forgetting"—is a form of "illusory gnosis."[69] Etymology is a "quest for an original secret"—a knowledge hidden even from those who spoke the language one turns to, as Heidegger saw the Greeks as oblivious to the meaning of being.[70] What troubles Blanchot here is the view of history as a "successive continuity" which, in the interest of imposing a certain trajectory of thought, forgets the disaster and contingency of interpretation. For instance, as Blanchot notes, Heidegger's reading of *aletheia* dismisses Plato's alternative *alé-theia*, "divine wandering"—a reading that would foreground an exilic, Levinasian form of truth, rather than the enrootedness of being.[71] The thought of the disaster gives Blanchot a way to contest the premises on which etymology constructs its vision, opening a different thought of history. The enigma of the disaster, in its refusal of completeness, opens a politics rooted in the "principle of insufficiency," which responds to the fragmentary in its submission to dying.

It is quite apparent, then, that the enigma becomes a central figure for both thinkers in the years following *The Infinite Conversation*. As Elisabeth Bosch writes of Blanchot's literary work, the enigma makes possible "an infinity of nuances and creates an atmosphere of mystery where there is place for events and phenomena which situate themselves beyond rational understanding."[72] Like literature, the enigma of revelation or writing may—or may not—lead to engagement and responsibility. In this we see Levinas and Blanchot reworking one another's concepts, transforming them and opening them to further questioning through their multiple encounters. This builds, in many ways, on Blanchot's earlier

68. Blanchot, *Writing of the Disaster*, 134–35.
69. Ibid., 97.
70. Ibid., 114. See Heidegger, "End of Philosophy and the Task of Thinking," in *Basic Writings*, 444–48.
71. Blanchot, *Writing of the Disaster*, 94–95.
72. Bosch, "L'énigme comme force Structurante du Récit," 153.

conception of the ambiguity of literature and politics, as discussed in the opening section of this chapter. The enigma allows them both to conceive a form of immanent transcendence—linking alterity with justice, passivity with writing, and conceiving the infinitude of responsibility. Levinas and Blanchot rethink responsibility in large part through responding to one another—questioning either the impersonality of the neutral, or the unity of God, as a limit to the enigma's obscurity, and thus to the shape of human responsibility. One could say that it is their difference on the nature of the enigma—as manifesting or refusing transcendence—that shows its irreducible multiplicity, and its refusal to be captured by one interpretation.

The dynamic here, as a case study in interreligious friendship, should be illuminated. Both think for themselves by thinking through the words of the other. It is in light of the other's speech, and on the other's behalf, that the thought which is most their own emerges. One's singularity, then, is inseparable from the response to the other, and the movement of the other's writing. This displacement from within is where their friendship resides—in a questioning whose critical edge enigmatically testifies to their fidelity.

In their different responses, one thing that emerges is the demand for multiple, ceaseless voices—plural forms of writing and speech. It is through plural speech that one hears, and can thus respond to, the cry of multiple others. Given this, it is not surprising that commentary, and its ability to integrate multiple voices and perspectives, becomes a central focus in their thought and their intellectual practice. Thus, the next chapter will explore their literary and Talmudic commentary as ethical and political practices, in part to explore how their inter-readings develop their sense of commentary as a model for community and politics.

SIX

These and These Are the Words of the Other
Commentary and the Infinite Conversation

THE RELATIONSHIP BETWEEN LEVINAS and Blanchot has been extensively chronicled in recent years. From their early days at Strasbourg to Blanchot's work to protect Levinas's family during the Nazi occupation of France, their interactions have become central to numerous interpretations of their work—though the relationship is still discounted or ignored by many scholars.[1] In interviews and testamentary writings, both Levinas and Blanchot emphasized the other's importance; as Levinas said in one interview, "He always chose the way the least taken and the most noble, the most difficult."[2] Blanchot likewise concludes *Pour L'Amitié* with a testimony to his intimate friendship with Levinas.[3] While perhaps not the "legendary" friends Blanchot and Bataille would become, in Derrida's terms, it was in response to the other that each pushed his reflection to the limit.

All the same, both the authors themselves and their critics have focused almost exclusively upon the thought of these authors. While thought was clearly central to their lives and work—as Blanchot said, philosophy was the "clandestine friend" that accompanied him and Levinas[4]—the forms of writing through which they generated their thought warrants further reflection. Both were involved in a range of intellectual projects and a variety of publications. It is particularly striking that both Levinas and Blanchot turned to commentary as a privileged form of writing, particularly from the early 1960s onward. Beginning in 1960, Levinas gave (and, for the most

---

1. It should be noted that two of the studies most extensively devoted to Levinas's religious writings—Richard Cohen's *Ethics, Exegesis, and Philosophy*, and Samuel Moyn's *Origins of the Other*—hardly reference Blanchot's presence or centrality for Levinas's thought. By contrast, Large's *Emmanuel Levinas and Maurice Blanchot*, de Vries' *Minimal Theologies*, and Toumayan's *Encountering the Other* make the relationship far more central to their work.
2. Poirié, *Emmanuel Levinas*, 73.
3. Blanchot, *Pour l'Amitié*, 35.
4. Blanchot, "Our Clandestine Companion," 42.

part, published) annual Talmudic commentaries, while Blanchot shifted away from narratives (*recits*) and novels to a more oblique, "plural" style of fragment writing that operates through commentary on other texts.

This chapter focuses on the role of commentary in their later work, and its significance for them as a literary and philosophical form of writing. Commentary, as I use the term here, is a distinctive style of writing that eludes generic classification. For Levinas, while it operates at the level of biblical and Talmudic interpretation, commentary is often a philosophically informed discourse, straddling and troubling the "Jewish/philosophical" distinction that Levinas offers to classify his texts. Likewise, while Blanchot remains suspicious of the term "commentary," his critical writings on literature and philosophy unsettle any strict distinctions between philosophy, poetry, and prose. As a polyphonic form of writing, commentary holds the possibility of speech in the "third relation," exposure to the neutral that is the experience of literature. For both thinkers, the unsettling aspects of commentary become clearer over the course of their work, and their works shift in style and tone so as to hold open this possibility.

As their views of commentary[5] become clearer over the course of their work, a study of their practice of commentary relates to a number of central issues. For both authors, commentary provides a way to speak (or write) philosophically that avoids the closure and finality of Heideggerian interpretation. As commentary may be a form of writing that opens itself to the other's response, it undoes the unifying authority with which philosophical truth has often been imposed. In undoing this force, it makes possible a more responsible speech, one open to the voice of the other or the neuter. In their emphasis on commentary, what emerges is a shared commitment to a conception of plural speech—speech open to otherness and resistant to totality. All the same, how commentary is written remains a central point of contention between them, in large part informed by the aesthetic conflicts discussed in the preceding chapters.

This chapter begins with a study of Levinas's Talmudic commentaries. It explores how Talmudic study—which involves listening to and participating in the conversation of commentary—becomes more central over the course of Levinas's writings, and how an openness to the plurality of commentary becomes a defining mark of holiness in reading, especially

---

5. While Blanchot criticizes the term, I will use it here for simplicity, and to emphasize the parallels in their approaches. The differences that remain will be addressed more extensively below.

in his later work. The parallel discussion of Blanchot's commentary begins by exploring some of his wartime literary criticism, recognizing how these writings served as a central transition from the journalism of the 1930s to the better-known criticism of *The Space of Literature* and thereafter. It concludes with a commentary on *The Infinite Conversation*, where Blanchot comments on Levinas's first major work, articulating the ideas of fragment writing and the indestructibility of humanity. Both of these issues would become central thematics in Blanchot's later writings. For both Levinas and Blanchot, their conceptions of commentary shift over the course of their careers, particularly in moving from a unitary conception of interpretation and responsibility toward a pluralized, polyphonic form of writing. By thus tracing the respective paths of commentary within Blanchot's and Levinas's works, the significance of commentary as a responsive form of writing will emerge, in ways that show both their deep affinity and the gulf that separates them on the question of religion.

RITUAL, DISCIPLINE, AND STUDY

In examining Levinas's Talmudic commentaries, several critical issues shape how one reads these complex and intricate texts. Levinas's own description of these commentaries raises the question of how they relate to his more explicitly or self-consciously philosophical work. Levinas describes his Jewish or "Hebrew"[6] writings as separate from his philosophical explorations, and the independence of these writings should be respected such that they can be read on their own terms; however, a neat demarcation between the two groups of works does not really hold up. This is, in part, because there are clearly overlaps between the conceptualities at work in the Talmudic writings, and Levinas's contemporaneous philosophical work—as shall be discussed further with regard to the issue of "youth." Second, however, Levinas's practice of reading the Talmudic texts is perhaps best seen as a philosophical form of exegesis, as Robert Gibbs and others have argued, and significant questions have been raised about how deeply his commentaries root themselves in the Jewish tradition.[7] Finally, as shall be explored below, there are shifts in emphasis within Levinas's own commentaries in terms of how he articulates the relation between Talmudic commentary and ethical

---

6. See Gibbs, *Correlations in Rosenzweig and Levinas*, 156–58.
7. Kavka, "Is There Warrant for Levinas's Talmudic Readings?" 170–71.

responsibility—shifts which parallel, and I would argue play into, his revaluations of Christianity, philosophy, and politics.

> That which is more profound than the conscience, than interiority—
> it is books.[8]

Over the course of Levinas's lectures, Talmudic study takes a more and more central place as a redemptive, ethical practice. As shall be discussed below, whereas earlier lectures emphasize various liturgical and ritual dimensions of Judaism as central to the cultivation of an openness to ethical responsibility, in the later essays it is Talmudic study itself—as commentary—that is more closely linked with responsibility. For Levinas, what is particularly central to Talmudic study—as represented by both the Talmud as the expression of the oral Torah and the practice of commentary on the Talmud—is its opening of the scriptural texts to new meanings and interpretations. This openness exposes the subject to the prophetic responsibility to the poor, the widow, and the orphan; where the Scriptures cry out, "Interpret me!" study *responds* to this cry and command. As there is always the risk of foreclosing the significance of Scripture and shutting down conversation, the Talmud as study makes possible a relation to infinity through its pluralization, demystification, and the "endless return" of reading. As Levinas writes, commentary is "the reading or study of a text that protects itself from eventual idolatry of this very text, by renewing, through continual exegesis—and exegesis of that exegesis—the immutable letters and hearing the breath of the living God in them."[9]

This emerging emphasis on study carries important ramifications for Levinas's conceptions of ethics and politics. In shifting the inspiration of responsibility from particular liturgies of Judaism to commentary and study, Levinas implicitly recognizes the possibility of a revelation (like the oral Torah itself) that exceeds the written Scriptures given at Sinai. This shift, I would argue, is part of what enables him to give more attention to what Derrida terms a "revelation before Sinai,"[10] in which other nations and their forms of thought may participate. At the same time, however, the shift to study makes possible new forms of political critique, and even begins to articulate a new form of political praxis. "Study" resonates closely with two important movements in political and ethical philosophy. First,

---

8. Interview of Levinas in Poirié, *Emmanuel Levinas*, 160.
9. Levinas, *In the Time of Nations*, 59.
10. Derrida, *Adieu to Emmanuel Levinas*, 117–20.

it comes very close to the "educative" form of divine violence that Walter Benjamin briefly discusses, as the central form of messianic life that challenges the mythical violence of the state. In its valorization of the proximity of humanity, and its refusal of political power and violence, study incarnates the messianic transcendence that contests and breaks apart the closed political world of war and combat.[11]

Secondly, and in an equally intriguing way, Levinas argues that study (in the Talmudic sense) cannot be a purely intellectual or cognitive exercise. Rather, as a form of openness and attentiveness that demands obedience to the commands that are its focus, Talmudic study combines doing and learning. It thereby models a form of thought that is also a way of life, to use Pierre Hadot's term.[12] To see Talmudic study as a way of living, and as a cluster of spiritual exercises, makes it both more like philosophy (in the ancient sense) and yet still distinctive, in terms of the particular form of life it makes possible.

The emergence of Levinas's Talmudic work in the late 1950s is well documented. As Levinas himself says on many occasions, particularly within his Talmudic lectures, though he was taught in "the square letters" of Hebrew, he had not received any formal Talmudic learning in his youth. His most significant and enigmatic influence was the mysterious M. Chouchani, who guided Levinas in Talmudic studies beginning in the late 1940s, and who passed away suddenly during the publication of the first volume of lectures in 1966 (*Difficult Freedom* was dedicated to him). Levinas often credited Chouchani with modeling a way of reading that avoided pietistic, religious, or mystical readings of a text, but rather sought to read the Talmud in light of a contemporary problematic or issue. As Levinas says in the introduction to his first published Talmudic commentaries,

> He has made a dogmatic approach based purely on faith or even a theological approach to the Talmud altogether impossible for us. Our attempt must attest to this search for freedom even if it does not attest to a freedom already possessed . . . Without it, the sovereign exercise of the intelligence recorded in the pages of the Talmud can change itself, too, into the litany or pious murmur of a consent given beforehand, a reproach that could be made to Talmudists whose familiarity with these pages is nevertheless to be envied.[13]

11. See Benjamin, "Critique of Violence," 297–98.
12. See Hadot, *Philosophy as a Way of Life*.
13. Levinas, *Nine Talmudic Readings*, 8–9.

Levinas presented his Talmudic readings in the annual Colloquium of French-Speaking Jewish Intellectuals.[14] In these forums, Levinas's Talmudic work would be preceded by others' lectures, to which he often refers in his comments.

While a range of recent studies has examined Levinas's Talmudic work in great detail from both sympathetic and critical perspectives, the variance and change within Levinas's Talmudic work over time has received less attention. I would like to open a path for exploring the chronology of his work, while recognizing that the issues raised here warrant further scrutiny. Specifically, what is intriguing is how the ritual practice of Judaism becomes less central to Levinas's interpretations as one moves from the earlier to the later commentaries. On one level, this is not surprising, as Levinas confines himself to haggadic commentary, rather than work with the legal concerns of halakhah. However, when one looks at the significance of ritual in Levinas's early Talmudic readings, its absence becomes more noteworthy in his later writings.

In Levinas's early texts, the central significance of ritual is the discipline it creates. While not directly ethical, rituals open the subject to responsibility and to a recognition of the other's vulnerability. Ritual thus creates a space for the inter-human. In Levinas's first reading, this occurs through a discussion of the festival of Sukkot, in which living in the booths reminds the Jewish people of the impermanence and fragility of the state and its institutions—thereby opening them to transcendence in a way that other peoples refuse.[15] Ritual and liturgy thus guard against the ontological closure that might otherwise occur; as Gibbs writes, the festival "creates a concrete exceptionality to the security and the power of the state."[16] Ritual also serves as a demarcation between Judaism and other religions and cultures—notably, philosophy and Christianity—as the Talmudic view is that other nations would reject Sukkot and disrespect religion.

Jewish ritual also plays a critical role in several of Levinas's essays and commentaries from the early 1960s. In "The Ark and the Mummy," he links it with the practice of demystification, by which holiness and ethics emerge

---

14. See Gibbs, *Correlations in Rosenzweig and Levinas*, 155. Gibbs provides a very helpful chronology of the lectures (175) as well, to which I am indebted in tracing the development of Levinas's Talmudic work.

15. Here, I am relying on the reading by Gibbs in "Levinas, the Messianic, and the Question of History," 271-84.

16. Gibbs, "Levinas, the Messianic," 279-80.

from the sacred. "The people who wish to demystify the world nonetheless have a life that is subject to those numerous prohibitions which constitute the practices of Jewish ritual . . . the learned foundation of these disciplines . . . was for centuries the guarantee of this independence of spirit."[17] Even for more secular or liberal Jews today, the tradition of this "disciplined and highly inconvenient life" creates the ethical identity of Judaism. A more extensive discussion of this point is found in "A Religion for Adults," where Levinas again refers to ritual law as "austere discipline."[18] The point of ritual, for Levinas, is in its regular training and shaping of identity, so that one may then be for the other. As he writes,

> The law is effort. The daily fidelity to the ritual gesture demands a courage that is calmer, nobler and greater than that of the warrior . . . The Talmudist does not hesitate to link this royal awakening to the sovereign power of a people capable of the daily ritual . . . The law for the Jew is never a yoke. It carries its own joy, which nourishes a religious life and the whole of Jewish mysticism.[19]

A vivid and specific discussion of ritual's ethical dimension comes in Levinas's first published Talmudic commentary, "Toward the Other." In his discussion of the Day of Atonement, Levinas examines which offenses God may forgive directly—and which may only be forgiven by other people. Ritual offenses, he argues, are forgivable by God, while God cannot forgive on behalf of others; only repentance and requesting forgiveness from the victim can bring forgiveness for these.[20] Given this distinction, one would expect Levinas to emphasize sins against one's neighbors and responsibility for these as the central aspects of Judaism. Yet, in a surprising reversal, he argues that the ritual offenses and sins against God impact ethics even more deeply than particular offenses. The passage is worth quoting at length:

> It could be concluded a bit hastily that Judaism values social morality above ritual practices. But the order could also be reversed . . . does calling these ritual transgressions "transgressions against God" diminish the gravity of the illness that the Soul has contracted as a result of these transgressions? Perhaps the ills that must heal inside the Soul without the help of others are precisely the most profound ills, and that even where our social faults are concerned, once our

17. Levinas, *Difficult Freedom*, 54.
18. Ibid., 18.
19. Ibid., 19.
20. Gibbs, "Returning/Forgiving," 73–91.

neighbor has been appeased, the most difficult part remains to be done. In doing wrong toward God, have we not undermined the moral conscience as moral conscience? The ritual transgression that I want to erase without resorting to the help of others would be precisely the one that demands all of my personality; it is the work of *Teshuvah*, of Return, for which no one can take my place.

To be before God would be equivalent then to this total mobilization of oneself. Ritual transgression—and that which is an offense against God in the offense against my neighbor—would destroy me more utterly than the offense against others. But taken by itself and separated from the impiety it contains, the ritual transgression is the source of my cruelty, my harmfulness, my self-indulgences.[21]

In destroying the conscience—destroying one's sense of responsibility—ritual transgression opens the possibility of evil and violence against the neighbor. Thus, inversely, ritual figures as either that which heals the conscience (as in repentance before God, on Yom Kippur), or that which guards against such illness. Ritual is a "total mobilization," which protects from evil and prepares one for ethical action.

These selections indicate that in his early commentaries Levinas saw ritual practice as a central, essential component of ethical responsibility. This is important, in my view, because over the course of the next thirty years this ritual emphasis will diminish. The shift can be marked, in some ways, within the deeply intriguing commentary "The Youth of Israel," which opens the second volume of Talmudic writings, *From the Sacred to the Holy* (published in English as part of *Nine Talmudic Readings*). In this commentary from 1970, Levinas discusses the Nazirate (the institution and ritual life of Nazirites, individuals who consecrate themselves to God for a period), as a figure of "youth." In accord with Levinas's emphasis on how the texts speak to us today, he chose this text because of an article from *Le Monde*, in which like the Nazirites, the youth of France refused to cut their hair as a protest against their society. The Nazirite's exceptional life thus becomes a figure of youth, posing a challenge to his society's norms.[22]

Within the commentary, however, a shift occurs. The first part of the commentary discusses the practices of the Nazirite, and gives an interpretation of them. A Nazirite takes the following vows for a set period of time: not cutting one's hair, avoiding contact with the dead, and avoiding all fruits and products of the vine (including wine). Levinas gives a philosophical

21. Levinas, *Nine Talmudic Readings*, 17.
22. Ibid., 121.

interpretation; he argues that avoiding death is a way of avoiding nihilism or despair, abstinence from the vine gives lucidity and vigilance (don't sleep like Samson!), and long hair is a way of being "straightforward" and unconcerned about appearance. What intrigues Levinas most about the rite, however, is that at the end of the Nazirate (the period of the vow), the adherent must cut all his hair off to avoid the vanity that would come from long hair: "Why is one obligated to shave one's head as soon as the vows of the nazirate are over? Perhaps to prevent the noble violence one has done to oneself from becoming sweet custom and the protest against institutions from becoming an institution."[23] The rites of the Nazirate thus create the temporality of youth, maintaining a dynamism and movement, refusing to get stuck in the past (perhaps unlike some Deadheads and other aging hippies today), through a constant undoing of identity. "Long hair worn as a uniform—that is the great scandal of long hair." Through these rites, the Nazirite comes to embody disinterestedness, the movement beyond being that opens one to the ethical and displaces one's identity. The rite and its revocation exemplify the dialectic of saying and said discussed in chapter 5, opening one to alterity and guarding against a good conscience through the unsaying of one's vow.[24] As in the previously discussed writings, ritual cultivates a disciplined responsibility.

Toward the end of the essay, however, Levinas traces a shift in the Talmudic text, and this shift is, I would argue, emblematic of the trajectory of his work. After discussions of exceptions to the rites, the final section turns to the study of Torah as that which gives youth. Here, it is in knowing and studying the Torah that one becomes a Nazirite, and from such study one brings youth and peace to the world.

> The children of Israel, students of the Torah, are youth par excellence. They are the ones who, in receiving the Torah, renew it . . . Great is the peace of your builders. To receive while building. To bring peace into the world by renewing it constructively, that is the youth of the nazirate, that is youth.[25]

As study renews the world, and creates a receptivity that Levinas calls a "youth before youth," it becomes the religious practice that embodies ethical responsibility par excellence.

---

23. Ibid., 124.
24. For more on this connection see Young, "Betrayals of Vulnerability."
25. Levinas, *Nine Talmudic Readings*, 134.

While caution is required here, this text does mark a notable shift: in the ensuing Talmudic commentaries, ritual practice is rarely referenced, and its place as a disciplinary, formative ethical practice is far less central. By contrast, the practice of *study* of the Talmud takes on far greater significance, and it becomes a form of ethical practice. One could certainly argue that the study of the Law and its practice go hand in hand; however, there is a rhetorical shift that warrants reflection.

My hypothesis as to the change in Levinas's rhetoric would be that his shift in emphasis parallels the broader philosophical shift that he undertakes in moving from *Totality and Infinity* to *Otherwise than Being*. "The Youth of Israel" was written at the same time as the central essay "No Identity," in which Levinas articulates a parallel conception of youth from a phenomenological vantage point. This view of youth also becomes central to the discussion of vulnerability in *Otherwise than Being*.[26] The shift from ritual to study thus parallels the philosophical shift away from a substantial identity that responds to the other, to a sense of ethics as the way that one is "hollowed out" through vulnerability, or undergoes a de-coring, (*denucléation*), such that one is exposed to a uniqueness and singularity beyond identity. As a vulnerable subject, alterity emerges from within oneself, in what William Large terms an "inclusive" relation, rather than one based on exteriority.[27]

The shift away from ritual makes sense, in part, because Levinas had frequently interpreted ritual as building or disciplining character, so as to *create* a certain identity. By contrast, in study one is already bound by the text's alterity, hostage to the voices and readings both therein and of other people. Study, then, is something that undoes identity, rather than reinforcing it. As inter-human life, Talmudic study is both a preparation for and the practice of ethical responsibility, as it is defined in Levinas's later work.

The shift from a valorization of practice to the valorization of commentary is significant, in part because of the deontologized form of subjectivity it underwrites—one much closer, in many ways, to Blanchot's. This will become significant, as both authors revise their understanding and practice of commentary, in ways that are remarkably similar. However, there are other dimensions to this shift as well. In the later Talmudic writings, Levinas adopts a less polemical approach to Christianity than in the

26. See Young, "Betrayals of Vulnerability."
27. Large, *Emmanuel Levinas and Maurice Blanchot*, 32–33.

writings of *Difficult Freedom;* he also articulates politics more as an extension of ethics in the name of justice, rather than as the "betrayal" or collapse of the ethical into an ontology of violence.[28] This is a significant move, since it is the perceived failure of his earlier works to move beyond a "negative" moment that has brought Levinas in for extensive criticism in political theory.[29] Perhaps, one could say, study becomes the mode of thought that enables a redemptive politics.

DIRTY HANDS, HOLINESS, AND SCRIPTURAL COMMENTARY

With his increased emphasis on scriptural study in the later Talmudic works, Levinas addresses in several places the question of holiness in Judaism. A central question that arises is how one recognizes a revelatory scripture, and thus distinguishes a source of holiness from a mythical or "sacred" text. Levinas addresses this issue by exploring debates regarding the canon of Holy Scripture[30] among the rabbis. What is most intriguing, here, is that Levinas defines the revelatory character of scriptures negatively—via the misuse or misinterpretation to which they may give rise. The ways that holy scriptures can "make the hands dirty" or create an impurity in the reader are precisely what reveal them to be transmissions of revelation. This is in part because it is the *risk* of impurity—or, one could say, of thematizing reduction—that creates the space for an ethical *reading* of the text. In many ways, this returns us to the enigmas discussed in the last chapter. Holiness, like responsibility, takes an enigmatic form.

The issue of impure hands arises in two of Levinas's later Talmudic commentaries—"For a Place in the Bible" (1981) and "The Translation of Scripture" (1984). They are the opening essays of *In the Time of Nations*, his

---

28. Here, I follow Oona Ajzenstat, "Levinas in the Key of the Political."

29. On this point see Dussel, "'The Politics' by Levinas." One could thus see Levinas's later work as moving toward a more constructive position, rather than simply negating the view of politics as war by other means that he sees as implicit in Heideggerian ontology. However, I would caution that the move from ethics to constructive politics for Levinas is not a straightforward one, and may give readers pause. I would refer the reader to Howard Caygill's *Levinas and the Political*, 187–98, which raises some necessary questions about Levinas's response to the massacres in the Palestinian refugee camps in 1982.

30. In calling scripture "holy scripture" as opposed to "sacred scripture," I am holding to Levinas's distinction between the sacred and the holy, as between that "sacred" which remains within the mythical or ontological and that "holiness" which opens to the infinite, responsibility, and thus revelation.

next-to-last published collection of Talmudic lectures. In different ways, both address the relationship between holy scripture and other texts. In "For a Place in the Bible," the issue is the limits of the biblical canon, while "The Translation of Scripture" focuses on whether the language of Scripture can find appropriate expression in Greek and other languages. Interestingly, both texts focus on the scroll (or book) of Esther as a text that raises unique problems and issues of interpretation. I will focus on this more extensively below.

Levinas explicates the phrase "make the hands impure" extensively in "For a Place in the Bible." Impure hands are *asqaniot*—"always busy, taking hold of everything."[31] This grasping and searching suggests to Levinas a certain approach to the texts that does violence:

> And is the hand just a hand and not also a certain impudence of spirit that seizes a text savagely, without preparation or teacher, approaching the verse as a thing or an allusion to history in the instrumental nakedness of its vocables, without regard for the new possibilities of their semantics, patiently opened up by the religious life of tradition? Without precautions, without mediation, without all that has been acquired through a long tradition strewn with contingencies, but which is the opening up of horizons through which alone the ancient wisdom of the Scriptures reveals the secrets of a renewed inspiration. Touched by the impatient, busy hand that is supposedly objective and scientific, the Scriptures, cut off from the breath that lives within them, become unctuous, false or mediocre words, matters for doxographers, for linguists and philologists. Therein lies the impurity of these inspired texts, their latent impurity.[32]

As Jacob Meskin writes, "Touching the 'uncovered Torah scroll' here means approaching the Torah *de novo*, without any respect for or acknowledgement of the traditional requirements of preliminary study and prior formation of mind and character."[33] While Meskin is right that Levinas highlights a formational dimension of reading—one lacking in *Wissenschaft*-style approaches to scripture—there are additional dimensions to the impurity that concerns Levinas here.

In "The Translation of Scripture," Levinas says that the reading of inspired scripture requires wisdom—"a wisdom without which the message

---

31. Levinas, *In the Time of Nations*, 24.
32. Ibid.
33. Meskin, "Critique, Tradition, and the Religious Imagination," 96.

buried deep within the enigma of the text cannot be grasped."[34] Impurity, then, is to lack or ignore such wisdom. One must *have* wisdom, to *gain* inspiration from scripture! What Levinas means, apparently, is that inspiration by scripture calls for a certain form of reading: first, to read a biblical text in relation to other scriptural passages, and second, to read as part of a community, in light of authoritative and communal readings that precede one's own subjectivity. Impurity, then, would presume to already know what the text could say, whereas wisdom would require a humility that opens itself to others' voices and an intertextual dimension of interpretation.

These two dimensions of wisdom are reflected to different degrees in the two lectures' interpretations of the book of Esther. In "For a Place in the Bible," Levinas highlights the ways that arguments both for and against Esther's inclusion in the Bible proceed via intertextuality. For example, Proverbs 22:20 argues for committing maxims to writing—"Three times and not four!" As Esther is the fourth story of the Israelites' struggle with the Amalekites, this verse suggests that her story should *not* be canonical. However, other verses, which emphasize that one should "write this for a remembrance" (Exod 17:14) are set forth by other rabbis as applying to the scroll of Esther, and thus as arguments for inclusion.

"The Translation of Scripture" explores the issue of the translatability of scripture, with several rabbis arguing that scriptures can be translated into any language without losing their holiness. In any language, they would still "make the hands impure." Others argue that the meaning can be translated, but the Hebrew letters must be retained.[35] However, a competing view is that the Scriptures are more translatable into certain languages—most notably, Greek, as demonstrated in the centrality of the Septuagint. This translatability is significant, for Levinas, both in terms of its connection with philosophy, and in how it allows for a connection between the holiness of the Scriptures and the everyday life of the people,[36] even while risking assimilation and a loss of identity.

Esther becomes central in terms of the debate over untranslatability. The Talmudic discussion begins with a textual argument, like those discussed above. Esther is written "to the Jews," which would suggest a particular audience and thus no need for translation. Moreover, the text risks a confusion of Hebrew and Aramaic, which seems to be the primary

34. Levinas, *In the Time of Nations*, 39.
35. Ibid., 42.
36. Ibid., 47–48.

concern for this debate. On this basis, Rav Pappan and Rav Nahman argue it should remain untranslated; however, the arguments set forth by Rav Pappan and Rav Nachman are, ultimately, suspended: the Talmud decides neither for nor against their position.

The Talmud thus records a disagreement without resolving it. The particular arguments, set forth by individuals, are respected and heard without being closed down. This openness of interpretation within the Talmud is crucial to Levinas. As he writes, "That Law lives through the multiplicity of persons and despite the aspiration to agreement, a hope that is never suspended, but that finds dogma distasteful."[37] Through its form—over against a philosophical reasoning where one view vanquishes or subordinates others—Talmudic reasoning maintains difference, respecting the plurality of the different views, and opening a space for future readers' engagement.

While the form of Talmudic reasoning is thus central for Levinas, the particulars of this debate further illuminate the ethical problematics of translation. As Levinas highlights, Esther is the biblical story of persecution in the Diaspora; it therefore raises the question of who can understand the experience of persecution and suffering:

> The Scroll of Esther, a book about persecution, a book on anti-Semitism, is intelligible only to Jews in their language and their writing. The suffering of anti-Semitic persecution can only be told in the language of the victim. It is conveyed through signs that are not interchangeable. It is not, whatever the sociologists may say, a particular case of a general phenomenon, even if all the other problems taken up in the Scriptures are inter-human and can be translated into all languages . . . Here, in the Scroll of Esther, there is persecution . . . Is the word "holocaust" not too Greek to express the Passion?[38]

In translation, the story of anti-Semitic persecution becomes generalized, reducing the uniqueness of suffering to a particular case of a general rule. Since, as Levinas writes in the epigraph to *Otherwise than Being*, anti-Semitism attacks the unique, irreducible subjectivity of humanity prior to any identity,[39] such translation inevitably distorts and thus participates

---

37. Ibid., 43.

38. Ibid., 46.

39. The epigraph reads: "To the memory of those who were closest among the six million assassinated by the National Socialists, and of the millions on millions of all confessions and all nations, victims of the same hatred of the other man, the same anti-semitism."

in the suffering of the victim. To refuse to translate suffering, to refuse to comprehend it, is to hear the cry within the story; as Levinas writes in "Useless Suffering," the ethics of being for the other begins from this unassumable suffering that both manifests evil and creates a space for the inter-human.[40] Thus, while translation is necessary, its ineluctable distortion of suffering must be recalled, as a form of "unsaying" that conditions any act of translation.

As is clear from Meskin's article, one concern in Levinas's discussion of "the impatient, busy hand" that "cut off" the Scriptures from "the breath that lives within them" is the historicist treatment of scripture. This is a concern that runs from early in his Talmudic commentaries through the later ones, and has been addressed by a number of scholars.[41] For Levinas, a historicist interpretation would preclude the possibility of exegesis, in which the text could speak to other generations or have a meaning that transcended its original historical context. As should be clear in light of preceding discussions, such transcendence is not an eternal or ethereal meaning—but, rather, the ability of a text to have significance in other times and places, and especially in the current intellectual climate. Levinas argues in multiple essays that the Talmud presents a counter-historicist perspective, particularly insofar as it presents an openness and dynamism within the biblical scriptures themselves. A reading that "grasps" the text, so as to constrain it to a particular historical meaning or source, contracts and ultimately chokes off the life of interpretation which the text enables.

While Levinas's explicit target in many of his comments on "dirty hands" is historical criticism—be it that of Spinoza,[42] or more recent versions—his interpretation of this image of impurity warrants further reflection. First, in reading these essays today, one may be struck by how much his critique could be applied to literalist, anti-modern readings of Scripture (often simplistically labeled "fundamentalist"). Such readings—

---

40. Levinas, "Useless Suffering," 371–74. What "Useless Suffering" also highlights—as does the epigraph of *Otherwise than Being*—is the universality of its victims, as anti-Semitism may target the humanity of anyone, either Jew or non-Jew.

41. In preparation for this discussion, the following sources have been especially central: Moyn, "Emmanuel Levinas's Talmudic Readings" and *Origins of the Other*; Ajzenstat, *Driven Back to the Text*, 236–75; and Gibbs, "Levinas, the Messianic, and the Question of History." I would particularly highlight Moyn's and Ajzenstat's discussions of the "messianic texts" from *Difficult Freedom*, as they provide sharply opposed readings of Levinas's position and the level of fidelity to tradition that it displays.

42. See "Spinoza's Background" in Levinas, *Beyond the Verse*, 168–73.

Jewish or Christian, and there could be analogues in other religions—"grasp" a text, taking it as something that can be read in plain view, and with the unbridled authority of the individual reader. Levinas's emphasis on Talmudic reading, then, would seem to challenge these anti-modern approaches, and provide an alternative religious hermeneutic.[43]

While such an application is intriguing, in my view there is another target lurking in the shadow of these references. A hermeneutic in which a hand "grasps" that which it takes to be ready at hand, "unveiled" to it as something for its appropriation? As so often with Levinas, behind the historicist mantle one finds him wrestling once again with Heidegger. On the one (dirty) hand, to reference Heidegger here is puzzling, because his Scriptural references are negligible. However, what I would suggest is that Heidegger's method of "grasping," even within philosophy, appears impure to Levinas precisely because it denies the possibility of holiness. More concretely, Heidegger represents a certain impurity insofar as his practice of interpretation forecloses other interpretive possibilities and meanings—thereby shutting down a sociality of commentary that hears and responds to others.

A brief illustration, followed by the contrast with Talmudic reading, may show where Heidegger goes wrong. In his form of questioning—for example, the question "What is Being?"—Heidegger articulates his problematic in a way that excludes all answers but one; the ontological difference becomes the only way to think through the meaning of Being, and thereby of temporality and history. Effectively, this dismisses all prior responses—from Plato through Nietzsche—as unable to consider the problem properly. In a way that perhaps epitomizes historicism, the panoramic view situates all other views as historically located (or ontically determined), and thus lets Heidegger interpret in a way reminiscent of Bentham's "god-effect"—to see others without being seen. This interpretive positioning insulates Heidegger's approach from criticism, and silences other voices—effectively reducing ontology to a single view.

By contrast, Levinas highlights the ways that in a Talmudic discussion, disagreement and minority opinions are preserved as a way of retaining the

---

43. In a very different context, Hans Frei often used the Talmud, and more broadly the practice of midrash, as a model for reconceiving the literal sense of Scripture on Christian terms, in ways that preserved an openness and ethical sensibility that are analogous to Levinas's concerns regarding polyphony, while still working within the particularity of his tradition. See Young, "Identity of the Literal Sense," 631–32.

openness of the text. Thus, reading Scripture in light of the Talmud requires a different form of questioning, one that participates in and reopens a conversation, whose plurality of voices signifies the irreducible plurality of meanings in the text. As Levinas writes,

> Rabbinicial hermeneutics [is] . . . an act of soliciting which issues from people whose eyes and ears are vigilant and who are mindful of the whole body of writing from which the extract comes, and equally attuned to life: the city, the street, other men. An act of soliciting which issues from people in their uniqueness, each person capable of extracting from the signs meanings which each time are inimitable . . . It does . . . amount to understanding *the very plurality of people as an unavoidable moment of the signification of meaning*.[44]

One can, and should, question whether Levinas's approach to the Talmud accurately portrays the relations between different people within the text, and in reading it. The lack of any discussion of authority, as a component of commentary, is especially notable. That said, the connection of ethics and hermeneutics within Levinas's view emerges with clarity: to read Scripture through the Talmud requires attentiveness to the uniqueness of others; one speaks in response to and in light of these other voices—as responsible to them, so as to open further possibilities of speech for others. One does not interpret in a way that closes off discussion or gives the last word, but rather leaves it to whomever will follow. In this light, Levinas's frequent admissions of his "amateur" status in reading the Talmud—even in light of his years of study with M. Chouchani—take on a different significance. Levinas's readings are philosophical, but they are also readings that open the texts to readers who lack a professional or scholarly training. Not that any reading thereby becomes viable, so much as that any reader who performs an "act of soliciting" from the plurality of voices in the text would be offering a legitimate textual interpretation. Could the Talmud disseminate the interpretive authority that Heidegger and historicists would accord to themselves? At the least, the contrast in their interpretive stances is striking, and may help us to understand why Levinas turned to Talmudic commentary as a central practice of his intellectual work. Perhaps against the agonistic struggle of Heideggerian thought, Levinas's commentary presents an irenic possibility. With this later emphasis on the plurality of interpretive voices in mind, we may now turn to Blanchot's commentary.

44. Levinas, *Beyond the Verse*, 110; emphasis added.

CRITICISM IN THE SHADOW OF WAR: BLANCHOT'S EARLY LITERARY CRITICISM

Blanchot's earliest literary reviews were central to his development within the French and Parisian cultural milieu. Through his wartime writings, he gradually transitioned from political journalism to literary criticism proper, as well as the novels and *recits* that marked his singular authorship. As Leslie Hill describes, there is a shift from the polemical journalism of 1937 to the detached voice of 1947, when his literary and critical books were first published.[45] Much like his character Thomas in *Thomas l'Obscur*, he worked by day as a journalist and reviewer, while writing novels by night. Beyond the material support his reviews provided, then, the critical writings of this period help to trace his transition from the early nationalist politics that have dogged his career to a "politics of refusal" that sought to resist cooptation through a rigorous literary practice. Significantly, these reviews also emerged in the wake of his initial encounter with Georges Bataille, the friendship which, along with that with Levinas, would shape Blanchot's thought most profoundly.[46] In these reviews, his conceptions of poetry and the novel start to diverge from Heidegger, marking the path for both the critical works and the novels that follow. As with Levinas, I would argue that there is a shift in the form and the focus of Blanchot's criticism, with an emerging focus on plural speech and resistance to interpretive closure in Blanchot's later writings. This emerging focus on pluralization—which has just been highlighted in Levinas's work—represents a significant, though overlooked, dimension of their intellectual friendship.

The reviews collected and published in *Faux Pas* were initially published in the *Journal des Debats*, a highly conservative and nationalist journal. Blanchot had written for the *Journal* since 1933, and served as *redacteur* until 1940.[47] During the war, the *Journal* was supported by the Vichy government; Blanchot apparently refused any involvement beyond weekly reviews, and he wrote these reviews most likely due to economic hardship. While economic hardship may justify some choices, the volume's title indicates Blanchot's own view of his work in this setting—*Faux Pas*

---

45. Hill, *Blanchot: Extreme Contemporary*, 48–50.

46. For more on their friendship, see Kaufman, *Delirium of Praise*, 18–36.

47. For further examination of the interwar writings, their nationalist elements, and their relative obscurity in Blanchot's reception, see Ungar, *Scandal and Aftereffect*, 81–136.

indicates that he saw his own work as a false step, or one he should not have taken.[48]

While ostensibly withdrawing from direct political involvement, the implicit politics of Blanchot's writings did lead to occasional censorship. A consistent concern throughout the essays in *Faux Pas* is the form of literary discourse proper to the novel. As Blanchot writes, the novel's artistry consists in its realization of a certain poetic possibility. With few exceptions he saw the French novels of the period as falling short of this. As he writes in "The New Novel," "The French novel is undergoing a sort of crisis."[49] The crisis consists in writers choosing to borrow from everyday life—remaining within social and linguistic conventions, exhibiting a "puerile taste for realism." This artistic focus on imitation means literature "borrows from external truth the verisimilitude that makes a coherence"; stories gain their coherence from their relation to actual historical events. Such grounding of novelistic discourse in mimesis and a correspondence to historical truth, however, leads to a literary conformism that Blanchot labels "decadence." A similar aesthetic also shapes the literary criticism, as Blanchot discusses how René Lalou sees the novel as "the mirror of an era" in "The Enigma and the Novel."[50]

As Hill notes, the rhetoric of "The New Novel" strongly echoes Blanchot's political writings of the 1930s, with its focus on the loss of French identity, decadence, and a certain weakness of spirit that blindly holds to convention and tradition.[51] It bears echoes of anti-semitism. When one considers that this was published in May 1941 under the Vichy regime, one cannot help but consider its political import. However, I would suggest that while these texts still bear traces of Blanchot's earlier politics, the catastrophic defeat of France turns this rhetoric in a new direction—via what I would term a subterranean resistance. The French novel—and, perhaps, France—must be saved from itself, but this requires a break with both liberalism and the reactionary politics he had associated with before the war. This is a dangerous game, and Blanchot remains responsible for his complicity with a Vichy-sponsored publication, but there is an emerging shift here in terms of how a French renewal could occur.

48. Blanchot also discusses this in *Pour l'Amité*, 12–16.
49. Blanchot, *Faux Pas*, 183.
50. Ibid., 189.
51. See Hill, *Blanchot: Extreme Contemporary*, 240 n. 7.

The renewal of the novel can only occur through a poetic revolution, as poetic language "destroys" daily language, transforming the novel through a break from mimesis.[52] For Blanchot, the demand for mimesis arises when writers "perceive the monster that a prose narrative would represent, composed of a mass of interchangeable details."[53] To many novelists, such randomness and contingency would be chaos, unless external order was imposed—yet there is an alternative. A poetic novel, for Blanchot, strives for its necessity through its internal form, drawing its coherence and logic from the words and symbols that compose it, rather than from an external correspondence to reality. The novel's form should determine the narrative—*not* the resemblance to or imitation of social conventions. An artistic novelist must strive for a "Mallarmé-like novel," which Blanchot describes as follows:

> We cannot perceive why the novelist, by the mere fact that he writes in prose, should not protect what he creates by the very scruples, refusals, and resistance to ease that are, in poetry, the guarantee of a certain purity ... Why should he not understand the word *creation* with all the force that he must win from it? Rejecting the absence of constraints that allow him everything only to condemn him to doing nothing, why should the novelist not be concerned with a particular necessity outside of which his work can only be an imitation and a symbol of untruth? The novelist must give himself a law, and the true value of this law, as well as the more or less strong urge to reject all that does not conform to it, alone will measure the solidity of his work. To write nothing and to do nothing that might mark a premeditated defeat of chance and, thus, its victory, is the first thought that a writer must have if he truly wants to be an author.[54]

As Hill notes, Mallarmé was hardly a neutral figure in France, seen by many on the right as a symbol of the decadence of modernity. To conceive the novel as a poetic work sees it opening beyond the world, a passage toward exteriority that breaks with traditionalism. How such a work involves "resistance" might also give us further pause.

The political significance of this break becomes more apparent when one examines where, in spite of the general crisis of the French novel, Blanchot locates traces of poetry within literature. In a profound reading

---

52. Blanchot, *Faux Pas*, 138.
53. Ibid., 190.
54. Ibid., 169.

of Balzac, Blanchot describes how his work follows its own internal necessity, while making use of realism to that end. Balzac's force, then, is in moving beyond mimetic constraint, letting the work demonstrate its own logic, separate from that of the world. Balzac demonstrates the "extreme lucidity" of madness that Gerald Bruns locates in Blanchot, "the mind led by itself beyond itself into a formidable darkness of which the creator knows nothing."[55]

Among Blanchot's contemporaries, Jacques Audiberti and Raymond Queneau stood out as breaking through the constraints of realism. Blanchot lauds their work for its inventiveness and rupture from realistic narrative. What strikes Blanchot about their work is how it straddles and even blurs the border between the novel and poetry. Like myth, Queneau's language keeps us at a distance from what is actually happening. As Blanchot writes in "Mythological Novels," "One could say that such myths are destined to make us penetrate things, not by introducing us to their mystery but by leaving us eternally outside. To see the outside of objects is to put oneself in the best position to discern their secret."[56] The enigmatic character of poetry distances language from us, preventing its grasp or comprehension, and making it strange. Like Queneau, Audiberti's work is one of creation, where the work follows from itself, impassively separate from the world. With Audiberti, however, Blanchot is somewhat more critical insofar as his work becomes symbolic, with the meanings borne by the characters introducing an "artificiality" into the poetic work of the novels.[57]

Blanchot renders a similarly split decision regarding one of the period's most famous novels, Camus's *The Stranger*. The story intrigues Blanchot, for the Stranger's fate emerges from within the events of the story, and from his own character: it is from taking the gun, sleeping at his mother's funeral, and his general distance from the world, that he condemns himself to execution. There is, here, a "destiny that chooses us" beyond what we choose, think, and feel—or fail to feel. Yet while Blanchot praises both the novel's fatality and its refusal to exculpate the Stranger, the work's ending remains its one evident flaw:

> A rather annoying change of tone occurs between the almost absolute objectivity of the narrative, an objectivity that is its profound truth, and the final pages in which the stranger expresses what he

55. Ibid., 181. See Bruns, *Maurice Blanchot*, 148.
56. Blanchot, *Faux Pas*, 199.
57. Ibid., 211.

thinks and feels faced with death and life. It would seem that the more destiny closes around him, the more his sobriety, his silence, his "I do not think, I say nothing" should also grow. The fatality that overwhelms him because he cannot explain himself should not, as it crushes him, separate him from his silence.[58]

To bring in the explanatory voice threatens to undercut the work's strangeness, its exteriority, which Blanchot contrasts with Faulkner's rendering of his characters in the silence of their misery. The danger, here, would be in returning the work's strangeness to the realm of the everyday. Camus makes possible the thought of the outside—yet seems to retreat in the last pages.

While Blanchot is judicious in his praise of these writers, his privileging of their work is significant on several fronts. As shall be discussed below, Blanchot's criticism gives us a way to conceive the strangeness of his own literary work—attempting to poetically revive the French novel. It also lays the initial groundwork for the more explicit disagreement with Heidegger that emerges after the war. However, there are aspects of his criticism that more directly relate to its wartime context. First, many of the writers praised in *Faux Pas*—for instance, Faulkner and Woolf—are foreign. Those writers who are French write, as with Camus, in a way that estranges them from the everyday. In effect, Blanchot argues that France must open itself to these foreign literary voices, in order to rediscover its "own" literary identity—a strange, veiled turn from the nationalist rhetoric of the 1930s.

What is equally noteworthy is Blanchot's principle of selection among French authors. The authors he reviews favorably were, in various ways, connected with the French Resistance. There is thus, implicitly, a correlation between an anti-realist aesthetic and a stance of resistance to the Vichy government. Of course, one could ask how much Blanchot was aware of their activities at the time, but the consistency is quite notable. To praise consistently authors involved with the Resistance in a journal sponsored by the Vichy government is a subversive, ironic gesture of solidarity. In light of the broader context, one may certainly (and, in my view, rightly) ask if such solidarity is enough—but the poetic criticisms Blanchot published under this regime suggest a complexity to his apparent complicity.

To conclude this section, let me briefly discuss how the criticism of *Faux Pas* gestures toward Blanchot's later work. First, there is a notable consonance between the style of his early novels, *Thomas l'Obscur* and

58. Ibid., 221.

Aminadab, and the poetics articulated in these reviews from the same period. These novels have an ethereal feel, and make it difficult for the reader to be grounded in any sense of verisimilitude. Particularly in *Aminadab*, where the architecture of the house gives a feeling of instability and uncertainty—one can rarely, if ever, locate where one is in relation to other rooms in the house—the novel creates a space, in language, that draws one outside of the everyday. Likewise, the feel of *Thomas l'Obscur* is one in which "the entry into a foreign element" predominates, with regard to both Thomas and to Anne's dying as a separation from the everyday world.[59] It is clear, then, that the emphasis on literature as exteriority, and Blanchot's refusal of mimesis, traverse both Blanchot's criticism and his novels.

The emphasis on exteriority also marks the initial stages of a disagreement with Heidegger that becomes more pronounced after the war, particularly in *The Work of Fire*. In *Faux Pas*, it is clear that poetic language takes its distance from the world. It gestures toward what is impossible, rendering community and identity unsettled. This leads into Blanchot's claim, in a reading of Holderlin in *The Work of Fire*, that the impossibility of the poet's task ruins the totality of the world, rendering the sacred absent. The poet, like the critic, is to be divided from him or herself, unable to accomplish fulfillment or a sense of unity. Poetry, then, cannot serve as an origin or founding of identity.[60] In making this argument, Blanchot is reading Holderlin against Heidegger, who interprets poetry as the language which, in giving possibility, becomes "the originary language of a historical people," gathering a community. As Heidegger writes, "The Sacred is transformed by poets' silence into gentleness of a communicable and communicating word."[61] For Blanchot, by contrast, poetry comes to be that which calls the hearer (or reader) *away* from an identity, and discloses the inaccessibility of the sacred—the impassive, incommunicable distance that creates the demand for further speech.

While literary criticism thus becomes a way for Blanchot to interrogate and rethink identity and the significance of language, there is nonetheless a limit to his distance from Heidegger at this point. For, one could say that exteriority, and the voice by which poetic language opens to the outside,

---

59. See Toumayan, *Encountering the Other*, 68–71.

60. See Blanchot, *Work of Fire*, 126; and also Hill, *Blanchot: Extreme Contemporary*, 86–88.

61. Heidegger, *Erlauterungen zu Hölderlins Dichtung*, 71; translation here by Leslie Hill in *Blanchot: Extreme Contemporary*, 85–86.

remains unitary: the critic's understanding of the poet closes off further discussion, defining his unique perspective at the expense of others. There is still a unitary voice at work in this early criticism. Blanchot's work would undergo further mutation, in ways that depart dramatically from the style of these earlier writings—and their residually traditionalist politics as well. Blanchot's critique of unitary criticism develops in one of his most influential works of commentary, *The Infinite Conversation*, which extends his disagreements with Heidegger while taking up Levinas's thought.

COMMENTARY BEYOND THE BOOK: *THE INFINITE CONVERSATION*

In the 1960s, commentary became more central to Blanchot's writing than it had been previously. Blanchot gave up the writing of narrative in this period, adopting an elliptical style that, like the writing he terms literature, elides classification as criticism, poetry, or prose. From *Awaiting Oblivion* to *The Step Not Beyond*, or from *The Infinite Conversation* to *Friendship*, his writings unfold through an engagement with others' texts, as well as through multiple voices within a text. Commentary, then, takes the form of a conversation (*entretien*), maintaining difference through both its relation to other works and the multiple voices within it. Commentary becomes a re-saying of the work, which, "said perfectly and incapable of being said again, nonetheless irresistibly tends to say itself over again, requiring the infinite speech of commentary."[62] Here, Blanchot's practice of reading, which Hill describes as finding a detour through closely following a text, finds its articulation as the retracing of the work's uniqueness opens a way for further speech.

Given commentary's parallel emergence in Levinas's work as an alternative to philosophical inquiry, this emergence of commentary in Blanchot's work warrants focus. Moreover, much of Blanchot's commentary in this period concerns itself with issues raised by Levinas's work, most notably in *Totality and Infinity*. Throughout *The Infinite Conversation*—and not just in the essays that engage Levinas directly—exteriority, *autrui*, and the impossibility of speech inflect Blanchot's reading of numerous texts. One could say that the thought of the neutral, plural speech and the critique of the book emerge through Blanchot's repetition of these Levinasian ideas,

---

62. Blanchot, *Infinite Conversation*, 390.

as they take a turn (*detour*) that recognizes the uniqueness of Levinas's thought in Blanchot's distancing from his work.

This section explores the significance of commentary for Blanchot by focusing on *The Infinite Conversation*, a collection of essays written between 1953 and 1965 that were revised for publication in 1969. The discussion traces how Blanchot's thought moves in his commentary on *Totality and Infinity*, and where the thought of the neuter breaks with Levinasian alterity. Second, and importantly, since *The Infinite Conversation* illustrates the movement of fragmentary writing and plural speech—to the extent that this is possible—it sets up an intriguing comparison with the movement of commentary in Levinas's Talmudic writings. For both authors, commentary is significant in its exteriority and its ability to open thought to new voices and further conversation. However, how one articulates this infinity remains the central disagreement between them. In light of this comparison, Blanchot's critiques of theology can be reexamined to determine whether or not Levinas's approach to commentary falls under the "demand for unity" that Blanchot thinks effaces the neuter, and thereby misconceives alterity.

While disparate in their origins, the essays collected under the subtitle "Plural Speech" focus intensively on the question of exteriority. The opening essays explore how questioning, while often finite and in search of an answer, can nonetheless open a form of relation that extends beyond the whole; the Sphinx, in its "profound question" that figures the passing of humanity, asks a question that makes the Greek order shudder. It is only by responding on a general level—"But what is man?"—that Oedipus can reinscribe this trembling and confine it, restoring order to the city through the exclusion of death. What this and other writings show, however, is that one can begin to conceive a questioning that exceeds totality, such that language could be the site for a relation that has heretofore remained silent.

Blanchot's reading of Yves Bonnefoy, in "The Great Refusal," turns the conversation toward the central issues of Levinas's work. Bonnefoy explores the ways that the sacred, as immediacy, is impossible—refusing any manifestation or presence. The immediate's immediacy, as Blanchot says, renders it infinitely distant. This ruptures the Hegelian dialectic, as negation no longer captures and makes use of this immediacy, which only recedes behind its dissimulation. The only relation to immediacy, then, is impossibility—a relation that exceeds all labor and grasping. The immediate, in its impossibility, is "nothing other than the mark of what we so readily call experience, for there is experience in the strict sense *only where something radically other is in play.*"63 As what is radically other, the immediate separates us from ourselves, opening the way to exteriority.

If the immediate is impossible, then how is one to think it? Blanchot approaches this question by reflecting on the relationship between speech, possibility, and violence. All relations within the world, as possible relations, are rooted in force; power and possibility establish the being of the world:

> Possibility, in this new sense, is more than reality: it is to be, plus the power to be. Possibility establishes and founds reality: one is what one is only if one has the power to be it . . . Never are we purely and simply, we are only on the basis of and with regard to the possibilities that we are; this is one of our essential dimensions. The word possible becomes clear, then, when it is placed in relation with the word power [*pouvoir*], first in the sense of capacity, then in the sense of a power that is commanded or a force [*puissance*].64

The relation between power and possibility determines speech as a form of force, an engagement in the powers and forces of the world. Speech thus becomes violent, even as it struggles against death: "All speech is violence, a violence all the more formidable for being secret and the secret center of violence."65 While speech limits and masters violence, it still remains within the purview of force, and thus cannot bring violence to an end.

If speech, violence, and possibility go together, then this implicitly links impossibility with non-violence: to relate to the impossible is to break with the force and violence that constitute the speech of the world. As a relation of *passion*, an undergoing or suffering (*subissement*), this relation delivers us to another time, "A time without event, without project, without possibility . . . an unstable perpetuity in which we are arrested and incapable of permanence, a time neither abiding nor granting the simplicity of a dwelling place."66 Exteriority, exposing us to suffering and the neuter, also opens the impossibility of nonviolence, a relation that exceeds the world and refuses—without resisting—the violence of everyday speech. This would be incommunicable, except that

---

63. Ibid., 46; emphasis added.
64. Ibid., 42.
65. Ibid.
66. Ibid., 44.

> Such a sentence ["communication is impossible"] is not meant to negate scandalously the possibility of communication, but to alert us to that other speech that speaks only when it begins to respond to the other region that is not governed by the time of possibility.[67]

This "other speech" would break with force, then, only through a relation to alterity. Here, poetics becomes politics; the articulation of an alternative speech becomes the way to undo the force and violence of the world.

As the essay leading into the essays focused on Levinas, "The Great Refusal" evokes numerous traits of Levinas's thought, in its reading of Bonnefoy's poetics. The "other speech," of course, evokes the peacefulness of the face, which speaks as a refusal of violence, saying "Thou shalt not kill" as its primary manifestation.[68] Moreover, the connection of immediacy and alterity evokes Levinas's thought of the face as that which ruptures consciousness and ontology, breaking in without mediation while remaining separate and other from the subject. Blanchot's reading resonates with Levinas on a deep level, yet in that resonance carries overtones that begin to mark their distance from one another.

Like Levinas, Blanchot locates the relation to otherness in language, and this relation calls into question the possibility—and power—of the subject. However, the central question between them is where otherness (*autrui*) occurs. Speech is where the strangeness of the other can be heard. The infinity of the relation is clear: "My relation with *autrui* is irreducible to any measure, just as it excludes any mediation and any reference to another relation that would include it."[69] But Blanchot locates this absolute otherness within the realm of the human: "Only man is absolutely foreign to me."[70] While Levinas agrees that foreignness resides within human relations, Blanchot here rejects the link between alterity and God that Levinas maintains. Such a link, for Blanchot, limits otherness, and indirectly reinscribes the ontology that Levinas strives to escape. It is in moving beyond this limit that the "third relation" begins to emerge as a relation of irreducible human strangeness.[71]

Blanchot's rejection of theological otherness shapes much of his commentary through the rest of *The Infinite Conversation*—not least, ironically

---

67. Ibid., 47.
68. Levinas, *Totality and Infinity*, 199.
69. Blanchot, *Infinite Conversation*, 59.
70. Ibid., 59–60.
71. Ibid., 68.

enough, his affirmation of the significance of Judaism. The issue with a theological construal of otherness is its conceiving otherness on the basis of unity—thinking difference within the terms of the One. Theology—especially, though clearly not solely, in monotheism—precludes the relation to the neutral, and prevents a truly plural speech or thought from emerging. The neutral is plural, in its discontinuity and interruption, breaking up the "flow" of time through which the process of becoming can be homogenized. It is also plural, however, in that it involves a double dissymmetry, as the two people speaking to one another become both other and subject. The consequence of this is that, in responding to the impossible, in exposure to the neutral, *one never knows who is speaking*: speech is neither personal nor impersonal, but somewhere beyond their opposition.[72] This other speech, found in writing, opens an alterity that resides in dispersal, and a different relation to humanity: "he who does not yield to the same nor is exalted in the unity of the Unique."[73]

Blanchot incisively articulates the significance of Judaism, and more specifically of being-Jewish, in the essay "The Indestructible." While the essay resonates harmoniously with much of Levinas's post-1962 thought in terms of language and responsibility, its location between largely affirmative discussions of Simone Weil and Nietzsche turns Levinas's thought in some unexpected directions; Levinas had sharply criticized Weil's writings in the 1950s for their interpretation of the Hebrew Bible.[74] By contrast with Levinas, Blanchot sees Weil as gesturing toward an attention to the good, and interprets Weil as desiring an absolute renunciation of the world. Attention, as a waiting without object, is the mode of being that opens one beyond being; Weil's desire for the good, as incessant, prevents any satisfaction or stasis, even in her argument that giving oneself to abandon unites one with God.[75] It is with her articulations of affliction and attention as the proper loci of thought that Blanchot turns to the question of Judaism.

For Blanchot, "Being-Jewish" is a way of being that attends to affliction, and does so through sojourning from itself. Drawing from the historical experience of the Jewish people, beginning with the story of Abraham and Sarah, Judaism defines itself through its going-outside, leaving a residence

72. Ibid., 76–77.
73. Ibid., 74.
74. Levinas, *Difficult Freedom*, 133–41.
75. Blanchot, *Infinite Conversation*, 117–18. For more on Blanchot's conception of attention, see Winfree, "On the Lineage of Oblivion," 249–69.

or stable dwelling. This is not negative—à la Hegel—but rather an affirmation of the outside and the search for a "nomadic truth": "Doesn't this nomadic movement affirm itself not as the eternal privation of a sojourn, but rather as an authentic manner of residing, of a residence that does not bind us to the determination of place or to settling close to a reality forever and already founded, sure, and permanent?"[76] Anti-Semitism is thus, at least in part, a refusal of exteriority, an unwillingness to exit one's dwelling place—much like Levinas's analysis of the rejection of Sukkot discussed earlier in this chapter. However, Blanchot rejects the theological as a central element of Jewish life. With sharp frankness he writes, "I would rather say, brutally, that what we owe to Jewish monotheism is not the revelation of the one God, but the revelation of speech as the place where men hold themselves in relation with what excludes all relation: the infinitely distant, the absolutely Foreign."[77] Speech is exile, but it is also the human relation to otherness that founds community: "Speech, in this sense, is the promised land where exile fulfills itself in sojourn since it is not a matter of being at home there but of being always Outside, in a movement wherein the Foreign offers itself, yet without disavowing itself."[78] Human speech is thus the relation to that which is absolutely foreign, the otherness that disperses and questions unity, so as to remain open to an alternative sociality.

While the emphasis on speech as inter-human already creates distance between Levinas and Blanchot, Blanchot's comments on Roger Antelme's *The Human Race* attend to a level of desubjectification which, at least on the initial publication in 1962, Levinas's thought had not yet explored. These are, as mentioned in the conclusion of chapter 4, dimensions that resonate far more with Levinas's work in *Otherwise than Being*. Antelme's account of the camps emphasizes the utter loss of subjectivity that occurred: prisoners were not just reduced to the level of basic need (the root of subjectivity, for *Totality and Infinity*), but even to a point where their identity or personhood was destroyed. The "trap of affliction" is that it desituates itself, reducing "the man of the camps" to utter powerlessness, "leaving him to an anonymous presence without speech and without dignity."[79] One's self becomes another—unknown, estranged, without place, community or speech. In this lack, one is reduced to a condition of bare life, losing

76. Blanchot, *Infinite Conversation*, 127.
77. Ibid., 127.
78. Ibid., 128.
79. Ibid., 132.

relation with oneself and rendering speech impossible. In order to find any hope in this situation, Blanchot says there must be a "Self-Subject," a subject who speaks in and for the individuals whose identities have been lost, "as what can receive the unknown and the foreign, receive them in the justice of a true speech." Such a self gives the dispossessed their sole hope for resistance, seeking justice in restoring their humanity, first and foremost by recognizing the humanity of those whose identities have been erased. A "just speech" counters the violence of the camps by responding to the demand for speech that the other's silence creates, recognizing this indestructibility in the midst of the ruins of destruction.[80] While an infinite responsibility for the other is present here, Blanchot's discussion highlights the extreme demand placed upon speech: the one who speaks must respond to the other—hearing the other's cry—but, also, must respond in a way that allows the other to speak, even (and perhaps especially) where the other can no longer do so. To speak in a way that disperses speech, founding a community that becomes hospitable to difference—plural speech calls for an Abrahamic hospitality that not only sees three men as God, but perhaps even sees the *Muselmann* as the one to be welcomed.

As one of the interlocutors in "The Indestructible" asks, that this vision of humanity as able to be destroyed with "no limit" raises the specter of nihilism. While confronting the bleakness of existence, Blanchot refuses nihilism, which leads him to turn to Nietzsche. Nietzsche's work is instructive because of the rigor with which he thought through nihilism, especially with regard to the eternal return. Part of this thought, however, lay in his mode of writing, and Nietzsche's work thus provides an illustration of how the "just speech" discussed above, which takes the form of fragment writing, cannot guard itself from being misappropriated in the name of force or ideology.

For Blanchot, the reception of Nietzsche's work traces the history of an error. From his sister's desire to "make Nietzsche a true philosopher"[81]

---

80. As Blanchot writes, humanity is "the indestructible that can be destroyed" (*Infinite Conversation*, 130). While Agamben takes issue with this formulation (which is rendered incorrectly in the translation), it is largely so as to emphasize that there is not an essence to humanity that precedes this division, but rather that humanity is the relation or separation between the speech and the destruction, even as these go together (what Agamben calls their noncoincidence). My sense is that Blanchot's own notion of the exigency of speech is, in fact, quite close to Agamben's notion of testimony. See Agamben, *Remnants of Auschwitz*, 136–37.

81. Blanchot, *The Infinite Conversation*, 137.

(and to publish a work that would be well-received and profitable), and perhaps also from Nietzsche's occasional requests for understanding, Nietzsche's work was published in a form that systematized it, making the will to power its central thematic. The collection of aphorisms in *The Will to Power* simplifies and distorts his thought—which, for Blanchot, has no central theme, as his thoughts exist separately and in isolation from one another. From this error arises the "myth of Nietzsche" appropriated by the Nazis, which some of his critics (like Lukacs) rightly criticize. The challenge that Blanchot articulates is to read Nietzsche differently:

> Remain unsatisfied until one has found that which contradicts what one has asserted about him; maintain amidst the contradictions [of his thought] the exigency of the whole that is constantly present, though constantly dissolved by them; never conceive of this whole—which is non-unitary—as a system, but as a question, and as the passion of the research in its impetus toward the true, one with the critique of all that has been acquired in the course of the research; grasp anew "the real dialectic": thought as the play of the world, text as fragment.[82]

To read Nietzsche in this way is to think the fragmenting of totality; that the whole of his thought is constituted by its fragmentation and separation, its necessary insufficiency. To grasp the interplay of his texts, their noncoincidence, is essential for Blanchot, because *reading Nietzsche as a fragmenting of totality enacts the thought of the Eternal Return.*

Blanchot reads the Eternal Return as the thought which piercingly gazes upon the meaning of nihilism. While the overman announces the end of humanity and of history, his open field of possibility is but a dialectical negation; he remains, on Blanchot's view, within the thought of the same. His negation of being depends upon being—the overman reveals the incessance of being, its unsurpassability. It is only with the Eternal Return that Nietzsche's thought moves to the outside, beyond that which one can will and the realm of power. The Eternal Return is "the most extreme form of nihilism," because it shows that being is all there is: "It says the impotence of nothingness, the false brilliance of its victories . . . Midnight is only a dissimulated noon, and the great Noon is the abyss of light from which we can never depart—even through death and the glorious suicide Nietzsche recommends to us."[83]

82. Ibid., 140–41.
83. Ibid., 149.

While the Eternal Return thus renders ontology inescapable, the *thought* of being in its eternity—as infinitely repeating itself—also, in a strange reversal, does open a path of evasion. This requires no longer seeing Nietzsche as a philosopher, but rather discerning within his work the trace of a "very different language, the writing of effraction."[84] Blanchot thus turns Nietzsche away from nihilism through the notion of fragment writing. Fragment writing breaks up becoming into discontinuity and separation. It operates through repetition, undoing the totality that presents itself as the final word through a displacement. This is the stance that Nietzsche's thought, on occasion, takes with respect to philosophy, "taking its distance from dialectical philosophy less in contesting it than in repeating it."[85] As a writing that renders separation, ensuring that the becoming of being is never complete, it is a writing that imitates the Eternal Return, but also moves outside it, "designating to thought by its fissure that thought has already left itself."[86] Here, the significance of reading Nietzsche becomes clear. To read Nietzsche as a fragmentary writer is to read him in a way that breaks up totality, thinking the play of thought without end, and thereby opening his work to the outside—a reading that enacts, or reenacts, the Eternal Return in its very movement.

In its plurality, fragment writing guides much of the ensuing discussion in *The Infinite Conversation*. Its repetition makes possible "true" thoughts, which exceed the predication and comprehensibility of "developed" thought. Moreover, it is through this doubling of repetition that the neutral emerges, not as something distinct, or something that would unite opposed terms, but rather as an irreducible separation that enables speech. As Blanchot writes of René Char's poems, it is an arrangement "that accepts disjunction or divergence as the infinite center from out of which, through speech, relation is to be created."[87] The plural speech that emerges from such writing is beyond a simple dialogue: "Plural speech, inasmuch as in its simplicity it is the seeking of an affirmation that, though escaping all negation, neither unifies nor allows itself to be unified but rather always refers to a difference always more tempted to defer."[88] Plural speech, in its neutrality and dispersal, responds to the otherness that exceeds language,

84. Ibid., 151.
85. Ibid., 159.
86. Ibid., 158.
87. Ibid., 308.
88. Ibid., 215.

opening a way out of being through its refusal of force, and responding in a way that lets others respond.

The question remains, then, what Blanchot's writings on the neuter and otherness suggest about the significance of commentary. Throughout his work, commentary has an ambivalent significance. At times, commentary or criticism may seem to close off a work, as the critic may be "the one who speaks last."[89] A critic may speak with power, and thus close off what can be said, arresting the movement of the neuter. At the same time, in its interpretation of a work, commentary can gesture toward the worklessness (*désoeuvrement*), the neuter, that dwells within a poem, novel, or even philosophical discourse. Commentary, then, may be what restores the book to its sovereign unity, or a repetition of the book that opens it to its outside.

One could propose the following: *commentary is workless when it pluralizes speech*. This thesis would seem to accord with several shifts in Blanchot's own writings: for instance, turning away from narrative recits, and frequently adopting a dual-voiced approach in the writings of *The Infinite Conversation*, such that what "Blanchot" says about a work cannot be reduced to a single position. It is also worth highlighting the shift to the fragment, and to literary conversation, from the more monological form of his earlier criticism. Blanchot's writing is plural, in terms of the multiple voices at work at once: he offers critiques of one author through another's work, troubling the divisions between author, critic, and audience; the between-being of these writings gestures toward the neutral. This is the demand of commentary: to speak in a way that attends to the other's affliction, in part by creating an opening in which the other may speak. Blanchot's later writings, it would seem, attempt to turn commentary toward the outside—opening both the works and his own writing to the movement of the neuter.

While Blanchot's views and practice of commentary closely resemble Levinas's, questions remain. In one of the fragments from "The Absence of the Book," a series of theses that conclude *The Infinite Conversation*, Blanchot takes up the relation of midrash to the biblical text, in relation to his conception of fragmentary writing. The issue, here, is whether this commentary serves to constitute or render absent *the book*. The book, for Blanchot, is a way that writing becomes a receptacle of knowledge, and a totality or unity "restoring to culture the mutation that threatens it."[90]

89. Ibid., 326.
90. Ibid., 425.

The book thus contains the plurality and neutrality of writing, rendering it conceivable within the terms of unity. One might think, then, that the Talmud as the "oral Torah" would open the book of the written Torah to exteriority, but Blanchot cautions otherwise:

> Let us attempt to examine this surprising proposition by relating it to what might be an experience of writing yet to come. There are two kinds of writing, one white, the other black: one that renders invisible the invisibility of a colorless flame; the other that is made accessible in the form of letters, characters, and articulations by the power of the black fire. Between the two there is the oral, which, however, is not independent, it being always involved with the second kind of writing inasmuch as it is this black fire itself, the measured obscurity that limits and delimits all light and makes all light visible. Thus what we call oral is designation in a present of time and a presence of space, but also, first of all, the development or mediation that is ensured by a discourse that explains, receives and determines the neutrality of the initial inarticulation. The "oral Torah" is therefore no less written than the written Torah, but is called oral in the sense that, as discourse, it alone allows there to be communication, that is, allows the word to be enunciated in the form of a *commentary* that at once teaches and declares, authorizes and justifies: as though language (discourse) were necessary for writing to give rise to general legibility, and perhaps also to the Law understood as prohibition and limit.[91]

If the oral Torah is the "black fire" of characters, then it is a measuring and a confinement of obscurity; rendering the written Torah legible, and authorizing only certain readings (one is reminded of Levinas's remark that one does not read the Bible without the Talmud), it serves in a way to limit interpretation—even while opening up a field of possibilities. On this point, one might consider how intertextuality is often defended as a practice that gives the Bible its coherence and unity. Talmudic commentary, as teaching and declaring, would here be that which covers over or effaces plural speech.

Where does this leave us with respect to Levinas? Blanchot's critique of the oral Torah as Law that "determines neutrality" reprises his earlier critique of Levinas's theological notion of alterity. To think otherness within a theological framework—as personal, unique, and giving unity to the work—effectively homogenizes alterity. For Blanchot, the neuter demands a thought that undoes unity, and unsettles the force of language.

91. Ibid., 430–31.

To achieve a radical pluralization, commentary cannot rest within the Talmudic realm. It must take on a still more fragmentary form, and engage with the writing that makes the thought from outside possible. For Blanchot, the idea of unity is, in many ways, the last myth, and it is only through the demystification of the One that Blanchot thinks the hold of the sacred can be broken. If, as de Vries and others have noted, Levinas thinks that the aesthetic is a necessary but preliminary stage on the way to ethics or holiness, one could argue that for Blanchot it is only in the demystifying of religion that one truly steps outside. The passage beyond the sacred is necessary for both Levinas and Blanchot—but their journeys toward this pass one another in the sacred's dark night.

It is at this point that the concerns of the first part of this chapter—the shifts within Levinas's Talmudic interpretation, and his emphasis on the pluralization of voices within Talmudic study—become especially important. For, one could argue that the discontinuous, nonsynthetic arguments of the Talmud—along with the way it opens itself to further interpretation—*do* embody a form of fragmentary writing. Here, it would be especially important to note how Levinas reads (or, learns to read, over time) in a way that opens texts, and gives voice to other readers. Commentary, precisely through its refusal of confinement—to genre, to univocity, or to a telos—may enact a form of infinite thought that never rests, but calls forth further responsibility. It is possible, then, to read Levinas's commentary as enacting a form of religious reading that responds to the demand of the neuter. The movement here is complex: Levinas is, in many ways, adopting a Blanchotian conception of reading, for the reading of sacred texts—but, thereby, he is refuting Blanchot's argument regarding the monological nature of theology, as foreclosing the neuter's plurality.

While their disagreement over religion and art remains throughout their work, it is striking to see how the pluralization of voices becomes far more central for both authors in their later work. It is equally striking that for both Blanchot and Levinas, commentary becomes one of the forms of writing that most fully lets this plural speech exist, and the way for thought to break from myth. Perhaps it was through repeating and displacing the other's commentary, turning it back on itself so as to put it in question, that Blanchot and Levinas sustained the conversation that bound them to one another even in their infinite separation.

PART THREE

Julia Kristeva *and*
Catherine Clément

SEVEN

Analyzing the Soul of Religion

THE THIRD FRIENDSHIP TO be examined differs dramatically in shape from the first two. While Catherine Clément and Julia Kristeva worked and lived in the same Parisian circles for years, they had not collaborated or drawn on one another's work in nearly thirty years of writing.[1] On several levels, their careers have been quite similar; both offered extensive critiques of Lacanian psychoanalysis, and moved in different ways away from their political focus of the late 1960s and 1970s. In recent years, both have also turned to novels as one of their preferred forms of reflection, and both have focused increasingly on the subject of religion in their work.

It is perhaps because of these mutual interests that Kristeva and Clément collaborated on an exchange of letters in 1997 titled *The Feminine and the Sacred*. The volume that brought them together only shows how far they have diverged from one another, and not only in the distance of transcontinental emails and faxes. In *The Feminine and the Sacred*, Kristeva and Clément explore the world of religion from a variety of perspectives. Their concerns run the gamut, from the analysis of trances of Senegalese women during a Catholic mass to the self-immolation of Hindu widows, and on to the anorexic discipline of Catherine of Siena. Through these various discussions, the complex relation of both authors to psychoanalysis emerges as one of the defining contrasts in their work. Their other commitments and disciplinary practices deeply shape their interpretations of psychoanalysis. Clément's Marxist, anthropological, and philosophical training shapes her understanding of psychoanalytic theory and practice. This becomes clearest in her critical appropriation of Lacan's work and her challenge to the norms of the psychoanalytic community. On the other hand, Kristeva's interests in semiotics, linguistics, and her experience as an analyst lead to her recognition of the importance of countertransference, and her focus on analysis as a theater in which semiotic discourse can reshape the drives and desires of the body.

1. The sole exception is *Sollers: La Fronde*, Clément's volume on Philippe Sollers, Kristeva's husband; see 40–42.

Not surprisingly, given these differences, Kristeva and Clément disagree sharply in their interpretations of religion. Most notably, they disagree over the relation between Judaism and Christianity and other religions; however, this argument also brings together their disagreements over the significance of the body, language, art, and politics. In many ways, the exchanges of *The Feminine and the Sacred* condense their life's work into a lucid yet complex argument, through which both friends see more clearly the shape of their own thought. The work of the next three chapters is to pull out the different threads of reflection that are woven together in their letters, tracing the paths and detours both have taken that led to this unusual yet provocative exchange.

As mentioned, their differences in interpreting religion constitute the central subject of *The Feminine and the Sacred*. Whereas Clément takes a more syncretistic approach, emphasizing the healing potential of Indian religious traditions, Kristeva's work generally privileges the symbolic, interiorizing discourse of Christianity, even as she works to maintain a critical distance from it. Their exchange thus illuminates two things. First, it highlights the potentially therapeutic aspects Kristeva notes in religious discourse, which have been largely overlooked in Kristeva scholarship, if not criticized in more recent years. As Cleo Kearns has argued, Kristeva's work perceives religion as a "cultural theory and practice offering communal and psychically supportive modalities for recognizing limit and handling abjection and pain."[2] At the same time, the contrast between Clément's and Kristeva's views highlights what Kelly Oliver terms a "lurking ethnocentrism"[3] within Kristeva's privileging of certain artistic and symbolic forms. What becomes clear, for both Kristeva and Clément, is that their interpretations of religion and the sacred are closely tied to their understandings of psychoanalytic practice. Beginning with their recent work, one can then reconstruct the theoretical positions underlying their amicable (though heated) epistolary disagreements.

One of Clément's early stories from *The Feminine and the Sacred* exemplifies the tensions between their views. Observing a Catholic mass in Dakar, she notes that on a regular basis women in the crowd give out a shriek and collapse. The women are carried from the gathering, but the regularity suggests to Clément that they are manifesting a relation to the

---

2. Kearns, "Suffering in Theory," 66. See also idem, "Art and Religious Discourse in Aquinas and Kristeva."

3. Oliver, *Reading Kristeva*, 123.

sacred "different from that of a Catholic mass." Entering trances, they manifest an alternative relation that challenges the order and hierarchy of the Catholic mass—as only the African women (who are lower on the social hierarchy of those present in terms of race, class, and gender) exhibit this phenomenon. While observing this, a Senegalese man turns to Clément and names the faintings "hysteria"—denying the sacral quality of the event by medicalizing it, and reinscribing class difference, since hysteria was first defined as an illness in working-class women.[4] Already in her description, several central themes of Clément's work regarding psychoanalysis manifest themselves: the sacred is disclosed in feminine bodies that introduce disorder and disruption into the order of language; there is a risk of psychoanalysis being used to maintain and reinforce class distinctions rather than truly seeking to heal; and, there is a mystical trance that can carry one beyond the subjectivity of Western culture—a "syncope," or rupture, that dislocates hierarchy and transforms social relations.

Kristeva's response likewise crystallizes her approach to analysis and religion. First, where Clément locates the sacred in the bodies of the women, Kristeva shifts terrain, focusing on the sacred as the border where bodies and language meet—in this case, where the women's bodies enact the meaning that they hear *in* the words of the mass. As she writes, "I claim that what comes back to us as 'sacred' in the experience of a woman is the impossible and nevertheless sustained connection *between life and meaning*."[5] In making this claim, she thereby connects the sacred, and the experience of giving meaning, with participation within organized religion, through its semiotic language. Like Clément, she recognizes the women's participation in the sacred—but sees this as occurring through the mass, rather than over against it. Moreover, Kristeva's interpretation revalues psychoanalysis as a practice that helps us to recognize that the sacred is a split within ourselves. Thus, the value Kristeva accords to the discourse of the mass in this case parallels the value she accords to psychoanalysis, as a language through which one can begin to acknowledge the strangeness within oneself, enabling us to live with one another through respect and love of the strangers in our midst—including ourselves.

This brief exchange in *The Feminine and the Sacred* highlights several of their key disagreements. In this light, the theoretical arguments undergirding this dispute can now be explored. This chapter explores how the

4. Clément, *Feminine and the Sacred*, 5–7.
5. Ibid., 14, emphasis added.

differences in Kristeva's and Clément's approaches to psychoanalysis, as configured throughout their work, play into their disagreements regarding the relation between religion and the sacred. Through their exchange, a nuanced psychoanalytic approach to religion becomes possible, one that does not reduce religion simply to an illusion or neurosis, but recognizes its therapeutic and transformative potential, as well as the risks its discourse bears.

KRISTEVA, PSYCHOANALYSIS, AND THE SACRED

Over the course of her career, Kristeva's work has developed a range of analyses of literature, culture, and art, as well as religion. Throughout her work—from *Revolution in Poetic Language* through *Strangers to Ourselves*, from *Powers of Horror* to *Murder in Byzantium*—Kristeva's writings develop an analytical approach as to the social, familial, and corporeal states and forces that give rise to various forms of discourse and representation. Her emphasis in many of these writings is showing the role of embodiment in the construction of thought. Through these disparate writings, she gives voice to the various forms of subjectivity that constitute cultural life, both in its extant forms and in the possibilities she hopes for. Central to such work has been her development of the idea of semiotic discourse, as a signifying practice irreducible to the predicative, thematic discourse of everyday speech (what she terms "symbolic" signifying practices). This is a form of signifying that "acts to open, in and beyond the scene of linguistic representation, modalities of pre- or trans-linguistic psychic inscriptions that one would call semiotic, in retrieving the etymological sense of the Greek *semeion*—trace, mark, distinctiveness."[6]

Over the course of her reflections upon the field of signification, and the modes of subjectivity represented therein, Kristeva's relation to religion has become more nuanced. Whereas in early work she refers to semiotic signification as "a-theological"—opposed to any orthodoxy or religious practice—her work with biblical semiotics and with the writings of the Christian tradition have led her to a recognition that religion is not simply a contemplative form of discourse that operates through the repression of the body (especially, the maternal body). Rather, the complexity of Christian discourse enables diverse modes of relation to corporeality

---

6. Kristeva, *Au commencement etait l'amour*, 14.

through its particular forms of semiotic discourse.[7] In this shift, she resembles one of the characters from her novel *The Samurai*, Hervé Sinteuil. Over the course of the novel Sinteuil (perhaps modeled on her husband, Philippe Sollers) shifts from a Maoist atheism that rejects any association with Christianity—he and Olga were married in a civil ceremony—to a complex appreciation for Christianity. He defends Duns Scotus and the Catholic Church as the "prime defender[s] of individual liberty."[8] His view of the connection between religion and freedom becomes even more provocative in his reading of Master Eckhart at his father's funeral:

> "We say therefore that a man should be so poor that he cannot himself be 'a place where God may act,' nor even have God in him. As long as a man has space within him, he also has difference. And that is why I pray for God to make me free of God."
>
> Master Eckhart was speaking through Hervé of Jean de Montlaur: his elegant simplicity was indeed a kind of poverty "free of God." Hervé thought his father had been an atheist, but that his atheism was another kind of belief . . .
>
> Olga gazed at him, as if trying to draw out his thoughts through that closed-up face and understand them. He had just placed his father, pragmatic and self-effacing to the point of invisibility, among the mystics. Jean de Montlaur had been "free of God," and his distance from heavenly grace was the guarantee of his humanity; but from him, in the moral peace of his own solitude, there emanated such pride that he needed no one. That was how Olga interpreted Eckhart's meditation as she stood clutching Hervé's hand.[9]

While Sinteuil and Kristeva are both far from orthodox, their shifting recognitions of the complexity of religious subjectivity carry with them important insights for philosophical, psychoanalytic, and religious reflection. These shifts can be traced by exploring Kristeva's own understanding of the semiotic from her early theoretical work, and then seeing how it develops in her later writings on religion.

Kristeva lays out the central facets of semiotic signification in her early work *Revolution in Poetic Language*, which explores the modes of signification specific to modern poetry. There, she defines the semiotic as a stage

---

7. It is important to note that this shift in her approach to religion also parallels her own training and practice in psychoanalysis, which has led to her adoption of it as a more central theoretical and practical discourse.

8. Kristeva, *Samurai*, 257–58.

9. Ibid., 295–96.

in the process of the subject that "logically and chronologically precedes the establishment of the symbolic and its subject."[10] In the semiotic, both biological and social forces combine to constitute the subject who can then give voice to symbolic (objective, thetic) signification. The semiotic "is articulated by flow and marks: facilitation, energy transfers, the cutting up of the corporeal and social continuum as well as that of signifying material, the establishment of a distinctiveness and its ordering in a pulsating *chora*, in a rhythmic but nonexpressive totality."[11] Semiotic discourse thus arises from the material conditions of speech, including the drives and emotions of the subject. While it precedes the symbolic (that is, rational discourse), its precedence is only apparent in light of poetry's rupture of the symbolic. Poetic signification, which foregrounds the materiality of the language, discloses the material conditions from which the symbolic subject emerges. Poetry discloses these conditions by "introducing into the thetic position the stream of semiotic drives and making it signify."[12]

In *Revolution*, Kristeva opposes poetic signification and semiotics to "theology," terming poetics an "a-theological" discourse that transgresses the repressive abstraction of "theological" symbolic language. She further develops the opposition through the contrast between sacrifice and artistic language. Sacrifice establishes the symbolic realm through the confinement or repression of drives. Artistic language establishes and then breaks down symbolic representation, precisely so as to give voice to the drives, sociality, and corporeality. The contrast with artistic discourse illuminates the way that, in Kristeva's early work, religion functions as a repressive and restrictive mode of discourse that silences the body. It may put the drives to use—incorporating their negativity and energy into its discourse—but this is in view of resituating the unified subject and the power relations supporting him or her. She writes,

> We thus find sacrifice and art, face to face, representing the two aspects of the thetic function: the prohibition of *jouissance* by language and the introduction of *jouissance* into and through language. Religion seizes this first aspect, necessary to the institution of the symbolic order . . . On the other hand, poetry, music, dance, theater—"art"—point at once to a pole opposite that of religious prohibition . . . *art takes from ritual space what theology conceals:*

10. Kristeva, *Revolution in Poetic Language*, 41.
11. Ibid., 40. See also Bové, *Language and Politics in Julia Kristeva*, 11–26.
12. Kristeva, *Revolution in Poetic Language*, 60.

trans-symbolic *jouissance*, the irruption of the motility threatening the unity of the social realm and the subject.[13]

Poetic discourse is revolutionary in that it pluralizes the subject, and contests the very possibility of a unitary subject by exposing the plurality of voices that shape its construction.

It is worth noting that in *Revolution in Poetic Language*, Kristeva likewise limits the efficacy of psychoanalysis, seeing it as still operating within the idea of a unified subject. Specifically, she argues that the horizon of analytic discourse is the intersubjective relation (transference) between analyst and analysand, which restricts the field of signification in ways that poetry does not. As Sara Beardsworth states, psychoanalysis provides the theory, but art (especially literature) provides the practice.[14] In this early work, then, both psychoanalysis and religion are conceived as restricting, and therefore to some degree repressing, the semiotic signification that links language to the body in the service of a unified subject of consciousness.

Over the course of her later works, however, this opposition between poetic and thetic discourse becomes more complicated. As mentioned above, this is perhaps partly due to her training in analysis, which was completed in 1979. Kristeva's attention to the particular signifying practices of analysis, including the phenomenon of countertransference and the modes of signification found in biblical and religious texts, brings to light a wide range of signifying practices, subjective positions, and relations to the other within religious life. Her psychoanalytic interest leads her to new questions regarding the functions of these practices. She turns the structuralist study of religion in a new direction, asking about its subjective configuration. As she writes in *Powers of Horror*,

> Why that system of classification and not another? What social, subjective and socio-subjectively interacting needs does it fulfill? Are there no subjective structurations that, within the organization of each speaking being, correspond to this or that symbolic-social system and represent, if not stages, at least types of subjectivity and society?[15]

In the trilogy of works from the 1980s (*Powers of Horror*, *Tales of Love*, and *Black Sun*), as well as the later *New Maladies of the Soul*, these new significations within religious discourse emerge with increasing clarity.

13. Ibid., 80; emphasis added.
14. Beardsworth, *Julia Kristeva*, 39–40.
15. Kristeva, *Powers of Horror*, 92.

Kristeva's analysis of religious subjectivity begins with her discussion of biblical semiotics—the signs of the Bible and their relation to the body. As discussed in *Powers of Horror*, biblical law establishes a system of signs founded on separation. This separative semiotics is rooted in the distinction between God and humanity, and the Levitical system maintains that distinction through an organized series of oppositions between pure and impure with regard to food, sexuality, and other aspects of material life, including mortality. "The semes that clothe the process of separation (orality, death, incest) are the inseparable lining of its logical representation aiming to guarantee the place and law of the One God."[16] By establishing what she terms the sphere of "biblical abomination," Jewish law enacts a separation between the speaking subject and those aspects of existence that would interfere with or disturb one's relation to God, which occurs within the symbolic order. In this taxonomy of abomination, the law breaks away from sacrifice, while incorporating the repression of violence that sacrifice signifies.

Not least in this taxonomy is the separation that signifies sexual difference; the male child, in being circumcised, is separated from his birth, and from the maternal. Women must ritually cleanse themselves to purify their bodies of the blood that defiles, signifying a material remainder that would disturb the transparent devotion to divine agency. As the maternal body thereby signifies impurity, much like a body that has a blemish, sexual difference becomes a separation that is articulated in the different ritual relations to the body for men and women, which thereby also place them in a social organization that relates them differently to divinity.[17]

For Kristeva, this taxonomy of abomination displays many different dimensions of social organization; the separation from the maternal body displays, on a social level, the desire to separate from the pagan fertility cults around Judaism. The dietary separation of meat from blood, and the separation of a kid from his mother's milk, signify obedience to the command not to kill (or, the repression of the desire to kill) and the forbidding of incest. On the psychic level, however, they also signify a fundamental separation from the body in its materiality—a separation that enables speech as the relation to God. Here, in the divisions of abomination, we see a passage to symbolic language, from the chaos and impurity of the semiotic.

16. Ibid., 94.

17. Ibid., 100–103. It should be noted that Kristeva builds off of Mary Douglas's work on Leviticus in *Purity and Danger*. Douglas, herself, has revised her position substantially in *Leviticus as Literature*.

However, it should be noted that Kristeva's analysis already separates the symbolic speech of the Law from sacrifice, as a sublimation of violence. Kristeva's shift away from *Revolution*'s approach to religion has begun.

The taxonomy of abomination is hardly the last word; while it constitutes a separation that enables speech, this taxonomy could also be repeated and turned against its practitioners in support of morality. As Kristeva explores, the prophets make use of the language of abomination as a moral critique of the life of Israel, to signify how injustice separates the people from their God, rendering them impure rather than on the side of purity. When Isaiah refers to the people as an "unclean thing" (59:3) and their hands as "defiled with blood" (64:6), he locates the demonic power that destroys subjectivity within the people themselves, as something from which they must purify themselves through repentance.[18] The prophetic discourse is designed to complete the separation from the maternally impure, completing the coming-to-be of the speaking subject constituted through the Levitical prohibitions. As Kristeva later writes in "Reading the Bible," Leviticus and the prophets "speak to me by locating me at the point where I lose my 'clean self.'"[19] Prophecy thus recounts the detachment that the subject must undergo in order to rise to speech, and the way that the subject may become aware of this process through the speech that signifies this organization of subjectivity.

Kristeva discusses how Christian scriptures—beginning with Jesus's welcoming of the impure, the defiled, and women—likewise develop this interiorizing of abjection, such that it becomes an aspect from which we cannot entirely separate ourselves. In Christianity, interiorization occurs through judgment and confession as practiced in the liturgy of the Eucharist, where believers both recognize and free themselves from the abject.[20] While this interiorization enables new relations to the body and the maternal, it still functions within the symbolic realm: "Henceforth reconciled with it [abjection], the Christian subject, completely absorbed into

---

18. Kristeva, *Powers of Horror*, 106–10.

19. Kristeva, *New Maladies of the Soul*, 119.

20. Cleo Kearns rightly points out that this sets up what amounts to a form of psychoanalytic supersessionism, in which the Christian discourse of the Eucharist would seem to surpass the Jewish form of legal and prophetic abjection. In what follows, I argue that Kristeva's treatment is more balanced and less supersessionist than it appears, but Kearns is right to say that "Regarded as a synchronic rather than a diachronic schema, Kristeva's work offers a religious wisdom here deeper than the discursive level of her argument quite indicates" ("Suffering in Theory," 64).

the symbolic, is no longer a being of abjection but a lapsing subject."[21] The symbolic nature of this reconciliation, then, largely stays within the abstract realm of the symbolic, directed toward thetic speech. This is clear not only in *Powers of Horror*, but also in *Tales of Love*, where Kristeva analyzes how Paul's epistles signify a new form of *agape*, but do so only through the death of the body:

> Christian love is an idea that changes my body into a worshiped name. The killing of the body is the path through which the body-Self has access to the Name of the Other who loves me and makes of me a Subject who is immersed (baptized) in the Name of the other. A triumph of idealization through a sublimatory elaboration of suffering and of the destruction of the body proper, *agape* marks, for that very reason, the end of sacrifice.[22]

Insofar as both Leviticus and the Christian scriptures remain symbolic, they still function through the repression of the semiotic from which they originated. Thus, while the biblical economy of meaning breaks with sacrifice, on Kristeva's view its symbolic nature remains opposed to the semiotic plurality of art. However, Kristeva does note two biblical texts in which the semiotic comes to the fore: the Eucharist and the Song of Songs. These discussions are especially significant, since they are largely neglected in the secondary literature on Kristeva.

While she suggests the *significance* of the Eucharist in *Powers of Horror*,[23] her most extensive interpretation is found in her later essay "From Signs to the Subject," in *New Maladies of the Soul*, which focuses on chapter 6 of the Gospel of John. In commenting on Jesus's words to the crowd, ("Truly, truly, I say to you, you seek me, not because you saw signs, but because you ate your fill of the loaves"[24]), Kristeva writes, "Through the words of Jesus, John thus adds a sensory layer to signs, and he interprets them as a satisfaction of the primordial need to survive."[25] A sign, on the Johannine model, only works as a sign if it acknowledges the affective, corporeal desires of the recipient—in other words, if it brings to light the semiotic dimensions that constitute subjectivity. However, while incorporating such affectivity, the text does not stop there: "It is a matter of going from these sign-foods of

---

21. Kristeva, *Powers of Horror*, 119.
22. Kristeva, *Tales of Love*, 146.
23. Kristeva, *Powers of Horror*, 117–20.
24. John 6:26.
25. Kristeva, *New Maladies of the Soul*, 128.

your needs to 'I,' to place your trust in 'I.' 'I am the bread of life' (6:35)."[26] The I who speaks (Jesus) is also sent from the Father, which further engages the body in its claim to a carnal genealogy; however, by moving the subject through the "sign-foods" to seeking fulfillment in the "I" who speaks, these signs also open a space in which the recipient is called to *trust* Jesus. Such trust requires interpretation, as the subject appropriates the meaning that relates Jesus to the Father. "The Son 'means' the Father, and this signification is to be deployed by *you*, as addressees of the evangelical narrative . . . Signification means trusting the other, whose own confidence binds him to his father."[27] In an almost Lutheran view of faith as trust, the affective language of Jesus both enables speech and reconnects with embodiment.

As Kristeva explains, by enabling trust these signs open up a new interiority. They also enable an identification between the believer and Christ, which the eucharist enacts. This identification, a "paroxysmal osmosis," turns the interpreters into subjects, as their interpretation opens them to a life that is not limited by death, and thus eternal. Moreover, as Kristeva writes:

> Symbolic identification with the Son of God, which is centered on speech, has a direct effect on the body. Here, we rediscover that signs have a sensory and affective foundation, which has been suggested from the beginning. And now there is a reversal, for by realizing that speech unites him with the absolute Subject, the believer discovers that his own body has been revitalized. This experience of sensory and corporeal regeneration through the effect of transport—of transference—onto the love of the other is imagined to be a guarantee of immortality and resurrection.[28]

Kristeva goes on to suggest that as challenging as such a subjectivity is, it "offers psychoanalysts an *exemplary* course of action."[29] By engaging the body, John's signs disrupt the thetic, exposing the semiotic dimensions of signification at the roots of subjectivity. However, by also calling the subject to trust, John's signs place "a hold on the violence of affects," as the drives are shaped by the relation to another. Moreover, in opening an infinite time of interpretation, and locating the subject in both the semiotic and symbolic realms, these signs pluralize the subject. Strangely

26. Ibid., 129.
27. Ibid.
28. Ibid., 132.
29. Ibid., emphasis added.

enough, the limits of psychoanalysis—as described in *Revolution in Poetic Language*—are overcome, in the biblical healing of Jesus!

The other biblical text that discloses a semiotic dimension is the Song of Songs. Kristeva highlights several important features of this text, as well as the process of its canonization in the Hebrew Bible. First, the text is a polyphonic dialogue; its polyphony brings the bodies of the two lovers (God, Israel, the Shulamite, Solomon, etc.) into speech. Moreover, in the repetition of phrases of praise ("How beautiful you are, my love, how beautiful you are"[30]), poetic discourse emerges, bringing the drives to light in an emphasis on both the materiality of the language, and the irreducible embodiment thereby signified. In staging dialogue, repetition, and letting the female subject speak, the text thereby opens onto the semiotic. As Kristeva writes, "At equal remove from both [Platonically ideal love and orgiastic fusion], sealed by law as much as based on a distance, a flight, even an impossibility, love in the Song of Songs turns over a completely new leaf in the experience of western subjectivity."[31]

While the "unnameable" corporeality of love in the Song does submit to law, as it takes place within the couple, as a wedding song, it nonetheless surpasses this boundary as well; the woman's voice becomes sovereign, in relation to the law without thereby being confined by it. Moreover, the Song of Songs brings out the semiotic dimension of love and subjectivity precisely in its repetition of prophetic discourse, thereby taking up the signs of abomination and abjection. For example, "My beloved thrust his hand through the hole in the door; I trembled to the core of my being"[32] echoes the language of Jeremiah 31:20, where God is "deeply moved" for Ephraim, the lost Northern Kingdom.[33] The Song thus transforms the taxonomy of abomination, opening a subjective, interior space from within it, uniting what had been separated in a healing, life-giving way. In Kristeva's words, "the intensity of love comes precisely from that combination of received jouissance and taboo, from a basic separation that nevertheless unites—that is what love issued from the Bible signifies for us, most particularly in its later form as celebrated in the Song of Songs."[34]

---

30. Song 4:1.
31. Kristeva, *Tales of Love*, 97.
32. Song 5:4.
33. On this point, see Ellen Davis, "Reading the Song Iconographically."
34. Kristeva, *Tales of Love*, 90.

Kristeva's analysis of these two passages shows clearly that Judaism and Christianity retain a semiotics that can enable incarnation, pluralization of interpretation and subjectivity, and relation to the feminine. They need not, then, be taken as simply discourses or practices of interpretation that remain symbolic, repressing the body so as to allow speech to flourish. Such a restriction is always possible—and Kristeva has been highly attentive to how the feminine is frequently silenced within Christianity and Judaism; however, this does not exhaustively define either religion. Moreover, it is important to note that this potential, for Kristeva, resides in *both* the Song of Songs (and thus, the Hebrew Bible and its rabbinic interpretation) and the Gospel of John (and its Christian interpretations). This is especially important to note because most of Kristeva's analyses of the poetic, artistic dimensions of religion focus on Christianity, which, along with the progression of the argument in *Powers of Horror*, could lead to a supersessionist or anti-Semitic reading.[35] This is not her intention; the Song of Songs, one might say, functions to challenge and disrupt the very idea of abstract religion through which Hegel stereotypes Judaism and thereby reduces its polyphony. Here, a convergence between Kristeva and Rosenzweig might emerge, as both see this text as representing a potential for psychic, subjective, and communal development.

Kristeva's interpretation of the value of biblical semiotics—and, especially, the exemplary semiotics of the Gospel of John—foregrounds the central place that she accords language within analytic practice. For Kristeva, language is important because it enables a countertransferential interpretation of the analysand's discourse. At its most basic level, countertransference is the analyst's desire for the analysand, as a result of the analysand's transference that makes the analyst the object of love. Countertransference uses symbolic language, along with affection, to re-link the symbolic and semiotic levels of discourse in the analysand. An analyst's speech is countertransferential because it expresses not only what she hears the analysand saying, but also the desire and psychic structure that the analyst brings to the interpretation. By bringing desire to bear on the analysis through her speech, the analyst hopes to give the analysand a language in which the repressed unconscious can be brought to light. As Kristeva writes,

> ... although the analyst's empathy and understanding are necessarily accompanied by a revival of his own psychological conflicts and unconscious elements, which no training analysis can suppress, this

---

35. See note 20.

notion of countertransference aims at introducing, seducing, and producing the same sort of psychological work in the patient—with the eventual possibility that the unnameable autosensuality will be converted into a compatible discourse.[36]

Particularly as such "psychological conflicts" unsettle the attempts to define psychoanalysis as an objective science, countertransference has frequently been rejected or suppressed within psychoanalytic theory. Within treatment, it also threatens to impose a possible violence on the analysand's speech, as an interpretation from a distance.[37] Nonetheless, drawing on the work of Melanie Klein, Kristeva argues that some form of countertransference is required for treatment to succeed: "If not through the acting out of their own unconscious reserve, it is difficult to see how analysts could part with a superegoistic or simply conscious listening in order to aim for the well-known yet enigmatic 'benevolent listening.'"[38] Without countertransference, the affective connection with the analysand's semiotic life could not develop.

Drawing on her unconscious, the analyst's speech is semiotic—both knowledge and desire—and thus provides a structure through which the analysand can give semiotic expression to her desire. Kristeva's growing emphasis on countertransference, as a necessary interpretation that passes through symbolic language, helps to explain why she sees the Johannine discourse as exemplary. Jesus presents his audience with an interpretation that is, at once, his interpretation of their desire, *and* an expression of his love for them. Through this discourse, and the love embodied therein, he moves them to an interpretation of and for themselves, which creates the subjective space in which they may find life and freedom. Christ's words, then, fulfill the analytic project by bringing together desire and knowledge. Like psychoanalysis, his discourse has a vitality "that grows out of the immanence of death (the discourse of knowledge) and resurrection (the discourse of desire)."[39]

In light of this potential, it is worth noting a couple of the ways Kristeva sees this interpretive practice as developed within the Christian tradition. In order to relate this to her discussion with Clément, I will

---

36. Kristeva, *New Maladies of the Soul*, 78.

37. Ibid., 34.

38. Ibid., 80. See also her discussion of Klein's work on countertransference, in *Melanie Klein*, 175–76.

39. Kristeva, *New Maladies of the Soul*, 35.

focus here on Bernard of Clairvaux and Catherine of Siena. In Bernard's work, Kristeva sees the possibility of a monotheistic passage to the sacred that breaks down the hierarchical, symbolic opposition of sexual difference. For Bernard, the human love of God always involves inhabiting a transitional, mediating space between the body and the spirit. In a letter, Clément argues that monotheism precludes an openness to mysticism as a dissolution of sexual boundaries. In response, Kristeva points to Bernard's work, especially his *Sermons on the Song of Songs*, where both God and believers take on bisexual attributes.[40] She writes,

> In his commentary on the Song of Songs, he insists at length on the ambiguity of the passage that describes the breasts of the beloved offering herself to the divine spouse, and does not hesitate to assert that the spouse himself possesses breasts . . . These are supposedly words addressed by the beloved to the husband . . . which suggests that the believer (if he is the beloved) and God (if he is the husband) would both be . . . equipped with breasts—hence maternal?[41]

The ambiguity of gender in Bernard's work is situated in the context of a broader transitional logic that Kristeva describes in *Tales of Love*. Bernard's work operates, psychologically, as a passage from the carnal to the spiritual. Human love always begins in carnal love, even if this is only meant to be a symbol of spiritual love. It is through the speculative passage from carnal to spiritual love that one relates to the desired object, which fulfills one's love even as it is (physically) lacking; for spiritual love, as Bernard writes in his *Sermons on the Song of Songs*, "seeking is finding." Bernard thus remains "within an ambiguity, torn between Self and Other, flesh and spirit, lust and harmony."[42] This ambiguous seeking opens a space and a discourse between desire and law, between drive and speech, enabling a passage from one to the other. By so opening love in this way, Bernard's work points toward an incarnational semiotics that is at least one possible outgrowth of Christian thought.

More sharply than Bernard, Catherine of Siena signifies what Kristeva terms the "violence of the Word"—the marked separation within Catherine that occurs through her fidelity to Christ. This fidelity, which led to her being named a doctor of the Church, led to acts of devotion from giving advice to popes to feeding the poor, from fasting in penance for the

40. See Young, "Song of Songs."
41. Kristeva, *Feminine and the Sacred*, 62.
42. Kristeva, *Tales of Love*, 165.

Church's sins to sucking the pus from lepers' wounds. Her fidelity, however, was also an aggressive defense against the violence of her family, in whose relations she risked being swallowed up (her renunciation of marriage, and spiritual marriage to Christ, occurred in the context of her family wanting her to marry her dead sister's husband). In this case, as Kristeva says, "the lethal sacred drives the machine of spiritual improvement,"[43] as the very participation in sacrifice that leads to Catherine's agency and authority in the community also cuts her off from her family and ultimately from her own life. Her devotion brings about the separation from her family, but is so complete that there is no space for self-love, or relation to others, on the worldly level; in Catherine's own words, self-centered love "destroys the city of the soul."[44]

The life of Catherine exhibits the tension within Kristeva's work on Christianity, as she both identifies with its tradition and yet distances herself from it. By identifying totally with the Word—her fasting signifying a complete sublimation of drive—Catherine exhibits the "tyrannical" danger of Christianity, as a drive for purity that can impose on and thus restrict subjectivity. Catherine's repression does enable subjectivity—and, notably, a certain ecclesiastical authority—as it is through her self-sacrifice that Catherine relates to the other. Kristeva, however, wants to "ease" the "draconian ideal" of Catherine's life, enabling one to relate to the sacred, while also recognizing and welcoming the otherness within oneself that remains irreducible to the symbolic realm of belief.

Kristeva writes to Clément that she sees it as necessary to traverse Christianity in order for a free, responsible subjectivity to emerge. "By traversing, that is, by knowing and analyzing: not by becoming imprisoned within it."[45] One must, then, inhabit Christianity, but also analyze the symbolics of discourse, so as to allow the discourse to come into contact with the bodies, desires, and psychic life of our world.[46] Through analysis, one finds an interpretive freedom in relation to this discourse linking its symbolics with affectivity. While Kristeva, then, may reject the objective truth of Christianity as a description of reality, she does see its discourse as

---

43. Kristeva, *Feminine and the Sacred*, 120.
44. See O'Driscoll, *Catherine of Siena*, 40.
45. Kristeva, *Feminine and the Sacred*, 165.
46. See also Kristeva, "Dialogue with Julia Kristeva," 9, where she argues for an "appropriation of religious traditions as part of revolt."

true for the subject, opening a space in which both knowledge and desire can reside.[47]

The freedom that comes from traversing signs through interpretation, then, is not a Hegelian self-consciousness that sublimates material form. Rather, Kristeva's project is best understood as a work of incarnation, a making-flesh of the word, allowing semiotic drives to inform and destabilize discourse, so as to make space for the otherness within us. This infusion of semiosis into symbolic language is an artistic, poetic endeavor. As shall be discussed at greater length in the next chapter, it is through artistic engagement with the symbolics of Christian discourse that one traverses them in interpretation, opening them toward a freedom that comes through love. Yet, clearly, such artistic passage need not be opposed to religion. If such passage involves an Augustinian "becoming a question to oneself," then religious discourse and practice become forms that may creatively lead to healing.[48] By passing to the artistic interpretation of religion, and the subjectivity such artistic appropriation enables, Kristeva articulates the psychic structure that informs her politics of strangeness and cosmopolitanism. Nevertheless, the privilege accorded certain verbal modalities highlights the limits of Kristeva's conception of materiality, embodiment, and religion. In order to explore this problematic further, it is necessary to turn to Clément's approach to psychoanalysis, and her accompanying interpretation of religion.

IRON SKELETONS: SACRED HEALING IN CLÉMENT'S WORK

While Kristeva's work has been very influential in contemporary North American critical theory, Catherine Clément's work has remained largely untapped in American circles. This is, perhaps, the result of a historical irony: Clément's commitment to contextual work, and her stylistic concern for accessibility (both of which relate to her Marxist slant), have made her *less* "theoretical," and thus less likely to translate into terms easily placed on the American intellectual scene. Nonetheless, over the course of her many intellectual endeavors—from teaching philosophy at the University of Paris, to founding a Marxist newspaper, to television production, and her many novels—Clément has cultivated a unique intellectual voice that deserves to be heard. Her work developed as a critique of the institutionalized

---

47. On this possibility, see Kearns, "Art and Religious," 117–19.
48. See Bouthors-Paillart, *Julia Kristeva*, 84–88.

practice of psychoanalysis for its failure to hear the embodied voices and disparate language of its patients. Her placement of herself "in the position of a valet"[49] in relation to philosophy likewise interrogates the discourses of philosophy and Western religious thought from the perspective of those they would forget. Thus, as with Kristeva, Clément's approach to psychoanalysis illuminates her analysis of religion—from her early work through *The Feminine and the Sacred* and onward to *Theo's Odyssey*, her novelistic journey through the world's major religions.

The central image that guides Clément's thought is that of the shaman. A shaman is, as she writes, one who "sets out on a journey, armed with imaginary wings and clad in an iron skeleton"[50] so as to bring about the healing of a trauma within a community. The shaman, the "medicine man," acquires the power to heal by having undergone such trauma and been healed himself. Clad in the iron skeleton, the shaman becomes able to take on the suffering and illness of the patient so as to bring healing. As Clément describes, for healing to occur, both the shaman and the patient must recognize and undergo the trauma that is causing the illness, entering into its trance. The shaman's healing thus moves outside of normal life, which "makes ordinary love impossible." Within psychoanalysis, Lacan played this role, "prodigiously well-read but determined to repeat what he had read in his own way, allowing language to make its own discoveries within his fertile imagination."[51] Lacan's challenge to the analytic establishment—including his dissolution of his own school—placed him outside the norms of society, in the service of a deeper healing than the culture could recognize.

Along with its practitioners' desire to be recognized as scientific, the professionalization of psychoanalysis led to its normalization, suppressing its potential for radical, transformative healing. In a similar way, Clément sees Western religion's focus on linguistic meaning as confining, repressing, and destroying the pluralizing, disruptive discourses of the sacred. It is in part through her appeal to Indian philosophy, as well as the figure of the shaman, that Clément seeks to restore the possibility of healing and an openness to the sacred to the analytical and religious cultures that risk foreclosing them. Examining the shape that language takes within these

---

49. Alluding to Hegel, this is Clément's description of her reading of Plato, Descartes, and Kant, in *Syncope*, 50.

50. Clément, *Weary Sons of Freud*, 51.

51. Clément, *Lives and Legends of Jacques Lacan*, 203.

institutions, and what remains beyond their purview, will highlight the significance and coherence of Clément's thought.

Clément's intellectual career developed in close proximity to psychoanalysis. She underwent psychoanalysis, and attended Lacan's seminars for many years, and his work has been central to her writing. All of these events shaped her understanding of the discipline, which involves a recognition of its healing potential, its distortion of Lacan's teaching in its failure to *listen*, and its loss of a sense of the need for social transformation.

As mentioned, Lacan's work oscillates between that of a prophet and a shaman. The difference is notable: The prophet, as she says following Bourdieu, speaks publicly; he "stands on the very edge of intelligibility, at the place where his linguistic innovations can still be understood by the group."[52] The shaman, however, no longer speaks ordinary language, and is often unintelligible; in many ways, Lacan practiced such discourse in his later seminars. However, for Clément, it was not his ability to speak abnormally, but to *hear* the abnormal that distinguished his analytic ability. His nonmedical writings on the discourse of madwomen illustrate how differently he heard them:

> The life experience of the paranoiac and the worldview it engenders may be thought of as a novel form of syntax, which enlists its own peculiar means of comprehension for the purpose of affirming the community of mankind. Understanding this syntax can, I think provide an invaluable introduction to the symbolic values of art and, more particularly, to the problems of style—an introduction, in other words, to art's peculiar virtues of conviction and human communion as well as to the paradoxes attendant upon its creation. These problems will always remain beyond the grasp of any form of anthropology that has not yet freed itself from the naïve realism of the object.[53]

By hearing what is unintelligible as discourse, Lacan moved beyond a "naïve realism" that sees language as pointing to a signified. For these women, the signification *itself* is what their speech signified. Lacan's studies of female criminals, paranoiacs, and saints sought to bring to light their alternative discourses that resisted everyday comprehension.

Such listening had dramatic effects, not least on Lacan himself. He frequently spoke in "midspeak," a half-speaking that intentionally remained

---

52. Ibid., 56.

53. Jacques Lacan, *Psychose paranoïaque*, 387–88; quoted in Clément, *Lives and Legends*, 57–58.

cryptic so as to prevent full comprehension. Yet to hear such discourses, he had to enter into this world of passion, a world where there is "the danger of too much closeness, the misfortune of one person's identification with another."[54] The mystic or the paranoiac collapses the distance that maintains proper social relations, and Lacan had, in Clément's words, "a pronounced taste for the abolition of distance."[55] However, since psychoanalysis also relies upon building the correct distance, so as to break transference and end the analysis, was such fusion really compatible with analysis? Clément says, in passing, that the analyst cannot build the distance; the analyst's role is precisely to build proximity through listening. This then lets the analysand build distance, repeating the mirror stage that leads to subjective formation and "untying the Gordian knot" that fills the place of the subject. In *listening*, the analyst breaks down the borders that establish normality—the boundary between genders, the boundary between the divine and the insane, the boundary between science and irrationality. It is in this sense, then, that "Lacan drew a lesson for psychoanalysis: the analyst too is one who gives what he does not have and who refuses to give what he does have. The psychoanalyst is a creature of love and psychoanalysis, an amorous discipline, an erotic theory, a craft of pure jouissance."[56] It is as listener that the analyst becomes a shaman—breaking with the distance of language so that the analysand may build that language and her subjectivity herself.

If one does not follow Lacan's path and avoids the passionate break with logocentrism, then a psychoanalyst becomes "an impoverished intellectual"[57] and a failure. Clément criticizes such failure within the analytic practice on several different occasions. First, within Lacan's own career, the movement to medicalize psychoanalysis risked losing the specific temporality of the analyst/analysand relation. Such debates led to a schism in 1953, and Lacan's expulsion from the IPA in 1964. Further, after founding his own school, Lacan dissolved the École Freudienne in 1980—according to Clément, because his followers no longer were really practicing analytic *listening*.[58]

Even before this dissolution, Clément criticized this failure of analysis, as its practitioners sought to present themselves as cultural, literary experts.

54. Clément, *Lives and Legends*, 76.
55. Ibid., 78.
56. Ibid., 143.
57. Ibid., 51
58. Ibid., 104–7.

The focus on producing books, as commodities, took away from the focus on healing—in the patient's discourse, "all the psychoanalyst hears is a novel."[59] Clément's primary criticism in *The Weary Sons of Freud* is that analysts used Lacan's critique of "American" normalization,[60] to justify a refusal to cure. Drawing from the life of their patients, while refusing to give life, such analysts become vampires, shutting off the possibility of radical individual and social transformation:

> Closed doors, family doors and no way out: when they reject the word healing, psychoanalysts shut the door. Even the doors of desire are locked, held in an implacable net whose implicit unspoken premises are that nothing can be done about it. But it's not true. If what Freud discovered is not used to change the world around us in order to realize the desire whose roots we now know, then it's just one more philosophical system, one more illusion. So many lives have been changed, so many transformations are accomplished every day after so much pain that we must keep on saying it again and again: it's not true, the doors are not closed.[61]

The "closing of doors" occurs within both psychic and political life as a result of this cultural, elitist determination of psychoanalysis. In its focus on being learned, and literate, the tragic irony of analysis is that it fails to hear and give voice to those voices whom Lacan thought analysis could serve. As Clément describes in the case of Mme Victoire, a cleaning woman who listens to those around her, and thus has knowledge of the unconscious, she displays a "will to heal, which will never be realized."[62] Because she cannot be trained, her ability to listen goes unnoticed and untapped. The analysts' failure to listen, and to cure, repeats a cultural failure to listen, and this potential for healing is forgotten.

In her critical appreciation for Lacanian psychoanalysis, and her disparagement of its normalization, Clément articulates the two modes of subjectivity that establish the field for her interpretation of religion. In the Lacanian attention to the founding of the subject in the mirror stage, and the attentive listening to the different languages of the psyche, she

---

59. Clément, *Weary Sons of Freud*, 38.

60. "Normalization" was the idea that psychoanalysis should be used so as to make patients well-adjusted to the society in which they lived, thereby making it a highly conformist and bourgeois practice.

61. Clément, *Weary Sons of Freud*, 47.

62. Ibid., 90.

finds a subjectivity that relates itself to the sacred, allowing its borderless, infinite energy (at once creative and traumatic) to saturate and desituate the subject. In normalized, cultural, and professional analysis, one finds a subjectivity that draws energy from the sacred, yet separates itself from and suppresses that event. In the broader context of her work, this distinction becomes paramount, as Clément identifies the normalizing, organizing subjectivity that represses the sacred with the dominant philosophical and religious conceptions of subjectivity within Western culture, while seeing Indian religion and practice as more open to the sacred.

Clément's interpretation of religion operates through a distinction between religion and the mystical, which she identifies with the sacred. The sacred thus becomes opposed to any hierarchical, organized, ordering discourse, and identified with the bodies, gestures, and languages that break down such established order. She writes to Kristeva,

> As for the religious, I can hardly imagine it without organization . . . the function of the religious always comes back to the organization of worship: one enters here, goes through there, here one prays, there one bows, one begins and ends; in short, time and space are well managed. The sacred does exactly the opposite: it eclipses time and space. It *passes* in a boundlessness without rule or reservation, which is the trait of the divine.[63]

Clément recognizes that mysticism, as a passage to the sacred, is possible through religious order and hierarchy, but only as the overturning or dissolution of the order. Western religion, as monotheistic, sets limits to this passage, and thereby retains an organization and hierarchy that distances its subjects from the sacred. In light of the distinction between religion and the mysticism, one could say that for Clément, Judaism, Christianity, and Islam are irreducibly religious.

For Clément the issue with monotheism is twofold: first, in the distinction between the one God and creation (*tawhid* for Islam, the oneness of God in Judaism, divine simplicity for Aquinas, etc.), monotheism relies upon an irreducible separation and organization. Moreover, in the identification of God as masculine, and without complement, monotheism also sets up an *impasse* between the sexes—a limit that cannot be crossed. The feminine, for Clément, is excluded from a religious conception of the sacred. In comparison with the "syncopated" culture of India, Clément thinks that monotheism even prevents access to the sacred, rather than simply diverting

63. Clément, *Feminine and the Sacred*, 30.

it. As she writes to Kristeva, "There is no doubt that a relation between man and God exists. But what about between man and the sacred? What if, by chance . . . the worship of the only god barred the masculine from acceding to the sacred?"[64] Even the more mystical trends within monotheism—for example, Sufism—remain in tension with the logic of monotheism, and thus of an order that passes beyond the religious order.

Clément glosses this analysis with the following statement: "On the side of Christian monotheism, I do not see how a male saint could identify with any female figure whatever, especially not the Virgin."[65] It is here that her differences from Kristeva become most apparent. As discussed above, Kristeva's rejoinder builds on her work with Bernard of Clairvaux, as a particular example within Christianity of how mysticism can unsettle and reshape religious hierarchy and organization from within. Clément seeks to pass beyond both the order of religion and the order of the subject in Western philosophy, as both refuse to listen to the voices and languages that would unsettle them and expose their construction. Kristeva likewise seeks to pass beyond the subject, but seeks to do so by working *within* these discourses to uncover the alternative possibilities and subjectivities that reside within their texts and practices. She thereby highlights a possibility that Clément would seem to neglect.

By contrast with Clément, one could see Kristeva's understanding of mysticism as close to that proposed by Archbishop Rowan Williams in his fine analysis of Teresa of Avila. Williams argues that mysticism is best understood in terms of its social function, as an internalization and transformation of a tradition's self-understanding.[66] As in the case of Teresa, mysticism functions to challenge social boundaries and practices, as Teresa's establishing of the Carmelites opened a way of life for anyone in early modern Spain, without regard to social status or "honor" as socially defined, and it provided a voice for a woman who otherwise would have been silenced in her culture. By attending to those signifying moments within Judaism and Christianity where new modes of subjectivity and relationality challenge the fixed, established subject of Western thought, Kristeva passes beyond logocentrism by reworking the tradition—passing to the sacred, *through* the religious. Clément—in part due to her generalizing

64. Ibid., 54.
65. Ibid.
66. See Williams, *Teresa of Avila*, 153. Also, as a note, Kristeva has recently completed a novel about Teresa's life, entitled *Thérèse mon amour*.

opposition between religion and mysticism—sees the need to shift terrain for access to the sacred to become possible, turning to those experiences and practices that have been ignored or appropriated in ways that both draw on and restrict their potential.

Clément's opposition between religion and mysticism is thoroughly modern and can be deconstructed quite easily, as Kristeva does via Bernard of Clairvaux. However, while Christian, Jewish, or Muslim mysticism may provide the access to the sacred that Clément finds elsewhere, her analysis does raise deeper questions regarding the relation to the sacred within these traditions, and particularly within Christianity. Specifically, she raises questions about the modes of mystical subjectivity enabled by Christian discourse, the exceptional status of mysticism within Christianity, and the appropriation of such sacred relations by normalizing institutions in our culture. Reference to the examples of mysticism already discussed will help to illustrate these points.

Theologians who write on Bernard of Clairvaux frequently make a distinction in interpreting his work: when Bernard describes union with God, he describes a "union of wills" in which one acts in accord with God, freely and lovingly. The implication, of course, is that he does not mean a union of essence, in which any distinction between God and the creature would be lost. This complicates how we understand the subjectivity of mysticism within Christianity. While Bernard does identify with Mary and with the bride of Christ in the Song of Songs—and encourages his audience to do likewise—thereby passing beyond sexual difference, he nonetheless remains distinct from God, such that the boundary between God and creature remains uncrossed. In this sense, at least, there is a limit to the "regression" (dissolution) of the subject. What Clément's analysis highlights, then, is that even in its access to the sacred, the subject remains intact within Christian discourse. Furthermore, it should be noted that mystics are treated as exceptional within the Christian community. Their access to the sacred, while perhaps reshaping the community, remains the purview of elites, and unavailable to most people.

Finally, in the cases of Bernard, Catherine, and Teresa, all three have been canonized by the Catholic Church, and are recognized as central contributors to both the history and culture of Western Christianity. When they are set forth as examples of devotion, and as examples of the intellectual and literary possibilities within Christianity, it becomes difficult to hold this together with their stringent critiques of religious practice in their times. Like the stories that analysts take from their sessions with patients (as Clément describes in *The Weary Sons of Freud*) so as to develop novels, the appreciation of their stories risks effacing these mystics' uniqueness, and the potential for change therein. To read Catherine of Siena as a doctor of the Church may give validity to her discourse, but it also can ignore the tenuous and complex relation to authority found in the very words of her letters and prayers (her *Dialogue*, for instance, does not take place via ecclesial mediation). This raises a question, then, as to how we hear their discourses: do we hear or read them as languages of otherworldly devotion—ecstatic language that says nothing to the particular societies in which they lived—or, do we read them as alternative signifying practices, with their own logics, and thus having import for cultural life today? In other words, will learning to hear these texts in all their complexity help us to learn to cure—or serve as stories for us to draw on, so as to appear more cultured? For all the flaws of her generalizations, Clément's questions remain important for the study of religion. Moreover, her emphasis on listening and regression qualifies Kristeva's focus on countertransferential speech, perhaps pointing to a more embodied dimension of the sacred than Kristeva's semiotic discloses.

In the space between their different perspectives, then, Kristeva and Clément trace out an alternative thought of religion—as a discourse through which one passes to a new, reflective, ethical mode of subjectivity that takes responsibility for desire, but also creates a space in which the other's desire can speak. Both see analysis as an affective discourse, and a form of listening, that can lead to the creation of new forms of subjectivity. And, especially as one moves to their later work, religion (or mysticism) comes to represent one form of this subjective creation. At the same time, both offer cogent and important critiques which may be useful in the study of religious traditions and theology. Bearing their criticisms in mind, then, may help one to hear Western religion with a new ear. However, to hear with a new ear requires a shift in interpretation, and an alternative approach to culture. The next chapter engages their cultural and artistic reflections, demonstrating the alternative hermeneutics that Clément and Kristeva bring to religion, building toward a discussion of their politics in chapter 9.

EIGHT

Keeping Time
Music, Philosophy, and the Feminine

If one objective of postmodernity is to move beyond the Cartesian subject, then a central question becomes what forms of subjectivity should take its place. One alternative is to redescribe the relations between the subject's different types of signifying activity. For instance, Rosenzweig and Rosenstock crafted their theory of speech-thinking as a challenge to Cartesian solipsism and ahistorical thought. Alternatively, Derrida's inversion of the relationship between philosophy and literature opens a field of grammatology and the time of the trace. Or, as discussed earlier, Levinas frees ethics from the constraints of epistemology, thereby disclosing a mode of subjectivity that is hostage to and for the other, and Blanchot opens the thought of the neuter—a form of writing that does not remain rooted in the world or the subject. By emphasizing different forms of writing or speech, new forms of agency, thought, and community can emerge.

Like these authors, Kristeva and Clément resituate the thinking subject by shifting its relation to other signifying practices, most notably those related to art. Drawing on their psychoanalytic training, both see art as signifying diverse states of psychic life with their own integrity and logic, which may not be recognized or properly interpreted within the philosophical tradition. Because of its connection with materiality and embodiment, artistic signification takes a special place within their work, disclosing the time, vitality, and energy of semiosis that philosophical discourse often seeks to suppress. To focus on the arts is to explore the otherness within ourselves, which both authors see as central to developing an effective postmodern politics, as shall be discussed further in the next chapter. While sharing this approach, it is in their discussion of the arts that their views diverge—deepening the debates over the relation between religion and the sacred discussed in the previous chapter.

In *The Feminine and the Sacred*, music is particularly central for Clément's articulation of the sacred, while Kristeva's interpretation of the arts focuses primarily on visual and literary arts. Clément's focus on music develops her account of the sacred as a mystical, ineffable experience; this focus draws from her account of syncope, her critique of opera as a dramatization of the violence of Western subjectivity, and her turn toward Indian philosophy. By contrast, Kristeva's emphasis on visual and literary work conceives embodiment in conjunction with language, and thus in a closer connection with the forms of subjectivity that have emerged within Christianity. For both authors, new modes of relation and subjectivity emerge through the analysis of such artistic and religious forms. Exploring how they listen to and interpret art will make apparent the differences in Kristeva and Clément's constructive projects, and lay the groundwork for their respective political engagements in the final chapter.

OFFBEAT: MUSIC, PHILOSOPHY, AND RAPTURE

Music is exhausting, carrying one away. It carries us to the heavens, while grounding us in dance. It is highly enigmatic: in speaking of music, is one speaking of melody's diachronic progression, or the synchronous difference of harmony? Is music reflectively ethereal, or rhythmically corporeal? In her reflections on music, Clément cites Claude Levi-Strauss, who wrote that, "since it is the only language with the contradictory attributes of being at once both intelligible and untranslatable, the musical creation is a being comparable to the gods, and music itself is the supreme mystery of the science of man, a mystery that all the various disciplines come up against and which holds the key to their progress."[1] Like the sacred, music dissolves the borders and oppositions that structure thought and communities. In light of Levi-Strauss's description of music as the "supreme mystery," Clément sees the philosophical interpretation and definition of music as illustrative of philosophy's classification and restriction of the sacred. Philosophy restricts the appearance of the sacred, so as to harness its energy and power, putting it to work productively through sacrifice—as is illustrated in the deaths of women and other marginal characters in opera. As a challenge to this philosophical approach, Clément accentuates the syncopative, elusive dimension of music that has so often been suppressed. As she writes to Kristeva, "Music takes hold of its listener via the slow movements of the internal organs. It draws its effects from visceral time . . . music, material and ideal, physical and spiritual, remains an unassailable roadblock for the

---

1. Clément, *Syncope*, 209.

sciences."[2] Beneath the philosophical confinement of music, and through conversation with Indian philosophy, Clément articulates an alternative relation to music, time, and the world.

Clément's recent novel, *Theo's Odyssey*, highlights the importance of music as well. *Theo's Odyssey* tells the story of Theo, a young French boy whose aunt seeks to find healing for his unknown, untreatable illness. In their journeys, they explore the rites of religious traditions on every continent, seeking an answer to the problem of evil (that is, *theodicy*). The story is replete with trances induced by religious music: Theo undergoes a trance in Egypt during a healing ritual of dancing.[3] His aunt enters a trance while dancing to drums in Senegal,[4] and music enchants them in Russian Orthodoxy, a Baptist choir, and with Sufi dancers. Music is thus an element of religion—or, more precisely, of what Clément terms mysticism—that is present in rites across religious traditions, and this emphasis leads to her syncretistic perspective. In each case, by bringing the dancer or listener into a trance, the music introduces a delay, a separation, into the rhythm of culture—what Clément terms a *syncope*.

What is syncope? It goes by many names—depression, darkness, gap, rupture. At its most basic level, it is delay: a waiting that throws time out of joint, unsettling anticipation or expectation. As in medicine, where it means a loss of consciousness (and a cessation of breathing), this delay seems to be derivative from consciousness, and dependent upon it. As Clément argues, however, syncope may have its own logic that operates under the surface of this gap. In the introduction to *Syncope: The Philosophy of Rapture*, Clément says that the question is not, "Where am I?" when one returns to consciousness; the real question is, "Where was I?" during the syncope. Where might this gap or delay take us? Syncope shines a dark light on our world, such that, "when one returns from syncope it is the real world that suddenly looks strange."[5]

Within Western culture, the movement of syncope has been suppressed and harnessed. This harnessing has been effected, in part, by the weakening of ritual practice. As the ritual life through which one enters syncope has diminished, its place within culture has diminished as well;

2. Clément, *Feminine and the Sacred*, 161.
3. Clément, *Theo's Odyssey*, 126.
4. Ibid., 462–63.
5. Clément, *Syncope*, 1.

the productive time of daylight, the time of the subject, pervades and determines our lives. Clément writes,

> Today's world watches with jealous care in order to limit these crossings over into nothingness . . . The work ethic and the energy invested in it take over benevolent night's territory; retirement, where the senses once sheltered from thought, now resounds like a bell with productive activity.[6]

In place of the syncopative rites, regression now occurs through depression, rupturing the social bond as an "echo of these lost initiations." The treatment of this illness, and its medicalization, shows the extent to which a desire for night, weakness, or rapture is not legitimized in Western culture.[7] Much as with Rosenzweig and Rosenstock-Huessy, changes in social time restructure psychic and social life; the modern world's emphasis on labor has lost the connection of holidays and retreats with sacred time. Now, Clément writes, "Hard working modernity denies this retirement to the social being. To 'take a breather,' as we say, vacations were invented; but they are the other side of working; they are an authorized interruption . . . It is impossible to go on retreat, as one used to say."[8] The focus on energy, productivity, and social being forecloses the relation to delay, weakness, and solitude that would enable a different, more harmonious way of being in the world.

In its desire for light and clarity—from Plato's allegory of the cave to the *Aufklarung*—philosophy likewise manifests the desire to contain syncope. Clément traces this tendency through a survey of the philosophical classifications of music. While Plato, in the *Republic*, does allow music that moves one toward the divine, he nonetheless restricts its operation on two levels. First, as with poetry, only music that is piously directed to the gods is admissible. But second, the music must not excite in any way that leads away from reason, or distorts the harmony of the soul. As she writes, "The poet is a carrier of the potential for delirium, and by neutralizing this, one is purged; one immunizes oneself. Then the process is repeated for music. Soft harmonies are dismissed, the ones that are 'suitable for banquets' and incite drunkenness."[9] Only through such purging and rationalization are

---

6. Ibid., 25.
7. See Clément, *Feminine and the Sacred*, 133–34.
8. Clément, *Syncope*, 25.
9. Ibid., 54.

music and syncope allowed into the *polis*, once deprived of their disruptive potential. Like the wild horse of the *Phaedrus*, music must be subdued under the guidance of sober reason.

In an intriguing, brief commentary on Kant, Clément illustrates the modern philosophical confinement of syncope in Kant's determination of the sublime. For Kant, the sublime is the rational transcending of feeling— for example, in the recognition of fear or the awareness of nature's majesty. In either case, there is a feeling of being sensibly overwhelmed, and yet subjectivity remains sovereign through reason's *grasp* of feeling overwhelmed. Music, as spiritual and sensible, thus becomes highly problematic. In order to reserve for reason the sublime transcendence of sensible feeling, Kant associates music entirely with physicality, as a "play of tones" that excites the intestines yet has no share in reason. He thereby denies music's syncopative power in human life:

> It is already enough if he will allow to pass, by detouring through a scrupulous and honorable analysis of the feelings and the arts, a little syncope in the sublime and a lot in laughter. For we must make the best of the intestines and the tickling, find pleasure a place in the sun without allowing it to be engulfed in the night. But great care is taken not to let it spill over.[10]

Indeed, building on Clément's analysis, one could say that this classification of music, so apparently tangential, is crucial to Kant's entire project: it is precisely by dissociating music from math and reason that Kant creates the need for subjectively postulating the reconciliation of the moral law and the telos of nature. The idea of God, as a subjective postulate of practical reason, only emerges as necessary through the suppression of sensibility's musical and immediate access to the sacred.

The exceptions to this systematic keeping of the beat are, not surprisingly, Kierkegaard and Nietzsche, whose poetic grasp of syncope unsettles the "Hegelian three-step." Kierkegaard, in particular, opens the possibility of syncope through his reflections on the abyssal separation and irreducible temporality of the balletic *leap*. His seducers, in their (aesthetic) fascinations with young virgin women, seek to break with morality, but also to suspend time, relating to the infinite by remaining off of the ground. As Clément writes, "This immoderate leap that suspends man's weight has the very lightness of fainting away: the magical grace of human time as

10. Ibid., 49.

it passes, of thought as it stops."[11] In addition to the seducer's fascination with the young girl's leap, Abraham's leap as the knight of faith carries Kierkegaard beyond the calm world of thought. As the knight who goes beyond the border of thought, Abraham enters into darkness: "Thinking about Abraham is another matter, however: there I am shattered . . . I am constantly repelled, and, despite all its passion, my thought cannot penetrate it, cannot get ahead by a hairsbreadth."[12] The teleological suspension of the ethical, his silence before Sarah, and the paradox of faith are all figures for the atemporal darkness or the moment of separation that constitutes syncope.[13] Faith passes into a moment of despair, sickness, or weakness that cannot be readily synthesized or recuperated, even if Abraham does believe that Isaac will be given back to him.

In his poetic thinking of syncope, Kierkegaard is a pivotal figure in Clément's analysis of Western religious and philosophical thought. His work marks the possible divergence of philosophy from itself, representing both the revaluation of syncope and the height of its confinement. These two approaches can be delineated as follows. The first path of syncope opens in the figure of Abraham, whose secrecy toward God cannot be determinatively interpreted, and whose faith introduces a gap into the subject. For, though Kierkegaard is not certain that he has ever met a knight of faith, he recognizes that this possibility destructures the subjectivity of every individual. In thus undermining the ego's foundation, Kierkegaard presages Lacan's mirror stage, as the undoing of the subject. Second, the seducer's desire for syncope, as figured by the desired young woman, epitomizes the operatic economy of syncope—which, ultimately, suppresses syncope's power and restores the order of light. Clément explores and displaces this second path in her well-known work *Opera, or the Undoing of Women*. A brief account of each path is required.

Kierkegaard's work leads to Lacan, as the "knight of faith's" leap introduces a fissure into the subject. As discussed in the last chapter, Lacan's insight into hysterical discourse was to hear it as its own language, with its own rationality. This listening enabled what Clément describes as Lacan's true psychoanalytic discovery, the mirror stage. The mirror stage is syncopative because it results from the delayed development of the child, who does not yet have motor coordination, and the anticipated resolution of

11. Ibid., 89.
12. Kierkegaard, *Fear and Trembling*, 33.
13. Clement, *Syncope*, 95–97.

this delay, as the reflection in the mirror presages what the infant wants to become (self-sufficient and in control of oneself). By locating this syncopation at the heart of the subject, Lacan's work raises the possibility of the subject's not-being. The work of the analyst then becomes introducing this gap into the subject, where identification with the Ideal-I would always attempt to cover over this gap—so that the subject can reengage in a creative process, rather than remain in stasis. To do this, the analyst must listen to the rhythm of the patient's speech, and *syncopate* it. Clément writes,

> Broken words, sobs held back or gasped out, empty or pregnant silences, laughter or tears, sweating or chocking are the materials gathered by the psychoanalyst, like the unknown music of a mysterious tribe. It takes a long time to hear and recognize the rhythms . . . The best way to put it would be to say that the psychoanalyst's job is to look for an effect of syncope during every session.[14]

It is precisely by emphasizing the fissuring of the subject that Lacan resisted "American" psychoanalysis with its utilitarian overtones of ego strengthening. To seek the mirror stage is to open oneself to the rhythm that precedes the subject, and thereby points to its dissolution. Thus, Kierkegaard's knight of faith lets Clément imagine a certain form of regression, as psychoanalysis allows for a limited, individual path to syncopation.

While Kierkegaard gives space to syncope in both the figures of young girls and Abraham, his attention to syncope is hardly innocent. For, particularly in *The Seducer's Diary*, once a young girl makes the leap, she is destroyed. On Clément's reading, the syncope of *The Seducer's Diary* is a spectacle of syncope, in which she leaps and dies for the seducer, who will then seek a new seduction. *He*, then, does not leap; the seducing subject remains intact. She dies, so that he may see the leap occur. One should not identify Kierkegaard with the seducer in any simple way, particularly in light of the pseudonyms in his work. Yet, in his complacency before this feminine lapse—watching the young girl throw the engagement rings in the air—Clément detects the appropriation and silencing of women that constitutes the operatic spectacle:

> Oh, I have read you over and over again, Soren, I understand perfectly well what you write so complacently. No, seduction is not only the act of making oneself be loved when one does not love; it is, above all, making the one who loves you know that you do not

14. Ibid., 125.

love—breaking her flight, clipping her wings, making her bend her neck.[15]

What *The Seducer's Diary* shows is the logic of opera, a spectacle in which women and marginal figures undergo suffering and death for the sake of heroism and the audience. As Clément describes in the Prelude to *Opera, or the Undoing of Women*, women who attend opera are "present for the dispatch of women like themselves."[16] Opera is, itself, a theater of seduction; it is a "double scene where two languages, the spoken and the musical . . . play inseparably."[17] While these are inseparable, the focus is always on the music, as we identify operas by their musical composers—Mozart, Verdi, Puccini. The librettos, and their authors, recede from view. Yet to ignore the librettos is also to forget the dead women strewn on the opera stage. By concealing the narratives, while playing them out, the music actually develops the narratives, subconsciously implanting the ideology that "maintains the harsh laws of family and politics."[18]

Behind the music, the worship of the autonomous subject continues, putting syncope to work to confirm its nobility. The dynamics become most apparent in Mozart's *The Magic Flute* (*Die Zauberflöte*), which Clément rereads as a "family quarrel" over a daughter.[19] "If there is an opera that clearly shows, with all its verbal and musical power, the crushing symbolics of men over women, it is *The Magic Flute*. Divine Mozart? This is he."[20] In this light, this Masonic ode to reason looks very different. Pamino is spirited away from her mother, and suffers loneliness while Tamino remains silent. The flute, which was in the Queen's possession, is returned to Zarastro, its rightful owner, and Tamino takes Pamina on a journey until they "arrive finally at light"—reason, wisdom, enlightenment.

While the narrative is familiar, Clément's analysis illuminates its violence. Pamina suffers from a kidnapping, and being separated from her mother. Papageno, of common birth, is portrayed as only worthy of sexual reproduction, and his mate Papagena is purely his double, with

15. Clément, *Opera, or The Undoing of Women*, 82.
16. Ibid., 5.
17. Ibid., 18.
18. Ibid., 178.
19. It is a measure of the difference in their reception that a recent article offers a feminist reading of *The Magic Flute* inspired by Kristeva, without any reference to Clément's work whatsoever. See Stuckey, "Light Dispells Darkness," esp. 11–14.
20. Clément, *Opera*, 75.

no independent identity. Only a few nobles are worthy of the journey to reason. The violence reaches its height, however, in the treatment of the Queen of the Night. She has the most beautiful, limitless arias—as, especially, in her lamentation of losing her daughter—and might be said to represent syncope's darkness, as her song is one of loss; however, she "speaks not to reason," in saying that her daughter is lost to her forever.[21] Her feat becomes her defeat (*defaite*, Clément's term for "undoing,") rendered hyperbolic and irrational. The journey only reaches its completion once she has tumbled from the stage; reconciliation between Zarastro and the Queen, an equality between them, could never happen. Night is suppressed and the Queen silenced in this journey toward reason. Clément's reading casts a shadow on Mozart—not to mention on Karl Barth's joke that the heavenly choir sings Mozart in their spare time.

In thus analyzing opera, Clément describes her work as one of education—confronting and exposing what opera teaches, in its demonstration of the "harsh laws of family and politics." By recovering the lost lives of these women, uncovering them from narratives and music that would justify their suppression, Clément performs a classically feminist gesture of retrieval of discourses from under the dominion of patriarchy. Yet, her project is not simply one of retrieval, but also of imagining a different future. She imagines writing "her heart's" version of *The Magic Flute*, one that is more honest and thereby moves toward less violence—or, more exactly, toward teaching the violence that is inherent in this story.

> In it the good priests with majestic voices would do what they really do, they would shove Pamina forcibly into the cubbyhole where Zarastro locks her up, they would beat up the Queen of the Night, they would kick Papageno, the truth at last . . . The complicity between the young boy and the men could be read, clear as day, as well as the oppression they impose heavily on the little birdcatcher, and the dishonor of the women they subjugate. The music would be no less divine; but it would then serve a more just cause . . . night would no longer be violent, day would no longer be so brutal. It would be another world, which does not yet exist.[22]

In this passage, we see Clément's vision of living in difference: a culture that allows syncope its place and time, does not seek only the light of

---

21. Clément, *Opera*, 75. See Mozart, *Magic Flute*, 134 (aria xiv, "So bist du meine Tochter nimmermehr").

22. Clément, *Opera*, 76.

wisdom, and thereby moves away from the violence dramatized on this stage. This proposal—in essence a syncretism of day and night—is further developed in *Syncope*, where she journeys from Western religions to Indian philosophy—a journey that takes her beyond the borders of the conscious subject. For syncope to emerge in its own right, to "choose night," one must go further, leaving the village and seeking the dissolution of the subject—not just its downfall. For this to occur, Clément steps beyond Western philosophy, journeying to India to grasp what happens in syncope, beyond the gap or lack the West perceives.

As this journey is central to her vision of cultural politics, it will be discussed further in the next chapter. Here, though, we can see the heart of Clément's thought of the sacred: the order and rationality of society (Western society, especially) harnesses syncope and the sacred, restricting its access and living off of the power that emerges from this suppression. To hear music differently, and give it its proper time, would require a reintegration of rites within society, and it is largely in the name of such reintegration that Clément adopts a syncretistic and ritually-focused view of religion. While Kristeva likewise would highlight the therapeutic dimension of artistic activity, her sense of art's relation to the sacred departs dramatically from Clément's syncretism.

THE SIGNIFICANCE OF ART

The significance of art, as an activity that reshapes relations to others, appears very clearly in Kristeva's work on depression and her analysis of Dostoyevsky's writing as a reshaping of the self in response to melancholy. Her use of Dostoevsky also highlights the limited but significant way that she draws from Christian theology, in articulating the significance of speech as a process of healing. Passivity and despondency are the marks of depression, leading to an utter loss of speech and signification. Melancholy is a living death of the subject. Under the "noncommunicable grief" of depression's black sun, one loses one's being. Kristeva describes melancholy's origins:

> The wound I have just suffered, some setback or other in my love life or profession, some sorrow or bereavement affecting my relationship with close relatives—such are often the easily spotted triggers of my despair. A betrayal, a fatal illness, some accident or handicap that abruptly wrests away from what seemed to me the normal category of normal people or else falls on a loved one with the same radical effect, or yet . . . All this suddenly gives me

another life. A life that is unlivable, heavy with daily sorrows, tears held back or shed, a total despair, scorching at times, then wan and empty. In short, a devitalized existence that although occasionally fired by the effort I make to prolong it, is ready at any moment for a plunge into death.[23]

In this depressive event, there is a loss of the loved object, and with that loss goes the signifying relation that maintained one's bond to the object. Speech fails. In the face of such loss, the avenues out of despair are suicide, terrorism (or murder), or an artistic sublimation of the abyss. All three are found in Dostoevsky's work, which proceeds in light of Christ's embodiment of the passage from suffering to forgiveness, through the act of donation. Dostoevsky's writing, as a writing of forgiveness, is a "continuous struggle to compose a work edge to edge with the unnamable sensuous delights of destructive chaos . . . works of art thus lead us to establish relations with ourselves and others that are less destructive, more soothing."[24]

The melancholic, in the face of absolute loss, can maintain a signifying stance through suffering. The paradigm for such suffering is Job, who is "patient" only in and through the radical protest of lamentation, which gives voice to the abandonment and anger he feels in God's silence. While he feels abandoned, or even persecuted by the God he loves, his speech nonetheless allows him to relate to God, even in God's apparent absence. By giving voice to his aggression and grievance, Job's speech tempers these affectivities and avoids the violence against himself—and perhaps, against others—implicit in his complaint that he wishes he had never been born. While, as a checking of hatred, suffering places a hold on violence, the one suffering remains within the purview of loss, which still constitutes the horizon that limits the subject's possibilities. Without an opening to the future, the reversion to violence and aggressivity always remains possible. In the terms of Dostoevsky's poetics, one may become suicidal like Kirillov, or murderous, like Raskolnikov. How, then, can one move beyond this limit?

Dostoevsky's work illustrates another way of responding to melancholy, which Kristeva terms "aesthetic forgiveness," the literary representation of the affect and thus of the loss. In writing, the passivity of the affect becomes causally effective, restoring signifying agency. Literature and perhaps visual art thereby create a space in which a new life of the subject

23. Kristeva, *Black Sun*, 3–4.
24. Ibid., 187–88.

can unfold.²⁵ It is as forms of literary creation that Kristeva highlights the theological aspects of Dostoevsky's work, beginning with forgiveness.²⁶ In the analytic setting, Kristeva terms this "tact," when one listens for the voice hidden within the representation of suffering, so that, when heard, one can begin again beyond it. Such forgiveness seems to say, "Through my love, I exclude you from history for a while, I take you for a child, and this means that I recognize the unconscious motivations of your crime and allow you to make a new person out of yourself."²⁷ Writing, as a separation from the object and renewal of love through symbolization, becomes a renewal and resuscitation of the subject. It remembers the loss of the beloved that gave rise to melancholy, the crime and violence that grew from the loss of signification, yet manages to assert meaning, thereby giving new possibilities to the subject, as an act of forgiveness. Through a new identification with the ideal, "it allows him [the subject] to live a second life, a life of forms and meaning, somewhat exalted or artificial in the eyes of outsiders."²⁸ While an act of love, forgiveness appears immoral because it refuses to directly or punitively address the crime. And yet, for the depressive subject to have a future, such amoral forgiveness may be necessary. Of course, Dostoevsky himself highlighted this amorality of forgiveness, as Raskolnikov learns that the "one person great enough to no longer be bound by the law" is not the murderer, but Christ—and, one could add, his disciple Sonia.

An Orthodox, Trinitarian theology underlies Dostoevsky's poetics, in its emphasis on the mutual indwelling of the persons of the Trinity. In particular, Kristeva locates Raskolnikov's aesthetic, symbolic identification with Sonia within the Orthodox understanding of the Holy Spirit's procession—from the Father *through* the Son (*per filium*), as opposed to the *filioque* (with the Son) of Western Christianity. While the debate surrounding the *filioque* frequently centers on the issue of subordination (if the Spirit proceeds from the Father and Son, then it seems the Spirit is subordinate to them), Kristeva locates the importance of the "through" (*per*) in its "pneumatological belonging"²⁹—the persons of the Trinity are identified precisely by their interpenetration and relation, merging with one another. The Father is the Father, and the Spirit is the Spirit, precisely

---

25. Colman, "Holbein's Work of Art in Kristeva's Political Thought," 90.
26. See Kearns, "Suffering in Theory," 68–69.
27. Kristeva, *Black Sun*, 204.
28. Ibid., 207–8.
29. Ibid., 210.

by the Father's proceeding *through* the Son. Whereas the Western conception leads toward a focus on the individuation and autonomy of the persons, the living-within of the *per filium* offers Orthodox Christianity a way to inspire a mystical indwelling of Christ and believers. As Symeon the New Theologian writes, as Jesus dwells with the Father, so too do saints dwell in Jesus, the Father, and ultimately in one another.[30] For Kristeva, this indwelling exemplifies an analytic creativity that allows new life to emerge through the analyst's engagement. Doestoevsky's aesthetic forgiveness, then, becomes a way to extend this indwelling life, opening a space in which the reader may also participate. As Kristeva writes,

> Writing causes the affect to slip into the effect—*actus purus*, as Aquinas might say. It conveys affects and does not repress them, it suggests for them a sublimatory outcome, it transposes them for an other in a threefold, imaginary, and symbolic bond. Because it is forgiveness, writing is transformation, transposition, translation.[31]

Literature, then, is a central modality of artistic subjectivity. As Kristeva has written recently, it creates a space for the recognition of subjects, without law or norms being imposed in a way that crushes them.[32]

Kristeva not only makes the theoretical argument that writing creates new life in response to radical, abyssal loss; she enacts it as well through her own writing of literature. Her novel *Possessions* also illustrates her view of writing as aesthetic forgiveness. *Possessions* is a mystery story revolving around the murder and decapitation of Gloria Harrison, a translator. As described by journalist Stephanie Delacour (who also appears in *The Old Man and the Wolves* and *Murder in Byzantium*), as a translator Gloria lived in two languages while teaching her deaf son to speak. She encounters his deafness as a resistance to speech—an embodiment that cannot be put into language, and his attempted speech only mimics hers. "Every word, phrase, or story was merely a kind of prosthesis, rarely containing the surprises that give parents so much delight . . . He sometimes returned the ball very neatly. But he never came up and smashed from the net."[33] Jerry's blind imitation, merely playing back for her what she had said, even described his painting activity, where he could technically reproduce

---

30. Symeon the New Theologian, *Church and the Last Things*, 72.
31. Kristeva, *Black Sun*, 217.
32. Kristeva, "Rethinking 'Normative Conscience,'" 222–23.
33. Kristeva, *Possessions*, 53.

a Picasso without fault, but showed no originality in doing so. In his lack of affect and creativity, Jerry models a certain form of melancholy, unable to find any non-mimetic form of speaking.

As the story unfolds, it becomes clear that Gloria clings to Jerry, possessed by her love for him. Delacour notes that Gloria had been extremely melancholic before Jerry's birth, and her attempt to give him speech, in love, is also her attempt to create herself anew—and yet, strangely, it replicates this melancholy within him. She suffers, then, from the trauma inflicted on him in his deafness, making it hers, such that to lose Jerry would wound her terribly. By so giving herself to Jerry, she finds renewed life, and yet, as Pauline Gadeau, Jerry's therapist, observes, "Self-denial is a delusion of grandeur disguising trauma."[34] Possessed by him, seeking to possess him, her love becomes aggressive, silencing him even in trying to make him speak.

While Gloria's murder is the result of her lover's sadism, the novel also depicts the conflict between such loves when they are not artistically sublimated. For Gloria's love is not the only one that seeks new life through attachment to Jerry. Pauline, his speech therapist, likewise recreates herself after losing her brother to drowning—she was no more in his loss.[35] Having attempted suicide over this loss, she now fears that Gloria will send Jerry away, repeating her loss and shattering her life once again. In finding Gloria dead, she acts out her anger through a horrific decapitation of Gloria—literally replicating the aggressivity captured in Jerry's replica of Picasso's *Woman with a Collar*. Once Gloria has lost her head, Pauline, who always wears high collars to cover her own scars, becomes the woman with a collar in Jerry's life.

Loss, aggression, violence, tone—all these play out in *Possessions*, which shows both the difficulty of bringing affects into language, and the necessity of doing so. For without language, forgiveness remains impossible, and one is trapped in one's history, as Gloria or Pauline is. The novel, then, may be read as Kristeva's attempt to represent these passions, so as to acknowledge them, and thereby create a space of freedom in relation to them. By linking body and thought, literature enables the forgiveness and relation to the sacred that Kristeva sees as ethical and politically necessary.

Kristeva's recent novel *Murder in Byzantium* also explores the ways that religion can temper affect—though the novel highlights the complex,

34. Ibid., 49.
35. Ibid., 201.

contradictory forces at work in its construction. *Murder in Byzantium* is a detective story, with Stephanie Delacour as the heroine who seeks to resolve a series of murders of members of a powerful, perverse religious sect. Intertwined with this is the story of historian Sebastian Chrest-Jones. The illegitimate son of a neglectful mother, Sebastian's historical study is as much a quest for his own origins as a study of migration and the Crusades. As someone who feels a strangeness at work deep within himself,[36] he struggles with the wound of neglect and rejection, striving to work through these.

Sebastian focuses his study on Anna Comnena, an eleventh-century princess whose writings demonstrate tremendous intellectual depth and learning while narrating the history of her royal family. Her erudition both unveils and enfolds the passions that drive her—giving a laudatory, selective account of her father's actions, and concealing any possible encounter with Ebrard, a crusading noble who later renounced the Crusades for their violence (and who, not coincidentally, may have been Sebastian's founding ancestor). Identifying with Anna's paternal identification, and longing for her strong maternal support, Sebastian sees in her an ideal he strives to attain.

Delacour's investigation of Sebastian's writings brings out the interweaving of history and psychic life. As she describes it, his history of Anna is "building a reasonable intellectual surface over an abyss of passions . . . Someone trying to save himself by idealizing a thousand-year-old colleague, a certain Anna Comnena, with her broken heart, a wound that resembles Sebastian's."[37] The idealized portrayal of Anna, which repeats her idealization of her father, leaves Sebastian's deeper aggression unaddressed. Ultimately, it is only when Chrest's attention turns from Anna to Ebrard, who gave up his dream of the crusade—in which violence would be the transformative mark of divine love—that Chrest's own affects undergo transmutation. Ebrard, as one who sacrifices love, dogma, and the violence that could go with it, enters into a "Byzantine" life that navigates the aggression of untransformed drive and abstract rationalism. In the end, singing the *Salve Regina* just before his death, Sebastian identifies with Ebrard's vision of Christianity as a form of inner peace that comes through re-narrating this history. History, suffused with emotion, becomes an aesthetic, literary form of forgiveness.

While Sebastian's journey is in some ways analogous to Kristeva's own "revolt" in turning back to Christian discourse as a repair of psychic

36. Kristeva, *Murder in Byzantium*, 7.
37. Ibid., 145.

space, *Murder in Byzantium* highlights some of the critical problematics of Kristeva's turn to religion. For, while Sebastian finds an inner peace through Ebrard, this does little for Fa, his pregnant lover, whom he killed when she wished to have her child without Sebastian (as he himself had been raised in his father's absence). It is Fa's brother Xiao Chang (who goes by Wuxian, the "Infinite Purifier") who kills Sebastian, and who had killed the members of the New Pantheon sect, in an aggressive quest for purification that would overcome his own lack of love. In the absence of maternal love, Sebastian and Xiao are placed in the depressive position—like Raskolnikov, faced with the choices of suicide, terror, or intellectual transformation. What is especially unclear, in the case of Sebastian, is the cause of his violence—whether it is a lack of maternal love that leads to violence and sets him on his journey, or his identification with the father, which also demands silencing of the mother who would live independently of the paternal law.

Sebastian's case—and his proximity to Xiao—highlights a central problem within Kristeva's poetic appropriation of religion. For, while she appropriates a certain image and conception of Christianity as a form of analytic healing, this identification with paternal language—the linking of affect to verbality—does seem to require a suppression or exclusion of certain forms of the feminine. Even in her articulation of a "herethique"—a heretical and feminine ethic, in *Stabat Mater*—Kristeva seems to conceive of the feminine as operating within and under the restriction of the language of the father. It is notable, for instance, that she often takes high modernist, avant-garde masculine poetics as figuring the most semiotically rich texts.[38] This is a point on which she has been criticized by many feminists, perhaps most notably and effectively Judith Butler. Butler highlights how many of Kristeva's writings figure homosexuality (and especially lesbianism) as "irretrievable self-loss"[39] and psychosis; even the bivalence of the maternal (source of pleasure and fusion/loss of identity and destruction) effectively restricts the conception of the feminine. Likewise, certain forms of the feminine would seem to be ignored in the construction of the aesthetic and forgiven subject. To be sure, Kristeva is not Sebastian, and there is a literary distance created by the narrator Delacour, but his character nonetheless

---

38. On this, and the political implications, see Watkin, "Melancholy, Revolution, and Materiality," 92–93, 97.

39. Butler, *Gender Trouble*, 87.

highlights a central issue in her work, in terms of the separation from the maternal and the ensuing conception of the feminine.[40]

It should be highlighted that throughout the novel, music is implicitly linked with aggression and even violence; Adhémar's beautiful chorus to Mary launched the passion of the Crusade, and music is Xiao's constant companion—it is "a language of hatred that leaves the human species on its ass."[41] Thus, despite the "musical" elements of the semiotic, it would seem that there is an aesthetic hierarchy at work, in which language and representation must shape artistry, in order for sublimation and the creative subject to emerge. This would mean, though, that music and alternative forms of femininity are *both* linked to psychopathy—dangers to the subject that would emerge from depression into speech.

The story thus provides a fitting rejoinder to Clément—and an opportunity for a mutual critique. Where Clément wants to emphasize music's dissolution of the subject and how it can ecstatically overturn rationality, Kristeva accentuates the potential for fanaticism and violence that lurks within such dissolution. Whereas Clément sees the need to move beyond the subject, for Kristeva the subject's speech serves as a limit to violence and creates the possibility of a future that need not return to one's origins or infinitely repeat a traumatic violence.

Clément's approach highlights how language is in the service of a social order, and that its production is inextricably linked with either the "forced leap" or the death of a feminine that would subvert its order. One might ask, then, if further attention to the aspects of music highlighted by Clément, especially in her readings of religious ritual, might serve to modify Kristeva's theory in ways that would help to construct a response to Butler's charge (and those of others) of a compulsory heterosexuality. Perhaps in the variance of rite, and the dissolution of the subject, a wider range of creative possibilities and ethical relations might emerge.

Sebastian's Ebrard—as a sort of "paternal feminine" figure—does not merely represent the analytic subject. Byzantium, for Kristeva, is a figure for a certain thought of Europe, a form of thought that cedes to the aggressive, exclusionary Christianity of crusaders from the West. Choosing peacefulness and an attention to history and literature, Byzantium figures an alternative subjectivity caught within the struggle of Islamic and Christian fanaticism. Written in 2005, the story alludes just under the

---

40. Margaroni, "Recent Work on and by Julia Kristeva," 795–97.
41. Kristeva, *Murder in Byzantium*, 207.

surface to the tensions between Europe and the United States, particularly around the war in Iraq. Ebrard's story, along with Anna Comnena, thus imagines a form of freedom and community that would traverse orthodox Christianity even while opening beyond itself—which, in many ways, is the story of Kristeva's later politics. Likewise, Clément's idea of an opera of equals—without the death of women, where "day and night," soprano and baritone, are given equal voice and equal power—imagines her own political vision of a syncretistic, polyphonic culture. Having explored their approaches to psychoanalysis and the arts, and seen how much these are linked with their interpretation of religion, we can now turn to the question of the politics envisaged by these two innovative thinkers.

NINE

The Stranger Within
Toward a Post-Analytic Politics

Having explored the work of Kristeva and Clément in psychoanalysis, art, and religion, we may now turn to the political dimensions of their thought. In *The Feminine and the Sacred*, both authors sketch the political implications of their theoretical work. As before, their approaches differ: Kristeva argues for a liminal politics, in which the encounter with the sacred leads into an incorporation of strangeness and alterity within one's psychic life. She argues, however, for the sublimation of this encounter, and, as in previous chapters, sees Christianity and Judaism as providing models for this voyage, provided they are interpreted analytically. As she recently quoted, in an interview, her character Stephanie Delacour, "I voyage myself" (*je me voyage*)[1]—the challenge we face is to question ourselves in ways that open us to the strangeness within ourselves, which may lead to respect or hospitality for those who are foreigners in the political realm.

By contrast, Clément sees Kristeva's emphasis on language and the analytical model of Christianity as still too repressive with regard to embodiment and cultural difference. Clément thus imagines a more pluralistic, mystical ecstasy, in which the structure of the self is dissolved rather than traversed. Out of concern for the effects of the sacred on women's lives and bodies, Clément argues strongly for a privatization of the sacred so as to avoid totalitarianism. As she writes, "The sacred belongs to the private sphere, from which the rite stems, even if it is collective . . . When the revolt contained within the sacred leaves the sphere of the private, it can become murderous."[2] For both authors, however, *The Feminine and the Sacred* illustrates the turn in their later work toward the political possibilities of psychoanalysis—as indicated in Kristeva's writings on religion, cosmopolitanism, and her reworking of Hannah Arendt's political theory.

---

1. Kristeva, "Crossing Borders," 165–66.
2. Clément, *Feminine and the Sacred*, 176.

Clément's syncretistic approach comes forth in both her work on transforming French culture and her turn to Indian philosophy and Gandhi's nonviolence as a counter-narrative to Western subjectivity.

WELCOMING THE STRANGER: RUTH AND ISRAEL

In her political writings, as with her earlier biblical and literary interpretations, Kristeva interprets particular political and religious texts as exemplifying various states of subjectivity—from Athens, Israel, and the Pauline Christian community to Enlightenment France and Kant. While each state of subjectivity defines itself in part by its relation to the sacred and to embodiment, her political work focuses on how such subjective states construe the relation to the foreigner. In both *Strangers to Ourselves* and *Nations without Nationalism*, Kristeva constructs an alternative understanding of the nation as a transitional object that gives expression to the desires and drives that often foster violence and exclusion towards others. Her thought seeks to reshape these drives so as to enable a cosmopolitan community that transcends violence. Simultaneously, this involves reshaping cosmopolitanism,[3] making it more attentive to particularity through sublimation, rather than enacting an idealization whose repression would indirectly give rise to a reactive xenophobia. Reflecting on the rise in France of the National Front, and responding to its racism, she writes,

> Is there a way of thinking politically about the "national" that does not degenerate into an exclusory, murderous racism, without at the same time dissolving into an all-encompassing feeling of "S.O.S.-Absolute Brotherhood" and providing, for the span of an evening, all who represent groups (historical identities that have been respectively persecuted and persecuting) with the delight of being on a boundless ocean?[4]

The problem, for Kristeva, is to navigate between the dual dangers of an excessively abstract universal and the regression into a violently exclusive particularism. It is with this problematic in mind that she turns to religious and philosophical figures of the foreigner.

From the "barbarians" of ancient Greece to modern xenophobia, Kristeva argues that each figure of the foreigner represents a particular relation to the unconscious, and thereby a particular constellation of cultural

---

3. See Mowitt, "Strangers in Analysis," 47.
4. Kristeva, *Nations without Nationalism*, 51.

possibilities. By tracing this history, she hopes to illustrate the range of possibilities within Western culture while transcending its limitations, by helping the reader to welcome otherness through this cultural analysis. As she writes,

> It is through unraveling transference—the major dynamics of otherness, of love/hatred for the other, of the foreign component of our psyche—that, on the basis of the other, I become reconciled with my own otherness-foreignness, that I play on it and live by it. Psychoanalysis is then experienced as a journey into the strangeness of the other and of oneself, toward an ethics of respect for the irreconcilable.[5]

One of the central chapters in this unraveling is the story of Ruth, who introduces foreignness into the story of Israel and Christianity.[6] As David's ancestor Ruth "was praised . . . for opening the sovereignty of David to an ineffaceable strangeness: it is she, in fact, who opens royal security to a permanent inquietude and spurs the dynamic of its drive for perfection."[7] Ruth thus exemplifies the analytic and political significance of religion, in the development of Kristeva's politics of hospitality.

The story of Ruth is fairly straightforward, but its exposition is helpful for both explaining and extending Kristeva's analytic politics. During a famine, Elimelech, his wife Naomi, and their two sons emigrate from Judea to Moab, a foreign land whose inhabitants had been inhospitable to Israel, and thus were barred from ever becoming "sons of Yahweh" (Deut 25). The sons marry two Moabite princesses, Orpah and Ruth, who are left in Naomi's care when Elimelech, Mahlon (Ruth's husband), and Chilion die. Orpah reluctantly returns to her family, but Ruth accompanies Naomi back to her people in Bethlehem. In need of food, Ruth gleans in the field, where she attracts the attention of Boaz, receives his protection, and then (at Naomi's prompting) pleads for him to become Naomi's redeemer, restoring the name of Naomi's family. Boaz agrees, and does so by buying the land of Elimelech's family, marrying Ruth and conceiving a child who continues Naomi's line, taking the place of Mahlon as her protector, and becoming the great-grandfather of King David (as well as an ancestor of Jesus).

5. Kristeva, *Strangers to Ourselves*, 182.

6. Alternately, it might be better to say that she intensifies it, as the Israelites had already experienced being foreign in the sojourn, slavery, and exodus from Egypt.

7. Kristeva, *Feminine and the Sacred*, 102.

For Kristeva, the story of Ruth embodies the biblical injunction to welcome the stranger. As Israel had been strangers in Egypt, the community is commanded by God to welcome strangers in its midst, showing them hospitality. Such hospitality points toward a "biblical universalism," as "the foreigner himself [or, in this case, herself] might chance to be God's unwonted although inevitable unveiler."[8] When Boaz accepts Ruth as his wife, and when the community blesses the marriage, the community thereby welcomes her strangeness into its midst, and recognizes Ruth as one of their own, based on her *hesed* (loyalty, or fidelity) to Naomi. However, Kristeva argues that Ruth exemplifies the necessary assimilation to the Torah and to the love of God, thereby participating in the "choice founded on ordeal" that founds the covenant (involving, as a minimum, recognizing the Noahide law). "The *ger-tochav* maintains his identity as a foreigner but, whether or not he resides in Israel, he obeys Mosaic laws; these are moral laws that are indispensable to society; they endow one, in the spirit of Judaism, with a spiritual dignity equal to that of the Jew himself."[9] Such assimilation clearly differs from modern tolerance, and manifests a hospitality toward the stranger—even the stranger who appeared to be an enemy. The possibility of such inclusion, moreover, shapes the psychic space of those who participate in the covenant. Such hospitality to the stranger dramatically breaks with the "barbarism" of Greece—namely, its hostility toward barbarians as irrevocably other.

While Kristeva's analysis of the story of Ruth as a story of welcoming the stranger is insightful, particular features of the story complicate her interpretation. First, it is difficult to say that Ruth "assimilates" to the covenant, since there is no noticeable change in her behavior. Second, as Kristeva herself notes, Ruth is effaced at the end of the story for the sake of the lineage of the family. This at least suggests that the conclusion effaces the role of the foreigner, restoring the proper lineage that leads to David. As Jack Sasson writes, "the narrator missed the opportunity to reward properly a heroine who risked all to accompany her mother-in-law to Bethlehem."[10] It may also suggest that *hesed* is above all loyalty to a *particular* family, in this case the Davidic line.[11] Most provocatively, interpretation may reduce Ruth to the role of a surrogate mother—leaving one to wonder if she is

---

8. Kristeva, *Strangers to Ourselves*, 66.
9. Ibid., 68.
10. Sasson, *Ruth: A New Translation*, 169.
11. Such is the gloss of the HarperCollins Study Bible, among others.

truly welcomed into the family and the nation at all, or if, as with the metics in the Greek city-state, she is only welcomed for her economic and political reproductivity.[12] Given these problems, more clarification is needed to unpack how Ruth inspires a "drive to perfection" within the Jewish and Christian communities that descend from David. Addressing these issues can clarify Kristeva's analysis in light of the narrative.

First, there is a definite passage of assimilation in the book of Ruth—but it is not Ruth's assimilation. Rather, her embodiment of the essence of Jewish law acts to assimilate the surrounding Jewish community to the law, moving them towards a deeper understanding of *hesed* (as charity, or grace). In the process, loyalty to family and the propriety of patriarchy are both undermined. The initial contrast in the narrative is between Naomi and Ruth. Naomi orders Ruth and Orpah to return to their families (and their gods), where they can have security and new life. Such a return—like Naomi's return to Bethlehem—could be read as a return to origins in the face of the loss of family and identity. This option is appealing, as Kristeva writes, when "the fragmentation of individuals [has] reached the point where we no longer know what we are and take shelter, to preserve a token of personality, under the most massive, regressive common denominators: national origins and the faith of our forebears."[13] Orpah agrees to go, but Ruth refuses. Her well-known declaration of loyalty follows:

> Do not press me to leave you, or to turn back from following you!
> Where you go, I will go; where you lodge, I will lodge;
> Your people shall be my people, and your God my God.
> Where you die, I will die—there will I be buried.
> May the LORD do thus and so to me, and more as well,
> If even death parts me from you! (1:16–17)

It is worth noting that there is no mention of family here. Ruth's action, rather, is that of welcoming the stranger—even though the stranger has been her mother-in-law. Her mother-in-law is a stranger, from another land, and worshipping another God. Naomi is also a stranger in other ways: she has no family, as the names of her husband and sons will be wiped from memory, and she is poor. While she wishes to return to a national and religious identity, she has *no* identity at this point. Thus, when Ruth cleaves to her, she fulfills the command of Deuteronomy with respect

---

12. Vanessa Ochs, "Reading Ruth," 296.
13. Kristeva, *Nations without Nationalism*, 2.

to both the foreigner and the strangers *within* the community—the poor and the widow:

> For the LORD your God is God of gods and Lord of lords, the great God, mighty and awesome, who is not partial and takes no bribe, who executes justice for the orphan and the widow, and who loves the strangers, providing them food and clothing. You shall also love the stranger, for you were strangers in the land of Egypt. (Deut 10:17–19)

Ruth's *hesed*, then, fulfills the very law that would exclude Moabites. She remains loyal to Naomi, who would be without social place, and gives her food, clothing[14] and a family in Obed.

Naomi, however, is less welcoming of the stranger. As mentioned before, she thinks Ruth should return to her family, and that she cannot be welcome in Bethlehem. It is suspicious, moreover, that she does not warn Ruth about harassment and assault in the fields *before* her first day of gleaning.[15] Only when Ruth returns with food does Naomi bless her. However, over the course of the narrative, Naomi does begin to welcome Ruth—calling Ruth her daughter, and no longer describing herself as empty. Likewise, when Boaz confronts the first *go'el*, the *go'el*'s response privileges his immediate family over care for the widow and stranger—again, resistance to welcoming the stranger is found within the Israelite community. Both Boaz's and Naomi's warnings about the harvesters also suggest that others in the community will likewise see her presence as an opportunity for violation and injustice. Only when Boaz says he will marry Ruth does the community come to welcome her. Thus, for many of the characters of the story, we see *them* assimilated to the law over the course of the book; they learn the full meaning of the Deuteronomic command to love the stranger, as they recognize its figuration in Ruth.

For a story about welcoming the stranger, the ending of the narrative is strange, since Ruth disappears from view. This can be read suspiciously, as mentioned above. However, it can also be read as including the reader within the movement of the narrative. For, the "effacement" of Ruth makes it the reader's responsibility to *remember* her, to *welcome* her into the

---

14. When Ruth asks Boaz to spread his cloak over her, it also extends to protection for Naomi.

15. On this point, and for a generally skeptical reading of the story, see Fewell and Ginn, *Compromising Redemption*, 46.

lineage, to remember the "fertility of the other"[16] that inspires the Davidic line. It thus creates a space within which, like Boaz, the reader is asked to remember Ruth's *hesed*, and thereby includes the reader in the narrative's assimilation of the community to the parameters of the law. Can the reader be faithful to Ruth as she has been faithful to Naomi?

This inclusion of the reader within the text's assimilation of the community to the law—as the community is called forth to become like Ruth, whose reward is perfect—points toward an understanding of the "drive for perfection" that the story inspires. The text works semiotically: Naomi gives voice to the tribalism within us, particularly when we are wounded and without place; the first redeemer speaks to the self-interest that motivates many actions. Yet, the text also moves us beyond these affective discourses, subsuming them within the desire to be loyal to God—to renounce the object of one's nation, to renounce self-interest or being-at-home, and in such renunciation to create space for the other. As Kristeva writes, "If David is also Ruth, if the sovereign is also a Moabite, peace of mind will then never be his lot, but a constant quest for welcoming and going beyond the other in oneself."[17] Here, one finds a different happiness—"the happiness of tearing away, of racing, the space of a promised infinite."[18] To welcome the stranger within oneself requires breaking with comfort, security, and stability—to live, in a sense, both in exile and in welcome of the other, finding joy in going where the other goes.

Kristeva's reading of Ruth highlights how the text both opens up a space of hospitality and yet, in its demand for assimilation, nonetheless may restrict this welcome. A similar dialectic conditions hospitality in many of her other analyses. For readers who would dismiss religion as a narcissistic return to one's origins, Ruth complicates matters. Moreover, the text seems to burst through Kristeva's reading, in light of her later work. For, in her affirmation of life, attention to Naomi's otherness, and emphasis on being-with others, Ruth could epitomize the "feminine genius" of Kristeva's later work, which becomes a central component in her rethinking of the political import of psychoanalysis.

---

16. Kristeva, *Strangers to Ourselves*, 75.

17. Ibid., 76.

18. Ibid., 4.

CITIZENS IN THE HOUSE OF GOD: PAULINE AND AUGUSTINIAN PSYCHOLOGY

> A miracle of flesh and thought, the banquet of hospitality is the foreigners' utopia—the cosmopolitanism of a moment, the brotherhood of guests who soothe and forget their differences, the banquet is outside of time. It imagines itself eternal in the intoxication of those who are nevertheless aware of its temporary frailty.[19]

The significance of Ruth, for Kristeva, is her injection of strangeness into the political constitution of the Jewish community. As with the prophets, who internalize the abject within the Jewish community, this breaks from the pagan sensibility in which abjection is something foreign, *xenos*, outside the community. However, as with her analysis of abjection, Kristeva argues that another level of internalization is necessary—from inside the community to the interior of individuals. This further internalization of strangeness is historically figured by Pauline and Augustinian Christianity, which open a new chapter on both the universalism of a politics that welcomes the stranger, and the negotiation between hospitality and assimilation that defines the border of a community.

As mentioned briefly in chapter 7, Kristeva analyzes Pauline Christianity as the "triumph of idealization" that proceeds to *agape* through the death of the body. Politically, this signifies that the Christian community, the *ecclesia*, constituted itself in the spiritual realm by breaking with the body politics of first-century Mediterranean communities. Paul's letters appealed to those who were strangers within Mediterranean society, taking marginal places in economic and social exchange—wayfarers, merchants, and sailors. Where they had been "strangers" within their world—and, as Gentiles, also strangers to God and Judaism—they now become "citizens in the house of God."[20] Paul's rhetoric inscribes itself in the lapse, or gap, of his followers' experience of not-belonging to a city; he thereby constitutes a community of wanderers who follow in the journey of Christ to God. As Kristeva writes, "Such marginal people, women, foreigners who remained bound to their native culture, nevertheless created among themselves bonds of solidarity, mutually welcoming each other in holy places where, precisely, the foreigner was safe from any affront, while he had, as we have

---

19. Ibid., 12.
20. Eph 2:19.

seen, only very few rights in the *polis*."²¹ The Pauline missives create a subjective space in which wandering becomes a new form of dwelling.

Since it is Christ who has broken down the barriers between Jew and Gentile, the *ecclesia* of strangers calls its members from their political communities to a new life, constituted by faith in Christ and the practice of *agape*. This effects a twofold break, as signified by the phrase that in Christ there is "neither Jew nor Gentile." On the one hand, as performed in the Letter to the Romans, Pauline Christianity breaks with Jewish nationalism by overturning the requirement of assimilation to the Law. Simultaneously, Paul subsumes the paganism of the Gentile nations under faith in Christ as the "unknown God," as described in the letters to Corinth and his visit to Athens.²² Paul thus makes himself "all things to all men," so as to welcome the strangers and model how they could be inscribed within this ideal, imagined community in the body of Christ. Here, we see the opening of a new universalism; extending the messianism and *xenophilia* found in the story of Ruth, Kristeva writes, "The well-known messianism of the Jews was changed into a messianism that includes all of humankind: the Ecclesia was to be the universality of the 'people' beyond peoples, gathered in the isolation and solitude of the desert in order to receive the words of a new Alliance."²³

With Augustinian Christianity, the relation to strangeness takes on the contours of a pilgrimage. As Augustine writes in *De Doctrina Christiana*, the world is a country far from our homeland, to which we seek to return. One does so through an interpretive journey, in which one learns to see things in the world as signs to be used toward the enjoyment of God. On such a journey toward the eternal, we recognize ourselves as strangers to the world, and to ourselves as well, detached from the memory, understanding, and love of God in which we can find rest and our home. Through identification with Christ—as discussed in "From Signs to the Subject"—Kristeva describes how one makes the pilgrimage toward God, but also toward love of one's neighbors. For, in love of God, one also discovers one's neighbors to be in the image of God, and also to be strangers in this world. To love them on account of God (*propter Deum*) is to love the strangeness within them, which likewise identifies them with oneself in an act of charity: "*Caritas* is

---

21. Kristeva, *Strangers to Ourselves*, 79.
22. Acts 17:22–28.
23. Kristeva, *Strangers to Ourselves*, 80.

infinite . . . thus welcoming foreigners who have become similar in their very distinction."[24]

The peregrine shape of early Christianity was evident in the hostels that offered hospitality to traveling Christians on their journeys from one city to another. Such welcome enacted the use/enjoyment dynamic of Augustinian theology, treating one's homeland, possessions, and house as being for the sake of God and any neighbor, welcoming him or her on behalf of God. In such acts of welcome, the church began to take on its universal shape, moving beyond the national or imperial boundaries of the earthly city, toward embodying the heavenly city of God.

However, such a hospitable community, while dissolving national boundaries, quickly conditioned itself through the boundaries of belief, extending hospitality only to fellow Christian travelers (often in order to maintain separation from the inns that were seen as dangerous).[25] A certain assimilation, or sameness, thus became a precondition for the welcome of foreigners *as* neighbors. In this restriction, Kristeva sees the borderlines of religious hospitality:

> A means of proselytism, or even of pressure, such hospitality when all is said and done forced the pilgrim to be a pilgrim of Christ, and forced every wandering person to become a Christian. Dogmatism raises its head in the unfolding of that universalism, which was real nevertheless and was able to go beyond the political particularisms of antiquity. But as soon as it reached its golden age in the fourth and fifth centuries, and while displaying that breadth of mind that endowed it with its early seduction and strength, Christian cosmopolitanism bore in its womb the ostracism that excluded the other belief and ended up with the Inquisition.[26]

---

24. Ibid., 85.

25. While Kristeva's reading does not address this, it is worth noting that Augustine seemed to be aware of this tension within Christian love. On the one hand, he does argue for love of the other person as a neighbor—insofar as he or she may be in God, and thus with a certain emphasis on sameness. Love of neighbor is the one eternal, unchanging law.

However, at the same time, Augustine's discussion of justice does demand attention to particularity, and does recognize that attending to the shifting demands of justice (based on the particularities of the other, and one's community) is an integral component of loving one's neighbor. Christianity—including Augustine himself—has found such a demand too much to handle, but perhaps it is in Augustine's notion of justice that Christian hospitality can become more welcoming of the stranger as stranger.

26. Kristeva, *Strangers to Ourselves*, 87.

Kristeva offers little explanation, in either *Strangers to Ourselves* or *Nations without Nationalism*, as to how Christian cosmopolitanism unfolds into ostracism. However, her tracing of the psychic space of the Johannine and Pauline writings in *Tales of Love* gives an indication that it is the tension between their messages that unleashes this powerful hospitality of the early church while nonetheless restricting its welcome. As Kristeva describes, the identification of God with love in the Johannine writings makes love an "internal turn within the subject"—love is no longer love *for* something. "Johannine love sketches out the space of a relationship between I and You, Son and Father, *an exclusive, absolute one in which They—third parties—are only intermediaries.*"[27] However, the effect of this turn is that love is now for those who share the love, in a way that is not found in Pauline writings. Thus, it seems that one can say that on Kristeva's reading, the Johannine writings, and their canonization by Christian communities, speak to a desire for unity, intimacy, and belonging on the part of Christian communities that shapes the pilgrim church and ultimately limits hospitality.

It appears, then, that there is a tension within Kristeva's political thought here: the same Johannine discourse that serves as an example to psychoanalysis in *New Maladies of the Soul* is also the discourse that limits and undoes cosmopolitan hospitality. This is particularly significant since psychoanalysis is the "ethical course . . . which can develop patient, complex discourses, involving everyone's meditation,"[28] and can, on Kristeva's view, help with reconceiving the nation. How can the example of the discourse that opens a new political future, also be at the root of ostracism?

As Sarah Beardsworth has noted, many of Kristeva's discussions of religion end with a critical stance. Thus, it may be the case that in religion, the "symbolic elaboration overreaches abjection," or more broadly that the symbolic suppresses semiotic affect.[29] Yet, at the same time, many of Kristeva's later writings point toward a more constructive, positive reading of religion. What is even more striking, as her exchanges with Clément make clear, is that her affirmation of religious discourse frequently emphasizes those aspects of religion where language shapes emotion and drives—in short, where the semiotic and symbolic are intertwined. Indeed, it seems to me that a psychoanalytic listening to religious discourse must hear both its potential for healing and the places where such repair may be blocked.

27. Kristeva, *Tales of Love*, 148; emphasis added.
28. Kristeva, *Nations without Nationalism*, 51.
29. Beardsworth, *Julia Kristeva*, 139.

This dual stance—which one might call sympathetically critical—is perhaps best exemplified in Kristeva's discussion of forgiveness.

THE PROMISE OF FORGIVENESS

In one letter to Clément, Kristeva asks why the pope is the only public figure to defend life:

> I think it is a shame that the pope is the only modern figure to defend the desire to live and the right to life. It is not because "eternal life" does not exist that life has no meaning. On the contrary, it is the experience of the "nothing" that gives the meaning of life, the fight for the most ordinary life, its sudden piquancy.[30]

By invoking John Paul II's idea of a "culture of death" and the need for a politics of life, Kristeva appears to be aligning herself with a conservative, traditionalist politics.[31] This is not quite the case; while she will argue that "life" provides a potential point of solidarity between the French left and Catholic social teaching,[32] she is adopting a somewhat unorthodox political stance, arguing that the "life" of analysis, in its struggle for meaning, plays a crucial role in culture, thus marking a distance from a more traditionalist view.[33] In so doing, Kristeva both follows and extends the similarly unorthodox work of Hannah Arendt, one of the most influential political philosophers of the twentieth century. It is against the background of Arendt's work, and especially her notions of rebirth and forgiveness, that Kristeva articulates the political side of her analytical affirmation of a life that is social, literary, and makes space for re-creation and renewal.

Kristeva's most extensive discussion of Arendt is in the first volume of her trilogy on "feminine genius," which also explores the work of Melanie Klein and Colette. One of the most significant aspects of Arendt's work, from Kristeva's perspective, is her conception of narrative, which underwrites her distinctively human conception of life (*bios*, as opposed to *zoe*).

---

30. Kristeva, *Feminine and the Sacred*, 82.

31. The charge takes on a bit more bite when one considers that similar charges have been leveled against Philippe Sollers for his approach to issues of freedom and authority. See Bourdieu, "Sollers *Tel Quel*."

32. Kristeva, *Intimate Revolt*, 264.

33. This dynamic is also evident in some of her most recent writings, including an essay in memory of John Paul II, and a critique of Benedict XVI's views on faith and reason. See "N'ayez pas peur de la culture européene," in *Cet incroyable besoin de croire*, 183–88, and "Rethinking 'Normative Conscience.'"

Narrative is not strictly textual; rather, it is the telling of an action, as seen and remembered by others.

> The possibility that we can envision birth and death, that we can contemplate them within time and that we can speak about them with the other by sharing with other people—in a word, the possibility that we can tell a story—is at the heart of the specific, nonanimalistic, and nonphysiological nature of human life.[34]

The event of a narrative is the decisive political action, because the act is done, and the story is told, for their own sake (what Arendt would term a moment of *poesis*, not *praxis*). This frees human action from the necessity of production, in labor, and it also creates a political bond, as the telling of the act joins agent, author, and audience: "The [narrator's] gaze is neither the *bios theoretikos* of pure thought nor the solitary disclosure of pure poetry, but the contemplation of the actions put into words in the city-state."[35] Narrative raises human activity beyond biological reproduction, into the dramatic realm of action and spectators. Part of the significance of this, for Kristeva, is that in the narrative body and language meet; narrative, then, is a political form of the semiotic.

Likewise, in Arendt's notion of being-plural as the "essence" of humanity, Kristeva finds a political analogue to the polyphony of semiotic speech. Totalitarianism, in suppressing this being-plural, tries to efface the uniqueness of each person, rendering them superfluous (most evidently, though not solely, in the anti-Semitism, dispossession of citizenship, and systematic elimination of the Jews by the Nazis) by suppressing emotion and affect. This takes away the possibility of thinking—to "see things from another's perspective," in Arendt's words.[36] As Kristeva writes,

> By suppressing our internal ability to begin, and by destroying the common space in which we can move and which is the political space, totalitarian terror, "lest anybody ever start thinking," ultimately targets the human quality par excellence that is thinking, which is synonymous with birth and rebirth.[37]

If politics requires both act and narration, involving judgment and thought on the part of the spectator, then Eichmann's inability to think obliterates

---

34. Kristeva, *Hannah Arendt*, 41.
35. Ibid., 75.
36. Arendt, *Eichmann in Jerusalem*, 49.
37. Kristeva, *Hanna Arendt*, 141.

the possibility of politics. It is only in love, as thought put into action, that one really affirms the uniqueness of individuals—their *haecceitas*, in Scotist terms, which is a new creation in each person. Reducing the Jews to a category, and himself to a functionary, he treats all people as "what" they are, rather than "who," effecting the totalitarian reduction of humanity beginning with his own person.

However, if others' judgments of our actions or the promises by which we bind ourselves define our characters, then history becomes the limit for politics. Errors and unforeseen complications can prevent renewal, and vengeance risks cutting off new forms of sociality. Forgiveness thus becomes necessary. As Arendt writes, "Without being forgiven, released from the consequences of what we have done, our capacity to act would, as it were, be confined to one single deed from which we could never recover."[38] Arendt therefore locates humanity between Nietzsche's "animal who makes promises" and the power to forgive. Forgiveness, for her, is an eminently political concept, freeing one from the past so that new political actions ("beginnings") are possible. As Kristeva writes,

> It is impossible to undo what has already been done, and it is impossible to imagine how one can forgive in solitude. Perhaps Arendt believes that forgiveness would be a mere inhibition if it were deprived of the space of appearance and the words of other people. But she can tolerate the idea that men, among themselves and at the heart of the frailty of their actions, free themselves from their doings and past actions whose consequences they had not foreseen or they cannot accept.[39]

One forgives the person, not the action, suspending but not eliminating the judgment that is central to politics, so that it may begin again.

Thus far, Kristeva reaffirms Arendt's political philosophy, as it emphasizes the social, signifying life of thought as constitutive of humanity. However, Kristeva also extends Arendt's vision through a psychoanalytic supplement, as Arendt was largely averse to psychoanalytic theory. The first extension is literary. With her Aristotelian approach to philosophy, Arendt privileges a coherent, linear narrative form over against poetry, nonverbal arts, and avant-garde literature. In so doing, she discounts literature that highlights intra-psychic conflict or dialogue. This privilege of narrative excludes psychoanalysis from the political realm, while also determining

38. Arendt, *Human Condition*, 237.
39. Kristeva, *Hannah Arendt*, 232.

Arendt's approach to embodiment, in ways that largely repress our specific and sexual differences.

What is significant about the artistic forms that Arendt ignores is their relation to psychic forms of revolt, which could extend the idea of revolution beyond the social.[40] These forms represent the negativity, energy, and trauma that constitute the psyche, and shape the consciousness of political agents. In some cases, these can also help to display the forces at work in cruelty, sadism, and intentional evil—the forms of evil which Arendt does not really address at length. Analysis, then, is a form of thinking in which one can judge and comprehend past psychic events; in those cases where forgiveness is possible, it enables a new internal beginning, and thereby new relations to others. Analysis also helps to build the imaginary through poetic, semiotic links between language and the body. As we saw in the last chapter with Kristeva's discussion of Dostoevsky, it is precisely through this imaginary development that forgiveness and new life can be found. As Kristeva writes in *Intimate Revolt*, "To give meaning to suffering and begin the associative speech that will transform malady and death into a narrative of life, a new life: this is how the value of analytical interpretation as pardon can be defined."[41] By enabling a fuller engagement with the semiotic, an extension of literature into its more modernist forms can complexify our conception of narrative and create a more extensive form of forgiveness.[42] Such forgiveness, as Kelly Oliver writes, is "a process of questioning in order to open onto otherness"[43]—a revolt that keeps the subject open to further creativity, allowing renewal without forgetting the past.

Arendt's discussion of Adolf Eichmann exemplifies how this analytic extension could transform her political vision. While many readers misunderstood Arendt as excusing Eichmann, the sentence she declares at the end of *Eichmann in Jerusalem* is a notably severe judgment, affirming his execution while rejecting the court's reasoning. It deserves quoting:

> Let us assume, for the sake of argument, that it was nothing more than misfortune that made you a willing instrument in the organization of mass murder; there still remains the fact that you have carried out, and therefore actively supported, a policy of mass murder. For politics is not like the nursery; in politics obedience and

40. Ibid., 92–93.
41. Kristeva, *Intimate Revolt*, 24.
42. See Kristeva, "Forgiveness: An Interview," 287.
43. Oliver, "Forgiveness and Community," 11.

support are the same. And just as you supported and carried out a policy of not wanting to share the earth with the Jewish people and the people of a number of other nations—as though you and your superiors had any right to determine who should and who should not inhabit the world—we find that no one, that is, no member of the human race, can be expected to want to share the earth with you. This is the reason, and the only reason, you must hang.[44]

In his lack of thought, Eichmann has lost his personhood—and thus, for Arendt, his ability to be forgiven. He deserves death, for refusing to be part of the plurality or the being-with of humanity. As Gillian Rose has argued, Arendt adopts this unforgiving stance toward Eichmann—and thus toward modern, "mass" society—by separating its determinism from politics in her proper sense.[45]

Psychoanalysis, however, may carve a path toward forgiveness. Eichmann's inability to speak in anything but stock phrases and clichés suggests a depression of his psyche: this collapses his obedience to the moral law within himself (which he knows he ought to obey) into obedience to Hitler's laws. If, as Kristeva argues, analysis helps to re-create subjects and gives them speech, then this could also lead Eichmann to a new position with respect to what he has done: through receiving another's interpretation, he could realize for himself the wrongness of the actions, and why the punishment is justified.[46] In this act of judgment, he might restore to himself his forgivability, in a way that he could not during the trial. In short, by bringing to light the inner drama that creates the psychic conditions in which totalitarianism may take control—and also giving the literary and semiotic creativity that can revolt against this—analysis can contribute to understanding and judging the banality of evil and the origins of totalitarianism.[47] It could help to create citizens who, by working through and speaking the traumas and violence within themselves, "ask themselves to what extent they would still be able to live in peace with themselves after committing certain deeds," in a Socratic dialogue, as doubters and

---

44. Arendt, *Eichmann in Jerusalem*, 279.

45. See Rose, *Broken Middle*, 230–40.

46. As Kristeva argues in "Forgiveness: An Interview," 283, analytic forgiveness would not preclude punishment. She sees such forgiveness as confined to the individual or private sphere, only perhaps tempering but not suspending the punishment that represents the judgment of public life. See also Ruth Kluger's critical response in the same volume, "Forgiving and Remembering."

47. See Kristeva, *Intimate Revolt*, 20–22.

questioners, with the knowledge that "Whatever else happens, as long as we live we shall have to live together with ourselves."[48]

From Arendt, Kristeva develops a vision of human freedom that she associates with "European" politics. She contrasts this with another form of post-Enlightenment freedom—the "American" freedom of capitalism and globalization "to achieve the best results by adapting to the logic of cause and effect: that is, free to adapt to the market of production and profit."[49] Euro-freedom is a spoken freedom, found in Socratic dialogue; because this freedom is more social and less production-oriented, it can attend to and affirm social difference and plurality: "This other model is animated by a concern for human life in its most fragile singularity."[50] Without arguing *against* the American form of freedom, Kristeva argues that it needs to be balanced by this European form. This social freedom, as enabling individual possibilities of revolt, and in its concern for psychic as well as social health, extends the politics of hospitality discussed in the preceding section.

Bringing psychoanalysis into conversation with political theory makes Kristeva's approach intriguing. She articulates a strong sense of how psychoanalysis contributes to literary as well as cultural life.[51] However, the issue of balance between European and American approaches raises the question of cultural pluralism once again. Clearly, she argues that the privilege of the European model is in its allowing for a diversity of expression and experience, letting varied cultures and individuals live in their differences together. As we will see, Clément's politics is more polyphonic and embodied than Kristeva's; thus, the question is whether the balance so achieved really enables religious and cultural diversity, or if the tendency toward literary representation—even in avant-garde and poetic forms—continues to privilege certain cultural expressions and forms of alterity. If language, for Kristeva, always takes priority over the body—as she says in commenting on Arendt, Eurydice must become Orpheus to be remembered—then this literary form marks the limits of her cosmopolitanism. We will return to this issue after exploring the embodied syncretism of Clément's approach.

48. Arendt, "Personal Responsibility under Dictatorship," in *Responsibility and Judgment*, 44–45.

49. Kristeva, *Intimate Revolt*, 262. This was republished as "Europhilia, Europhobia."

50. Kristeva, *Intimate Revolt*, 264.

51. For a view that sees Kristeva's emphasis on revolt as breaking with her earlier, "revolutionary" poetics, see Watkin, "Melancholia, Revolution, and Materiality," 98–100.

DREAMS OF POLITICS: PARTICIPATORY ENGAGEMENT AND CULTURAL DIVERSITY

As we have seen in the preceding chapters, Clément and Kristeva disagree over the privileged place of Christian discourse with regard to religion and the sacred, and this disagreement is substantially rooted in their diverging views on aesthetics. As has been discussed, Kristeva emphasizes the semiotic potential of poetry, in its relation between body and language, as a figure for the sacred, while Clément privileges music as a non-representational, ego-dissolving creativity. Not surprisingly, in light of these aesthetic and religious disagreements, politics also becomes a disputed topic in their exchange of letters. As we have just discussed, Kristeva's discussion of politics as a form of cosmopolitanism that makes space for particular affinities while remaining part of a broader community, and her notion of revolt as a reworking of traditions and their symbols, are both practical corollaries to the critical theory and analysis of her earlier works. Clément's disagreement on the subject of politics follows from several aspects of her work: her engagement with the status of minority communities within France, her syncretistic approach to both culture and religion, and finally, an emphasis on conceiving history as a contested narrative in need of interrogation, to prevent a totalizing or monolithic interpretation. Through these topics, the distinctiveness of her political approach, and its interrogation of Kristeva's work, will become clear.

Clément's disagreement with Kristeva is, in part, due to a shift within Clément's own work, which can be traced via the chronology of her writings on opera. In an early work, *Miroirs du Sujet* (*Mirrors of the Subject*), opera occupies a central place. First, she relates opera to the narration of myth—providing listeners with a way to pass through the symbolic realm of culture.[52] The arias, moreover, in saturating the narrative with song, provoke a regression to the mirror stage. The most intriguing aspect of her discussion, however, is her discussion of opera as an "excess of the real": with the integration of music and language, opera carries myth beyond the realm of the imaginary, provoking a point of contact with the real. Drawing on Brecht, she argues that this jouissance of opera, its unreal play, unsettles the symbolic and political orders. Song, as pure signification, defers the signified to which it appears to refer. Opera is unique, she writes, as "song

---

52. Clément, *Miroirs du Sujet*, 270–71.

in representation,"[53] but in this work she emphasizes the musical regression rather than the symbolic order of narratives and character.

Of course, as discussed in the last chapter, her position changes markedly by the writing of *Opera, or the Undoing of Women*, where the appropriation of syncope and the deaths of characters reinscribe patriarchal narratives rather than unsettling them. However, there is also an important discussion of opera in a work on cultural politics, *Rêver Chacun Pour L'Autre* (*To Dream, Each for the Other*). This collaborative book explores the possibility of a "cultural politics" of the left, following François Mitterand's election as president in 1981, which carried the left out of the opposition for the first time in generations. Here, Clément takes a critical stance with respect to opera's social location vis-à-vis other arts, and particularly in relation to the circus. Combining music, dance, stories, and spectacle, circus and opera share similar forms, yet they have vastly different histories with respect to political power. Opera is the art of the city, located in towns and cities, and supported by the establishment as an event of official culture. The circus, by contrast, is itinerant—on the fringe of a town, without location, wandering from city to city.[54] This raises the question whether opera, in relation to its sociopolitical setting, reinforces this conservative order, even if the songs and narratives (for instance, *La Boheme* or *Carmen*) might seem to trouble it. Clément thus asks whether a leftist politics should support opera, or rather shift attention to more marginal and socially transformative art forms. The question is even more complicated in that, in postindustrial society, opera is now becoming a marginal art form treated as antiquated or the purview of a small elite. There is also the danger that support for an itinerant art may sterilize its innovative potency—co-opting the circus's outsider stance.

What is significant about this shift in Clément's position regarding opera is that early in her career, her formalist focus on the artistry itself led to an interpretation of opera largely in keeping with Kristeva's view of the semiotic, or of the sacred—as a form of language that, in bringing the drives and energies of the body into contact with symbolic speech, has a liberating or transformative potential. Later, the social setting of this speech and its institutional history make Clément more skeptical of this potential. In a sense, then, this shift in her view on opera illuminates her disagreement with Kristeva's analytic politics.

53. Ibid., 309.
54. Clément, *Rêver Chacun de l'Autre*, 96–100.

Rêver Chacun L'Autre is a collaborative work in which Clément sets forth her own views on culture and politics through interaction with several thinkers, including philosophical dialogues with several influential members of the French artistic establishment. While the book covers a range of philosophical and political issues, several are especially pertinent for this study: the relation between a centralized, national culture and its minority communities, the artistic relation to history, and the issues of audience and participation. While it is striking to note the absence of religion from this discussion, the issues of plurality and multiculturalism which Clément addressed display a syncretistic logic similar to that developed later in her writings on India and her novels. The image she uses here is that the task of politics is to be a gardener: to help culture to grow, in an artistic repetition of what has come before, but also thereby which opens new creative possibilities and potentials.

In 1981, as part of its program and platform, the left had promised to support and develop the varied ethnic and regional cultures. In a nation whose self-understanding revolves around liberty, equality, and fraternity, such an emphasis on difference runs counter to the momentum of French history. Yet, as Clément points out, "The same principles which had guaranteed equality in one time, which had protected against racism, had been reversed against [cultural] differences."[55] She therefore argues that what is needed is not a broad, hegemonic, national culture, but rather "little spaces" where various art forms and communal traditions can flourish alongside one another, rather than being pushed aside or assimilated in the name of the greater French culture. However, this program had been attacked by more conservative, traditionalist politicians and critics, such as Michel Debré, as "suppressing French culture," even wanting to "destroy everything," and "reversing the History of France"![56] Behind such rhetoric rests the idea of a French national culture, which requires giving up one's particularity—ethnic or regional—and sees French history as the synthesis and overcoming of these regional-cultural differences.

Against this argument, Clément raises several objections. First, she argues that the critics are grandstanding and fearmongering by imagining that national identity can only be conceived as a homogeneous unity. Drawing on Levi-Strauss, she argues that welcoming fringe communities, and letting them renew or transform the national culture, maintains and

---

55. Ibid., 108.
56. Ibid., 111–12.

strengthens a national identity. A culture that promotes "little spaces"—perhaps, even, with little spaces for opera and other "official" arts—would enrich and complexify French culture, rather than destroy it.[57]

The deeper concern of Clément, however, is how Debré attacks cultural diversification as a "reversal" of history. For, it suggests that French national identity must be idealized, as the standard by which others are judged—while beyond judgment itself, without critique or fault. This, Clément points out, glosses over the history of France's relation to its minorities—the exclusion and persecution of gypsies, anti-Semitism, and the violent assimilation of regional cultures under one national banner. Invoking national unity, Debré "forgets the repression, the deaths, the buried, the memory . . ."[58] In short, by ignoring how the national definition of France has related to its minority communities, Debré forgets French history, far more deeply than Clément's retrieval and support for a multifaceted culture.

Far from wanting to destroy everything, as Debré charges, Clément has a more specific destructive task in mind: the artistic task is to break "the image of history" that serves as a consoling, secure fantasy, and thereby can legitimate violence against others. She invokes the image of the theater in Chaillot, which is set in the ruins of a traditional theater. This illustrates that theater today performs a dual function: it communicates a tradition of art—be it Molière or the circus—but it also communicates its history of transmission. As performed in a now-ruined theater built in the grand style of fascism, drama reveals both art's complicity in this history *and* its ability to break away from it. When art "breaks the image of history," and reveals the gaps and stories that have been repressed or willfully ignored, then art contributes to a politics that builds community and seeks justice for its society.[59] To recognize the fissured character of history is to open it to other voices and perspectives, in ways that enable a more responsible memory and a creative future. A leftist politics, then, would be one in which multiple, diverse traditions would interact and develop in relation to one another, contributing to a broader cultural vision that does not totalize, but rather displays the fractures and wounds of its history. To dream each for the other—to relate the dreams, imaginary, and creativity of multiple communities and individuals, so that culture can develop—

57. Ibid., 115.
58. Ibid., 134.
59. See Clément's discussion with Antoine Vitez in ibid., 160–86.

might give "little spaces" to each other's dreams without assimilating them into a unified vision.

Another problem that Clément raises with regard to the development of culture is the issue of participation and elitism. If a culture, as a body of knowledge and a tradition of practices, defines itself over against other practices, and as elite, then how one develops a culture that involves and engages the people, and contributes to their happiness becomes a problem. An intellectual, sophisticated culture often involves a hierarchical model of transmission,[60] and its forms (for example, theater) may be accessible only in very small numbers, over against the audiences of film and television.

In music and theater, Clément sees two different models for how elitism can be addressed. The musical model she learns from Maurice Fleuret, who draws his pedagogy from traditional Bali society and its participatory orchestra. On this model, the involvement of everyone in the production, learning, and playing of music is essential. To experience the vibrations of the instrument, or one's voice, in one's own body, overcomes the passivity of being a consumer or listener in the cultural sphere. For this approach, the participation in performance is more important than the thematic content or form of what is performed, countering the tendency of mass culture to make the populace into viewers. In the theater, a different model is at work. It is hierarchical, in a sense that the transmission of theatrical art must pass from a small community of performers to a small audience, and only from there into the broader cultural stream.[61] While not immediately accessible to all, through this subterranean mode of transmission, theatrical arts can nonetheless influence a populace and impact how non-artists live their daily lives.

Rêver Chacun Pour L'Autre does not address religion specifically; it is largely concerned with the development of culture and politics in an overwhelmingly secular society, particularly in terms of the French left. However, it is noteworthy for Clément's work in general, because both her syncretistic understanding of culture and her views on the problems of transmission in an egalitarian politics become central to her interpretation of the religious dimensions of politics.

---

60. See Certeau, *Culture in the Plural*, 86–87.
61. Clément, *Rêver Chacun de l'Autre*, 149–57.

MINDING THE GAP: INDIAN PHILOSOPHY, GANDHI, AND THE POLITICS OF SYNCRETISM

If Lacan's mirror stage brings us to a syncopated subject, but this remains at the individual level, then the question becomes where one can turn to cultivate a life in which syncope is given its due. Clément turns to Indian philosophy, in large part, because it offers models of ritual practice for analysis that counter the rite-less depression of Western society. Foremost among these is the tradition of renunciation, developed first in the Upaniṣads and later by Saivism and Tantrism. which introduced syncope into Indian social and cultural life. A brief discussion of this tradition will help to frame Clément's discussion of the problems of elitist renunciation, the appropriation of syncopatic energy, and the politics of social renunciation.

In the Upaniṣads, there is a reversal of the cosmic order of Vedic sacrifice, by which the Brahmins mimetically embodied the life of the gods. In the Vedas, sacrifices were offered both to and *with* the gods, uniting the sacrificer with Prajapati. This *imitatio dei* pursued immortality through the transient: one could overcome death, in one's priestly role, through sacrificial killing and the fathering of sons. Other social classes, to the extent they supported this activity, participated in derivative ways. Through an internalization of sacrifice, the Upaniṣads transvalued the Vedic symbolic order—sacrifice, sex, and wealth became worthless as transient things. It was only one's inner being, *atman*, that could give immortal union with Brahman, the absolute being.[62] One could only achieve this union through the renunciation (or, perhaps better, interiorization) of sacrifice, and the goods associated with it; moreover, yoga, as a meditation on breath and turning-inward of thought, provided a practice that embodied this interiorization. The Upaniṣads, then, provided a symbolic structure that supported a life of renunciation over against the stable, productive life of the Brahman.

Many of the subsequent developments in Indian philosophy—in Buddhism and Jainism as well as Hinduism—can be understood as growing from the tensions between the Vedic order centered on Brahman sacrifice and the worklessness of renunciation. Indian thought sought to either cultivate or appropriate the "gap" the Upaniṣads introduced.[63] Broadly

---

62. This concept is set forth most fully and clearly in the Katha Upanaisad, where Naciketas has a dialogue with death.

63. This tension was, from very early on, manifest in the Brahmin community itself. See, in particular, Patrick Olivelle, *Asrama System*, for an intriguing and compelling interpretation of the history of renunciation and the ritual hierarchy.

speaking, one could say that the *Bhagavad Gita*, the *asrama* system, and the Puranas have been attempts to integrate renunciation's difference into the social order, in ways that are more productive and less destabilizing. These all give different forms and goals to renunciation, such that dying to the world reaffirms the cosmic order. For instance, Arjuna learns that renunciation is giving oneself to one's role ("discipline is renunciation," in the *Bhagavad Gita*), so as to bring about the cosmic sacrifice that unites the world with Krisna. The *asrama* system makes renunciation into stages in life, rather than a separate path, so that it does not threaten the perpetuation of the priestly class; the Puranas, while shifting the symbolic order, perpetuate the class order by creating a "popular" version of ritual life that is accessible to non-Brahmins—all the while reaffirming the distinction of religious classes.

By contrast, other movements in the Hindu tradition suspend or sustain the social dissonance of the renouncer. Left-hand Tantrism, by inverting Brahmanic ritual, turns away from social purity and order, creating an enraptured state of ecstasy. Moreover, its symbolic and philosophical outworking in Saivite worship emphasizes the dissolution of the self through the breakdown of its borders, as the practitioner unites with Siva and Shakti, burning away desire much as Siva destroyed Kama, becoming like the "erotic ascetic" himself, unleashing a destruction that is also fertile and creative. The *tapas* of yoga burns away one's social and external self, to unite with the cosmic being of Brahman. Finally, *bhakti*, as ecstatic devotion to a god (generally, to Krishna or Siva) poetically figures a loss of self in song, dance, and prostration. *Bhakti* devotion is coupled with a loss of social identity and the undoing of hierarchy: not only is it a divine-human erotic union, it is open to men and women of all castes, and undoes traditional gender roles. Radha, the consort of Krishna, and Mirabai, the poet, commit divine adultery, leaving or "betraying" their spouses.[64] Moreover, much of *bhakti* poetry is androgynous, as male poets become feminine in their relation to the god, challenging standard gender divisions of Indian society. These movements, by inverting or challenging the ritual order, resist recuperation and unsettle the social hierarchy. It is this subversive tradition that interests Clément in her studies of Indian philosophy and religion.

Drawing on the work of Sudhir Kakar, Clément gives an analytic interpretation of these ritual and ascetic developments as providing a philosophical counterpoint to the Western traditions. In these diverse forms,

---

64. Clément, *Syncope*, 184–85.

Hinduism offers ritual practices that enhance the syncopative, "nighttime" side of life, philosophically (if not socially) balancing it with the life of quotidian productivity. Furthermore, in this array of rituals, particularly in yoga and *bhakti*, the culture offers ways for syncope to become central to the lives of many Indians, rather than the purview of artists and a few elite analysands. As Clément quotes Kakar,

> The ideal of *moksha*, applicable in principle to every Hindu . . . gives him the possibility of living, even at a preconscious level, a "mystical experience." The fact is that in India, the concept of *moksha* does not represent a phenomenon of deviance, but occupies a central position in the culture."[65]

The Hindu cosmos sets Cartesianism to the side, conceiving a "dividual," split subjectivity in which creative dissolution becomes possible in a more egalitarian way than in Western culture.

In examining Clément's interpretation of Indian philosophy, it is important to bear in mind that she focuses on the analytic potential it holds—setting it up, in many ways, as an ideal construct over against continental philosophy. This is particularly important when one bears in mind the ways that dividual identity can become collectivist. *Bhakti* is perhaps especially illustrative. Where Clément locates Indian thought between the individualism of the West and "collective" Chinese thought, the emotive force of *bhakti* can become collectivist as well. This has become quite evident in recent years, as various forms of *bhakti*—particularly devotion to Rama that has centered on Ayodhya—have been exploited for nationalist and "Hinduist" ends by the VSS (Viswakarma Service Society) and BJP (Bharatiya Janata Party).[66] Clément emphasizes the significance of dividuality for a single person, and for communities of individuals, yet she also remains well aware that the path of renunciation has traditionally been an elitist, Brahman path: "The Brahman system, even when later altered, is directed by a strict and pitiless hierarchy, of which the exclusion of those who dared not die next to the river is but an example; only an elite is capable of inspiring the village." [67] It falls to Buddhism and Jainism to move beyond this social hierarchy (albeit by reinstating an alternative, monastic

---

65. Ibid., 154, quoting from Kakar, *Moksha*, 47.

66. See the essays by Philip Lutgendorf, Peter van der Veer, and Susan Devalle in Lorenzen, *Bhakti Religion in North India*, 253–322, which deal with the relationship between *bhakti* and the recent rise in Hindu nationalism.

67. Clement, *Syncope*, 174–75.

one in many cases). The radical potential of syncope may require analysis, so as to prevent subjective dissolution from becoming a form of collective assimilation, or reverting to hierarchy.

Clément locates syncope's most radical potential in the person of Mahatma Gandhi. Taking on the renouncer's simple life, opening his *ashrams* to all castes, fasting on behalf of Indian independence and peace, Gandhi's life embodied a revolution that was at once traditional and modern. Gandhi "ungoverns," fissuring the political-economic order through the adaptation of renunciation and *bhakti*, reinterpreting the epics and myths of Hinduism in accord with nonviolent noncooperation. "Noncooperation," *satyagraha*, was a step outside productive activity, a refusal to be part of the economic order.

The importance of Gandhi to Clément cannot be overestimated. Building on her discussion of Gandhi in *Syncope*, Clément would later write and design a short, popular book on his life titled *Gandhi: The Power of Pacifism*, which traces his political involvement and gives an analytic interpretation of this quasi-androgynous, celibate, and pacifist "mother" of India.[68] Gandhi's approach to everyday life in India, and his appreciation for the simple yet difficult rural Indian life, is also central to Clément's recent commentary on a collection of photographs titled *Desert Eves*. In these photographs of Indian woman from the Thur Desert, she comments that they have the "spirit of Mirabai," a freedom and strength beyond the Brahman order—a power that comes from being outside the social strictures of the upper classes. Clément eloquently describes Gandhi's appreciation for the beauty and strength of Mirabai's challenge to Brahman hierarchy:

> The aged Mahatman so dearly loved the songs of Mira Bai, that he listened to them to his last breath. This is not entirely innocent. For Princess Mira also sang about the lovers of her god Krisna, including the lowliest among them. These were the women of Bhil, women considered worthless, dirty . . .
>
> The god does not care that the woman is low-born. Dirty and common, the impure woman found the best of the plums, and she entrusted them only to the papillae of her tongue. There is no greater misdeed, no finer love. In the sixteenth century, even for a princess using it in a poem, it is a revolutionary thought.[69]

68. Clément, *Gandhi: The Power of Pacifism*, 126.
69. Clément, *Desert Eves*, 13.

It was, in her view, this freedom and simple beauty, as well as the sense of sacredness that accompanies it, that Gandhi loved so much on his travels through the Indian countryside. This led him to challenge the hierarchy of caste, and gave him a strength and a vision that went beyond the purview of modern, coercive politics.

The significance of Gandhi for Clément's work is perhaps best illustrated by the following quote, which brings together syncope, religion, and politics:

> For the syncope-person whose struggle consisted in abstaining from food, sex, and fighting, for this man who remained silent one day a week, this new country for whom he was the birth mother was still too fraught with ethnic violence; no affiliation or fellowship, not even with India, could justify bloodshed. Not to be Indian became a virtue for him: India was a universal negative coalition considered as a country.
>
> Nationalism and patriotism do not enter the mindset of this person; spontaneously holding back from life, on the verge of holding back from death, they are *spontaneously syncretic, spontaneously without a country*. Gandhi walked through the Indian countryside always carrying three books: the Bhagavad Gita, the Koran, and the Bible. Nothing further was required to be brutally massacred.[70]

If syncope dissolves the borders of the subject, here we see its full implications in the syncretic and universal dissolution of religious and national identity. With Buddhist compassion, or perhaps a Jain-like sense of non-injury (*ahimsa*) toward all beings, Gandhi refused nationalism, even while fighting for independence; while drawing from the Bhagvad Gita, Qur'an, and Bible, his belief in divinity transcended the representation of any particular tradition. And yet, by stepping outside the positions of authority and power granted by society, this "weak" abstainer revolutionized modern civilization (which, of course, he said would be a "good idea"). In his multinational, global syncretism, Gandhi symbolizes the cultural and religious politics that Clément advocates, which lead to her resistance to Kristeva's Eurocentrism.

This does not, however, lead to a neglect of biblical and European traditions. Rather, Clément sees a return to these as possible, in light of reflecting on India. As with syncope, everything looks different from here.

---

70. Clement, *Syncope*, 247, my emphasis.

As she writes in *Desert Eves*, the desert of India is, in many ways, the desert of the Bible:

> Trudging along like the people of God led by the prophet Moses and his brother Aaron, here are the caravans, donkeys, and camels carrying bundles attached by cords . . . here are the running children, the houses made of earth and thatched with straw . . . and at last, the women, all beautiful and all Eve, even the oldest one, whose smile reveals missing teeth.[71]

Here, we see the essence of Clément's wager: in engaging with other traditions, the heart of one's own may be illuminated in a new way. For Clément, syncretism is not meant to desiccate a tradition of its particularity. Rather, by emphasizing the commonality of practice, music, ritual—the embodied aspects of religion—she hopes to undercut the Eurocentric and elitist hierarchy that would privilege certain analytical or theological discourses. Indeed, as one studies their exchanges, one wonders whether, despite Kristeva's emphasis on the semiotic aspects of discourse, Clément's emphasis on a diversification of arts, participation, and her embrace of Gandhi's political noncooperation is more attuned to the variance and polyphony of engaged democratic practice.

To help illustrate the point, one could return briefly to Arendt. Kristeva largely embraces Arendt's notion of political action as narrative, while seeking to open such narrative to more polyphonic and fragmented forms of discourse. However, she thereby still operates within the *praxis/poiesis* opposition which, according to Sheldon Wolin, truncates Arendt's conception of politics. On Wolin's reading, Arendt's conception of politics forces one to leave out—or silence—those voices and concerns which would emphasize social and class difference, creating agonism and struggle within the *polis*.[72] Wolin also highlights Arendt's ignoring the "darkness" of everyday culture, in which the practical and poetic may not be so easily distinguished—and, religion might be first and foremost among such forms of socio-political formation.[73] If Kristeva's approach adopts Arendt's conception of narrative, then it would seem she is subject to a similar critique, and it is striking that her two forms of freedom seem to downplay the importance of class struggle and solidarity.

71. Clément, *Desert Eves*, 9.
72. Wolin, "Hannah Arendt," 294–95.
73. Ibid., 300.

One could, I think, defend Kristeva from this charge. To the extent that the semiotic incorporates drives, desires, energies—in short, the more embodied aspects of life—the semiotic could, in principle, include the social dynamics and interactions that Wolin wants to emphasize. It is therefore possible that Kristeva's corrective to Arendt could be read as a rejoinder to Wolin's critique. However, the examples which Kristeva gives, in her literary and political "minor histories," still seem to downplay this possibility. By reading Kristeva in tandem with Clément, however, one might deepen and diversify the presence of the semiotic in symbolic and political discourse, creating an avant-garde that is less elitist and more a chorus of voices from a range of traditions, communities, and economic standpoints. Likewise, Clément's account of subjective dissolution might guard itself against collectivization, through a further reappropriation of Jewish and Christian discourse and practice—as Gandhi exemplified in his own way. Thus, the friendship of Kristeva and Clément both clarifies the trajectory of their thought, crystallizing their distinctive approaches, and provides a way for each thinker (or those of us who follow them) to extend and revise their approaches in the future.

Finally, the exchanges between Clément and Kristeva point toward the irreducible strangeness of religion: it is at once both how we become open to alterity, and a way that we become bound to certain traditions, people, and places. For all their criticisms, it would seem that in the end, an ethical form of politics requires religion—perhaps as a mode of life to be analyzed, and certainly as situated in engagement with other traditions and practices. It is, ultimately, a form of strangeness that we have in common, and its shared importance for these two atheists may testify all the more strongly to our "unbelievable need to believe," as a form of community where we find ourselves even in our continued restlessness.[74]

---

74. Kristeva, *Cet incroyable besoin de croire*.

Conclusion
Questioning Friendship

From the preceding explorations of these three friendships, the centrality of interreligious friendship to modern religious thought emerges with clarity. In terms of clarifying a problematic, adopting a discourse, or refining the trajectory of one's thought, the friendships help us to trace the turning points and innovations in the work of these seminal thinkers. The relationships shed light on a dimension of their intellectual context that is often overlooked or minimized by certain interpretations. Eliding simple classification, and troubling the categories by which we often schematize religious thought, these friendships may help us to attend to marginal aspects of their work, and of interreligious friendship more generally.

In this conclusion, I would like to consider the significance of these interreligious friendships in terms of how we conceive of friendship. For, while clearly bearing some resemblances to more traditional or common conceptions of friendship, these relationships also can help us to envisage friendship in new ways. Specifically, they highlight the significance of questioning and listening as practices of friendship, which become especially important for relationships that transgress or subvert established boundaries. Moreover, each friendship models a different dynamic of friendship that may serve as a model—or, in some ways, a cautionary tale—regarding the shape that interreligious friendship may take. Attending to these different patterns may help us to think more fully about the varied forms that friendship may take in our lives.

THE QUESTION OF FRIENDSHIP:
WHERE FRIENDSHIP WAS, THERE I SHALL BECOME

In different ways, each of these relationships highlights the importance of questioning as a central aspect of friendship. Rather than friendship being the guarantee of an essence, or something that confirms the sameness or identity of two individuals, these friendships center on a moment of interrogation in which one's assumptions, prejudices, and certainties are thrown into doubt. This is not, to be sure, a Cartesian doubt, in which one's ego calls the world into question and then finds its own inner certainty. Rather, it would seem that the ego itself is called into question by the friend's discourse—which, in an odd reversal, then becomes the discourse by which one is able to repair, and retrieve, one's conception of religion and of redemption. Because the other loves me, I am questioned; we think, and therefore I can become.

This would suggest, then, that the temporality of such interreligious friendships is not, in a strict sense, presence. Rather, it is a proximate relation that allows for creativity, renewal, and development, enabling a *process* of subjectivity. In this process, there, no doubt, could be hostility and even destruction, as renewal may require separation or a breakdown of previously established patterns of thought and/or behavior. Such hostility or criticism, however, is undertaken in light of seeking a higher good; these friendships are ecstatic relations, carrying the friends beyond themselves. In the terms of these thinkers, friendship is the not-yet of redemption, the exposure to the *il y a*, or the affective break that dissolves the subject, enabling its rebirth in new forms of speech. These friendships, then, can help us to transform and re-create traditional conceptions of friendship on several levels.

In many ways, such questioning is similar to the frankness of speech (*parrhesia*) discussed in the introduction, particularly as it developed in Stoic and Ciceronian traditions. However, there are several crucial differences. First, in Stoicism, frankness is supposed to help a friend to remain rational, so that she or he can practice virtue. This suggests, in some ways, that the highest level of subjectivity is a stable, self-sufficient rationality.[1] However, in the friendships discussed here, the questioning of friendship opens beyond rationality—for instance, into the space of ethics or literature, for Levinas and Blanchot. Likewise, both Kristeva and Clément would emphasize the affective dimension of analysis and religion, such that the process of subjectivity cannot develop simply through a repression or negation of emotion. Thus, the openness to the process of questioning modifies the frankness of traditional models of friendship.

---

1. Of course, one might argue that the Stoics don't think we ever achieve this, and thereby that subjectivity is more of a process, but the goal defined by the "wise man" is nonetheless fixed.

In this light, one might see this openness as more like the *epektasis* of Gregory of Nyssa, who saw the infinite striving for virtue as our closest approximation to God's infinite being. It was, for Gregory, in such infinite striving that one becomes a friend with God.[2] One might further link this with an Augustinian "becoming a question" that seeks rest only in God. To be sure, especially for Kristeva, the Augustinian idea of questioning becomes more and more central in her later work, as an aspect of Arendtian being-plural that recognizes singularity, but such continued striving is something that all of the thinkers share, to varying degrees.

While the parallels are significant, once again the differences from classical friendship require recognition: the body is no longer what should be suppressed or transcended, but rather must be taken up in its affectivity and vulnerability, as the way the subject becomes open to transcendence. In both the relationships and the concepts of these thinkers, transcendence becomes immanent—it is in history and translation, literature and enigmas, or music and analysis that one's response to alterity embodies the infinitude of love.

It is at this point that the interreligious aspect of these friendships becomes especially significant. For, in each of these exchanges, attention to religious difference becomes a central aspect of making thought immanent. It demands historical, literary, and philosophical analysis, not to mention highlighting the aesthetic dimension of thought. Through such engagement, the friends must question the adequacy of their conceptual approach, and it is often through the other's thought that they are able to rework this in ways that are illuminating and reparative. This is, in my view, most evident in the repeated engagement of Levinas and Blanchot, where the adoption of the other's writing, via a critical engagement, leads to innovation within each author's work—Blanchot's notion of plural speech, Levinas's enigmatic transcendence, and both authors' later views on criticism and commentary. This instance shows, moreover, that religious difference need not simply be opposition or disagreement; rather, if subjectivity is an ongoing questioning, then the engagement with, and even appropriation of, the other's thought and tradition can lead to moments of agreement or solidarity, even where difference persists.

There is an important corollary to this claim: if engagement with religious difference intensifies the questioning dimension of subjectivity, then the ignorance of such difference likewise serves to limit thought. This is not

2. Gregory of Nyssa, *Life of Moses*, 116.

surprising; as our thought develops through our participation in different traditions and communities, there is a contextual and historical finitude to its development. However, it remains important to emphasize this, in order to critically draw out the workings of these relationships. Within each relationship, the limits of a friend's engagement with the other frequently block their reflection. Rosenstock remained resistant to Rosenzweig's Judaism (perhaps because of his own conversion), and struggled to see its significance even in his later historical and philosophical reflections. Blanchot, and to some degree Clément, both reject monotheism in reductive ways that preclude their recognizing the variance and complexity of these traditions. Kristeva and Levinas, for all the ground that they traverse, nonetheless limit the significance of various artistic and religious traditions, even as we have seen that their views on these questions are more complex than is often recognized.

It would seem, then, that an emphasis on questioning by itself is not sufficient. Rather, listening takes on a particularly central role. In their best moments—for instance, Rosenzweig and Rosenstock on translation, or Blanchot's interrogation of *Totality and Infinity*—these friends attended to one another through an act of listening that lets them be affected by the other. Listening, in many ways, could be compared to Levinas's description of the "*affection* of the finite by the infinite," in the idea of the infinite that subverts the cogito. Listening pulls one out of one's "mineness," or one's own way of thought—"toward a thought that thinks more than it thinks, and does better than think."[3] It is in such listening that one becomes other than oneself, pluralized, and thus able to question responsibly. The failure to listen that occurs in each relationship may also be what leads to the reductive, overly schematic views that the friends set forth. Nowhere is this more apparent than with Rosenzweig and Rosenstock, whose typological and schematic approaches to history and society undercut their innovative and illuminating analyses, not to mention their relation to one another.

The significance of listening should not be underestimated. It is a moment of receptivity, a challenge to the sovereignty of one's thought or ego. As a "straining toward a possible meaning," or an openness to a resonance beyond the philosophical subject, listening goes beyond what we can readily understand.[4] As Romand Coles has argued, it is perhaps the most significant dimension of building the sorts of cross-communal solidarity requisite

3. Levinas, *Entre Nous*, 220–21.
4. Nancy, *Listening*, 6.

for a radical politics. Listening is often central to cultivating real friendship where differences exist, but in many ways does not fit within a philosophical tradition that privileges solitary, monological reflection and agency.[5] At times, in these friendships, we see such solidarity emerge—and we see its failure as well.

In looking at the three friendships together, there is a further aspect to this limitation of reflection that must be addressed. In a sense, all three of these friendships involve a certain exclusion of Islam. This is most evident between Rosenzweig and Rosenstock, where one is free to decide whether Rosenstock's outright ignorance (in defining humanity as pagan or Christian) or Rosenzweig's systematizing caricature of Islam is more offensive. Kristeva, in a letter to Clément, likewise recognizes that their exchange leaves Islam largely to the side as well,[6] and one can only think that attention to Muslim approaches to commentary might further complicate both Levinas's and Blanchot's discussion of this issue. On many levels, this claim is not new. However, if it is through engagement with religious difference that one becomes more engaged in the world—and thereby moves toward transcendence of the world—then this glaring gap in their reflection should give us pause.

While thus far I have largely discussed the three relationships in tandem, they clearly differ greatly from one another in their histories and trajectories. If attending to singularity is an appropriate ethical goal, then simply assimilating the friendships to one model would fail in the very act of setting them forth. Thus, a brief consideration of the shape of each friendship, in both its dynamic and its history, is warranted—and may help us to recognize the different shapes other friendships take in our lives as well.

THE SHAPES OF FRIENDSHIP

Beyond playing a central role in the development of some of the twentieth century's most innovative and influential religious thinkers, what is the significance of these friendships? One aspect that deserves attention is the distinctive shape each friendship takes, as none of them conforms to a standard or canonical model of friendship. Indeed, I would argue that each

---

5. Coles, *Beyond Gated Politics*, 217–29. See also Coles and Hauerwas, *Christianity, Democracy and the Radical Ordinary*, 81, 196–97.

6. Kristeva, *Feminine and the Sacred*, 165–67.

represents a different model of friendship, as their temporal forms differ dramatically. A brief consideration of each friendship, in its singularity, can help us to see how such relations contribute to intellectual and religious engagement in different if overlapping ways. In what follows, the images of the friendships are meant to capture both their beauty and their flaws, which may ultimately be inseparable.

Rosenzweig/Rosenstock-Huessy: Variant Fidelities

At first glance, Rosenzweig and Rosenstock's friendship would seem to have faded over time, as they became more distant from the intense conversations that set Rosenzweig on his path back to Judaism in 1913. From their epistolary exchange, to the *Star of Redemption*, through Franz's passion for Gritli, into their later work on translation and adult education, the disagreement between them only intensified over time. Indeed, it is understandable that one would see Rosenstock's significance as largely confined to Rosenzweig's early work, with Rosenzweig's Jewish interlocutors becoming more prominent upon his move to Frankfurt. Moreover, if one follows the respective paths their reputations have taken since, the opposition between Rosenzweig's rise to prominence and Rosenstock's relegation to marginal academic status only serves to confirm that they went their separate ways.

And yet, within this divergence, a parallel emerges. As discussed, both remained deeply committed to speech-thinking as the center of their philosophy, and their thought ranged through historical, legal, and educational problems. In different ways, both sought to combat what they saw as the creeping homogeneity of modern culture—its loss of the range of possibilities of speech, the assimilative understanding of Judaism, and the reduction of education through its dissociation from labor (or from daily Jewish life). Thus, in a paradoxical way, it was precisely through their disagreement, divergence, and perhaps even in their infidelity—each seeking a different path toward the truth—that they remained surprisingly faithful to one another.

The image that best captures the interplay between these two forceful thinkers is that of an improvisational competition between virtuoso musicians—playing variations on a common theme, like dueling violinists or guitarists. Their antagonism was, in many ways, shaped by a competitive desire to both imitate and outdo the other. As Rosenstock wrote in the introduction to their correspondence, "The two partners found themselves reluctantly put under the compulsion to face up to one another in a struggle with no quarter to be given or asked for."[7] One dimension of this competition was its being *for* Gritli—for her affection and admiration, if not her possession. Throughout the exchanges, from the arguments over whose people is closer to God to the most effective approach to adult education, these friends sought to outdo the other in intellectual and practical excellence. They borrowed from each other's work, taking it in new and more radical directions, striving to master the other's discourse and thought and improvise new forms.

Such competitive virtuosity was a struggle, as neither wanted to play second fiddle. As Rosenzweig wrote in a late essay on the phonograph, in describing the status that such virtuoso improvisation conferred,

> Only here the virtuoso may exercise the seigneurial right of the first night in the century of scientific editions: to invent on the basis of what he finds; a right, which today seems so wrong, indeed nearly blasphemous . . . that makes us shudder slightly as if to say: "But is that allowed?"[8]

The "seigneurial right" demands others' recognition and cannot be shared. It was only through one-upmanship, and the refusal to agree, that the friends could push one another to the heights for which they strove. Of course, attempting to improvise on a theme may become constraining, or fail to really ring true, and at times their work seems forced, forcing a system or model onto a situation or problem to which it is ill-suited. Furthermore, the costs of such competition, to both men as well as Gritli and Edith, will remain uncountable and should not be overlooked. Nonetheless, this competition provided a path for thinking that led to some of the most innovative attempts to integrate work, faith, and thought under the conditions of liberal capitalism and the pressures of assimilation. For those of us who see such issues as persistent concerns for religious communities, their efforts are laudable, even where the results of their endeavors no longer resonate with the same persuasive force they may once have held.

---

7. Rosenstock, Introduction in Rosenzweig, *Die "Gritli"-Briefe*, 638, cited by Harold Stahmer in the introduction to *Judaism despite Christianity*, 4. (Originally published in 1935, this volume did not include the Gritli letters, nor many other letters between Rosenstock and Rosenzweig.)

8. Rosenzweig, "Concert Hall on the Phonograph Record," in *Cultural Writings of Franz Rosenzweig*, 135.

Levinas/Blanchot: An Ecstatic Sobriety

In many ways, the friendship between Levinas and Blanchot would appear to be the most conventional friendship of the three studied here. Friends for more than fifty years, with Blanchot having rescued and sheltered Levinas's family during the Nazi occupation, both engaged in an incessant conversation with their "clandestine companion," philosophy. Their friendship almost appears Aristotelian in its combination of intellectual and moral virtue. And yet, ironically, if their friendship were constant and unchanging—rooted in their essential being, rather than the other's alterity—then neither of them would recognize it as friendship.

Though Blanchot articulates it more forcefully and more frequently, for both thinkers friendship demands an attentiveness that interrupts and ultimately dissolves the subject. It requires recognizing the contingency, the murmur of the *il y a,* which unsettles the being of the friend—both letting his singularity emerge, and conditioning it through death and hunger. Friendship, then, is a relation of dispossession. As Blanchot writes in memoriam of Bataille,

> Friendship, this relation without dependence, without episode, yet into which all of the simplicity of life enters, passes by way of the recognition of the common strangeness that does not allow us to speak of our friends . . . the movement of understanding in which, speaking to us, they reserve, even on the most familiar terms, an infinite distance, the fundamental separation on the basis of which what separates becomes relation. Here discretion . . . is the interval, the pure interval that, from me to this other who is a friend, measures all that is between us, the interruption of being that never authorizes me to use him, or my knowledge of him, and that, far from preventing all communication, brings us together in the difference and sometimes silence of speech.[9]

This passage resonates with Levinas's and Blanchot's work on many levels: alterity as the interruption of being; the relation of proximity—rather than fusion or respect—that enigmatically brings together what remains infinitely distant; and the privilege of the *saying* that elides use, thematization, or appropriation. Do the engagements of Levinas and Blanchot with one another's work live up to Blanchot's formulation?

In their patient attention to one another's work, I would be inclined to say they do. What is perhaps most striking about their friendship is

---

9. Blanchot, *Friendship,* 291.

the austere, sober devotion to the other's thought that each displays in his writings. This requires, first, letting the other speak, in ways that question and unsettle one's own thought. This is evident in both authors' references to the other's work, as in *The Infinite Conversation* and *On Maurice Blanchot*. It then demands a questioning of that author's work—not on one's own terms, but rather in and through the words of the other. This is a more cryptic, hermetic form of interrogation, as seen in Blanchot's challenge to Levinas's notion of substitution in *The Writing of the Disaster*, or Levinas's appropriation of the enigma as a mode of transcendence. There is little, if any, "delirium of praise," to use Eleanor Kaufman's phrase, which captures the spirit of many of the friendships these two men (especially Blanchot) shared.[10] Rather, it is a commitment that seeks to articulate the "plural speech," or the polyphonic commentary, that Blanchot and Levinas locate as the heart of responsibility. Theirs is a relation of proximity, rather than unity.

Their friendship, then, breaks with canonical forms; it cannot be "legendary," as Derrida described Blanchot's friendship with Bataille.[11] Rather, it would seem closest to an inversion of Stoic friendship. In his letters to Lucilius, Seneca articulates the purpose of friendship for a Stoic—whose emphasis on virtuous self-sufficiency would seem to preclude any need for friends whatsoever:

> The wise man, I say, self-sufficient though he be, nevertheless desires friends if only for the purpose of practicing friendship, in order that his noble qualities may not lie dormant. Not, however, for the purpose mentioned by Epicurus in the letter quoted above: "That there may be someone to sit by him when he is ill, to help him when he is in prison or in want;" but that he may have someone by whose sick-bed he himself may sit, someone a prisoner in hostile hands whom he himself may set free.[12]

For the Stoics, the purpose of friendship is the exercise of virtue—that one's "noble qualities may not lie dormant." By looking within, one constructs what Marcus Aurelius called the "inner citadel,"[13] in which one's agency and thought give protection against fortune's vicissitudes.

---

10. Kaufman, *Delirium of Praise*, 29.
11. Derrida, *Politics of Friendship*, 293. See Kaufman, *Delirium of Praise*, 37.
12. Seneca *Epistulae Moralae*, in Pakaluk, *Other Selves*, 121.
13. See Hadot, *Philosophy as a Way of Life*, 179–205.

For Blanchot and Levinas, friendship likewise calls one to a friend's sickbed—it is, after all, the *other's* death that concerns me, not my own. Once there, however, they break from the Stoics. For, in the face of the other's death, one's agency and self are rendered radically insufficient—one becomes passive, vulnerable, exposed to the outside. Friendship puts the subject into question, rather than confirming his or her virtue. It thereby temporalizes responsibility, disclosing both the uniqueness of the other and the singularity of one's own responsibility before them. Rather than protect one from fortune, it exposes the subject to the contingency of being. In this disruption of finitude, an element of goodness shines forth—either in the trace of God for Levinas, or the radical solidarity of being-human for Blanchot. The sober companionship of the gaze that reflects on the neuter and substitutes itself for the other—only in this immersion within the world does an escape from nihilism become possible.

In this light, one could borrow Kevin Hart's term, and name Blanchot and Levinas's friendship a "counterspiritual" exercise.[14] Blanchot's refusal of unity and theology and Levinas's refusal of a traditional conception of religion and transcendence repeatedly lead them both back to the other's work. It is through the reading and attention to one another's work, putting each other and themselves into question, that they seek to hear the cry that resounds within the chatter of speech—the cry of the suffering, the cry of the persecuted—the humble truth that enigmatically resounds within our everyday world and language. Theirs is a sober vigilance, in which the noble solidarity of humanity can only be thought in facing the worst violence and destruction that we visit on ourselves.

Kristeva/Clément: Open Chords

As Kristeva writes to Clément in *The Feminine and the Sacred*, the essential thing in friendship is "a hesitation . . . that wagers on what is to come."[15] Their friendship takes a different form than the others, in terms of its temporality, as they join together in their work after years of independent scholarship. Somewhat like Rosenstock and Rosenzweig, their careers have been quite parallel, as both began their work in psychoanalysis, shifted onto more artistic and religious terrain, and have turned in recent years to the novel as one of their preferred discourses. However, these paths led

---

14. Hart, *Dark Gaze*, 229–30.
15. Kristeva, *Feminine and the Sacred*, 17.

toward their engagement with one another, rather than away from it, and in their letters they pursue the same goal of healing—individually and socially—through a sustained disagreement.

Clément and Kristeva's work, in many ways, manifests an almost magnetic relationship—though, as a form of repulsion, where two magnets with the same polar orientation resist contact. Their exchanges, while frequently in agreement, situate this agreement in a way that pushes them apart. For both, the sacred may be that which dissolves boundaries and unsettles the order of society, but how one relates to the sacred remains a node of disagreement.

In contrast with the reworkings and mutual appropriations practiced by the previous friendships, in drawing upon and adapting one another's thought, it is striking that Kristeva and Clément's later work seems largely unchanged by their exchange of letters. Kristeva's conception of feminine genius, as set forth in her discussion of Arendt, Klein, and Colette, bears few traces of Clément's analytic or interpretive approach. Rather, her emphasis on life, attachment to others, and birth echoes the thematics of her letters to Clément. Clément's later novels, likewise, remain committed to a syncretistic approach, with a strong emphasis on rites and embodiment.

However, to see their exchange as two ships passing in the night misses the creative tension that the exchange creates. It is precisely through their differentiation that they can put each other into question. For Kristeva, the sacred requires a certain form of questioning, not least a questioning of the self, which defines thinking (in some ways that are close to Arendt's definition of thought as a form of being-plural).[16] As each is called to respond, the differences in their views introduce this thought into their discourse, preventing its stasis. This divergence further fractures the reader, who is left "without conclusion," as Kristeva writes near the end of their exchange. Avoiding resolution, the form of their correspondence leaves the reader open to further questions.

From Clément's perspective, one could argue that the exchange likewise exemplifies a proper mode of thought on several levels. First, the exchange leads Kristeva to address the significance of music and rite, thus reintegrating embodiment and language. The exchange of examples—as Clément writes, "you say 'cathedral,' and I say 'yoga'"[17]—likewise lends

---

16. Kristeva, "Rethinking 'Normative Conscience,'" 220.
17. Clément, *Feminine and the Sacred*, 147.

a certain syncretism to the exchange, dissolving the privilege Kristeva accords to Jewish and (especially) Christian forms of discourse.

The image that would seem to capture this dynamic is that of an open chord—an interval of a fifth, which may be either major or minor, tonic, dominant, or subdominant. In such a chord, each note resounds in harmony with the other, while maintaining its difference, and the chord sounds both complete and open to further revision. This is, moreover, a chord form that is central to blues, one of the musical forms that gives voice to affect, and helps re-create the depressed subject. Creative, ecstatic, joyous, melancholy—an open chord resonates with the multiple dimensions of Clément and Kristeva's mutual questioning, and its place in the broader corpus of their work.

BEAUTY, TRUTH, AND THE GOOD LIFE

In looking at these friendships, both the challenges and the transformative dimensions of interreligious friendship stand out. As in Blanchot's protection of Levinas' family, they can create moments of unexpected, transcendent solidarity. Alternately, as Kristeva and Clément show, they open up new dimensions of inquiry for how we think about religion, art, and politics, and the friendship between Rosenzweig and Rosenstock provides the pair with a path for both thought and life, in the movements from speech-thinking to education. At the same time, these friendships may display prejudicial or overly negative evaluations (Rosenstock and Rosenzweig), misunderstandings and mishearing (in Clément's and Kristeva's discussions) and even laudatory distortions, as in Blanchot's praise of Judaism and Levinas's discussions of the neuter. In both their successes and their failings, their friendships can serve as educational models for all of us—demonstrating the wide range of forms friendship can take, and highlighting the importance of questioning as a dimension of friendship, if it is not to collapse into essentialist, exclusionary identification.

What is clear though, is that, at their best, these friendships practice a sort of hospitality to strangeness; a willingness to hear what is other, and make room for it in one's conception of life, faith, and thought. There is a receptivity here—perhaps what Levinas would term vulnerability—that unsettles any static or fixed religious identity. That is as true for the atheist thinkers as for those committed to a particular faith. In this, there is a unity of aesthetics, understanding, and ethics—in short, a new form of harmony among the transcendentals of beauty, truth, and goodness. From their exchanges with one another, new dimensions of beauty and religious aesthetics emerge with greater clarity—as, for instance, in Levinas and Blanchot's challenge to Heidegger's conception of art. This emergence of beauty calls the prevailing notion of truth into question, leading to a search for new understanding, much as in Rosenzweig's sonorous translations of Jehuda Halevi and the Bible. From this comes a new relation—perhaps a different form of alterity, or a new way of speaking—that enables new forms of goodness, be they ethical or political, as in Clément's polyphonic conception of cultural life. The interrogation of aesthetics, then, is a central moment in these thinkers' movement toward reformulating religion, politics, and ethics. Interreligious friendship, then, not only challenges our prevailing conceptions of ethics, but can create new forms of beauty, truth, and goodness that transcend their more traditional conceptions.

It is notable, in my view, that this harmony is most often found in these authors' approach to music; even the authors who emphasize music less still turn to it to represent the nonrepresentational dimensions of art and religion. It may be that music is the ultimate enigma, through which the responsibility that calls us to transcendence emerges. Its resistance to order calls us beyond ourselves in ways that are both transformative and troubling. As an inherently temporal artistic form, with its merging of immanence and transcendence and its demand for listening, music may be the best figure for the beauty that emerges from interreligious friendship. As with music, it may be in learning to listen in interreligious friendships that we are carried beyond ourselves into history and the world, toward new forms of thought and friendship.

In both its aesthetic and reflective dimensions, interreligious friendship points beyond the limits of tradition. And yet, as a way of being faithful to the world we live in, a world created by God, such friendship extends and deepens our religious life. As a way of being faithful to our neighbors and friends—who may or may not believe—it demands engagement with their religious life as well. It is perhaps in these friendships, which neither synthesize nor divide, that we can imagine a new form of love—one that, in its rhythms and harmonies, echoes the creative love that brings light from chaos, speech from silence, friendship from hostility, and life from death.

Bibliography

WORKS BY PRIMARY AUTHORS

Maurice Blanchot

Aminadab. Translated by Jeff Fort. Lincoln: University of Nebraska Press, 2002.
Awaiting Oblivion. Translated by John Gregg. Lincoln: University of Nebraska Press, 1997.
La Communauté Inavouable. Paris: Minuit, 1983.
Death Sentence. Translated by Lydia Davis. Barrytown, NY: Station Hill, 1978.
Faux Pas. Translated by Charlotte Mandell. Stanford: Stanford University Press, 2001.
La Folie du jour. Paris: Gallimard, 2002.
Friendship. Translated by Elizabeth Rottenberg. Stanford: Stanford University Press, 1997.
The Gaze of Orpheus, and Other Literary Essays. Translated by Lydia Davis. Barrytown, NY: Station Hill, 1981.
The Infinite Conversation. Translated by Susan Hanson. Theory and History of Literature 82. Minneapolis: University of Minnesota Press, 1993.
The Instant of My Death. Translated by Elizabeth Rottenberg. Stanford: Stanford University Press, 2000.
The Most High. Translated by Allan Stoekl. Lincoln: University of Nebraska Press, 1996.
The One Who Was Standing Apart from Me. Translated by Lydia Davis. Barrytown, NY: Station Hill, 1993.
"Our Clandestine Companion." In *Face-to-Face with Levinas*, edited by Richard A. Cohen, 41–52. Albany: SUNY Press, 1986.
Pour l'Amitié. Paris: Fourbis, 1996.
The Space of Literature. Translated by Ann Smock. Lincoln: University of Nebraska Press, 1992.
The Step Not Beyond. Translated by Lycette Neslon. Albany: SUNY Press, 1992.
Thomas l'Obscur. Paris: Gallimard, 1950.
Vicious Circles: Two Fictions and "After the Fact." Translated by Paul Auster. Barrytown, NY: Station Hill, 1985.
When the Time Comes. Translated by Lydia Davis. Barrytown, NY: Station Hill, 1985.
The Work of Fire. Translated by Charlotte Mandell. Stanford: Stanford University Press, 1995.
The Writing of the Disaster. Translated by Ann Smock. Lincoln: University of Nebraska Press, 1995.

Catherine Clément

Desert Eves: An Indian Paradise. Translated by Lory Frankel, photographs by Hans Silvester. New York: H. N. Abrams, 2002.
The Feminine and the Sacred. Coauthored by Julia Kristeva, translated by Jane Marie Todd. New York: Columbia University Press, 2001.
Gandhi: The Power of Pacifism. Translated by Ruth Sharman. New York: H. N. Abrams, 1996.
The Lives and Legends of Jacques Lacan. Translated by Arthur Goldhammer. New York: Columbia University Press, 1983.
Miroirs du Sujet. Paris: Unions Générale d'Éditions, 1975.
The Newly Born Woman. With Hélène Cixous, translated by Betsy Wing. Theory and History of Literature 24. Minneapolis: University of Minnesota Press, 1986.
Opera, or The Undoing of Women. Translated by Betsy Wing. Minneapolis: University of Minnesota Press, 1988.
La Psychanalyse. Paris: Larousse, 1976.
Rêver Chacun de l'Autre: Sur la Politique Culturelle. Paris: Fayard, 1982.
Sollers: La Fronde. Paris: Éditions Juilliard, 1995.
Syncope: The Philosophy of Rapture. Translated by Sally O'Driscoll and Deirdre M. Mahoney. Minnesota: University of Minnesota Press, 1994.
Theo's Odyssey. Translated by Steve Cox and Ros Schwartz. New York: Arcade, 1999.
The Weary Sons of Freud. Translated by Nicole Ball. London: Verso, 1987.

Julia Kristeva

Au commencement était l'amour: psychanalyse et la foi. Paris: LGF, 1997.
Black Sun: Depression and Melancholia. Translated by Leon S. Roudiez. New York: Columbia University Press, 1989.
Cet incroyable besoin de croire. Paris: Bayard, 2007.
Colette. Translated by Jane Marie Todd. Female Genius 3. New York: Columbia University Press, 2004.
"Crossing Borders." *Hypatia* 21 (2006) 164–77.
"Dialogue with Julia Kristeva." *Parallax* 4 (1998) 5–16.
"Europhilia, Europhobia." *Constellations* 5 (1998) 321–32.
The Feminine and the Sacred. Coauthored by Catherine Clément, translated by Jane Marie Todd. New York: Columbia University Press, 2001.
"Forgiveness: An Interview." *Proceedings of the Modern Language Association* 117, no. 2 (2003) 281–87.
Hannah Arendt. Translated by Ross Guberman. Female Genius 1. New York: Columbia University Press, 2001.
Hannah Arendt: Life Is a Narrative. Translated by Frank Collins. Toronto: University of Toronto Press, 2001.
Intimate Revolt. The Powers and Limits of Psychoanalysis 2. Translated by Jeanine Herman. European Perspectives. New York: Columbia University Press, 2002.
"Is There a Feminine Genius?" *Critical Inquiry* 30 (2004) 493–504.
Melanie Klein. Translated by Ross Guberman. New York: Columbia University Press, 2001.
Murder in Byzantium. Translated by C. Jon Delogu. New York: Columbia University Press, 2006.

Nations without Nationalism. Translated by Leon S. Roudiez. New York: Columbia University Press, 1993.
New Maladies of the Soul. Translated by Ross Guberman. New York: Columbia University Press, 1995.
Possessions: A Novel. Translated by Barbara Bray. New York: Columbia University Press, 1998.
Powers of Horror: An Essay on Abjection. Translated by Leon S. Roudiez. New York: Columbia University Press, 1982.
"Rethinking 'Normative Conscience': The Task of the Intellectual Today." *Common Knowledge* 13 (2007) 219–26.
Revolt, She Said. Translated by Brian O'Keefe. Cambridge: MIT Press, 2002.
Revolution in Poetic Language. Translated by Margaret Waller. New York: Columbia University Press, 1984.
The Samurai: A Novel. Translated by Barbara Bray. New York: Columbia University Press, 1992.
The Sense and Non-Sense of Revolt: The Powers and Limits of Psychoanalysis 1. Translated by Jeanine Herman. European Perspectives. New York: Columbia University Press, 2000.
"Some Observations on Female Sexuality." Translated by Sophie Leighton. *Annual of Psychoanalysis* 32 (2004) 59–68.
Strangers to Ourselves. Translated by Leon S. Roudiez. New York: Columbia University Press, 1991.
Tales of Love. Translated by Leon S. Roudiez. New York: Columbia University Press, 1987.
Thérèse mon amour. Paris: Fayard, 2008.

Emmanuel Levinas

Alterity and Transcendence. Translated by Michael B. Smith. New York: Columbia University Press, 1999.
Beyond the Verse: Talmudic Readings and Lectures. Translated by Gary D. Mole. Bloomington: Indiana University Press, 1994.
Collected Philosophical Papers. Translated by Alphonso Lingis. Pittsburgh: Duquesne University Press, 1987.
En Découvrant l'Existence avec Husserl et Heidegger. Paris: J. Vrin, 1967.
Difficult Freedom: Essays on Judaism. Translated by Seán Hand. Baltimore: Johns Hopkins University Press, 1990.
Emmanuel Levinas: Basic Philosophical Writings. Edited by Adriaan T. Peperzaak, Simon Critchley, and Robert Bernasconi. Bloomington: Indiana University Press, 1996.
Entre Nous: On Thinking-of-the-Other. Translated by Michael B. Smith and Barbara Harshav. New York: Columbia University Press, 1998.
Ethics and Infinity: Conversations with Philippe Nemo. Translated by Richard A. Cohen. Pittsburgh: Duquesne University Press, 1985.
Existence and Existents. Translated by Alphonso Lingis. Pittsburgh: Duquesne University Press, 1988.
God, Death, and Time. Translated by Bettina Bergo. Stanford: Stanford University Press, 2000.
Humanisme de l'Autre Homme. Montpellier: Fata Morgana, 1972.
In the Time of Nations. Translated by Michael B. Smith. Bloomington: Indiana University Press, 1994.

New Talmudic Readings. Translated by Richard A. Cohen. Pittsburgh: Duquesne University Press, 1999.
Nine Talmudic Readings. Translated by Annette Aronowicz. Bloomington: Indiana University Press, 1990.
On Escape. Translated by Bettina Bergo. Stanford: Stanford University Press, 2003.
Otherwise than Being, or Beyond Essence. Translated by Alphonso Lingis. Pittsburgh: Duquesne University Press, 1997.
Outside the Subject. Translated by Michael B. Smith. Stanford: Stanford University Press, 1994.
Proper Names. Translated by Michael B. Smith. Stanford: Stanford University Press, 1996.
Time and the Other and Additional Essays. Translated by Richard A. Cohen. Pittsburgh: Duquesne University Press, 1987.
Totality and Infinity: An Essay on Exteriority. Translated by Alphonso Lingis. Duquesne Studies, Philosophical Series 24. Pittsburgh: Duquesne University Press, 1969.
Unforseen History. Translated by Nidra Poller. Urbana: University of Illinois Press, 2004.
"Useless Suffering." In *The Problem of Evil: A Reader*, edited by Mark Larrimore, 371–74. Malden, MA: Blackwell, 2001.

Eugen Rosenstock-Huessy

Works marked with an asterisk (*) were accessed through *The Collected Works of Eugen Rosenstock Huessy on DVD* (Norwich, VT: Argo, 2005).

*"Arbeitsgemeinschaft." *Daimler Zeitung* 2 no. 7 (July 29, 1920) 89–90.
*"The Army Enlisted against Nature." *Journal of Adult Education* (1934) 271–74.
*"Die Akademie der Arbeit in der Universtät Frankfurt a.M." *Die Arbeitsgemeinschaft* 3 (1922) 147–52.
*"Biblionomics." In *Bibliography: Eugene Rosenstock-Huessy Biography*, by Kurt Ballerstedt, 13–25. New York: Four Wells, 1959.
The Christian Future, or The Modern Mind Outrun. New York: Harper & Row, 1966.
The Fruit of the Lips, or Why Four Gospels. Pittsburgh Theological Monograph Series 19. Pittsburgh: Pickwick, 1978.
*"The Generations of Our Faith." *Hartford Theological Quarterly* 1 (1961) 1–16.
I Am an Impure Thinker. Norwich, VT: Argo, 1970.
**Ja und Nein: Auto-Biographische Fragmente.* Heidelberg: L. Schneider, 1968.
Judaism despite Christianity: The Letters on Christianity and Judaism between Eugen Rosenstock-Huessy and Franz Rosenzweig. New York: Schocken, 1971.
Magna Carta Latina: The Privilege of Singing, Articulating, and Reading a Language and of Keeping It Alive. Pittsburgh: Pickwick, 1975.
*"An die Mitarbeiter der Akademie der Arbeit." Eugen Rosenstock Archives, Frankfurt, Werner und Winter GmbH. March 13, 1922.
Out of Revolution: Autobiography of Western Man. Norwich, VT: Argo, 1966.
The Practical Knowledge of the Soul. Translated by Mark Huessy and Freya von Moltke. Norwich, VT: Argo, 1988.
*"The Purpose of William James." Unpublished manuscript. Four Wells, VT, 1940.
*"The Social Function of Adult Education." *Bulletin of the World Association for Adult Education* 44 (1930) 10–16.
Speech and Reality. Norwich, VT: Argo, 1970.
*"What They Make Us Think." Lecture for the Civilian Conservation Corps, Dartmouth, May 1940.

Franz Rosenzweig

Cultural Writings of Franz Rosenzweig. Translated by Barbara E. Galli. Syracuse: Syracuse University Press, 2000.
Franz Rosenzweig: His Life and Thought. Edited by Nahum N. Glazer. New York: Schocken, 1961.
Franz Rosenzweig's "The New Thinking." Translated by Alan Udoff and Barbara E. Galli. Syracuse: Syracuse University Press, 1999.
God, Man, and the World: Lectures and Essays. Translated by Barbara E. Galli. Syracuse: Syracuse University Press, 1998.
Die "Gritli"-Briefe: Briefe an Margrit Rosenstock-Huessy. Tübingen: Bilam, 2002. Online: http://www.argobooks.org/gritli/index.html.
"Jehuda Halevi: Ninety-Two Hymns and Poems." In *Franz Rosenzweig and Jehuda Halevi: Translating, Translations, and Translators*, by Barbara Ellen Galli, 1–286. Montreal: McGill University Press, 1995.
"Life." In *Franz Rosenzweig and Jehuda Halevi: Translating, Translations, and Translators*, by Barbara Ellen Galli, 94, 231–33. Montreal: McGill University Press, 1995.
Der Mensch und sein Werke: Gesammelte Schriften, I.2: Briefe und Tagebucher. Edited by Rachel Rosenzweig and Edith Rosenzweig-Scheinmann. The Hague: Nijhoff, 1979.
On Jewish Learning. Translated by Nahum Glatzer. New York: Schocken, 1956.
Scripture and Translation. Co-authored by Martin Buber, translated by Lawrence Rosenwald with Everett Fox. Bloomington: Indiana University Press, 1994.
The Star of Redemption. Translated by William H. Hallo. Notre Dame: University of Notre Dame Press, 1971.
Understanding the Sick and the Healthy: A View of World, Man, and God. Translated by Nahum Glatzer. Cambridge: Harvard University Press, 1999.

SECONDARY SOURCES

Aelred of Rievaulx. *Spiritual Friendship*. Translated by Mary Eugenia Laker. Cistercian Fathers 5. Kalamazoo, MI: Cistercian, 1977.
Agamben, Giorgio. *Remnants of Auschwitz: The Witness and the Archive*. Translated by Daniel Heller-Roazen. Albany: Zone Books, 1999.
———. *The Time That Remains: A Commentary on Paul's Letter to the Romans*. Translated by Patricia Dailey. Stanford: Stanford University Press, 2005.
Agnon, S. Y. "Friendship." In *Twenty-One Stories*, translated by Misha Louvish, 72–78. New York: Schocken, 1970.
Ajzenstat, Oona. *Driven Back to the Text: The Premodern Sources of Levinas' Postmodernism*. Pittsburgh: Duquesne University Press, 2001.
———. "Levinas in the Key of the Political." In *Difficult Justice: Commentaries on Levinas and Politics*, edited by Asher Horowitz and Gad Horowitz, 63–77. Toronto: University of Toronto Press, 2006.
Antelme, Robert. *The Human Race*. Translated by Jeffrey Haight and Annie Mahler. Marlboro, VT: Marlboro, 1992.
———. "Principles Put to the Test." In *On Robert Antelme's The Human Race: Essays and Commentary*, translated by Jeffrey Haight, 23–26. Evanston: Northwestern University Press, 2003.

Bibliography

Antrick, Otto. *Die Akademie der Arbeit in der Universität Frankfurt a.M.: Idee, Werden, Gestalt.* Darmstadt: Roether, 1966.

Arendt, Hannah. *Eichmann in Jerusalem: A Report on the Banality of Evil.* New York: Viking, 1964.

———. *The Human Condition.* Chicago: University of Chicago Press, 1958.

———. *Responsibility and Judgment.* New York: Schocken, 2003.

Aristotle. *Nicomachean Ethics.* Translated by Terrence Irwin. Indianapolis: Hackett, 1999.

Augustine, Bishop of Hippo. *The Confessions.* Translated by Maria Boulding. New York: Vintage, 1998.

Balthasar, Hans Urs von. *Die Apokalypse der Deutsche Seele.* 3 vols. Leipzig: Pustet, 1937–39.

Batnitzky, Leora. "Dialogue as Judgment, Not Mutual Affirmation: A New Look at Franz Rosenzweig's Dialogical Philosophy." *Journal of Religion* 79 (1999) 523–45.

———. *Idolatry and Representation: The Philosophy of Franz Rosenzweig Reconsidered.* Princeton: Princeton University Press, 2000.

———. "The Philosophical Import of Carnal Israel: Hermeneutics and the Structure of Rosenzweig's *Star*." *Journal of Jewish Thought and Philosophy* 9 (1999) 127–52.

———. "Rosenzweig's Aesthetic Theory and Jewish *Unheimlichkeit*." *New German Critique* 77 (1999) 87–113.

———. "Translation as Transcendence: A Glimpse into the Workshop of the Buber-Rosenzweig Bible Translation." *New German Critique* 70 (1997) 87–117.

Beardsworth, Sara. *Julia Kristeva: Psychoanalysis and Modernity.* Albany: SUNY Press, 2004.

Benjamin, Walter. "Critique of Violence." In *Reflections: Essays, Aphorisms, Autobiographical Writings*, translated by Edmund Jephthcott, 277–300. New York: Schocken, 1978.

———. "Theses on the Philosophy of History." In *Illuminations: Essays and Reflections*, translated by Harry Zohn, 253–64. New York: Schocken, 1968.

Bernasconi, Robert. "A Love that is Stronger than Death: Sacrifice in the Thought of Levinas, Heidegger, and Bloch." *Angelaki* 7 (2002) 9–16.

———. "No Exit: Levinas' Aporetic Account of Transcendence." *Research in Phenomenology* 35 (2005) 101–17.

———, and Simon Critchley, editors. *Re-Reading Levinas.* Bloomington: Indiana University Press, 1996.

Berry, Wendell. "Damage." In *What Are People For?* 3–8. Berkeley, CA: North Point, 1990.

———. *The Hidden Wound.* Berkeley: North Point, 1989.

———. "The Idea of a Local Economy." In *In the Presence of Fear: Three Essays for a Changed World*, 11–33. Great Barrington, MA: Orion, 2003.

———. *The Unsettling of America: Culture and Agriculture.* New York: Avon, 1977.

Bident, Christophe. *Reconaissances: Antelme, Blanchot, Deleuze.* Paris: Calmann-Lévy, 2003.

———. "The Poetics of the Neuter." In *After Blanchot: Literature, Criticism, Philosophy*, edited by Leslie Hill, Brian Nelson, and Dimitris Vardoulakis, 13–34. Newark: University of Delaware Press, 2005.

Bloechl, Jeffrey, editor. *The Face of the Other and the Trace of God: Essays on the Philosophy of Emmanuel Levinas.* New York: Fordham University Press, 2000.

Bonhoeffer, Dietrich. *Letters and Papers from Prison.* Editd by Eberhard Bethge. New York: Collier, 1972.

Bosch, Eisabeth. "L'enigme comme force Structurante du Récit. Blanchot et Bataille." *Rapports* 50 (1980) 150–59.

Bourdieu, Pierre. "Against the Policy of Depoliticization." In *Firing Back: Against the Tyranny of the Market 2*, 38–52. New York: New Press, 2003.

———. "Sollers *Tel* Quel." In *Acts of Resistance: Against the New Myths of Our Time*, translated by Richard Nice, 11–14. Cambridge: Polity, 1998.

Bouthors-Paillart, Catherine. *Julia Kristeva*. Paris: Association pour la diffusion de la pensée francaise, 2006.

Bové, Carol Mastrangelo. *Language and Politics in Julia Kristeva: Literature, Art, Therapy*. Albany: SUNY Press, 2006.

Braiterman, Zachary. *The Shape of Revelation: Aesthetics and Modern Jewish Thought*. Stanford: Stanford University Press, 2007.

Brenner, Michael. *The Renaissance of Jewish Culture in Weimar Germany*. New Haven: Yale University Press, 1996.

Brody, D. H. "Emmanuel Levinas: The Logic of Ethical Ambiguity in *Otherwise than Being, or Beyond Essence*." *Research in Phenomenology* 25 (1995) 177–203.

Bruns, Gerald. *Maurice Blanchot: The Refusal of Philosophy*. Baltimore: Johns Hopkins University Press, 1997.

Bryant, M. Darrol. "The Grammar of the Spirit: Speech, Time, and Society." In *Eugen Rosenstock-Huessy: Studies in His Life and Thought*, edited by M. Darrol Bryant and Hans R. Huessy, 233–60. Lewiston, NY: Mellen, 1986.

Burrell, David B. *Friendship and Ways to Truth*. Notre Dame: University of Notre Dame Press, 2000.

Butler, Judith. *Gender Trouble: Feminism and the Subversion of Identity*. New York: Routledge, 1990.

Caygill, Howard. *Levinas and the Political*. London: Routledge, 2002.

Certeau, Michel de. *Culture in the Plural*. Minneapolis: University of Minnesota Press, 1997.

Ciaramelli, Fabio. "Comparison of Incomparables." *Parallax* 8 (2002) 45–58.

Cohen, Richard A., editor. *Face-to-Face with Levinas*. Albany: SUNY Press, 1986.

———. *Ethics, Exegesis, and Philosophy: Interpretation after Levinas*. Cambridge: Cambridge University Press, 2001.

Coles, Romand. *Beyond Gated Politics: Reflections for the Possibility of Democracy*. Minneapolis: University of Minnesota Press, 2004.

———, and Stanley Hauerwas. *Christianity, Democracy, and the Radical Ordinary*. Theopolitical Visions 1. Eugene: Cascade, 2007.

Collin, Françoise. *Maurice Blanchot et la Question de l'Ecriture*. Paris: Gallimard, 1986.

Colman, Athena. "Holbein's Work of Art in Kristeva's Political Thought." *Southern Journal of Philosophy* 52 (2004) 88–95.

Cools, Arthur. "Revisiting the *Il y a*: Maurice Blanchot and Emmanuel Levinas on the Question of Subjectivity." *Paragraph* 28 (November 2005) 54–71.

Cristaudo, Wayne. "Redemption and Messianism in Franz Rosenzweig's *The Star of Redemption*." In *Messianism, Apocalypse and Redemption in 20th Century German Thought*, edited by Wendy Baker and Wayne Cristaudo, 259–72. Adelaide: Australasian Theological Forum, 2006. Online: http://www.waynecristaudo.com/writings.html.

———. "Revolution and the Redeeming of the World: The Messianic History of Eugen Rosenstock-Huessy's *Out of Revolution*." In *Messianism, Apocalypse and Redemption in 20th Century German Thought*, edited by Wendy Baker and Wayne Cristaudo, 243–58. Adelaide: Australasian Theological Forum, 2006. Online: http://www.waynecristaudo.com/writings.html.

Critchley, Simon. *Very Little, Almost Nothing: Death, Philosophy, Literature*. London: Routledge, 1997.
Davies, Paul. "A Fine Risk." In *Re-Reading Levinas*, edited by Robert Bernasconi and Simon Critchley, 201–26. Bloomington: Indiana University Press, 1996.
Davis, Ellen. "Reading the Song Iconographically." *Journal of Scriptural Reasoning* 3, no. 2 (2003) n.p. Online: http://etext.lib.virginia.edu/journals/ssr/issues/volume3number2/ssr03-02-e02.html.
Derrida, Jacques. *Adieu to Emmanuel Levinas*. Stanford: Stanford University Press, 1999.
———. "Différance." In *Margins of Philosophy*, translated by Alan Bass, 1–27. Chicago: University of Chicago Press, 1982.
———. *Monolingualism of the Other, or The Prosthesis of Origin*. Translated by Patrick Mensah. Stanford: Stanford University Press, 1998.
———. *Politics of Friendship*. Translated by George Collins. New York: Verso, 1994.
Dobbels, Daniel. *On Robert Antelme's The Human Race: Essays and Commentary*. Translated by Jeffrey Haight. Evanston: Northwestern University Press, 2003.
Douglas, Mary. *Leviticus as Literature*. New York: Oxford, 2001.
———. *Purity and Danger: An Analysis of the Concepts of Pollution and Taboo*. London: Routledge, 2002.
Drabinski, John. *Sensibility and Singularity: The Problem of Phenomenology in Levinas*. Albany: SUNY Press, 2001.
Dussel, Enrique. "'The Politics' by Levinas: Toward a 'Critical' Political Philosophy." In *Difficult Justice: Commentaries on Levinas and Politics*, edited by Asher Horowitz and Gad Horowitz, 78–96. Toronto: University of Toronto Press, 2006.
Farrell, Michael. *Collaborative Circles: Friendship Dynamics and Creative Work*. Chicago: University of Chicago Press, 2001.
Feidel-Mertz, Hildegard. "Der lernende Lehrer: Rosenzweigs Schulkritik und die Erneuerung judischer Erziehung und Bildung nach 1933." In *Juden im Kassel: Eine Dokumentation anläßeszett des 100. Geburtstages von Franz Rosenzweig*, 109–118. Kassel: Thiele & Schwarz, 1987.
Feld, Scott, and William C. Carter. "Foci of Activity as Changing Contexts for Friendship." In *Placing Friendship in Context*, edited by Rebecca G. Adams and Graham Allan, 136–52. Cambridge: Cambridge University Press, 1998.
Fewell, Danna Nolan, and David Miller Ginn. *Compromising Redemption: Relating Characters in the Book of Ruth*. Louisville: Westminster John Knox, 1990.
Foucault, Michel. "Sex, Power, and the Politics of Identity." In *Ethics: Subjectivity and Truth*, translated by Robert Hurley et al., Essential Works of Michel Foucault, 1954–1984, vol. 1, 163–73. New York: New Press, 1997.
Fox, Everett. "Franz Rosenzweig as Translator." *Yearbook of the Leo Baeck Institute* 34 (1989) 371–84.
Friedman, Marilyn. *What Are Friends For?* Ithaca, NY: Cornell University Press, 1993.
Galli, Barbara. *Franz Rosenzweig and Jehuda Halevi: Translating, Translations, and Translators*. Montreal: McGill University Press, 1995.
Gibbs, Robert. *Correlations in Rosenzweig and Levinas*. Princeton: Princeton University Press, 1992.
———. "Levinas, the Messianic, and the Question of History." In *Difficult Justice: Commentaries on Levinas and Politics*, edited by Asher Horowitz and Gad Horowitz, 271–84. Toronto: University of Toronto Press, 2006.

———. "Returning/Forgiving: Ethics and Theology." In *Questioning God*, edited by John D. Caputo, Mark Dooley, and Michael J. Scanlon, 73–92. Bloomington: Indiana University Press, 2001.
———. *Why Ethics? Signs of Responsibilities*. Princeton: Princeton University Press, 2000.
Glatzer, Nahum. "The Frankfort Lehrhaus." *Adult Jewish Education* (Fall 1958) 3–17.
Goldhammer, Jesse. *The Headless Republic: Sacrificial Violence in Modern French Thought*. Ithaca: Cornell University Press, 2005.
Gordon, Peter E. "Response to My Critics." *Jewish Quarterly Review* 96 (2006) 413–422.
———. *Rosenzweig and Heidegger: Between Judaism and German Philosophy*. Berkeley: University of California Press, 2003.
Gregory of Nyssa. *The Life of Moses*. Translated by Abraham J. Malherbe and Everett Ferguson. New York: Paulist Press, 1978.
Hadot, Pierre. *Philosophy as a Way of Life*: Spiritual Exercises from Socrates to Foucault. Oxford: Blackwell, 1995.
Handelman, Susan. *Fragments of Redemption: Jewish Thought and Literary Theory in Benjamin, Scholem, and Levinas*. Bloomington: Indiana University Press, 1991.
Hart, Kevin. *The Dark Gaze: Maurice Blanchot and the Sacred*. Chicago: University of Chicago Press, 2004.
———. "From the Star to the Disaster." *Paragraph* 30 (2007) 84–103.
———. "The Right to Say Anything." *The European Legacy* 9 (2004) 7–17.
———, and Geoffrey Hartmann, editors. *The Power of Contestation: Perspectives on Maurice Blanchot*. Baltimore: Johns Hopkins University Press, 2004.
Hauerwas, Stanley. "Gay Friendship: A Catholic Thought-Experiment." In *Theology and Sexuality: Classic and Contemporary Readings*, edited by Eugene F. Rogers Jr., 289–305. Oxford: Blackwell, 2002.
———. *Performing the Faith: Bonhoeffer and the Practice of Nonviolence*. Grand Rapids: Brazos, 2004.
Heidegger, Martin. *Basic Writings: From Being and Time (1927) to The Task of Thinking (1964)*. Edited by David Farrell Krell. San Francisco: HarperSanFrancisco, 1993.
———. *Erläuterungen zu Hölderlins Dichtung*. Gesamtausgabe 4. Frankfurt: Klostermann, 1944.
Hendricks, Christina. Review of *The Feminine and the Sacred*. *Journal of Speculative Philosophy* 18 (2004) 161–4.
Higton, Michael. *Christ, Providence, History: Hans Frei's Public Theology*. London: T. & T. Clark, 2004.
Hill, Leslie. "Affirmation without Precedent: Maurice Blanchot and Criticism Today." In *After Blanchot: Literature, Criticism, Philosophy*, edited by Leslie Hill, Brian Nelson, and Dimitris Vardoulakis, 58–79. Newark: University of Delaware Press, 2005.
———. *Blanchot: Extreme Contemporary*. London: Routledge, 1997.
———. "The World Is Not Enough." *Angelaki* 7 (2002) 61–8.
Hollander, Dana. *Exemplarity and Chosenness: Rosenzweig and Derrida on the Nation of Philosophy*. Stanford: Stanford University Press, 2008.
———. "On the Significance of the Messianic Idea in Rosenzweig." *Cross Currents* 53 (2004) 555–65.
Horowitz, Asher, and Gad Horowitz, editors. *Difficult Justice: Commentaries on Levinas and Politics*. Toronto: University of Toronto Press, 2006.
Iyer, Lars. *Blanchot's Communism: Art, Philosophy, and the Political*. London: Palgrave, 2004.
———. "The Workless Community: Blanchot, Communism, Surrealism." *Paragraph* 26 (2003) 51–68.

Kakar, Sudhir. *Moksha: Le Monde Interieur*. Paris: Belles Lettres, 1985.
Kaplan, Gregory. "In the End Shall Christians Become Jews and Jews, Christians? On Franz Rosenzweig's Apocalyptic Eschatology." *Cross Currents* 53 (2004) 511–529.
Katz, Claire Elise. *Levinas, Judaism, and the Feminine: The Silent Footsteps of Rebecca*. Bloomington: Indiana University Press, 2003.
Kaufman, Eleanor. *The Delirium of Praise: Bataille, Blanchot, Deleuze, Foucault, Klossowski*. Baltimore: Johns Hopkins University Press, 2001.
Kavka, Martin. "The Ethics of Verification: Does Rosenzweig's Neighbor Speak?" Unpublished manuscript, presented to the UCLA Mellon Sawyer Seminar on "The Ethics of the Neighbor," Los Angeles, CA, March 2004.
———. "Is There Warrant for Levinas' Talmudic Readings?" *Journal of Jewish Thought and Philosophy* 14 (2006) 153–73.
———. *Jewish Messianism and the History of Philosophy*. Cambridge: Cambridge University Press, 2005.
———, and Randi Rashkover. "Toward a Modified Jewish Divine Command Theory." *Journal of Religious Ethics* 32 (2004) 387–414.
Kearney, Richard. "Dialogue with Emmanuel Levinas." In *Face-to-Face with Levinas*, edited by Richard A. Cohen, 13–34. Albany: SUNY Press, 1986.
Kearns, Cleo McNelly. "Art and Religious Discourse in Aquinas and Kristeva." In *Body/Text in Julia Kristeva*, edited by David R. Crownfield, 111–24. Albany: SUNY Press, 1992.
———. "Suffering in Theory." In *Suffering Religion*, edited by Robert Gibbs and Elliot R. Wolfson, 56–72. London: Routledge, 2002.
Kern-Ulmer, Brigitte. "Franz Rosenzweig's *Judisches Lehrhaus*: A Model for Jewish Adult Education." *Judaism* (1988) 202–14.
Kierkegaard, Soren. *Fear and Trembling*. Translated by Howard and Edna Hong. Princeton: Princeton University Press, 1983.
Kluger, Ruth. "Forgiving and Remembering." *Proceedings of the Modern Language Association* 117, no. 2 (2003) 311–13.
Kofman, Sarah. "Antelme's 'Hands': Postscript to Smothered Words." In *On Robert Antelme's The Human Race: Essays and Commentary*, translated by Jeffrey Haight, 119–22. Evanston: Northwestern University Press, 2003.
———. *Smothered Words*. Translated by Madeleine Dobie. Minneapolis: University of Minnesota Press, 1998.
Konstan, David. *Friendship in the Classical World*. Cambridge: Cambridge University Press, 1997.
Kuhn, Thomas S. *The Structure of Scientific Revolutions*. Chicago: University of Chicago Press, 1962.
Lacan, Jacques. "Le problème du style et la conception psychiatrique des formes paranoïques de l'expérience." In *De la Psychose paranoïaque dans ses rapports avec la personnalité suivi de Premier Écrits sur la paranoia*, 387–88. Paris: Seuil, 1975.
Large, William. *Emmanuel Levinas and Maurice Blanchot: Ethics and the Ambiguity of Writing*. Manchester: Clinamen, 2005.
Lescourret, Marie-Anne. *Levinas*. Paris: Flammarion, 1994.
Lorenzen, David, editor. *Bhakti Religion in North India: Community Identity and Political Action*. Albany: SUNY Press, 1995.
Mack, Michael. "Franz Rosenzweig's and Emmanuel Levinas's Critique of German Idealism's Pseudotheology." *Journal of Religion* 83 (2003) 56–79.

Mader, Mary Beth. "Fore-given Forgiveness." *Southern Journal of Philosophy* 52 (2004) 16–24.
Malka, Salomon. *Franz Rosenzweig: La Cantique de la Revelation*. Paris: Cerf, 2005.
Margaroni, Maria. "Recent Work on and by Julia Kristeva: Toward a Psychoanalytic Social Theory." *Signs: Journal of Women in Culture and Society* 32 (2007) 793–808.
Marion, Jean-Luc. "The Voice without Name: Homage to Levinas." In *The Face of the Other and the Trace of God*, edited by Jeffrey Bloechl, 224–42. New York: Fordham University Press, 2000.
Meilaender, Gilbert. *Friendship: A Study in Theological Ethics*. Notre Dame: University of Notre Dame Press, 1981.
Meir, Ephraim. *Letters of Love: Franz Rosenzweig's Spiritual Biography and Oeuvre in Light of the Gritli Letters*. New York: Peter Lang, 2006.
Mendes-Flohr, Paul. *Divided Passions: Jewish Intellectuals and the Experience of Modernity*. Detroit: Wayne State Press, 1991.
———. "Franz Rosenzweig and the Crisis of Historicism." In *The Philosophy of Franz Rosenzweig*, edited by Paul Mendes-Flohr, 138–61. Hanover: University Press of New England, 1988.
———. *German Jews: A Dual Identity*. New Haven: Yale University Press, 1999.
Meskin, Jacob. "Critique, Tradition, and the Religious Imagination: An Essay on Levinas' Talmudic Readings." *Judaism* 47 (1998) 90–106.
Midttun, Birgitte. "Crossing the Borders: An Interview with Julia Kristeva." *Hypatia* 21 (2006) 164–77.
Moses, Stéphane. *System and Revelation: The Philosophy of Franz Rosenzweig*. Translated by Catherine Tihanyi. Detroit: Wayne State University Press, 1992.
Mowitt, John. "Strangers in Analysis: Nationalism and the Talking Cure." *Parallax* 4 (1998) 45–63.
Moyn, Samuel. "Emmanuel Levinas's Talmudic Readings: Between Tradition and Invention." *Prooftexts* 23 (2003) 338–64.
———. *Origins of the Other: Emmanuel Levinas Between Revelation and Ethics*. Ithaca, NY: Cornell University Press, 2005.
Mozart, Wolfgang Amadeus. *The Magic Flute: In Full Score*. Libretto by Emanuel Schikaneder. New York: Dover, 1985.
Myers, David N. *Resisting History: Historicism and Its Discontents in German-Jewish Thought*. Myers. Princeton: Princeton University Press, 2003.
Nancy, Jean-Luc. "The Inoperative Community." Translated by Peter Connor. In *The Inoperative Community*, 1–42. Minneapolis: University of Minnesota Press, 1991.
———. *Listening*. Translated by Charlotte Mandell. New York: Fordham University Press, 2007.
Ney, Steven, and Mary Douglas. *Missing Persons: A Critique of Personhood in the Social Science*. Berkeley: University of California Press, 1998.
Ochs, Peter, and Michael Cartwright. Introduction in *The Jewish-Christian Schism Revisited*, by John Howard Yoder, 1–29. Grand Rapids: Eerdmans, 2005.
Ochs, Vanessa. "Reading Ruth: Where are the Women?" In *Reading Ruth: Contemporary Women Reclaim a Sacred Story*, edited by Judith A. Kates and Gail Twersky Reimer, 289–97. New York: Ballantine, 1994.
O'Driscoll, Mary, editor. *Catherine of Siena: Passion for the Truth, Compassion for Humanity*. New York: New City, 1994.

Oppenheim, Michael. "Franz Rosenzweig and Emmanuel Levinas: A Midrash or Thought-Experiment." *Judaism* 42 (1993) 177–92.
Olivelle, Patrick. *The Asrama System: The History and Hermeneutics of a Religious Institution.* New York: Oxford University Press, 1993.
Oliver, Kelly. "Forgiveness and Community." Supplement to *Southern Journal of Philosophy* 42 (2004) 1–15.
———. "Julia Kristeva's Feminist Revolutions." *Hypatia* 8 (1993) 94–114.
———. *Reading Kristeva: Unraveling the Double-Bind.* Bloomington: Indiana University Press, 1993.
Pakaluk, Michael. *Other Selves: Philosophers on Friendship.* Indianapolis: Hackett, 1996.
Poirié, François. *Emmanuel Levinas: Essais et Entretiens.* Arles: Actes Sud, 1996.
Preiss, Jack Joseph. *Camp William James.* Norwich, VT: Argo, 1978.
Purcell, Michael. "On Hesitation before the Other." *International Journal of Philosophy of Religion* 60 (2006) 9–19.
Rancière, Jacques. *The Future of the Image.* Translated by Gregory Elliott. London: Verso, 2007.
———. *The Politics of Aesthetics.* Translated by Gabriel Rockhill. London: Continuum, 2006.
Rashkover, Randi. *Revelation and Theopolitics: Barth, Rosenzweig, and the Politics of Praise.* New York: T. & T. Clark, 2005.
Robbins, Jill. *Altered Reading: Levinas and Literature.* Chicago: University of Chicago Press, 1999.
———. "Responding to the Inifinity between Us: Blanchot Reading Levinas in *L'entretien infini.*" In *The Power of Contestation: Perspectives on Maurice Blanchot*, edited by Kevin Hart and Geoffrey Hartmann, 66–79. Baltimore: Johns Hopkins University Press, 2004.
Rogers, Eugene F., Jr. *After the Spirit: A Constructive Pneumatology from Resources outside the Modern West.* Grand Rapids: Eerdmans, 2005.
———. "The Stranger as Blessing." In *Knowing the Triune God: The Work of the Spirit in the Practices of the Church*, edited by James Buckley and David Yeago, 265–83. Grand Rapids: Eerdmans, 2001.
Rohrbach, Wilfrid. *Das Sprachdenken Eugen Rosenstocks: Historische Erörterung und systematische Explikation.* Stuttgart: Kohlhammer, 1973.
Rose, Gillian. *The Broken Middle: Out of Our Ancient Society.* Oxford: Blackwell, 1992.
Rouner, Leroy S. *The Changing Face of Friendship.* Boston University Studies in Philosophy and Religion 15. Notre Dame: University of Notre Dame Press, 1994.
Santner, Eric L. *On the Psychotheology of Everyday Life: Reflections on Freud and Rosenzweig.* Chicago: University of Chicago Press, 2001.
Sasson, Jack. *Ruth: A New Translation with a Philological Commentary and a Formalist/Folklorist Interpretation.* Sheffield: Sheffield Academic, 1995.
Seneca, Lucius. "On Tranquility of Mind." In *The Stoic Philosophy of Seneca*, translated by Moses Hadas, 75–106. New York: Norton, 1968.
Simmons, Terry. "The Bridge-Builder in Quest for Community." In *Eugen Rosenstock-Huessy: Studies in His Life and Thought*, edited by M. Darrol Bryant and Hans R. Huessy, 131–44. Lewiston, NY: Mellen, 1986.
Sjoholm, Cecilia. *Kristeva and the Political.* New York: Routledge, 2005.
Spire, Arnaud. "The Future of a Defeat." Interview with Julia Kristeva. *Parallax* 9 (2003) 21–26.

Stahmer, Harold. "Christianity in the Early Writings of Eugen Rosenstock-Huessy." In *Eugen Rosenstock-Huessy: Studies in His Life and Thought*, edited by M. Darrol Bryant and Hans R. Huessy, 31–48. Lewiston, NY: Mellen, 1986.

———. "Franz Rosenzweig's Letters to Margrit Rosenstock-Huessy, 1917–1922." *Yearbook of the Leo Baeck Institute* 34 (1989) 385–409.

———. "*Speak That I May See Thee!*" *The Religious Significance of Language*. New York: Macmillan, 1968.

Stout, Jeffrey. *Democracy and Tradition*. Princeton: Princeton University Press, 2003.

Stuckey, Priscilla. "Light Dispels Darkness: A Feminist Reading of *The Magic Flute*." *Journal of Feminist Studies in Religion* 11 (1995) 5–39.

Symeon, the New Theologian. *The Church and the Last Things*. Vol. 1 of *On the Mystical Life: The Ethical Discourses*. Translated by Alexander Golitizin. Crestwood, NY: St. Vladimir's Seminary Press, 1995.

Thomas Aquinas. *Summa Theologiae*. Madrid: Biblioteca de Autores Cristianos, 1951.

Toumayan, Alan. *Encountering the Other: The Artwork and the Problem of Difference in Levinas and Blanchot*. Pittsburgh: Duquesne University Press, 2004.

Ungar, Steven. *Scandal and Aftereffect: Blanchot and France Since 1930*. Minneapolis: University of Minnesota Press, 1995.

Vries, Hent de. *Minimal Theologies: Critiques of Secular Reason in Adorno and Levinas*. Translated by Geoffrey Hale. Baltimore: Johns Hopkins University Press, 2005.

Wachtel, Andrew. *Making a Nation, Breaking a Nation: Literature and Cultural Politics in Yugoslavia*. Stanford: Stanford University Press, 1998.

Watkin, William. "Melancholia, Revolution, and Materiality in the Work of Julia Kristeva." *Paragraph* 26 (2003) 86–107.

Williams, Rowan. *Teresa of Avila*. Harrisburg: Morehouse, 1991.

Winfree, Jason. "On the Lineage of Oblivion: Heidegger, Blanchot, and the Fragmentation of Truth." *Research in Phenomenology* 35 (2005) 249–69.

Wolin, Sheldon. "Hannah Arendt: Democracy and the Political." In *Hannah Arendt: Critical Essays,* edited by Lewis P. Hinchman and Sandra K. Hinchman, 298–306. Albany: SUNY Press, 1984.

———. *Politics and Vision: Continuity and Innovation in Western Political Thought*. Boston: Little, Brown, 1960.

Wright, Melanie J. *Religion and Film: An Introduction*. London: Tauris, 2007.

Young, William W. III. "Betrayals of Vulnerability: Beyond Sovereign Responsibility." *Philosophy Today* 53 (2009, SPEP Supplement) forthcoming.

———. "Healing Religion: Aesthetics and Analysis in the Work of Kristeva and Clement." *Cross Currents* 55 (2005) 152–61.

———. "The Identity of the Literal Sense: Midrash in the Work of Hans Frei." *Journal of Religion* 85 (2005) 609–33.

———. "The Patience of Job: Between Providence and Disaster." *Heythrop Journal* 48 (2007) 593–613.

———. *The Politics of Praise: Naming God and Friendship in Aquinas and Derrida*. Aldershot: Ashgate, 2007.

———. "The Song of Songs: From Affliction to Healing through the Text." *Journal of Scriptural Reasoning* 3, no. 2 (2003) n.p. Online: http://etext.lib.virginia.edu/journals/ssr/issues/volume3/number2/ssr03-02-r19.html.

———. "The Worklessness of Love: Agamben's Messianic Redemption." Presented as part of a panel on "Agamben and Messianism" at the AAR national meeting, San Diego, CA, November 19, 2007.

Zank, Michael. "Christlich-Jüdisches Gespräch im 1. Weltkrieg: Eine Analyse Des Briefwechsels von Eugen Rosenstock und Franz Rosenzweig aus dem Jahre 1916." Wissenschaftliche Hausarbeit gemäß der Vereinbarung mit der Prüfungskommission der Pfälzischen Landeskirche vom 14.10.85, im Fach Kirchengeschichte vorgelegt bei Herrn Prof. G. Seebaß an der wissenschaftlich-theologischen Fakultät der Universität Heidelberg. Edingen, 1986.

———. "Franz Rosenzweig, the 1920s, and the email Moment of Textual Reasoning." In *Textual Reasonings: Jewish Philosophy and Text Study at the End of the Twentieth Century*, edited by Peter Ochs and Nancy Levene, 229–50. Grand Rapids: Eerdmans, 2002.

———. "The Rosenzweig-Rosenstock Triangle, or What Can We Learn from Letters to Gritli? A Review Essay." *Modern Judaism* (2003) 74–98.

Index

abjection, 212, 219–22, 261, 264
Abraham, 77–78, 200, 202, 241–42
Academy for the Science of Judaism, 92–93
Acéphale, 142
adult education, 19, 25, 60, 84–87, 96–116, 288–89
Aelred of Rievaulx, 2
Agamben, Giorgio, 82, 202
Agnon, S. Y., 1, 112, 139, 148, 150
Ajzenstat, Oona, 183n28, 187n45
Akademie der Arbeit, 86, 97–100
Antelme, Robert, 143, 145–50, 201
anti-semitism, 85, 186–87, 191, 201, 266, 274
Arendt, Hannah, 115, 254, 265–70, 281–82, 285, 293
Aristotle, 1, 10
assimilation, 11n26, 68, 73, 83, 84–88, 91, 93, 109, 111, 257–58, 260–62, 274, 279, 289
Augustine of Hippo, 2, 263–64

Baden-Baden, 19n4, 23, 54
Barth, Karl, 46, 50, 51, 79, 112, 244
Bataille, Georges, 128, 142–43, 147, 173, 190, 290–91
Batnitzky, Leora, 32n41, 33n48, 34–36, 44n75, 45, 53n91, 66n24, 67n31, 69n33
Baudelaire, Charles, 131n25, 152–55
Beardsworth, Sara, 217, 264
Benedict XVI, 265n33
Benjamin, Walter, 12, 72, 82–83, 147, 177

Bernard of Clairvaux, 225, 233–34
Berry, Wendell, 105–6
bhakti (devotion), 277–78
Bident, Christophe, 145, 147, 167
Blanchot, Maurice, 4, 5n15, 8, 12, 14–15, 132, 136–38, 140, 142, 146, 148–49, 150–56, 157, 164, 165–72, 173–75, 182, 189, 190–207, 236, 284–87, 290–92, 294–95
  Faux Pas, 190–96
  Friendship, 290
  The Infinite Conversation, 123, 136, 145, 150, 156, 165–67, 171, 175, 196–207, 291
  Pour L'Amitié, 121, 145, 173
  The Space of Literature, 121–27
  The Step Not Beyond, 146, 150, 165–67, 170, 196
  The Unavowable Community, 142–44
  The Work of Fire, 151–56
  The Writing of the Disaster, 136, 137, 150, 167–71, 291
  See also disaster, enigma, literature, neuter, plural speech
Bosch, Elisabeth, 171
Bourdieu, Pierre, 116n83, 229, 265n31
Bové, Carolyn, 216n11
Braiterman, Zachary, 21–22, 32n43, 44n74, 53n91, 75n48
Brenner, Michael, 110n61, 114n78
Brody, D. H., 164
Bruns, Gerald, 193
Bryant, M. Darrol, 77n53

Buber, Martin, 25, 37, 40, 42, 48, 72–75, 80–82, 88, 112, 114
Burger, Anton, 89n8
Burning Bush (Ex. 3), 159
Butler, Judith, 251–52

calendar, 55–65, 65–71, 72, 81, 90–91
Calvin, John, 44, 51–52, 55
Camp William James, 87, 96, 100–107
Camus, Albert, 193–94
Cartwright, Michael, 3n11
Catherine of Siena, 211, 225–26, 235
Caygill, Howard, 183n29
Celan, Paul, 131n25, 139–40
Char, René, 152–55
Chouchani, M., 177, 189
Ciaramelli, Fabio, 163n42
Civilian Conservation Corps (CCC), 101–5, 108
Clément, Catherine, 4–5, 8–9, 12–15, 211–14, 225–35, 236–45, 252–54, 271–82, 284, 286–87, 292–95
  on cultural dialogue, 271–75
  Desert Eves, 279, 281
  The Feminine and the Sacred, 211–14, 232, 237–38, 292
  Gandhi: The Power of Pacifism, 279
  The Lives and Legends of Jacques Lacan, 228–30
  Opera, or the Undoing of Women, 243–45, 272
  on psychoanalysis, 227–31
  on religion, 211–14, 231–35, 237–38, 276–82
  Rêver Chacun Pour L'Autre, 272–75
  Syncope: The Philosophy of Rapture, 237–42, 277–80
  Theo's Odyssey, 238
  The Weary Sons of Freud, 228, 230–31
Cohen, Hermann, 27, 68, 87, 92–93, 112
Cohen, Richard, 173n1
Coles, Romand, 286–87
Collin, Françoise, 125n11, 127n13

commentary, 15, 20, 31, 35, 122, 172, 173–207
communism, 8, 60, 143. *See also* Marxism
community, 2–3, 6–7, 10, 25, 27–28, 33–36, 35, 38, 43, 45, 47–49, 52, 55, 56, 57, 60–69, 72, 73, 76, 81, 82, 85, 87–93, 97, 102, 104–12, 116–17, 122, 135–36, 141–44, 149, 185, 195, 201–2, 226, 228–29, 230, 234, 253, 257–63, 268, 274–76, 282
  and aesthetics, 13–14
cosmopolitanism, 227, 254–55, 261, 263–64, 270–71
Cristaudo, Wayne, 54n2, 56, 71n38, 77n59
Critchley, Simon, 155n12
Cross of Reality, 34, 45–48, 76–77

Davies, Paul, 170n67
Debré, Michel, 273–74
Derrida, Jacques, 89n11, 134, 156, 166, 169, 176, 236, 291
disaster, 167–72
divine command, 27, 31, 51, 72–75, 80–82, 162, 164, 176, 177, 198, 218, 257–59
Dostoevsky, Fyodor, 245–47, 268
Drabinski, John, 128n16, 158n21, 159n23
Duras, Marguerite, 142–43
Dussel, Enrique, 149n83, 183n29

Ehrenberg, Rudolf, 23
Eichmann, Adolf, 265–66, 268–69
enigma, 15, 122, 124, 138–39, 144, 148–49, 224, 285, 291–92, 295
  in Blanchot's early work, 150–54
  in Blanchot's later work, 165–72, 183, 185, 193
  in Levinas' transitional period, 156–61
  in *Otherwise than Being*, 161–65
Esther, Book of, 184–86
Eternal Return (Nietzsche), 165–66, 202–4

Eucharist, 4, 219–21

Farrell, Michael, 7
fatigue, 128–30, 133, 135
Feidel-Mertz, Hildegard, 112n69, 113, 115n82
Feld, Scott, 12n28
feminine, the, 213, 223, 232, 242, 251–52, 277
feminine genius, in Kristeva, 260, 265, 293
forgiveness, 179, 246–50, 265–69
Foucault, Michel, 9, 122
Fox, Everett, 42n70, 44n74
frankness (*parrhesia*), 11, 201, 284
Freies Judisches Lehrhaus (House of Jewish Learning), 20, 86–87, 92–93, 108–17
Freud, Sigmund, 7, 231
Friedman, Marilyn, 3
friendship, 1–16, 19–22, 55, 86, 116–17, 121–24, 137, 141, 142–44, 148, 150–51, 172, 173, 190, 211, 282, 283–95
and art, 13–15, 294–95
French Revolution, 63, 71

Galli, Barbara, 37
Gandhi, Mahatma, 255, 279–82
Genesis, Book of, 30–31, 34–35
Gibbs, Robert, 30, 33, 175, 178, 187n41
Glatzer, Nahum, 54n1, 112, 114
God, 1, 2, 4, 22, 24, 25, 26, 28–38, 41, 43–46, 49, 51–52, 58–60, 66–67, 73–74, 78, 82, 123, 128, 138–40, 144, 159–61, 167, 172, 176, 179–80, 188, 199–202, 215, 218, 221–22, 225, 232–34, 240–41, 257–64, 277, 279, 281, 285, 292, 295
Gordon, Peter, 40n65, 68, 69n33, 72, 82
Gospels, 46, 48–51
of John, 1, 49, 223
of Luke, 48
of Mark, 49
of Matthew, 48–49

grammatical thinking, 25–31, 33, 49, 57, 94
Gregory of Nyssa, 285
Gritli. *See* Rosenstock-Huessy, Margrit

Hadot, Pierre, 177, 291
Halevi, Jehuda, 37, 39–43, 52, 91, 295
Handelman, Susan, 12n29
Hart, Kevin, 143n64, 168n58, 292
Hauerwas, Stanley, 2, 3n8, 4n14, 79n64, 287n5
Heidegger, Martin, 121–22, 128, 137–38, 150, 153, 156–57, 171, 174, 295
and historicism, 188–89
and philosophy of art, 130–33, 190, 194–96
Hill, Leslie, 127n14, 190–92, 195n60, 196
historical criticism, 32, 45–46, 48, 92, 187
historicism, 23–24, 54, 88, 188
history, philosophy of, 4, 35, 80–83, 90, 137
in Blanchot, 168–71
in Clément, 271, 273–74
and forgiveness, 267
in Levinas, 178, 184
in Rosenstock, 55–65, 71, 75–79
in Rosenzweig, 65–71, 74, 81–83
holidays, 54, 56–57, 61–62, 64, 68, 239
holiness, 144, 174, 178, 183–85, 188, 207
Hollander, Dana, 55n3, 80–81
Holy Spirit, 2, 46, 48, 85, 96–97, 107, 247
hospitality, 15, 160, 202, 254, 256–57, 260–61, 263–64, 267
The Human Race, 145–48

Il y a (there is), 134, 136, 153, 168, 284, 290
immanence, 138, 224, 295
interreligious friendship, 3–5, 10, 13–16, 122, 172, 283–85, 294–95
Islam, 80n65, 232, 252, 287
Iyer, Lars, 123, 144n65

James, William, 97, 102
Jesus Christ, 34, 48–50, 76–77, 108, 148, 219–22, 224, 248, 256
Job, Book of, 30, 42, 168–69, 246, 265
John Paul II, 265
Journal des Debats, 190–94
Judaism, 8, 12, 23–25, 27–30, 34–36, 44, 50, 55, 66, 68–75, 78–83, 87–93, 108–12, 117, 121–22, 134, 150, 176, 178–79, 183, 200, 212, 218, 223, 232–33, 254, 257, 261, 286, 288

Kakar, Sudhir, 277–78
Kant, Immanuel, 228n49, 240, 255
Katz, Claire Elise, 134n33
Kaplan, Gregory, 79–81, 83
Kaufman, Eleanor, 148, 190n46, 291
Kavka, Martin, 67n29, 70, 74n46, 110n59
Kearney, Richard, 148n80
Kearns, Cleo McNelly, 212, 219n20, 227n47, 247n26
Kern-Ulmer, Brigitte, 112n70, 114n80
Kierkegaard, Søren, 240–42
Klein, Melanie, 224, 265, 293
Kluger, Ruth, 269n46
Kofman, Sarah, 144, 147
Konstan, David, 11n25
Kristeva, Julia, 4–5, 8–9, 12–13, 15, 211–14, 215–27, 233–35, 236–37, 245–53, 255–71, 280–82, 284–87, 292–94
    on the Bible, 217–23, 246, 255–63
    Black Sun, 245–48
    The Feminine and the Sacred, 213, 225–26, 265, 292
    on forgiveness, 245–48, 265–70
    Hannah Arendt, 265–68
    Intimate Revolt, 265, 268–70
    Melanie Klein, 224
    Murder in Byzantium, 249–53
    Nations without Nationalism, 255, 258, 264
    New Maladies of the Soul, 219–21, 224
    Possessions, 248–49
    Powers of Horror, 217–20
    on psychoanalysis, 245–49, 264–65, 267–70
    on religion, 214–23, 233–35, 236–37, 246–48, 249–53, 255–70
    Revolution in Poetic Language, 215–17
    The Samurai, 215–17, 219
    Strangers to Ourselves, 255–63
    Tales of Love, 220–21, 225, 264
Kuhn, Thomas, 5–7, 9

Lacan, Jacques, 211, 228–31, 241–42, 276
Large, William, 124, 138n49, 156n16, 173n1, 182
law
    in Judaism, 25, 43, 54, 59, 65, 72–75, 80–82, 95, 111, 139, 144, 179, 182, 206, 218–19, 222, 257–60
    moral, 240, 269
    paternal, 243–44, 248
    in Paul, 262–63
    of poetry, 192
    See also divine command
Lescourret, Marie-Anne, 121n2
Levinas, Emmanuel, 4–5, 8, 12–15, 121–24, 127–45, 148–51, 156–65, 167, 172, 173–89, 190, 196–97, 199–201, 205–7, 236, 284–87, 290–92, 294–95
    on art, 129–33
    Beyond the Verse, 187, 189
    Difficult Freedom, 179, 183, 187
    En Découvrant Existence avec Husserl et Heidegger, 156–61
    Entre Nous, 286
    Existence and Existents, 127–36
    In the Time of Nations, 176, 183–87
    on literature, 138–42
    on music, 129, 139
    Nine Talmudic Readings, 177, 180–82
    Otherwise than Being, 161–65, 186
    Proper Names, 137–42
    on Talmud, 173–89
    Totality and Infinity, 196–97, 199, 201, 286

Levi-Strauss, Claude, 237, 273
Leviticus, 218–20
listening, 45, 50, 52, 66, 70, 77, 129, 174, 229–31, 235, 241, 264, 286–87, 295
literature, 95, 122, 124–27, 137–36, 171–72, 192–95, 217, 246–52, 267–68, 284–85
liturgy, 23, 53, 55, 59, 65–66, 95, 157, 178, 219
Luther, Martin, 40–45, 51, 58–60, 63, 71, 89, 221

The Magic Flute, 243–45
Malka, Salomon, 19, 21n8
Marion, Jean-Luc, 159n26
Marxism, 60, 147, 155. *See also* communism
Meilaender, Gilbert, 3
Meir, Ephraim, 21n9
Melancholy, 245–49, 294
Mendelssohn, Moses, 44, 52
Mendes-Flohr, Paul, 24n16, 85, 88n6
Meskin, Jacob, 184, 187
Messianism, 1, 49, 55, 71, 79–83, 91–92, 143, 150, 177, 187n41, 262
mirror stage, 230–31, 241–42, 276
monotheism, 144, 168, 200, 201, 225, 232–33, 286
Mosès, Stéphane, 30, 34
Mowitt, John, 255n3
Moyn, Samuel, 173n1, 187n41
Mozart, Wolfgang, 243–44
music, 13, 216, 236, 252, 295
    in Clément, 237–45, 271–72, 275, 281, 288, 293–94
    in Kristeva, 252–53
    in Levinas, 129, 132–33, 139–40, 149
    in Rosenzweig, 32, 33, 41–43
Myers, David, 24n16, 55n3
mysticism, 15, 179, 225, 232–35, 238

Name of God, 38, 43–45, 144, 167
Nancy, Jean-Luc, 4n14, 142
narrative, 45–46, 48–49, 76, 79, 174, 192–94, 243–44, 258–60, 265–68, 272, 281
Nazirate, 180–81
Nazism, 71, 86, 103, 114, 121, 145–48, 173, 203, 266, 290, 298
neuter, 138, 140, 143, 151, 166–67, 169, 174, 197–98, 205–7, 292, 294
"New Thinking," the, 22–23, 54–55, 65, 84, 116
Ney, Steven, 116n84
Nietzsche, Friedrich, 123, 147, 166, 188, 200, 202–4, 240, 267
normalization (of psychoanalysis), 228, 231

Ochs, Peter, 3n11
Ochs, Vanessa, 258n12
Olivelle, Patrick, 276n63
Oliver, Kelly, 212, 268
opera, 33, 241–45, 253, 271–74

painting, 88–89, 131–32, 248
Paul, 48–49, 59–60, 107, 220, 261–65
Plato, 49, 107–8, 108n51, 171, 188, 228n49, 239
plural speech, 123, 165, 174, 190, 196–97, 200, 202, 204, 206–7, 285, 291
Poirié, François, 173n2, 176n8
polyphony, 188n43, 222–23, 266, 281
Preiss, Jack, 101, 102n41, 104n43, 108n52
prophecy, 26, 41, 58–59, 92, 111, 148, 156, 160–62, 165, 176, 219, 222, 229, 261, 281
Psalms, 33–35, 42, 92
psychoanalysis, 13, 15, 211–32, 236, 241–42, 253, 254, 260, 264, 267, 269–70, 292
Purcell, Michael, 162n35

Rashkover, Randi, 74n46, 110n58 and 61
redemption, 30–33, 35, 38–41, 49, 65–70, 72, 75, 79–82, 89, 110, 134, 144, 284
renunciation, 200, 226, 260, 276–79

Index

revelation, 15, 20, 21, 24, 26, 30–33, 35, 36, 39, 41–43, 45, 50, 64, 66–67, 74–75, 82, 122, 138, 144, 150–52, 156, 159, 160, 163, 171, 176, 183, 201
ritual, 49, 70, 175–82, 216, 218, 238, 252, 276–78, 281
Robbins, Jill, 123, 128n15, 139
Rogers, Eugene F., 3–4
Rohrbach, Wilfrid, 46n79
Rose, Gillian, 269
Rosenstock-Huessy, Eugen, 4, 5, 8, 11–12, 15, 19–29, 34–36, 38, 45–53, 54–65, 69–71, 75–79, 81–83, 84–87, 91, 94–108, 113–17, 121, 236, 239, 286–89, 292, 294
  on adult education, 96–108
  The Christian Future, 75–79
  The Fruit of the Lips, 45–50
  Judaism Despite Christianity, 21, 24–25, 34–36, 69–70, 78
  Magna Carta Latina, 94–96
  Out of Revolution, 55–65, 83
  The Practical Knowledge of the Soul, 22–23, 25–29
  on translation, 45–53
  See also *Akademie der Arbeit*, calendar, Camp William James, grammatical thinking, work camps
Rosenstock-Huessy, Margrit (Gritli), 5, 15, 19–22, 32, 52, 87, 113–14, 116, 288–89
Rosenzweig, Edith, 20–21, 289
Rosenzweig, Franz, 4, 11–13, 15, 19–25, 28–45, 46, 48, 50, 52–53, 54–56, 65–75, 78, 79–83, 84–93, 95, 106–17, 121, 223, 236, 239, 286–89, 294–95
  on education, 84–93, 95, 106–17
  on history, 54–56, 65–71, 72–75, 79–83
  Jehuda Halevi, 39–42, 52
  Judaism Despite Christianity, 34, 70, 78, 83
  on law, 72–75, 79–83
  Scripture and Translation, 42–45
  The Star of Redemption, 28–36, 65–70, 80
  on translation, 36–45
  Understanding the Sick and the Healthy, 37–39
  See also calendar, *Freies Judisches Lehrhaus*, historicism, revelation, Song of Songs
Rouner, Leroy, 3
Ruth, Book of, 255–62

sacred, 79, 81, 144, 163, 179, 183, 195, 197, 207, 212–14, 225–26, 228, 232–35, 236–40, 245, 249, 254, 255, 265, 271–72, 293
sacrifice, 78, 90, 139, 141, 159, 216, 218–20, 226, 237, 276–77
said, the (*le dit*), 143, 159, 161–65, 169
Santner, Eric, 70n37, 82n74
saying, the (*le dire*), 139, 143, 148, 151, 156, 159, 161–65, 167, 169, 181, 290
Schmitt, Carl, 72, 82
semiotic, 211, 213–18, 220–25, 227, 235, 251–52, 260, 264, 266, 268–69, 272, 282
Seneca, Lucius, 11, 291
shaman, 15, 228–29
Simmons, Terry, 97n28
skepticism, 163–64
sleep, 128, 133–34, 136
Sollers, Philippe, 211n1, 215, 265n31
Song of Songs, 8, 20, 31–35, 41, 66, 220, 222–25, 234. See also Bernard of Clairvaux, revelation
speech-thinking, 15, 25, 36, 37, 42, 45, 47, 52–53, 54–55, 57, 71, 83, 84, 86–87, 91, 93, 94, 95, 96, 115, 117
Stahmer, Harold, 20, 21n8, 26, 32n43, 55n3, 56n4, 77n58, 289n7
Stoicism, 1, 11–12, 80n65, 284
Stout, Jeffrey, 86, 101
stranger, 169, 193, 213, 257–63
Stuckey, Priscilla, 243n19
suffering, 52, 71, 77, 83, 100, 133–35, 138, 186–87, 198, 220, 228, 243, 246–47, 268, 292
Sukkot, 67, 178, 201

symbolic, 5, 68–69, 193, 271–72,
    276–77
  in Kristeva, 212–14, 216–27, 229,
    243, 247–48, 264
syncope, 213, 237–45
syncretism, 8, 245, 270, 280–81, 284
Symeon the New Theologian, 248

Talmud, 112–13, 176–77, 186–89, 197,
    206
Talmudic lectures, 15, 122, 172,
    176–89, 197
Talmudic study, 177, 182, 188–89, 207
Teresa of Avila, 233–34
Thomas Aquinas, 2, 232, 248
Toumayan, Alan, 173n1, 195n59
trace, 126, 139–40, 148, 156–61,
    162–64, 214, 236, 292
trace of God, 159–61, 292
transcendence, 1, 15, 134, 140, 148,
    150–51, 155–57, 159–60,
    162–65, 167, 172, 177, 178,
    187, 240, 285, 287, 291, 292,
    295. *See also* enigma
translation, 15, 20, 23, 33, 36–37,
    39–45, 46–53, 89, 90, 185–87,
    285–86, 288, 295
Trinity, 46, 247

unconscious, 223–34, 231, 247, 255
Ungar, Steven, 190n47

vulnerability, 138, 144, 146, 148, 161,
    170, 178, 182, 285, 294
Vries, Hent de, 131, 159, 173n1, 207

Wachtel, Andrew, 86
Watkin, William, 251n38, 270n51
Weil, Simone, 200
Williams, Rowan, 4n14, 233
Winfree, Jason, 200n75
Wolin, Sheldon, 107–8n51, 281–82
work camps, 95, 97–98, 100–104. *See
    also* Camp William James
work of art, 124, 153, 157
Wright, Melanie, 4n12
Yom Kippur, 23, 67, 179, 180

Young, William, 10n23, 79n64, 148n82,
    163n40, 169n61, 181n24,
    182n26, 188n43, 225n40
youth, 100–102, 104, 105, 175, 177,
    180–82

Zank, Michael, 19n4, 20n6, 24n17,
    34n50, 93n17, 108n53, 109n54

www.ingramcontent.com/pod-product-compliance
Lightning Source LLC
Chambersburg PA
CBHW021344300426
44114CB00012B/1071